The Causes of Molecular Evolu

OXFORD SERIES IN ECOLOGY AND EVOLUTION
Edited by Robert M. May and Paul H. Harvey

THE COMPARATIVE METHOD IN EVOLUTIONARY BIOLOGY
Paul H. Harvey and Mark D. Pagel

THE CAUSES OF MOLECULAR EVOLUTION
John H. Gillespie

The Causes
of Molecular Evolution

JOHN H. GILLESPIE

Center for Population Biology
University of California, Davis

New York   Oxford
OXFORD UNIVERSITY PRESS

Oxford University Press

Oxford   New York   Toronto
Delhi   Bombay   Calcutta   Madras   Karachi
Kuala Lumpur   Singapore   Hong Kong   Tokyo
Nairobi   Dar es Salaam   Cape Town
Melbourne   Auckland   Madrid

and associated companies in
Berlin   Ibadan

Library of Congress Cataloging-in-Publication Data
Gillespie, John H.
The causes of molecular evolution / John H. Gillespie.
p.   cm.—(Oxford series in ecology and evolution ; 2)
Includes bibliographical references (p.   ) and index.
ISBN 0-19-506883-1
ISBN 0-19-509271-6 (Ppbk)
1. Population genetics.   2. Variation (Biology)
I. Title.   II. Series.
QH455.G56   1991   575.1′5—dc20   91-16709

9 8 7 6 5 4 3 2

Printed in the United States of America

for John E. Cooper

Preface

Naturally occurring genetic variation is an enigma. Using modern molecular techniques, variation is found in all species, sometimes at astonishingly high levels. Yet, despite the ease of measurement, we remain essentially ignorant of the forces that maintain variation. There are few phenomena in biology that are so easy to observe and so hard to understand. The reason is simple: the forces that alter the genetic structures of populations tend to be very weak, operating on time scales of thousands to millions of years. Direct experimentation is, except in rare cases, completely uninformative. Instead, we must rely on indirect inferences based on models of the dynamics of genetic variation. The models serve up challenging mathematics, and the connections between them and the patterns of genetic variation are not always clear. Despite these obstacles, population genetics has made enormous strides over the past 25 years on one of the most intellectually challenging and exciting problems in biology.

As the study of naturally occurring genetic variation could be said to define population genetics, it is not surprising that population geneticists are constantly seeking new ways to measure it. In the middle and late 1960s population genetics entered the molecular age with the publication of seminal papers describing electrophoretically detectable variation in *Drosophila* by Lewontin and Hubby [190] and Johnson et al. [142] and in humans by Harris [116]. These papers showed that 5 to 15% of the examined protein loci are heterozygous in a typical individual. When extrapolated to the entire genome, these studies pointed to massive levels of variation, much more than had been predicted.

Even before these electrophoretic studies were started, protein sequencing studies had uncovered variation between species. Enough sequence data was available in 1962 for Zuckerkandl and Pauling [317] to notice an unexpected constancy in rates of amino acid substitutions leading them to postulate the existence of a molecular clock.

During the period just after the publication of the original electrophoretic studies, a flurry of theoretical activity showed that some form of balancing selection could account for protein polymorphism, even in light of load theory that was previously thought to rule out selection as a viable mechanism. In all of this discussion, no use was made of the species comparisons or of the molecular clock. By contrast, in 1968, Kimura [155] and, in 1969, King and Jukes [164] published papers arguing that amino acid substitutions, as revealed by species comparisons, were due to the action of genetic drift rather than natural selection. This was the birth of the neutral allele theory or, as King and Jukes called it in their provocative title, the theory of non-Darwinian evolution.

The paper that wedded polymorphism and molecular evolution data in a single theoretical framework was Kimura and Ohta's 1971 paper [161] "Protein polymorphism as a phase of molecular evolution." For me, this paper represents a great moment in population genetics as it is the first clear statement of a single mechanism for protein variation both within and between species. As with all great papers, it brings together elements that were previously only weakly connected. The neutral theory ascended from its initial skeptical reception to the dominant theory to account for molecular evolution and polymorphism in remarkably short time. Today, it is widely accepted, a testimony both to the theory and to the pioneering work of Kimura, Ohta, and others during the early 1970s.

There has been a persistent counterpoint to the neutral theory that has not come in the form of a mature theory, but rather as a diverse series of observations and theoretical works, each of which nibbles at just a small portion of the theory. The observations tend to be examples of protein variation that can be shown to have significant physiological consequences and, by implication, effects on fitness. The theoretical results tend to show that dynamics once thought to be the sole province of neutral alleles are shared by selected alleles as well. None of these, by themselves, are sufficient to topple the theory. Remarkably, they have never been accumulated in a single work to see if the neutral theory can be sustained in the face of their combined weight.

In this preface I will give a broad outline of what is to follow. This will help to bind together chapters that run the gamut from purely experimental to entirely mathematical.

The book is divided into three parts. The first consists of three chapters (Protein Evolution, DNA Evolution, and The Molecular Clock) that review the experimental observations on genetic variation. The second is made up of two chapters (Selection in a Fluctuating Environment and SSWM Approximations) that give a unified treatment of the mathematical theory of selection in a fluctuating environment. The final two chapters (Neutral Allele Theories and Selection Theories) combine the earlier chapters in a treatment of the scientific status of two competing theories for the maintenance of genetic variation. The three parts can be read independently; however, the third does depend in large part on the first two. Those not mathematically inclined may want to skip chapters 4 and 5 altogether.

The chapter on protein evolution begins with a series of examples of what I call microadaptations, where one or a few amino acid changes in a protein are implicated in an adaptation. Such examples are few and far between, leading us to question whether they are tantalizing apparitions of a general phenomenon lying just beyond the resolution of our experiments or anomalies positioned to mislead overzealous selectionists. As our story unfolds, I hope to convince the reader that the former is the true situation. Part of the argument involves a short treatment of the thermodynamics of protein folding designed to show that it is not chemically unreasonable for even conservative amino acid changes to alter kinetic properties of proteins.

A short section on rates of substitutions argues that the observation that certain proteins, like immunoglobulins, evolve two orders of magnitude faster than others, like histones, cannot be entirely understood by claiming that the latter are more "constrained" than the former. Rather, the argument must be expanded to include the effects of a changing environment: some proteins are more "environmentally challenged" than others and, as a consequence, evolve more rapidly. This view is motivated, in part, by the examples of microadaptations, all of which are in response to an aspect of the environment that changes through time or space.

The final section examines the extensive literature on electrophoretic surveys of protein polymorphisms. Despite the vastness of this literature, it serves up remarkably few insights into the forces responsible for the maintenance of the variation. Later in the book I will argue that most populations may be out of equilibrium due to linked hitchhiking events, suggesting that patterns of polymorphism are too dependent on historic events to be informative about mechanisms. One conclusion of this section that differs from the view of 10 years ago is that the enzymes used in electrophoretic studies may be more polymorphic than typical protein loci and may have misled us about the level of protein variation in the genome.

The chapter on DNA evolution concentrates on silent variation within coding regions. Two general questions are examined: does mutation limit the rate of silent substitution, and does the spectrum of silent substitutions match the mutational spectrum? Both questions are answered in the affirmative, although the available data are still too sparse to make these answers definitive. Next, the evolution of GC% and codon usage is discussed. I have taken the unorthodox view that the GC% is an evolved property, reflecting a value that is deemed optimal by natural selection and that this value has a marked impact on patterns of codon usage. Finally, patterns of DNA polymorphisms are reviewed.

The first two chapters allow us to contrast the dynamics of silent and replacement substitutions. One major difference seen in mammals is that silent substitutions appear to exhibit a generation-time effect while replacement substitutions do not. This difference will play a major role in our final judgment about the contrasting mechanisms of silent and replacement evolution.

The molecular clock is the focus of the third chapter. In it we see that rates of nucleotide substitution are anything but constant. Variation in rates may be partitioned into lineage effects, variation shared by all loci on a particular lineage, and residual effects, variation left over once lineage effects are removed. One example of a lineage effect is the generation-time effect.

Residual effects are quantified by $R(t)$, the ratio of the variance in the number of substitutions on a lineage to the mean number. The average value of $R(t)$ for replacement substitutions is over seven, while for silent substitutions it may not be significantly greater than one. A digression into the theory of point processes is used to argue that the variability in rates of protein evolution implies that protein evolution is episodic, with periods of quiescence marked by occasional bursts of substitutions.

In the fourth chapter we turn from data to mathematics. If we are to propose that molecular evolution is due to the action of natural selection, we need a mathematical theory to demonstrate that the dynamics of selection are compatible with the observations on molecular variation. It is my conviction that the only viable model of selection is one based on temporal and spatial fluctuations in the environment. The mathematics of selection in a random environment have never been systematically developed or brought to the point where they serve as a model of molecular evolution. Both situations will be remedied in this chapter. Unfortunately, the mathematics are very difficult. Yet, if molecular evolution is in response to a changing environment, then this is the sort of mathematical challenge that we must be willing to face. This chapter is littered with unresolved problems that should prove interesting to those with a mathematical bent.

The next chapter demonstrates how population genetic models that involve strong selection and weak mutation may be approximated by a technique that brings even the most difficult of problems into submission. The approximating models, called SSWM Markov chains, can be used to describe the genealogy of alleles. In this chapter I formulate a number of models that exhibit the same episodic pattern of substitutions inferred in the analysis of the protein evolution data.

The chapter on neutral allele theories, the first of two concerned with the fundamental scientific issues posed by the first three chapters, begins with an examination of the assumptions underlying the neutral theory, proceeds to examine the arguments that bear on the theory, and concludes that the theory should probably be abandoned for amino acid variation but may be valid for silent variation. Whatever neutral variation is present is likely to be far from equilibrium, reflecting historical events.

The final chapter presents the selection alternative. After summarizing the arguments supporting the role of natural selection on amino acids, a strong-selection model is described that is compatible with the episodic molecular clock. Some speculations on a unified theory of selection in a fluctuating environment are presented that should provide a springboard for further work.

This book is a statement of my own views on molecular evolution. It is not meant to be a review of molecular evolution or of population genetics. I have attempted to cite review articles where appropriate for the benefit of readers who may want more information. I have also attempted to cite those responsible for my views, either through written works or conversations. However, as many of the ideas in this book are in the "public domain," many are expressed without any attribution.

I am in debt to a number of people who made substantial contributions to this book. The book was the topic of the Zoology 270 seminar at Davis in the Spring of 1991. All involved made useful comments, particularly Jonathan Losos and Allen Briggs who shared the prize for finding the largest number of mechanical errors and Alan Orr who won the prize for the finding the most egregious scientific error. Much of the book was written at the Institute for Theoretical Dynamics in Davis while I was on sabatical. I would like to thank Joel Keizer for making space available at the Institute. The book was supported by NSF Grant BSR-8806548.

Dick Hudson, Masaru Iizuka and Montgomery Slatkin read large portions of the manuscript and offered many helpful suggestions. Michael Turelli, my colleague for the past ten years, has been a constant source of ideas and inspiration throughout the planning and writing of the book. His contributions to the theory of selection in a random environment permeate Chapter 4. His many suggestions greatly improved in the final four chapters. Most of what I know about diffusion theory I learned from Warren Ewens during the eight years that we were together at the University of Pennsylvania. Although he hasn't seen this book, his influence may be found throughout. A skeptical Larry Sprechman helped me understand the kinetic and thermodynamic arguments in Chapter 1. Finally, I must mention the special contribution of Chuck Langley. Ever since our graduate student days with Ken-ichi Kojima at the University of Texas, I have valued Chuck's unique scientific insights into molecular evolution. I fear that more of the book comes from his mind than I have been able to acknowledge.

My greatest debt is to my wife, Robin Gordon. Not only did she read and edit the entire manuscript, but she has been a source of encouragement and support throughout the writing. I could not have pulled this off without her.

The book is dedicated to my high school biology teacher and long time friend, John E. Cooper.

J.H.G.

Davis, Calif.
June 1991

Contents

The Causes of Molecular Evolution

1

Protein evolution

The study of protein evolution, like that of morphological evolution, is a multi-level enterprise. At the most fundamental level are those studies that infer what actually happened. At the next level are studies of rates of change. Once we know what happened, we want to know how quickly it happened. Finally, we want to know why these changes occurred. What are the mechanisms producing the changes in the amino acid sequences of proteins?

The *Atlas of Protein Sequence and Structure* [52] is the repository of much of the work on the first two levels. However, the *Atlas* is of little help on the issue of mechanism as it does not deal with functional aspects of proteins. Population geneticists, the natural custodians of the third level, have failed to reach a consensus despite many years of discussion.

That protein function has been shaped by natural selection has never been an issue. The controversy centers on the *fraction* of substitutions that contribute to adaptive evolution. Supporters of the neutral allele theory claim that less than 10% of all amino acid substitutions are functionally significant. Others claim that the fraction is much higher, perhaps as high as 100%. Why is it that we cannot agree to within an order of magnitude on an issue as fundamental as the mechanism of protein evolution?

Perhaps we are investigating phenomena that are below the resolving power of our current (and perhaps future) techniques. Selection coefficients for single amino acid substitutions as small as 10^{-4} to 10^{-3} are large enough to dominate genetic drift, yet are refractory to direct experimental investigations. In other words, most of protein evolution could be due to strong natural selection, yet we have no experimental protocol capable of measuring the selective differences. If this is so (as will be argued throughout this book) then what should be done?

One thing that we can to is to latch onto examples in which effects are large enough to measure and use them to gain insight into effects that will remain forever beyond our reach. I feel so strongly about this approach that I am beginning this book with examples of amino acid changes that appear to have functionally important consequences. These will guide our understanding of protein evolution to a point where the claim that most amino acid substitutions could cause fitness effects as large as 10^{-3} seems entirely reasonable. My view of these examples is that they are ordinary in their qualitative effects, but extraordinary in their quantitative effects.

1.1   Examples of microadaptations

What follows are a selection of my favorite examples of microadaptations in proteins. I call these microadaptations only to emphasize that the numbers of amino acid substitutions responsible for the adaptation are generally quite small, as are the (inferred, always unmeasured) effects on fitness. I don't mean to imply that the large adaptive differences between, say, fish and horse hemoglobins are the results of processes other than the microadaptations that are described in this section.

Each example contains a certain amount of background information. This was added under the assumption that, like myself, many readers will have forgotten some of their basic biochemistry.

Lactate dehydrogenase

Lactate dehydrogenase (LDH) is a tetrameric enzyme that catalyzes the interconversion of pyruvate and lactate and of NAD and NADH. In vertebrates, there are usually three major loci directing the synthesis of three distinct subunits, M (for muscle, also called A), H (for heart, also called B), and C. The subunits combine at random to produce isozymes. For example, a cell that synthesizes the H and M subunits will contain the H_4, H_3M_1, H_2M_2, H_1M_3, and M_4 isozymes in binomial proportions. In skeletal muscle the predominant isozyme is M_4 whereas in the liver and heart the predominant isozyme is H_4.

The muscle and heart forms play a key role in the *Cori cycle* as illustrated in Figure 1.1. In skeletal muscle glycolysis predominates with the consequent buildup of lactic acid. The lactic acid is transported through the blood to the liver where it feeds into gluconeogensis to produce glucose. The glucose is transported back through the blood to the muscles, thus completing the cycle. The M_4 isozyme favors the conversion of pyruvate to lactate whereas the H_4 isozyme favors the conversion of lactate to pyruvate.

Somero and his colleagues have studied adaptations of LDH in ectotherms in remarkable detail over the past 15 or so years (reviewed in [130, 269]). These studies were aimed mainly at understanding adaptations of LDH to different temperatures and pressures. They have examined various kinetic and thermostability properties of M_4-LDH from vertebrates with wildly different body temperatures ranging from an Antarctic fish (*Pagothenia borchgrevinka*) whose body temperature is near the freezing point of sea water, $-1.86°C$, to a desert lizard (*Dipsosaurus dorsalis*) whose temperature gets as high as 35-47°C.

The kinetic parameter that proved most interesting in these studies is the Michaelis constant, K_m, for the reduction of pyruvate. Their funda-

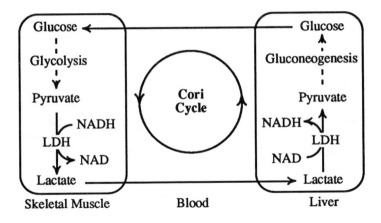

Figure 1.1. The Cori cycle.

mental observation is that K_m is conserved across species when the K_m from each species is measured at a temperature that falls within the normal range of body temperatures for that species [269, Figure 1]. In fact, the K_ms fell within the relatively narrow range of 0.15 to 0.35 mM of pyruvate. This twofold range is considerably narrower than the over tenfold range that is observed if K_ms are measured at temperatures outside the normal body temperatures of the species.

Why are the K_ms conserved? Or, why does there appear to be an optimal K_m? The answer, which will take us on a short digression into enzyme kinetics, is extraordinarily important for our appreciation of the microadaptations of enzymes.

The classic Michaelis-Menten model of enzyme catalysis involves the rapid binding and dissociation of the substrate with the enzyme and the rate-limiting catalysis and release of the product,

$$E + S \underset{\rightleftharpoons}{\overset{K_m}{}} ES \overset{k_{cat}}{\Rightarrow} E + P.$$

The rate at which the product is produced is given by the velocity

$$v = \frac{k_{cat}[E_t][S]}{K_m + [S]} \tag{1.1}$$

where the square brackets indicate the concentration and $[E_t]$ is the total concentration of the enzyme. Figure 1.2 illustrates the dependency of the reaction rate on the substrate concentration.

The maximum rate of the reaction,

$$V_{max} = [E_t]k_{cat},$$

occurs when the concentration of the substrate is high enough to saturate the enzyme. The Michaelis constant, defined by

$$K_m = \frac{[E][S]}{[ES]},$$

may be viewed as a measure of the strength of the binding between the substrate and the enzyme. Low values of K_m indicate tight binding; high values, weak binding. When the substrate concentration is equal to K_m, v is equal to one-half V_{max}, suggesting that K_m could also be defined as the concentration of the substrate at which the velocity of the reaction is one-half the maximum velocity.

When the substrate concentration is much smaller than K_m, the reaction behaves almost as a first-order reaction with velocity

$$v \approx \frac{k_{cat}}{K_m}[E_t][S] = \frac{V_{max}}{K_m}[S].$$

As intracellular substrate concentrations are usually less than K_m, it is commonly assumed that k_{cat}/K_m is the best measure of the in vivo activity of an enzyme [72].

Although the Michaelis-Menten model is a gross simplification of the dynamics of any particular enzyme-catalyzed reaction, it has proven to be a valuable guide for discussions of the major features of enzyme kinetics. For evolutionary studies, it focuses attention on three aspects of catalysis:

- The strength of binding of the substrate to the enzyme as measured by K_m.

- The efficiency of catalysis* as measured by k_{cat}.

- The in vivo velocity as measured by V_{max}/K_m.

With this background, we can return to our discussion of the conservation of K_m in ectotherms. If natural selection is responsible for the evolution of K_m to an intermediate value, we should be able to understand why it would be maladaptive to exhibit values that are much less or much greater than the intermediate value.

It has often been argued that K_m should be larger than the intracellular concentration of the substrate, $[S]$. This guarantees that the enzyme is far from saturation and thus has sufficient *reserve capacity* to respond to fluctuations in the substrate concentration [7,269]. In fact, the K_ms of most enzymes for which such data are available (including LDH) turn out to be 1 to 100 times the intracellular concentrations of their substrates [72, Fig. 12-7]. Thus, very small values for K_m are probably maladaptive.

On the other hand, if K_m is much larger than $[S]$, the velocity of the reaction in the cell is determined by V_{max}/K_m, which is a decreasing function of K_m. It is generally felt that it is advantageous for k_{cat}/K_m to be as

---

*There is no universally recognized measure of the efficiency of an enzyme. This is but one of several that have been used.

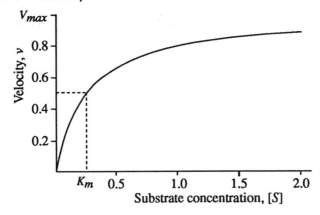

Figure 1.2. The velocity of an enzyme-catalyzed reaction under the Michaelis-Menton model.

large as possible to maximize the efficiency and transient performance of a pathway [63,295]. Thus, there will be an evolutionary force to decrease K_m to meet this requirement. Hochachka and Somero [130] point out that with a very large K_m an enzyme is not realizing a significant fraction of its *catalytic potential*—a bad thing. Thus, the "optimal" K_m is one that best satisfies the need for reserve capacity and high in vivo velocity.

Fersht [72] gives an entirely different evolutionary argument for the observation that K_ms usually fall between $[S]$ and $100[S]$. In general, we would expect evolution to maximize k_{cat}/K_m since this is the kinetic parameter that best reflects the rate of an enzyme-catalyzed reaction in vivo. Lowering K_m and increasing k_{cat} will obviously lead to increases in this ratio.

Suppose, however, that fundamental constraints in the structure of enzymes make the simultaneous increase of k_{cat} and decrease of K_m impossible (beyond some point), as seems likely. Tighter binding of substrates involves increases in the number and strength of weak bonds between the enzyme and the substrate. This, in turn, limits the conformational flexibility of the enzyme with a consequent reduction of its catalytic efficiency.

Suppose that k_{cat}/K_m is maximized at the value m. If k_{cat}/K_m equals m, then k_{cat} will equal mK_m. If this is plugged into equation 1.1, we see that the velocity of the reaction in the cell will be an *increasing* function of K_m, given our assumption that k_{cat}/K_m is held constant.

Increases in k_{cat} are more effective at increasing the velocity of the reaction than increases in K_m are at decreasing the velocity under the particular constraint that we employed ($k_{cat}/K_m = m$). The dependence of the velocity on K_m is concave. As K_m increases, the rate of increase in the velocity decreases. Fersht argues that evolution will increase K_m until such time as further increases do not result in significant increases in the velocity, at which point evolution stagnates.

Fersht's scenario nicely accounts for the high values of K_m because the slope of the curve of velocity versus K_m is large when $K_m \approx [S]$. Thus, evolution should have little trouble moving K_m to values that are larger than $[S]$. The weakness in the argument is its dependency on the exact relationship between K_m and k_{cat}.

As an alternative model, assume that

$$k_{cat} = K_m^\alpha, \alpha \leq 1,$$

making k_{cat} a concave rather than a linear function of K_m. Plugging this constraint into equation 1.1 shows that an intermediate value of K_m will maximize the intracellular velocity when

$$K_m = \frac{\alpha}{1-\alpha}[S].$$

If $\alpha \approx 0.9$, for example, then the K_m that maximizes the intracellular velocity is about $10[S]$. This small change in Fersht's argument changes our view of the adjustment of K_m from one involving evolutionary stagnation to one of optimization.

With two very different models for the evolution of K_m in hand, we cannot say for certain which—if either—is correct. However, at this point in our discussion it is important merely to accept that there are plausible reasons for K_m to be evolutionary adjusted to intermediate values. This forms the theoretical basis of our acceptance of the conservation of K_m in ectotherms as evidence for the action of natural selection in response to different thermal environments.

It would be of considerable interest if the conservation of K_m, which is apparent when creatures are examined with a wide range of body temperatures, could also be observed between closely related species with rather small differences in body temperatures. Two such studies have been undertaken.

Graves and Somero [111] compared four species of barracudas of the genus *Sphyraena* that live in the Pacific Ocean just off the coast of the Americas. The species are largely allopatric. Moving south from California to South America the species are, in order, *S. argentea* with a midrange body temperature at 18°C, *S. lucasana* at 23°C, *S. ensis* at 26°C, and *S. idiastes* at 18°C.

Thus, two of the species are temperate with similar midbody temperature ranges and two are tropical with ranges that are only 5-8°C higher. The measured K_ms are illustrated in Figure 1.3, which shows that the M_4-LDH K_ms have evolved in exactly the manner predicted by the pattern observed in species that are much more distantly related. Moreover, the evolution is in response to remarkably small differences in body temperatures.

There are no sequence data for these barracudas, but electrophoretic studies were performed. The two temperate species had identical electrophoretic and kinetic properties suggesting that they may have identical M

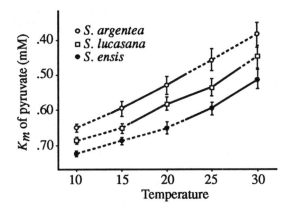

Figure 1.3. Michaelis constants for three species of barracuda as a function of temperature. The solid lines indicate the normal body temperature for each species. Redrawn from [111, Fig. 3].

chains. The two tropical species, on the other hand, could be distinguished from each other and from the temperate species by electrophoresis. The genetic identities of the four species, based on an electrophoretic analysis of 19 loci, suggests that speciation occurred 3 to 6 million years ago. If the average rate of evolution of LDH is about 3.4×10^{-10} amino acid substitutions per site per year [52, Table 1], then we expect that these LDHs differ by about 0.7-1.3 amino acids, assuming that the M chain is 329 amino acids long as it is in the spiny dogfish [52, p. 67]. Thus, the adaptive evolution of K_ms in these species may be due to only one or two substitutions per species.

The second study, by Graves et al. [110], used four pairs of fish species that have been separated by the Panama land bridge for approximately 3.1 million years. The fish on the Pacific side experience average temperatures that are 2-3°C colder than their close relatives on the Atlantic side.

Of the four pairs, two showed significant differences in their K_ms in the expected direction: Pacific fish have higher K_ms when the comparisons are made at the same temperatures. Electrophoretic analyses found that only one of the two pairs of M_4-LDHs could be distinguished among these two species, and only one pair could be distinguished between the two species pairs that failed to show significant kinetic differences. The former is probably due to the inability of electrophoresis to uncover all amino acid substitutions. The latter is more enigmatic. It could be that the substitution caused a kinetic change that was too small to be detected under the experimental conditions, affected some property of the molecule that is not expressed in the assay, or had no effect at all.

What is striking in these studies is that adaptive changes in LDH—adaptive as judged by their adherence to the general pattern of LDH evolution—occur with only a 2-3°C change in temperature. Temperature may be of extraordinary importance in the evolution of proteins, a point of view that has been convincingly championed by Somero and others for a number of years [268].

A second aspect of these studies is also important: the catalytic efficiencies of enzymes vary in such a way that cold-adapted species have higher catalytic efficiencies than warm-adapted species [130]. Enzymes speed up reactions by lowering the free energy of activation, $\Delta G^{\ddagger}$. A more efficient enzyme has a smaller $\Delta G^{\ddagger}$. Thus, cold-adapted species exhibit smaller $\Delta G^{\ddagger}$s. Warm-blooded animals, such as mammals, have less efficient enzymes. According to Hochachka and Somero [130, page 382], "no exception to this pattern of temperature compensation has been found." One explanation for this phenomenon involves an instance of evolutionary compromise.

As a general rule, enzymes undergo conformational changes when substrates are bound or released and during catalysis. These changes are necessary if the enzyme is to be an effective catalyst. Conformational changes are possible because the tertiary structures of intracellular enzymes are completely determined by weak bonds: van der Waals and hydrophobic interactions; hydrogen and electrostatic bonds. To be an efficient catalyst, an enzyme needs enough weak bonds to maintain the appropriate tertiary structure but not so many that it loses its ability to undergo conformational changes. Thus, an enzyme should be viewed as a compromise between structural stability and conformational flexibility.

Temperature plays an important role in that hydrogen and electrostatic bonds and Van der Waals interactions become less stable as the temperature increases. To prevent the tertiary structure from being disrupted, organisms with higher body temperatures must evolve enzymes with a greater number of weak bonds. As a consequence, there will be some loss of flexibility leading to higher $\Delta G^{\ddagger}$s. This is the essence of Somero's evolutionary explanation for the lower catalytic efficiency of enzymes in warm-adapted organisms [268,130].

Borgmann and Moon [21] favor a related hypothesis that focuses on the binding of ligands rather than the overall structure of the enzyme. They point out that ligands are bound by weak bonds and are thus subject to large temperature effects. Creatures living at higher temperatures will need to use more weak bonds to stabilize the enzyme-ligand complex, giving up some catalytic efficiency in the process.

As further evidence in support of the view that enzymes represent a compromise between stability and flexibility, it should be noted that enzymes from warm-adapted species tend to be more resistant to heat denaturation than those from cold-adapted species [130]. An enzyme denatures at temperatures that are far in excess of the lethal body temperature of the creature providing the enzyme. Thus, thermal stability should be viewed not as a property under direct evolution, but rather as an index of the number of the weak bonds stabilizing the tertiary structure. The weak bonds that raise $\Delta G^{\ddagger}$ in warm-adapted species also increase the thermal stability of their enzymes. A related observation is that enzymes that denature at higher temperatures also have longer half-lives in cells [104].

In the barracuda study, the catalytic efficiencies of the four species varied in exactly the pattern suggested by this discussion [111]. That is, the two temperate species had a higher catalytic efficiency than the two tropical species. Within the tropical species, the one living at a warmer temperature had a lower catalytic efficiency than the one living at a colder temperature. (Catalytic efficiency, in this case, is measured by k_{cat}, which is an exponential function of $-\Delta G^{\ddagger}$.) If our inference that the LDHs of these barracudas differ by very few amino acids is true, then these results are quite remarkable. The substitutions seem to have affected both K_m and k_{cat} in a way that is congruent with the evolution of these parameters in ectotherms generally and, at the same time, is compatible with a very appealing model of the effects of temperature on enzyme structure and function.

Studies that examine K_m and V_{max} separately illustrate one aspect of the evolution of enzymes to meet different thermal environments. Another aspect is captured in k_{max}/K_m, the pseudo first-order rate constant when the substrate concentration is well below K_m. When species from different thermal environments are compared, evidence for adaptation may often be seen in the behavior of k_{max}/K_m as a function of temperature [21]. The most carefully done studies on the evolution of k_{max}/K_m in LDH involve comparisons of alleles from within a species rather than comparisons between species. These studies were done by Place and Powers on two alleles of the heart form of LDH, LDH-B$_4$, in the fish *Fundulus heteroclitus*.

The common killifish, *F. heteroclitus*, is a small coastal minnow whose range extends from Newfoundland to Florida. This stretch of coastline has a very steep thermal gradient that averages about 1°C per degree of latitude. The mean water temperature ranges from about 7°C in the north to about 23°C in the south. A number of enzymes exhibit marked latitudinal gradients as well [241]. One of the most striking is the B form of LDH, which has two alleles: B^b, which is nearly fixed in the north and B^a, which is nearly fixed in the south. The enzymes from the three genotypes, B$_4^a$, B^a/B^b and B$_4^b$, have been isolated and their kinetics examined in extraordinary detail [239].

From our point of view, the most important aspects of this study are summarized in Figure 1.4, which illustrates the dependence of k_{cat}/K_m on temperature for both the forward (lactate oxidation) and reverse (pyruvate reduction) directions. Note that in both directions the northern genotype, LDH B$_4^b$, has a higher k_{cat}/K_m at colder temperatures whereas the southern genotype has a higher rate at warmer temperatures. The heterozygote rate tends to be intermediate over most temperatures, although not exactly so. This pattern is just what we would expect if natural selection favors large k_{cat}/K_m.

In addition to these kinetic differences, the genotypes also differ in their thermal stabilities in the expected direction. The southern genotype, B$_4^a$, is more thermally stable than the northern genotype, B$_4^b$, with the heterozy-

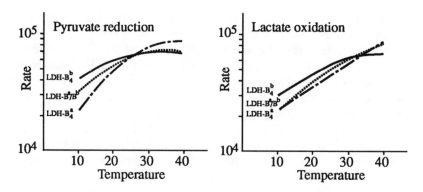

Figure 1.4. The rate of reaction for LDH genotypes from the fish *Fundulus hetero-clitus.* Redrawn from [239, Fig. 6].

gote falling in between. DNA sequencing reveals that these alleles differ by two amino acids, one affecting the electrophoretic mobility and one affecting the thermostability [Powers, pers. com.]. Alleles that were not detected electrophoretically have also been uncovered, promising a more complex story for the future.

At 10°C, the rate constant for LDH-B_4^b is about 40% higher than that of LDH-B_4^a. A difference this large might be expected to have some measurable physiological consequences. Indeed, this is the case. However, the evidence is not as clean as one would like because the enzyme concentrations differ among genotypes along with the kinetic parameters [49]. The evidence for physiological correlates with genotype will be presented first followed by some discussion of the relative roles of kinetic parameters and enzyme concentrations.

DiMichele and Powers [56] have shown that fish with different LDH genotypes vary in their ability to swim for prolonged periods of time. When fish are acclimated at 10°C, LDH-B_4^b fish swim longer and maintain a swimming speed that is about 20% higher than LDH-B_4^a fish.

The explanation for this difference appears to lie not with the Cori cycle, but rather with the effects of LDH on the concentration of ATP in the erythrocyte: levels of erythrocyte ATP are lower in LDH-B_4^a fish than in LDH-B_4^b fish. (The reasons for this are not understood at present.) ATP has the same effect on hemoglobin in fish as does 2,3-diphosphoglycerate in mammals: it lowers the oxygen affinity. Thus, LDH-B_4^b fish exhibit a lower oxygen affinity than LDH-B_4^a fish. More importantly, ATP also exaggerates the Bohr effect. At a lower blood pH, LDH-B_4^b fish will have an enhanced ability to distribute oxygen to the muscles, which may account for their increase in swimming performance at 10°C. These differences disappear at 24°C as expected from the kinetic studies.

The LDH variation is also correlated with hatching time. LDH-B_4^a fish hatch in 11.9 days, LDH-B_4^b fish in 12.8 days, and LDH-B^a/B^b fish in 12.4

days, exactly half-way between the times of the two homozygotes [55]. The eggs of *F. heteroclitus* are laid on grasses during spring tides in such a way that they develop above the water level. When the next spring tide arrives and the eggs are submerged, the respiratory stress caused by the low oxygen partial pressure in the water triggers hatching. Given that ATP levels affect the binding properties of hemoglobin, it is not surprising that the genotypes show differences in their hatching times. The direction of the difference suggests that it is the release rather than the binding of oxygen that is the key factor.

Recent work has shown that the enzyme concentrations of LDH in *Fundulus* are a function of both genotype and temperature [49]. That this fish possesses various mechanisms to adapt to temperature differences should not be surprising when one considers that the Q_{10} of enzymes is typically between two and three. Since *Fundulus* inhabits a stretch of coastline with a temperature difference of about 16°C at the extremes, all else being equal, the activities of northern fish would be less than half that of southern fish. Of course, all else is not equal. The northern genotype has a higher k_{cat}/K_m at cold temperatures than the southern genotype, it produces more enzyme as evidenced by higher levels of mRNA [49], and all *Fundulus* have the ability to increase the levels of LDH at colder temperatures by increasing the level of transcription of the locus. Crawford and Powers have argued that when all three factors are taken into account, the in vivo activity of northern fish in their native temperature regimes is equal to that of southern fish in theirs. This is a very provocative conclusion. It hints that evolution may strive to preserve the metabolic state of organisms, as summarized in substrate pool sizes and pathway fluxes, when a species experiences an altered thermal environment.

Our interpretation of the *Fundulus* results must be accompanied by the usual qualification: It may be that some of the physiological differences between genotypes are not due to activity differences between the LDH enzymes, but to linked loci.

Phosphoglucose isomerase

Phosphoglucose isomerase (PGI) sits at one of the great metabolic intersections. Glucose begins its trip through metabolism by acquiring a phosphate to become glucose-6-phosphate. From here it can go north to glycogen, east through the hexose-phosphate shunt, or south through glycolysis. The first step south is to fructose-6-phosphate, this step being catalyzed by PGI. It is hard to imagine a more important step in all of intermediary metabolism. Not surprisingly, PGI has received a great deal of attention from evolutionists interested in the functional consequences of enzyme variation. In some ways, the patterns of evolution parallel those seen for LDH. This is important in our quest for generalization. But PGI will also serve up some surprises. Most notably, it will give us overdominance (or underdominance) for kinetic parameters.

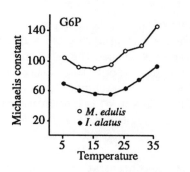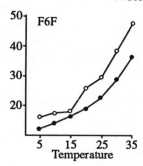

Figure 1.5. The Michaelis constants for two species of bivalves measured in both directions. Redrawn from [115, Fig. 2].

We begin our story, as we did with LDH, by looking at comparisons between closely related species. There are distressingly few such studies in the literature. The most complete that I could find is a comparative study done by Hall [115] of two bivalves from the Atlantic coast of North America. The northern species is the common (and tasty) blue mussel, *Mytilus edulis*. The southern species is the clam, *Isognomon alatus*. The two species are found in very different thermal environments. *Mytilus edulis* is seldom found in waters that are warmer than 20°C whereas *I. alatus* is a tropical species that inhabits waters from 25°C to 35°C.

When the Michaelis constants from these two species are compared over a wide range of temperatures, the results are remarkably similar to the pattern seen in LDH: the K_m of the northern species is higher than that of the southern species at all measured temperatures (Fig. 1.5). As a consequence, the K_ms from these two species are similar when measured at the temperature that each species inhabits. This is another manifestation of the conservation of K_m. Moreover, when the thermal stabilities of the two enzymes are compared, the southern enzyme is found to be substantially more thermostable than the northern enzyme. This also mimics the pattern seen in LDH.

The similarity to LDH begins to break down when we turn to k_{cat}. Hall gives data for V_{max} rather than k_{cat} even though the enzymes that he used were 97-99% pure and his V_{max} figures were normalized for enzyme concentration. This may reflect a feeling on his part that the enzyme concentration, E_t, can never be properly corrected for in an experiment designed to determine k_{cat}. This is, of course, a constant problem with all such studies.

In the forward direction, G6P→F6P, the V_{max} of *M. edulis* is generally higher than that of *I. alatus*; in the reverse direction, the opposite is true. The differences in V_{max} are quite small, but this result does go against the pattern that warm-adapted enzymes always exhibit lower k_{cat}s due to a trade-off of stability for flexibility.

In thinking about this contradiction, the Haldane relationship,

$$K_{eq} = \frac{[P]}{[S]} = \frac{k_{cat}^f/K_f}{k_{cat}^r/K_r},$$

which places a thermodynamic constraint on the forward and reverse Michaelis constants, K_f and K_r, and the k_{cat}s, needs to be considered. The four parameters must be such that the equilibrium constant for the reaction, K_{eq}, is not altered by the enzyme. Evolution is thus operating in a three-dimensional rather than a four-dimensional parameter space, ignoring, of course, other constraints imposed by the protein's structure that may further restrict the dimensionality of evolution on kinetic parameters.) As a consequence, we should not be surprised to see evolutionary changes among closely related species that do not fit broader patterns exhibited by more distantly related species.

A comparison of V_{max}/K_m reveals that this ratio is nearly the same for the two species at 5°C, but deviates steadily with increasing temperatures such that *I. alatus* always exhibits a higher value. At 35°C, there is about a twofold difference. Since V_{max} is nearly the same in the two species, the differences in V_{max}/K_m are due almost entirely to differences in K_m (see Fig. 1.5). Insofar as V_{max}/K_m is a measure of k_{cat}/K_m, it appears that *I. altatus* has a higher pseudo first-order rate constant at all temperatures. In this aspect of PGI, there is no evidence that the northern species is better adapted to colder temperatures than the southern species.

When we turn to comparisons between alleles within a species, there are many studies of PGI to choose from. The work of Watt and his colleagues stands out as the most complete at this time so will be taken up first.

Watt studies PGI in a species complex of sulfur butterflies, genus *Colias*, found in a particularly scenic area of Colorado. There are four common alleles segregating within these species*. With four alleles there are ten genotypes. Undaunted, Watt has characterized each genotype by at least 12 kinetic parameters (forward and reverse K_ms and k_{cat}s at three temperatures) and one thermostability parameter, or 130 observations (with replicates) [293,294]. For the more interesting genotypes he has included observations at different pHs as well. In addition, he has made extensive field observations to document fitness component and behavioral traits that correlate with the PGI genotypes. It is impossible to do justice to this excellent work here; only some of the highlights will be mentioned.

The basic obstacle to comprehending this work is the interactions that occur between alleles. Although heterozygotes tend to be intermediate, they are not exactly so. Moreover, under some experimental conditions and between certain pairs of alleles, overdominance is observed. To further complicate the story, thermostability does not appear to be correlated with kinetic parameters. For example, the ordering of alleles (numbered 2 to 5)

---

*As far as can be determined, there are only four alleles, although without sequence data there is always the possibility of some cryptic alleles.

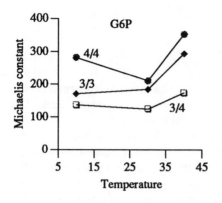
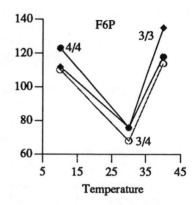

Figure 1.6. The Michaelis constants for the three genotypes of PGI in *Colias* measured in both directions. Data are from [294, Table 4].

by the thermostability of their homozygotes is $5 > 4 > 3 > 2$. By contrast, the ordering of K_ms for G6P is $4 > 3 > 5 > 2$.

There does not appear to be any simple way to summarize the data. This may be the most important message from the entire effort. It suggests that each amino acid substitution will affect several properties of a protein and that the effects are tangled. By this I mean, for example, that one amino acid substitution may lower both the K_m and the thermostability, while another may lower the K_m but raise the thermostability. There may be no low-dimensional property of amino acids that can be used to predict the full range of their consequences on the functional properties of the molecule. This is not a great insight. Were it otherwise, protein chemists would be able to tell us about the workings of a protein by knowing only its primary structure.

Alleles 3 and 4 have received the most attention. One reason is illustrated in Figure 1.6: there is marked underdominance for K_m at all temperatures. Since PGI is a dimer, the cells of heterozygotes have three forms of PGI. Presumably, the subunits of the 3/4 heterodimer interact in such a way that the K_m is outside of the range of the two homodimers. (This should be contrasted to LDH in *Fundulus* where we saw that the heterozygote was nearly intermediate in its kinetic properties.) V_{max}, on the other hand, is relatively similar in the these three genotypes. As a consequence, there is overdominance for V_{max}/K_m suggesting that these two alleles may be held in the population because of the superiority of the 3/4 heterozygote. If, that is, we accept that there is some advantage in having a larger V_{max}/K_m.

Butterflies follow the maxim "fly early, fly often." Viewed as a machine for turning nectar's simple sugars into eggs or sperm, it is easy to imagine that butterflies that begin their flights to the flowers first will accrue some advantage. These may well be the individuals that can fire up glycolysis the fastest in the chill of the morning. Since PGI is the first step in glycolysis, and since V_{max}/K_m of the 3/4 heterozygote is greater than that of the 3/3 or 4/4 homozygotes, it is natural to see if there are relatively more 3/4 individuals flying about early in the morning than at the warmer periods of the day. In fact, this is exactly what is observed. For example, in one study with six different samples, 3/4 heterozygotes made up a larger fraction of the early morning fliers than they did among the peak period flyers [296, Table 1]. This fits with the maxim's fly early component.

The 3/4 heterozygotes also fly more often. In one study in Tracy, California, it was observed that the 3/4 heterozygotes are active for a longer period of the day and that the 3/3 homozygotes were not far behind. The 4/4 homozygotes, on the other hand, flew for a distinctly shorter period of time [296, Fig. 1]. As can be inferred from Figure 1.6, this mirrors the relative positions of V_{max}/K_m for the three genotypes.

These observations were made at low to moderate temperatures (from a butterfly's point of view). Given the thermostability differences between alleles, it might be expected that some evidence for differential survival under heat stress could also be found. The 5/5, 4/5, and 4/4 genotypes are the most thermostable. There are two studies that suggest that the frequencies of these genotypes increase throughout the summer [296, Table 4]. This may well be due to their increased thermostability, although more direct evidence would be desirable.

The amount of information that Watt and his colleagues have amassed on the role of temperature in the biology of *Colias* in general and glycolysis in particular is staggering. The work of Kingsolver should also be mentioned as it extends the *Colias* story significantly [167,168]. While the details of this work are fascinating, from our point of view there are four general observations that are relevant to the theme of this book:

- There are significant kinetic and thermostability differences between alleles that segregate in *Colias* populations.

- Heterozygotes are generally intermediate in their properties, but never exactly so. In one important instance overdominance in V_{max}/K_m is observed at all temperatures.

- There are behavioral correlates with genotype that fit predictions based on the ordering of V_{max}/K_m among genotypes and the assumption that flight is limited by the flux through glycolysis.

- There is some evidence that natural selection favors more thermostable genotypes during hotter periods of the summer.

Except for the overdominance, this summary is remarkably close to that for LDH in *Fundulus*.

One could have argued that the role of temperature in the evolution of aquatic organisms may be very different from that of terrestrial ectotherms since the latter have the option of behavioral regulation of their body temperatures. The *Colias* results suggest that temperature may be even more important in terrestrial organisms due, in part, to the greater fluctuations in temperature and, in part, to the tendency for evolution to balance the advantages of longer periods of activity with the risks of moving about at extreme (hot or cold) temperatures.

Allelic variation in PGI has been examined in several other species as well. *Fundulus* has two segregating alleles that exhibit the same sort of cline along the Atlantic coast as seen in LDH. Van Beneden and Powers [285] have isolated the two alleles and shown that the southern allele is more thermostable than the northern allele although the kinetic parameters are generally the same. The one significant difference was in the binding constant for the inhibitor 6-phosphogluconate at temperatures above 30°C. No studies were performed to see if this difference has any physiological consequences. Similarly, Anthony Zera [315] found differences in thermostability and other kinetic parameters in two clinally varying PGI alleles from the water strider *Limnoporus canaliculatus* and Hoffman [131] has found kinetic differences between alleles in the sea anemone *Metridium senile*.

Hemoglobin

The major role of hemoglobin is to bind oxygen from the lungs or gills where the partial pressure of oxygen is relatively high, to transport it to regions of low oxygen partial pressure, and to release it in these areas for use by the cells.

The oxygen-binding properties of hemoglobin that make all this happen are illustrated in Figure 1.7. There are two important things to note about this graph. The first is that the curves are sigmoidal. This prevents hemoglobin from releasing oxygen continuously as it moves through the oxygen partial pressure gradient in the arteries. Rather, it holds onto oxygen until the partial pressure drops below a critical value before releasing it. The nonlinear binding of oxygen is called *cooperativity* since the binding of the first molecules facilitates the binding of subsequent molecules. The partial pressure of oxygen at which hemoglobin is 50% saturated, P_{50}, is called its *oxygen affinity*.

The second important aspect of this curve is the shift to the right as the pH is lowered. This is called the alkaline Bohr effect or, more often, simply the *Bohr effect*. The Bohr effect facilitates the release of oxygen in regions of low pH—frequently due to the buildup of lactic acid or carbon dioxide—signaling the need for oxygen. Various anions, including chloride, phosphate, D-2,3-bisphosphoglycerate (DPG), and inositol hexaphosphate (IHP), can exert a strong influence on the Bohr effect. Much of the variation in the properties of hemoglobins from different species have to do with the binding properties of these molecules.

Hemoglobin is a tetramer composed of two alpha chains and two beta chains. In humans and many mammals the alpha and beta chains are

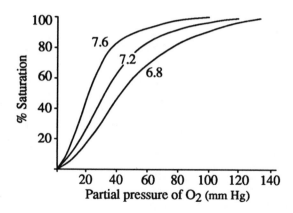

Figure 1.7. Oxygen affinity curves for human hemoglobin. The pH is indicated by the number next to each curve. Redrawn from [54].

made up of 141 and 146 amino acids, respectively. Each chain contains a histidine that is bound to a heme group, a porphyrin ring with an iron atom that can bind a single oxygen molecule. Since each subunit has one heme group, each hemoglobin molecule can bind four oxygen molecules. X-ray crystallographic studies indicate that the molecule should be envisioned as made up of two fairly rigid $\alpha\beta$ dimers that rotate with respect to each other by about 15 degrees when the molecule changes from the deoxy to the fully oxygenated state.

Cooperativity, the property yielding the sigmoid oxygen affinity curve, is due to configuration changes that occur in hemoglobin as oxygen is bound or released. At any instant in time, all four subunits of a hemoglobin molecule are in one of two states: The T (for *Tense*) state, which has a relatively weak affinity for oxygen, and the R (for *Relaxed*) state, which has a strong affinity. The equilibrium for the two states is strongly in favor of T when no oxygen is bound and strongly in favor of R when all four oxygens are bound. The shift from T to R usually occurs when two or three oxygen molecules are bound. As the partial pressure of oxygen increases, the first couple of oxygen molecules bind reluctantly because the hemoglobin is in the T state; when two or three are bound, the configuration changes to the R state allowing the final one or two oxygens to bind rapidly giving rise to the sigmoidal oxygen affinity curve. There is obviously a lot of room for evolutionary adjustment of oxygen affinity through alterations of the binding constants of oxygen to the T and R states or through changes in the equilibria constants for the T–R transitions.

The mechanistic explanation for the Bohr effect is more controversial [129,243]. There are two competing models. The simpler model attributes the Bohr effect to relatively few salt bridges between pairs of polar amino acids on the surface of the molecule [237]. Under this model the bridge between the final histidine in the beta chain (His β146) and aspartic acid β94 accounts for up to 50% of the Bohr effect.

The competing model spreads the Bohr effect over many more amino acids [248] including most of the histidines. This view is supported by both NMR (nuclear magnetic resonance) studies [129] and an electrostatic model [205]. Much of the confusion stems from the difficulty of attributing NMR resonances to particular amino acids and from the confounding effects of buffer conditions. Under some experimental conditions, for example, the contribution of His β146 to the Bohr effect is reduced to only 5% even though the total Bohr effect is not diminished at all [129].

The outcome of this highly technical debate will be of no small interest to evolutionists. Consider that the Bohr effect is but one—albeit an important one—attribute of the hemoglobin molecule. If a large fraction of the charged surface amino acids is shown to contribute to the effect, then it becomes less likely that substitutions of one polar amino acid for another will be inconsequential to the functioning of the molecule. Should other attributes also be due to effects of a similar number of amino acids, then we must conclude that changes in most amino acids will have a palpable affect on the molecule's properties.

The usual picture of the hemoglobin molecule is one where relatively few amino acids participate in functionally important activities such as ligand binding or determining the tertiary structure, and many more that are merely filling space in alpha helices [236]. The latter amino acids are free to evolve under the mild constraint that the amino substitutions are conservative, which means that they do not appreciably alter the polarity or the space occupied by the previous amino acid. Examples would include switches between glutamic and aspartic acids or between leucine and isoleucine.

In fact, most of the amino acid substitutions that have occurred in hemoglobin are conservative [54]. Some sites are invariant throughout the evolution of myoglobin and hemoglobin, whereas others change very rarely. Most of the latter have been shown to be critically involved in either the tertiary structure, the binding of the heme group or, in the case of hemoglobin, the contact between the subunits [54]. This supports the maxim that functionally important amino acid sites tend to evolve very slowly.

There are many examples of vertebrate hemoglobin adaptations to different life styles and environments (reviewed in [130,236,240,303]). Even among mammals, there are substantial differences in many properties of hemoglobins such as oxygen affinity (e. g., larger mammals tend to have higher oxygen affinities [251]), Bohr effect (e. g., larger animals have a smaller Bohr effect [242]), and ligand binding (e. g., DPG lowers oxygen affinities in most mammals but not cats, ruminants or lemurs [251]). In most cases, these adaptations have been uncovered by comparisons of species that are distantly related. Such species tend to differ by as many as 20 or 30 amino acids, making it difficult to investigate the contributions of individual amino acids to the adaptation. Perutz, in his fascinating review of this area [236], concludes that most of these adaptations may be attributed to very few of the amino acid substitutions while the remaining substitutions, he feels, are neutral.

One way to find support for the opposite point of view—that most amino acid substitutions have some adaptive significance—is to choose at random species whose hemoglobins differ by only a few amino acids and to attribute some adaptive significance to these changes. If this approach usually succeeded, we would eventually be persuaded that most amino acid substitutions are important. However, as an experimental approach this is far from satisfactory. While we may be able to find small functional differences between hemoglobins of closely related species, it is unlikely that we would be able to discover the environmental differences that selected for the altered function. Presumably, this is why such studies do not appear in the literature.

Alternatively, we could examine species from environments that differ in such a way as to suggest the adaptive changes that should occur in hemoglobin, and check to see if they do, in fact, occur. The obvious environmental property that should elicit adaptive changes in hemoglobins is the partial pressure of oxygen. Indeed, there is an extensive literature on the adaptations of hemoglobins in creatures living at high altitudes, underground, and under water.

Since at least 1936 [114] we have known that the blood of species living at high altitudes has a higher oxygen affinity than that of their lowland relatives. These species also exhibit an increased resistance to hypoxia (see [238]). The molecular bases for the adaptation can include a higher oxygen affinity of hemoglobin itself, a higher titer of hemoglobin, a lowered concentration of ligands, such as DPG, that reduce the oxygen affinity of hemoglobin, or a reduced sensitivity of hemoglobin to these ligands [238]. In addition, some species have evolved elaborate cascade mechanisms with multiple hemoglobins that differ in their oxygen affinities to, in effect, hand down the oxygen from one component to another [304]. Thus, it would be natural to expect that closely related species living at different altitudes might exhibit microadaptations in their hemoglobins in the direction that the highland species have increased oxygen affinities. In fact, there are several such examples in the literature.

There is a remarkable example of parallel evolution in the hemoglobins of the barheaded goose (*Anser indicus*) which lives above 4000 meters in the Himalayas (and flies above 9200 meters to get over Mt. Everest) and the Andean goose (*Chloephaga melanoptera*) which lives at 6000 meters in the Andes. Ducks and geese usually have two hemoglobins in the adult, hemoglobins A and D. The two hemoglobins have the same β chain but different α chains, α^A and α^D. The blood of the barheaded goose exhibits a higher oxygen affinity when compared to its close lowland relative, the greylag goose (*A. anser*) and the barheaded goose itself exhibits an increased resistance to hypoxia. This is due to properties of the hemoglobin molecule itself rather than to concentrations of intracellular ligands or hemoglobin titers [238]).

A comparison of the amino acid sequences shows that the beta globins of the barheaded and greylag geese differ by one amino acid (β125 glu→asp) [224], the α^A chains by three [224], and the α^D chains by four [123]. When these substitutions are examined in light of the three-dimensional structure of hemoglobin, one change, α^A119 pro→ala, stands out as a major contributor to the increase in oxygen affinity. The effect is thought to be due to the disruption of the van der Waals contact that α119 pro usually forms with β55 leu, shifting the equilibrium in favor of the R state and increasing the oxygen affinity [123]. This is supported by the fact that only hemoglobin A shows an increase in oxygen affinity and that abnormal hemoglobins in humans that break similar contacts tend to shift the equilibrium in favor of the R state [236].

A second substitution, α^A63 ala→ser, is predicted to cause a large change in the tertiary structure by moving the E and B helices apart by 1.5Å, thereby making an additional contribution to the increased oxygen affinity [224]. The difference in the oxygen affinities between the barheaded and greylag geese is amplified about tenfold in the presence of inositol pentaphosphate. The substitutions at both α^A119 and β125 are thought to contribute to this altered sensitivity [224].

The Andean goose is actually a closer relative of the mallard duck than of some other goose. When the sequences of the mallard and Andean goose were compared, it was discovered that they differed by five amino acids in the β chain and five in the α^A chain [122]. (The α^D chain has not been sequenced.) Remarkably, one of the substitutions is β55 leu→ser, a change that disrupts the very same van der Waals contact that is disrupted by the substitution α^A119 pro→ala in the barheaded goose. Since this is a change in the β chain, both hemoglobins A and D demonstrate an increased oxygen affinity. This is a very nice example of parallel evolution of function—increased oxygen affinity—and mechanism—changed van der Waals contact—by different amino acid substitutions.

The adaptive changes in the hemoglobins of these high altitude geese are attributed to three substitutions of eight in the barheaded goose and one of ten in the Andean goose. As far as I have been able to determine, no careful studies have been performed to try to identify functional changes that may be attributed to the other substitutions. It would be very interesting to change, say, greylag goose hemoglobin into barheaded hemoglobin one mutation at a time via site-directed mutagenesis. With each change, a careful analysis of the oxygen affinity, ligand binding, and Bohr effect should tell us whether these changes do alter the function of the molecule. It would be of particular interest to see if the disruption of the α^A119-β55 contact causes some auxiliary changes that are modified by some of the other amino acid substitutions.

There are a group of European and African vultures that often ascend to extraordinary altitudes. A rather unlucky Rüppell's griffon (*Gyps rueppelli*), for example, was hit by a commercial airliner over the Ivory Coast

Table 1.1. Amino acids from the α globins of the black vulture (BV), the white-headed vulture (WV), and Rüppell's griffon (RG) at positions that show variation between these species.

Locus	\multicolumn{6}{c}{Amino acid site}

Locus	12	34	38	104	123	137
BV α^A	thr	ile	pro	cys	ala	thr
WV α^A	thr	ile	pro	cys	ala	ser
RG $\alpha^{A'}$	asn	ile	pro	cys	ala	thr
RG α^A	asn	thr	pro	cys	ala	thr
BV & WV α^D	ala	ile	pro	cys	ala	thr
RG $\alpha^{D'}$	thr	ile	gln	asn	ser	thr
RG α^D	thr	ile	gln	cys	ser	thr

of Africa at 36,000 feet! The hemoglobins of several of these vultures including Rüppell's griffon, the black vulture (*Aegypius monachus*), and the white-headed vulture (*Trigonoceps occipitalis*) have been sequenced and their oxygen-binding properties examined [124,125,126].

All three species have high overall oxygen affinities due, in part, to amino acid substitutions at positions 34 and 38 in their α chains. This region of α globin, the *respiratory box*, is involved in $\alpha_1\beta_1$ and $\alpha_1\beta_2$ contacts. Substitutions in the respiratory box tend to have a marked effect on the relative concentrations of the T or R states.

All three vultures have proline at position $\alpha^A 38$ rather than glutamine as is usual for birds (Table 1.1). Black and white-headed vultures also have proline at $\alpha^D 38$, as does one of the two D hemoglobins of Rüppell's griffon (see below). All three species have identical β chains. The white-headed and black vultures also have identical α^D chains. The α^A chain of the white-headed vulture differs from that of the black vulture by a single substitution, $\alpha^A 137$ thr→ser, but the functional consequences of the substitution are not yet understood. It has been suggested that the substitution may affect the neighboring heme contact of $\alpha 136$.

Rüppell's griffon hemoglobin is particularly interesting as it contains four components, A, A', D, and D', which are thought to be due to duplications in both the α^A and α^D loci. Hemoglobins A and A' differ from each other by a single amino acid substitution $\alpha 34$ ile→thr. Paradoxically, this substitution lowers rather than raises the oxygen affinity as might be expected given the high-altitude flights of this bird. In addition, the two α^A chains differ from that of the black vulture by only one other substitution, $\alpha^A 12$ thr→asn.

Both D and D' have the substitution $\alpha^D 38$ pro→gln, which increases oxygen affinity through the stabilization of the R configuration. They also share the substitutions $\alpha^D 12$ ala→thr and $\alpha^D 123$ ala→ser. The former site varies quite a bit among birds, but the latter contains alanine in all birds except the starling, tree sparrow, and goshawk, each of these containing serine [126]. No functional significance is currently attributed to these two substitutions, although the parallel evolution of $\alpha^D 123$ is intriguing. The two D chains differ by $\alpha^D 123$ cys→asn, but no functional significance has been attached to this change either. The oxygen affinities of the four components are such that D/D' is highest, A' is next, and A has the lowest affinity. Thus, the griffon has evolved a cascade system where oxygen may be passed down through three stages. This may well account for the fact that the griffon is found flying at higher altitudes than either the white-headed or black vultures. Why a vulture should want to fly at 36,000 feet remains a mystery.

The microadaptations in the Rüppell's griffon is particularly noteworthy, with two substitutions of four exhibiting functional consequences that appear to be adaptations to flying at extremely high altitudes. However, this work is quite new so there are a few loose ends. Population samples should be examined from all three species to be sure that some of the "substitutions" are not polymorphisms. It would also be valuable to compare the properties of hemoglobin A in the black and white-headed vultures and the two D hemoglobins in the griffon. Such comparisons, if done carefully, might uncover some functional changes that are not predicted by the standard three-dimensional models.

The evolution of hemoglobins between populations of the deer mouse, *Peromyscus maniculatus*, follows a pattern similar to that we just described between species of birds. Deer mice are remarkable in their ability to live at different altitudes. The subspecies *P. m. sonoriensis*, for example, may be found below sea level in Death Valley, California, and at 4300 meters in the adjacent Sierra Nevada and White Mountains [267]. At 4300 meters the partial pressure of oxygen is about 56% that at sea level, a difference that is known to cause hypoxia when experienced by lowland animals.

The evolution of the oxygen transport system within *P. maniculatus* is extraordinarily complex. This is due, in part, to the fact that there are two tightly linked adult α-globin loci and three adult β-globin loci. Both α-globin loci and one of the β-globin loci are highly polymorphic, producing a bewildering array of hemoglobin molecules within the species. In addition to variation of the hemoglobin itself, deer mice exhibit variation in other aspects of the molecular environment of the erythrocyte as is typical of mammals living at different altitudes.

There is a strong positive correlation between oxygen affinity and altitude when subspecies are compared, but this correlation is not observed within subspecies. Snyder [267] argued that deer mouse migration rates are probably high enough to swamp out any local differentiation within the steep altitudinal gradients that are typically occupied by single subspecies, but are low enough between subspecies to allow the pattern to emerge. It is difficult to sort out the contributions of particular alleles to this pattern because of the large number that are segregating. To show that there is some effect, Chappell and Snyder [39] focused on a particular classification of haplotypes of the α-globin loci that was suggested by the extraordinarily high levels of linkage disequilibrium between these two loci.

The two α-globin loci are called *Hba* and *Hbc*. The alleles at each of these loci fall into two classes based on isoelectric focusing. These are called the a^0 and a^1 alleles at *Hba* and the c^0 and c^1 alleles at *Hbc*. The most frequent haplotypes in natural populations are a^1c^1 and a^0c^0. The "recombinant" types make up less than 0.015 of all haplotypes, on average.

As with oxygen affinity, there is a strong positive correlation between the frequency of the a^0c^0 haplotype and altitude across subspecies, but not within subspecies. (There may be differentiation within subspecies that is masked by the lumping of alleles into just two classes.) The frequency of a^0c^0 is nearly one in high-altitude subspecies and nearly zero in lowland subspecies. Thus, the geographic pattern is not at all subtle.

Oxygen dissociation studies showed that the P_{50} values for the three genotypes were ranked as expected [39]:

$$a^0c^0/a^0c^0 < a^0c^0/a^1c^1 < a^1c^1/a^1c^1.$$

These studies used genotypes from a number of different subspecies. The determinations of P_{50} used intact erythrocytes, so Chappell and Snyder had to go to some lengths to show that the effects were not due to intracellular concentrations of DPG.

The maximum oxygen consumptions for the three genotypes were also determined at two altitudes for mice subjected to stress through exercise or cold temperatures and were shown to differ in a rather interesting pattern. The maximum oxygen consumption was highest for a^0c^0/a^0c^0 mice subject to either form of stress when the experiments were performed at 3800 meters, but was highest for a^1c^1/a^1c^1 when they were performed at 340 meters.

The sequences of these alleles have not been determined so we cannot know at this time the number of amino acid differences that are responsible for the functional differences. The importance of this study is its demonstration that the same sort of functional differences that we observed between hemoglobins of closely related species may also be seen between alleles within a single species. Based on these observations, there is no reason to think that the processes that lead to variation between species are any different from those that lead to variation within species.

Osmoregulation

Many marine invertebrates adjust their osmotic pressures to match those of the surrounding waters by changing the concentrations of intracellular free amino acids. The most commonly used amino acids are alanine, proline, and glycine; some other amino acids are also used. Coastal species often live in environments with both temporal and spatial fluctuations in salinity. Such species have the ability to change their osmotic pressures in response to these fluctuations by increasing or decreasing the activities of enzymes involved in the production of osmoregulatory amino acids. These same enzymes are good candidates for genetically based variability in activity that is maintained by natural selection. Indeed, there are two striking examples of enzyme polymorphisms that appear to be involved with adaptations to salinity changes.

The copepod *Tigriopus californicus* lives in splash pools along the west coast of North America. These pools are subject to extraordinary fluctuations in salinity due to evaporation in dry periods and freshwater runoff in wet periods. *Tigriopus* has been shown to be able to tolerate salinities in the laboratory ranging from 15% to 300% that of seawater [32]. When a change in salinity occurs, the hemolymph osmotic pressure changes first followed by the cellular pressure. Within 3 hours after a salinity change, the free intracellular concentrations of proline, alanine, and glycine vary in the appropriate directions: increases for hyperosmotic stress and decreases for hypoosmotic stress. The response can continue for up to 24 hours, although at a much reduced rate.

The final step in alanine synthesis is catalyzed by glutamate-pyruvate transaminase (GPT). This enzyme, which is polymorphic in *Tigriopus* populations, takes the amino group from glutamate and sticks it on pyruvate to make alanine and α-ketoglutarate. I mention this because pyruvate is an end product of glycolysis and α-ketoglutarate is an intermediate in the citric acid cycle. Thus, GPT should not be thought of as an enzyme that is sitting in some remote corner of metabolism.

Burton and his colleagues have devoted a great deal of effort to understanding the role of the GPT polymorphism in the adaptation of *Tigriopus* to fluctuating salinities. In a population in Santa Cruz, there are two common electrophoretically distinguishable alleles, GPT^F and GPT^S [33]. The frequency of the GPT^F allele varies from 0.2 to 0.3 in this area. A simple experiment to check for a correlation of genotype with intracellular alanine concentrations showed that after 4 hours of hyperosmotic stress, the intracellular concentrations of alanine were 19.68, 9.88, and 6.57 parts per thousand for the genotypes GPT^{FF}, GPT^{FS}, and GPT^{SS}, respectively. The specific activity of GPT^{FF} is about 1.46 times that of GPT^{SS} in the alanine synthesizing direction. (It is 1.11 times as active in the alanine catabolizing direction.) Thus, the increased concentration of alanine is likely to be due to the effects of the GPT genotypes. In addition, GPT^{SS} larvae exhibit a significantly higher mortality under hyperosmotic stress than do GTP^{FS} or GTP^{FF} larvae in the laboratory.

Unfortunately, more detailed kinetics are not available. With the available data, it is impossible to know if the specific activity differences are due to the amino acid differences between the alleles or to differences in enzyme concentrations.

Koehn and his colleagues at Stony Brook have thoroughly studied the role of aminopeptidase-1 (called LAP from its former name, leucine aminopeptidase) in osmoregulation in the mussel *Mytilus edulis*. Like GPT, LAP catalyzes a reaction that results in the production of free amino acids used to adjust the mussel's osmotic pressure. LAP accomplishes this by digesting N-terminal amino acids from oligopeptides. There are five polymorphic alleles in *M. edulis* populations, three of which are relatively common. Although there are physiological and fitness differences correlated with LAP genotype, it appears that kinetic differences between alleles can account for only a small part of this [171]. In particular, one of the common alleles, Lap^94, has a higher k_{cat} than the other two, Lap^96 and Lap^98. Allele Lap^94 is more frequent in regions with higher salinities and individuals with this allele suffer a greater mortality at lower salinities. All this suggests that Lap^94 plays some role in adapting *M. edulis* to life at the higher salinities of the open ocean. There is much more to the *Mytilus* story than suggested by this small abstraction. Much of this, which is not directly applicable to the theme of this section, may be found in [127].

Insulin

The previous examples involved amino acid changes that modify kinetic or thermostability properties of enzymes. Insulin provides a nice example of evolution for another aspect of proteins: the hydrophobicity of the exterior.

Insulin plays a key role in the regulation of glucose metabolism in vertebrates. Insulin begins life in the β cells of the islets of Langerhans as *preproinsulin*, a protein subdivided into three regions: a signal peptide followed by the B, C, and A peptides. The signal peptide is cleaved off in the rough endoplasmic reticulum to give *proinsulin*. Proinsulin is packaged in storage granules along with proteases that remove the C peptide to produce insulin as the granules mature. (The A and B peptides are held together by disulfide bonds so the cleavage doesn't result in two unattached peptides.)

In most mammals, insulin associates into hexamers within storage granules. The formation of these hexamers is a two-step process. Two monomers come together to form a dimer, then three dimers form a torus with two zinc atoms in the interior. The zinc atoms bond to the histidine at the tenth position in the B chain.

The hystricomorph rodents, guinea pigs and friends, have departed from this pattern. They store their insulin as monomers rather than as hexamers. The reason for this is not understood, but the evolutionary adjustments that accompany the change make a fascinating story as told by Blundell and Wood [19].

The story focuses on a patch on the surface of the insulin molecule where the monomers are held together by hydrophobic bonds. In the changeover to the monomeric storage form, this patch must become hydrophilic so that the monomers will remain apart. The most important substitutions responsible for the disruption of the hexamer storage form are shown in Figure 1.8, which uses pig insulin as a basis of comparison. The substitutions indicated in the figure are some of the ones that would be needed to change pig insulin into guinea pig insulin. Obviously, guinea pigs did not evolve from pigs (despite the suggestive names). The ordinarily slow

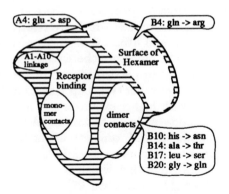

Figure 1.8. A projection of the major features of the pig insulin molecule onto two dimensions. Some of the amino acid changes that separate the pig from the guinea pig are indicated. Modified from [19, Fig. 1].

and conservative evolution of insulin in mammals and the very rapid evolution in the hystricomorphs allows us to use this comparison without being seriously misled.

Of the substitutions illustrated in Figure 1.8, none is more important than B10 his→asn since this is the histidine that binds to zinc to stabilize the hexamer. Of the hystricomorphs that have been sequenced, two (guinea pig and cuis) have asparagine at position B10 and two (coypu and caisiragua) have glutamine. Two other hystricomorphs, the African porcupine and the chinchilla, have retained the histidine even though they store insulin as monomers. Interestingly, these two also show much less of an acceleration in their rates of evolution than the four other hystricomorphs [12].

Three other amino acid substitutions have occurred within the hydrophobic dimer contact sites B14, B17, and B20. These changes are to larger and more hydrophilic residues. The substitutions at B4 and A4 are to larger and more basic amino acids. It should be emphasized that all of these substitutions are radical by almost any criterion. They all occur on the surface of the molecule and all contribute to an increase in the thermodynamic stability of the molecule in an aqueous medium [19].

Of the remaining 12 differences that separate the pig and the guinea pig, few would be called conservative. Not unexpectedly, there are many functional differences between these molecules as well. The most striking difference is the unusually low potency of guinea pig insulin even though their insulin receptors appear to be "normal." That is, their receptors bind more tightly to insulin from other mammals than to guinea pig insulin (as do the receptors from other mammals) [272].

Steiner et al. note that there are quite a few strange things about the role of insulin in guinea pigs that may be correlated with the accelerated evolution [272]. Among these are a higher level of insulin in the blood, a higher density of insulin receptors, greater growth factor activity, greater interactions with platelet-derived growth factors, and higher levels of IGF II in adults. Thus, it may well be that the shift from hexamer storage to monomer storage was part of a more general evolutionary shift in insulin function. In fact, since guinea pig glucagon also has an altered function, Seino et al. [252] feel that the entire gastro-entero-pancreatic hormonal system in hystricomorphs has undergone a major evolutionary change in the New World. They also point out that a similar rate acceleration is seen in the insulin of the New World owl monkey. They even speculate that there could be a common environmental factor responsible for both accelerations, although none has been identified.

Insulin was brought into the discussion at this point for two reasons. One was as an illustration of the evolution of surface properties of a protein. The other was to introduce the idea that an acceleration in the rate of evolution of a protein may often be used as an indicator that important adaptive changes have occurred. Although a more complete discussion of this will be postponed until the chapter on the molecular clock, it is worthwhile at this point to give some of the evidence that the rate of evolution is, in fact, higher in the hystricomorphs.

Among nonhystricomorph mammals, the rate of evolution of insulin is about 4.4×10^{-10} amino acid substitutions per site per year [52, Table 1]. This is about one-third the rate of hemoglobin suggesting that insulin should be viewed as a relatively slow-evolving protein. For example, pig and mouse I* insulins differ by only 4 amino acids even though these species have been separated for approximately 70 million years. By contrast, pig and guinea pig insulins differ by 18 amino acids, even though they have been separated for exactly the same length of time.

Beintema and Campagne [12] have used parsimony techniques to infer an insulin evolutionary tree for rodents and the pig. An abbreviated version is shown in Figure 1.9. The tree is based on amino acid sequences but the inferred number of substitutions along each branch are nucleotide substitutions. The branch lengths are drawn in proportion to the number of substitutions rather than in proportion to the length of time each lineage represents. This gives a dramatic visualization of the speedup in the hystricomorphs. Consider, for example, that the time from the junction of the pig and mouse branches to the tips of all of the branches is about the same. There is one inferred substitution on the pig lineage and 32 inferred substitutions from the rodent-pig split to the casiragua or about a 30-fold increase in the rate of amino acid substitution. Using an approach that does not involve parsimony, Kimura [160] estimated that the hystricomorph rate is more than 10 times the average rate in mammals.

It should be noted briefly that an alternative reason for the speedup in the evolutionary rate of insulin in the hystricomorphs is a "relaxation of

---

*Mice and rats have duplicate insulin genes.

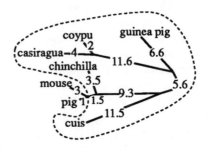

Figure 1.9. An unrooted maximum parsimony tree for insulin in rodents and the pig. The lengths of the branches and the number are the inferred numbers of nucleotide substitutions on the branches. The hystricomorph rodents are in the region surrounded by the dashed line. Modified from [12, Fig. 2].

constraints" that accompanies the shift from the hexamer to monomer storage forms [162]. This scenario claims that the substitution of asparagine for histidine at position B10 is an instance of the fixation of a deleterious allele by genetic drift. For some reason, the consequent changeover to the monomer storage form makes many previously constrained sites neutral, allowing rapid evolution. While this might be a plausible suggestion in the absence of other data, the fact that the amino acid substitutions made the exterior more hydrophilic and the fact that there are numerous functional consequences of the amino acid substitutions in this very important hormone make this hypothesis untenable.

Lysozyme c

Our final example, lysozyme c, is like insulin in that we will see an acceleration in the rate of evolution associated with a change in function of a protein. Also like insulin, the number of substitutions involved is fairly high, so it will not be possible to attach significance to all of them.

Lysozyme, an enzyme that attacks peptidoglycan in the cell walls of bacteria, is part of the antibiotic arsenal of many animals. It is found, among other places, in tears and saliva of mammals and in the whites of bird eggs. Artiodactyls (cows, deer, and the like) and leaf-eating monkeys (such as the langur) have independently recruited lysozyme as a means of digesting bacteria that flow from their rumins into their stomachs. Presumably, this allows them to retrieve some of the nutritional value that is contained in the bacterial cells. Lysozyme has independently evolved in cloven-hoofed mammals and langurs to resist digestion and to function in the low pH, protease-rich environment found in their stomachs. Some remarkable parallels in the amino acid substitutions that have occurred in the two groups. D. E. Dobson, Jacqueline and Pierre Jollès, Caro-Beth Stewart and Allan Wilson are the central figures in the work on parallel evolution in lysozyme although several others from Wilson's lab have contributed as well.

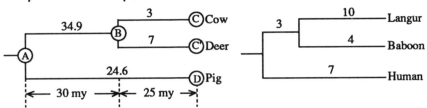

Figure 1.10. The left tree gives the maximum parsimony estimates of the number of amino acid substitutions in lysozyme among artiodactyls (modified from [146, Fig. 4]). The right tree gives the number of amino acid substitutions in lysozyme from primates (modified from [273, Fig. 4]).

We will look at the evolution of lysozyme in artiodactyls first, using this as a basis for examining evolution in the langurs. The history of amino acid substitutions, as inferred by parsimony techniques [146], is given in the left side of Figure 1.10. The most important thing to note is the apparent acceleration in the rate of evolution of lysozyme in the first half of the ruminant lineage followed by a deceleration in the second half. The rate along the AB branch (the early part of ruminant evolution) is about 1.16 substitutions per million years or about three times the typical mammalian rate of 0.4 substitutions per million years. The average rate along the BC branch (the later part of ruminant evolution) is about 0.2 substitutions per million years or one-half the typical rate.

As further support for rate variation, Jollès et al. [146] noted that for five other proteins the ratio of the number of substitutions on branch AB to those on branch BC was 0.9 as compared with about 6 for lysozyme. The acceleration occurs in the same branch where lysozyme was recruited for use in the stomach (assuming that the recruitment did not occur independently in each ruminant lineage). With some 34 amino acid substitutions on this branch, it is unlikely that we will ever know which ones play a role in the adaptation for life in the stomach and which ones, if any, are neutral.

Jollès et al. [146] attempted to identify the functionally most important substitutions. They began by summarizing those properties of lysozyme that are shared by deer and cows but are distinct from those of the pig. The assumption is that these properties are the very ones that adapt lysozyme to function in the stomach. The most important of these are as follows.

- The pH optimum of ruminant lysozyme is lower (a narrow profile centered at 5) than that of the pig (a broad profile from 5 to 8).

- The isoelectric points of cow and deer are both close to 7 while that of the pig is about 10. This appears to support the general adaptive strategy that enzymes that function at lower pHs should be less basic.

- The number of aspartyl and amide bonds is reduced in the ruminants relative to the pig (17-18 vs. 23-25). This is thought to confer stability at a lower pH. The pig asp-pro bond at sites 102 and 103, which is known to be sensitive to acid, is not present in the ruminants.

- The number of arginine residues is reduced in the ruminants (3-4, down from 7-9 in the pig). This is thought to make the enzyme more resistant to destruction by diacetyl, a common product of fermentation, or to attack by pancreatic trypsin.

By examining the placement of the amino acid substitutions on the three-dimensional structure of lysozyme, Jollès et al. conclude that at least 21 of the substitutions contribute to these adaptations.

The evolution of lysozyme in langurs is summarized in the right side of Figure 1.10. There appears to be an acceleration in the rate of evolution here as well. The branches leading to the langur and the baboon cover the same period of time, yet the number of amino acid substitutions on the langur branch (10) is 2.5 times that on the baboon branch (4). As with the ruminants, this acceleration is associated with the recruitment of lysozyme for use in the stomach. The most extraordinary aspect of this story, however, is the fact that five of the ten substitutions on the langur lineage are to amino acids that are found in the comparable positions in the cow lysozyme [273]. This is the most striking case of convergent evolution at the molecular level of which I am aware.

Equally intriguing is the fact that two of the three substitutions on the short branch leading from the human–monkey split to the langur–baboon split are also to the same amino acids as found in the cow suggesting that lysozyme may have evolved to some purpose in this lineage that preadapted it, in part, for use in the stomach of leaf-eating monkeys. In support of this, the baboon and langur lysozymes both exhibit a pH dependency that is nearly identical to that of the cow. It has been suggested that the substitution arg→ser at position 101, which is in the polysaccharide binding site, is a likely candidate for the downward shift in pH optimum [273].

The five substitutions in the langur lineage that converge to the cow lysozyme are on the surface of the molecule, well away from the active site. Three of these are from arginine, as are two of the nonconvergent substitutions. This is concordant with the ruminant pattern where the loss of arginines was thought to be adaptive. Three of the arginines are changed to lysines, whereas two are changes to glutamic acid. These latter two are interesting because glutamic acid is two mutational steps away from arginine. The contributions of these substitutions to the new role of lysozyme in the gut of langurs has not been examined directly. Our inference that these substitutions are functionally important is based on the acceleration of rates coupled with the parallel evolution with the cow lysozyme.

Chemostat studies

The results of a series of chemostat studies of selection for allelic forms of glycolytic enzymes in *Escherichia coli* by Dykhuizen and Hartl and their colleagues at Washington University stand in stark contrast to the examples examined thus far. Their basic approach is to engineer *E. coli* to produce two strains differing only in their alleles for a glycolytic enzyme and a neutral marker for T5 (a bacteriophage) resistance. The coupling of an enzyme allele with T5 resistance makes it possible to identify the genotype of a particular cell without having to resort to electrophoresis. As a consequence, they can follow the frequency of an allele in a chemostat with an accuracy of about 5% with a relatively small commitment of time.

Dykhuizen and his colleagues have examined naturally occurring, electrophoretically detectable alleles of five enzymes: phosphoglucose isomerase (PGI), glucose-6-phosphate dehydrogenase (G6PD), 6-phosphogluconate dehydrogenase (6GPD), phosphogluconate dehydrase (*edd*), and 2-keto-3-deoxygluconate aldolase (*eda*). The latter two, while not mainstream glycolytic enzymes, form a short pathway that allows glucose molecules that took a wrong turn into the pentose shunt to return forthwith to glycolysis.

The fitnesses of alleles from nature were compared with each other and to the allele found in the K12 strain of *E. coli* by following their relative frequencies over a 100-hour period in chemostats in which glucose or some other sugar is the limiting resource. The design allows the detection of fitness differences between alleles of approximately 1% in the earlier studies down to about 0.4% in the later studies.[*]

In addition to measurements of fitness differences, kinetic studies were also undertaken for some of the alleles. Thus, these experiments are similar to the ones reported earlier, differing only in that the objects of study are kinetics and fitness rather than kinetics and physiology. The results, in a highly condensed form, may be found in Table 1.2. What stands out in this work is the general failure to identify kinetic differences between alleles and the apparent neutrality of alleles when the competition occurs in glucose-fed chemostats. On the other hand, when sugars were chosen to feed into the pathways occupied by the locus under study, or when mutants were introduced to the same end, selective effects were observed in 9 of 24 cases (37.5%).

The most distressing aspect of these results is their failure to demonstrate kinetic differences between many of the electrophoretically distinguishable alleles. This disrupts our emerging generality that most alleles from natural populations differ kinetically. It could be that the examples from the previous subsections are a nonrandom collection of loci and that the *E. coli* study reflects a more typical situation. This possibility will be taken up in the next subsection. Here we will consider another possibility: the kinetic studies of *E. coli* enzymes were not performed with sufficient

---

[*]In the papers the resolution is given in units of hours rather than generations as we have done here.

Table 1.2. Measurable effects of allelomorphs of *E. coli* on kinetic parameters and fitness. The alleles column is the number of naturally occurring strains used in the studies. The left number in the kinetics column gives the number of strains that could be distinguished from the K12 allele based on enzyme kinetics. The right number is the number of strains that were examined. The left number in the fitness column gives the number of alleles with fitness effects large enough to be measured in a glucose-limited chemostat. (For 6PGD only six of the seven alleles were examined.) The right number is the number of alleles with measureable fitness effects in a chemostat with either a sugar other than glucose or a mutation meant to exaggerate fitness differences. ND means "not determined." The references refer to the original works, most of the data was obtained from [119].

Enzyme	Alleles	Kinetic	Fitness	Reference
PGI	5	1/5	0/1	[60]
G6PD	6	0/6	0/ND	[58]
6PGD	7	3/4	0/3	[61]
edd	6	ND	0/4	[59]
eda	6	ND	0/1	[119]

rigor to be reasonably confident that kinetic differences, if present, would be detected.

The kinetic studies reported in the previous subsections, in the main, included the following ingredients.

- Purified enzymes rather than crude homogenates were used in the determination of K_m, V_{max}, and k_{cat}.

- Kinetic parameters were measured in both the forward and reverse directions. This allows a check on the quality of the kinetic data via the Haldane relationship.

- The experiments were performed in a variety of conditions; most importantly, temperature and pH were varied. In addition, different buffers were explored as certain buffers tend to obscure kinetic differences.

- Each experiment was replicated enough times to allow a proper statistical comparison of the parameters.

The studies reported by Dykhuizen and his colleagues were not up to this standard. They were performed on crude homogenates, in one direction, under one set of conditions, and with, at most, two replicates. As a consequence, it is difficult to assess their power. In one paper it is claimed that the resolution is about 20% [58]. In another, it is reported that a kinetic difference was found using one lot of buffer but not when a subsequent lot from the same supplier was used [60]. This inconsistency, which remains unresolved, should be taken as an indication of the reliability of the kinetic data.

I belabor this point only because I am trying to establish in this book that naturally occurring alleles generally exhibit kinetic differences. The work of Dykhuizen and his colleagues has been widely cited as evidence against this point of view. By calling attention to the issue of experimental rigor, I hope to place the conclusions from the kinetic aspects of the *E. coli* studies on hold until proper experiments can be performed.

The failure to find measurable fitness differences under most experimental conditions should come as no surprise. The chemostat design is simply too crude to measure very small selective differences. Fitness differences of the order of 0.4 to 1% must be considered large by almost any standard. Such differences would characterize neutral alleles only if the effective size of the population were less than about 250 (the reciprocal of the selection coefficient). There is no compelling evidence that the effective population size of *E. coli* is this small. It would be very hard to reconcile, for example, the high levels of variation in *E. coli* populations with this number if the alleles were, in fact, neutral.

What should be emphasized in these experiments is that some fitness effects could be uncovered in 35% of the cases when some effort was made to exaggerate fitness differences by altering the environment or the genetic background. In this regard, these results are concordant with those of the previous subsections.

For example, the LDH alleles in *Fundulus* appeared to have no effect on lactate levels in resting fish or in fish that were exercising at a temperature where the kinetic differences are insignificant. They did, however, have effects on fish exercising at temperatures where the kinetic effects are substantial. Similarly, glucose-limited chemostats at 37°C with all the appropriate minerals undoubtedly represent a culture condition that minimizes physiological differences. A more informative design would be one that varies aspects of the culture conditions including temperature, pH, sugar type and concentration, flow rate, and other bacterial species. When one considers the extraordinary environmental fluctuations that *E. coli* must experience both within and outside of guts, it is hard to imagine that glucose-limited chemostats will reveal those selective forces that are acting in natural populations.

The significance of amino acid substitutions

This parade of examples leaves us with the impression that naturally occurring variation in the primary sequences of proteins, both within and between species, is likely to have kinetic and physiological consequences. In this summarizing section we will firm up this impression. In addition, we will consider some aspects of the physical chemistry of proteins that will help us to understand why such small changes in the structure of proteins can have such profound effects. Finally, some speculations on the evolution of kinetic parameters will be reviewed.

Much of what I hope to accomplish in this book rests on the generality that naturally occurring variation in proteins has functional significance. The effects need not be limited to kinetic parameters of enzymes, but may include structural and surface properties as well. While the examples in this section support this view, they cannot be wholly convincing since they were chosen from a literature in which the publication of negative results has been repressed. The *fraction* of investigations that uncover kinetic differences could be quite low, yet the literature could still be rich with examples of successes.

There are several ways to circumvent this problem. An experimentalist could choose at random, say, 10 polymorphic enzymes and perform detailed kinetics on each one. This represents an astonishing amount of work when one considers that each of the enzymes must be purified and kinetic evaluations performed under a variety of conditions. Another approach is to pick a species that receives a fair amount of attention and to see what fraction of a group of enzymes, chosen by some unbiased criteria, have reports of functional variation. Two obvious candidates are *Homo sapiens* and *Drosophila melanogaster*. While the former would undoubtedly prove enlightening, that literature is far too vast for the uninitiated. (Harry Harris, who is initiated, once concluded that 60% of a group of 30 polymorphic loci showed some kinetic differences between alleles.)

Drosophila melanogaster, on the other hand, is a perfect creature for this purpose. The initial problem is to choose a set of enzymes by criteria that are not biased with respect to the likelihood of finding kinetic differences. The enzymes that appeared in the first published survey of electrophoretic variation in *melanogaster* [222] appear to be a good choice. As anyone working at the time will verify, these enzymes were chosen mainly for technical or historical reasons, not because of any previous reports of kinetic variation. Ten loci were used in this study as shown in Table 1.3.

Of the six enzymes for which there are published data, all exhibit kinetic differences between alleles. I have been unable to find reports for the other four loci. Note that there are no studies that report a failure to find kinetic differences. The unreported cases may be cases of unreported negative (or positive) results or may be enzymes that simply have not received any attention. All of the enzymes that have been studied, with the exception of esterase-6, are glycolytic or nearly so. Of those that have not been studied, only xanthine dehydrogenase has a clearly defined role in metabolism suggesting that workers have adopted the reasonable strategy of investigating only those enzymes that are best known metabolically. Of the six well-known enzymes that have received attention, all exhibit measurable kinetic differences. Many of these have physiological correlates as well.

In filling in Table 1.3, I have generally cited the most recent papers for each enzyme to give the reader an entry into the literature. This does little justice to the extensive literature that exists for many of these enzymes. Alcohol dehydrogenase, in particular, could form the basis of an entire book.

The generality that allelic differences in the primary sequence of proteins

Table 1.3. A scorecard for the enzymes used in the original electrophoretic survey of *Drosophila melanogaster* [222] indicating those polymorphic loci for which kinetic, stability, or physiological differences between alleles have been reported. The question marks indicate my failure to find any relevant papers. Abbreviations not used previously are αGPD, alpha glycerophosphate dehydrogenase; Est, esterase; MDH, malate dehydrogenase; XDH, xanthine dehydrogenase; APh, alkaline phosphatase; ACPH, acid phosphatase.

Enzyme	Kinetic	Stability	Physiological	Reference
6GPD	yes	no	yes	[16,36]
G6PD	yes	yes	yes	[16,36]
αGPD	yes	no	yes	[208,211]
ADH	yes	yes	yes	[121,286]
Est-6	yes	yes	?	[306]
MDH-1	yes	yes	?	[2]
XDH	?	?	?	
Larval APh	?	?	?	
LAP-D	?	?	?	
ACPH-1	?	?	?	

tend to have structural or functional effects cannot help but to make us uncomfortable. How can changes in one or two amino acids out of the 200 or 300 in a typical protein possibly have any measurable effects? How can amino acids that are not involved with ligand binding or catalysis have an effect? The answer appears to rest with the idea that a protein is a compromise between structural stability and conformational flexibility. To achieve sufficient flexibility for efficient catalysis, proteins appear to be remarkably close to denaturation. We first encountered this idea in Somero's explanation for the evolution of k_{cat} to lower values in warm-adapted organisms.

Further evidence comes from studies on the physical chemistry of proteins. A common paradigm for protein folding is the reaction

$$\text{folded} \rightleftharpoons \text{unfolded}$$

whose equilibrium constant is defined as

$$K_u = \frac{[\text{unfolded}]}{[\text{folded}]} = e^{-\Delta G_u/RT}.$$

In the right-hand expression, ΔG_u is the difference in free energy between the folded and unfolded states, R is the gas constant, and T is the absolute temperature. When one considers the large number of bonds that stabilize the folded state of an intracellular enzyme, it is natural to expect that the free energy change will be large.

Remarkably, this is not the case. Typical values for ΔG_u fall within the range 3–15 kcal/mol under physiological conditions [232]. To calibrate this, consider that the energy changes associated with weak bonds are in the range of 1–7 kcal/mol. Thus, the addition or subtraction of a single weak bond could cause a protein to shift from being mostly folded to mostly denatured.

The explanation for the small free energy change rests with the large entropic cost of folding. A folded protein is in one of a very large number of possible states, the vast majority of which represent denatured states. The energetic cost of achieving this improbable state nearly offsets the energy of the weak bonds holding it together. For example, a net free energy change of 5 kcal/mol may represent a favorable energy of 300 kcal/mol from the weak bonding and an unfavorable energy of 295 kcal/mol from the entropic cost [232]. At 37°C the equilibrium constant when $\Delta G_u = 5$ is $K_u = 0.00029$. The loss of a single hydrogen bond could easily reduce ΔG_u to 3 kcal/mol with a resulting change of K_u to 0.0075, or about 26 times higher than before. Thus, our view of a protein should not be as a rigid structure that is immune to small changes in its components but rather as a delicate structure sitting on the edge of disaster that may be altered by even the smallest change in a component.

Partial support for this view comes from studies that exploit genetic techniques to change the amino acid sequences. In a review of this area, Pakula and Sauer [232] mention a number of studies in which mutations alter the stability of proteins. For example, T4 lysozyme has its ΔG_u lowered by 1.7 to 3.2 kcal/mol when an isoleucine that is about 80% buried in the hydrophobic core is changed to trp, tyr, ser, thr, or asp. Unfortunately, this and other studies using site-directed mutagenesis typically use assays that are somewhat crude from an evolutionist's perspective. Nonetheless, this direct experimental approach to questions of protein evolution holds extraordinary promise. Additional support comes from the common observation that alleles from warmer parts of a species range, or from warm-adapted species, tend to be more thermostable. It appears that even small temperature increases may necessitate the addition of a weak bond.

While this discussion may help to understand why we consistently observe kinetic differences between alleles, it places us squarely into a second dilemma: why should small kinetic or thermostability differences have any effect on the physiology or fitness of an organism? In certain cases, as in the evolution of hemoglobin for life at high altitudes, the answer is fairly straightforward. But what about glucose phosphate isomerase alleles? Why should a small kinetic change in an enzyme that catalyses a reversible reaction in a pathway that is regulated by some other enzyme have any consequences at all? If we adopt a steady-state flux view of metabolism, the answer may be that they have no effect. The steady-state flux through a pathway that is regulated by a single enzyme is insensitive to the activities of the other enzymes.

Watt, more than anyone else, has argued that the steady-state flux view of metabolism might be misleading [295]. The pathways of organisms faced with a constantly changing spectrum of food quality and physiological state may rarely achieve steady state. The transient dynamics of pathways will be sensitive to the kinetic parameters of each of the nonregulatory enzymes. The simplest demonstration of this is given by Easterby [63] who showed that the *transient* of a coupled enzyme system is the sum of the transients of the individual steps.

Consider a pathway that is regulated by the first enzyme

$$S \xrightarrow{v_0} I_1 \xrightarrow{V_1/K_1} I_2 \xrightarrow{V_2/K_2} I_3 \cdots I_n \xrightarrow{V_n/K_n} P$$

where v_0 is the rate of reaction of the regulated step and V_i and K_i are V_{max} and K_m for the ith step. Easterby showed that the concentration of the product at time t, when the initial concentrations of all of the intermediate substrates are set to zero, is asymptotically

$$[P_t] \sim v_0(t - \sum_{i=1}^{n} \tau_i),$$

where $\tau_i = K_i/V_i$ may be viewed as the lag or transient of the ith step.

The transient for the entire pathway may be roughly defined as the time of first appearance of the product, which is given by the sum of the transients of the individual steps. Clearly, each enzyme plays a role in the transient dynamics of the pathway. The least active enzyme makes the largest contribution; the most active makes the smallest. Moreover, if the activity of the least active enzyme is changed by, say 5%, this will have a larger effect on the transient than if the activity of the most active enzyme is changed by 5%. Kacser and Burn's "molecular democracy" [147] is a similar concept that applies to the steady-state flux through an unregulated pathway. It must be emphasized, however, that in simple models of regulated pathways such as Easterby's, the steady-state flux, v_0, is independent of the activities of the individual enzymes.

These comments may be helpful in understanding why Watt finds evidence for selection for PGI alleles in *Colias* while Dykhuizen finds no such evidence in *E. coli*. In essence, Watt's butterflies are operating away from steady state while Dykhuizen's chemostats are operating close to steady state. This contrast should be taken very seriously, particularly in light of the other examples of this section. Collectively, they clearly show that our ability to assess the importance of variation in enzymes depends on our understanding of the (internal and external) environmental factors that are relevant to an enzyme's role in metabolism.

In most of the examples, some background work on the ecology of the organisms was required to make sense of the variation. Often, comparisons between distantly related species provide hints about the forces that shape enzymes. The ecological factors were relatively transparent in the studies of temperature and LDH or altitude and hemoglobin. For insulin, the radical shift in the "internal ecology" of glucose metabolism provides the biological context in which the acceleration in the rate of evolution makes sense.

Negative results in experiments designed to measure physiological or fitness effects of alleles should be examined very carefully. While I do not want to close the door on the use of negative results to argue for neutrality, I do want to argue that an experimental program in this area is a major undertaking. The best work that has been done is by investigators who have devoted a major part of their careers to one or a few enzymes. The impact of their work should not be diluted by negative experiments that were performed with considerably less attention to the environmental context of the organism.

1.2   Rates of substitution

So much has been written about rates of amino acid substitutions that it is pointless to add yet another summary here. Rather, I will make a few observations that I hope will prove provocative. A more complete treatment of the facts may be found in the *Atlas of Protein Sequence and Structure* [52] or in Li and Graur's recent book [191].

Average rates of protein evolution present us with a rich phenomenology; the most striking is the extraordinary variation in rates of amino acid substitution exhibited by different proteins and by different sites within a protein. Table 1.4 lists the rates of amino acid substitution in units of substitutions per site per year for a selection of proteins taken from the *Atlas of Protein Sequence and Structure* [52]. From it we see, for example, that the rate for Ig kappa chain C region is 370 times that of histone H4 (and infinitely faster than ubiquitin).

The standard explanation for rate variation is that some proteins are more "constrained" than others. By that we mean that the chemical change caused by the substitution of one amino acid for another in some proteins has a much larger effect than in others. Since we imagine that changes of large effect are usually deleterious, it seems reasonable that the rate of substitution in tightly constrained proteins is lower than that in loosely constrained proteins.

The constraint explanation for variation in rates contains two components that are frequently confused. The first is concerned with the functional consequences of amino acid substitutions. An amino acid substitution at a site that is highly constrained will have a substantial functional consequence. We will call the consequence of a substitution the *site-effect* to avoid using the term constraint with all its implications about mechanism. A highly constrained protein is one with a large proportion of sites of large effect. The left side of Figure 1.11 illustrates a possible relationship between the chemical change embodied in a particular amino acid substitution and its functional consequence for sites of small and large effect.

The second component invokes a mechanism of evolution, usually some version of the neutral allele theory. Should this be the correct mechanism, then a monotonic relationship between the level of constraint and the rate of substitution is assured: less constrained sites will evolve more rapidly.

Table 1.4. Rates of amino acid substitution for various proteins. The units are substitutions per site per 10^9 years. Data are from [52, Table 1].

Protein	Rate /year
Ig kappa chain C region	1.850
Kappa casein	1.650
Ig gamma chain C region	1.550
Serum albumin	0.950
Hemoglobin alpha chain	0.600
Hemoglobin beta chain	0.600
Trypsin	0.295
Lactate dehydrogenase	0.170
Cytochrome c	0.110
Glutamate dehydrogenase	0.045
Histone H3	0.007
Histone H4	0.005
Ubiquitin	0.000

Suppose, however, that molecular evolution is not driven by mutation and genetic drift but rather by environmental change. Were this true, then we would require that slow-evolving proteins, like histones, function in an environment (intra-nuclear, tightly bound to DNA in this case) that has remained relatively unchanged over billions of years while rapidly evolving proteins, like immunoglobulins, are evolving in response to a rapidly changing environment (perhaps the environment of fast-evolving pathogens). We will call fast-evolving proteins that are responding to a changing environment *environmentally challenged*. Are histones evolving slowly because they are highly constrained or because they are not environmentally challenged? Are immunoglobulins environmentally challenged or loosely constrained? We really don't know.

These ideas are brought together in the right side of Figure 1.11. The constraint paradigm is restricted to the left side of the shaded area. Yet there is no reason why we should assume that that is the correct paradigm. If it were always true, as is claimed by Kimura in one of his five principles of molecular evolution, that "Functionally less important molecules or parts of molecules evolve (in terms of mutant substitutions) faster than more important ones" [159, p. 103], we might choose the constraint point of view. However, a glance at Table 1.4 leaves me undecided.

I can see no compelling pattern that more important molecules evolve more slowly. I would be hard put to argue that histones are more important that immunoglobulins or that glutamate dehydrogenase is more important than hemoglobin. (One could argue, based on our experience with sickle cell hemoglobin, that hemoglobins are more environmentally challenged than glutamate dehydrogenase.) The figure also points out that there are at least

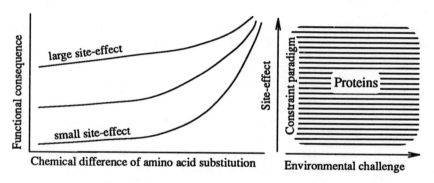

Figure 1.11. On the left, possible relationships between the effects of substitutions and their functional consequences; on the right, the space of proteins in the context of site-effects and environmental changes.

two dimensions involved: the site-effect dimension and the environmental-challenge dimension. Thus, the occurrence of a large fraction of sites of large effect does not necessarily imply that a protein will evolve more slowly.

I feel that, as suggested by Figure 1.11, our view of protein evolution is dimensionally inadequate. If proteins evolve to match the environment, as was strongly implicated in the previous section, then the rate of environmental change, as experienced by the protein, must be included in any explanation for variation in rates of substitution.

A closely related idea is expressed in another of Kimura's five principles of molecular evolution:

> Those mutant substitutions that are less disruptive to the existing structure and function of a molecule (conservative substitutions) occur more frequently in evolution than more disruptive ones.

Basically, substitutions with only a small site-effect occur more frequently than those with a large effect [159, p. 103].

The best quantitative demonstration of the conservative nature of substitutions in molecular evolution lies with the amino acids. There have been a number of papers graphing the chemical difference between pairs of amino acids versus the rate of substitution from one to the other, the most recent example being found in Kimura's book [159, Fig. 7.1]. This figure uses Miyata et al.'s [214] measure of chemical difference between amino acids, based on polarity and volume, and rates of substitution from McLachlan's 1972 paper [209]. Kimura shows that the relationship between rate, Y, and distance, X, is exponential

$$Y = 2.22e^{-0.376X}.$$

Thus, more conservative substitutions (those with a smaller X) occur more frequently.

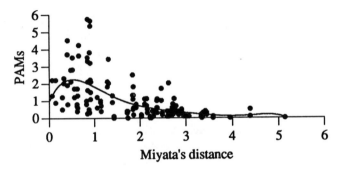

Figure 1.12. The relationship between the chemical difference between amino acids and their rates of substitution.

A reexamination of the relationship using more data and a slightly modified approach turned up a somewhat different result. McLachlan's rate estimates are not ideal for our purposes in that they are obtained from comparisons between proteins with a large number of amino acid substitutions. In contrasting his estimates with those used in *The Atlas*, McLachlan noted that the former apply to "closely related proteins" while his apply to cases where the "genetic relationship may be distant." Our interest is clearly with the instantaneous rates, making those from *The Atlas* more suitable.

However, even the rates from *The Atlas* need some refinement since they come from a somewhat artificial discrete-time Markov chain model called the PAM matrix model. Wilbur [307] has reexamined the estimation of rates using a continuous-time Markov process. His Table 1 appears to be the best estimates that we have for the rates of substitution between pairs of amino acids based on the protein sequences appearing in *The Atlas*.

Wilbur's single-step rates (those between amino acids that are one nucleotide substitution apart) are plotted against the chemical difference between amino acids using Miyata et al.'s index of chemical difference in Figure 1.12*. Remarkably, the figure shows that the most frequent substitutions are not between the chemically most similar amino acids, but rather between a group of amino acids with a chemical difference near one.

We cannot perform a statistical analysis on the scatter-plot because the points are not independent. Moreover, each point is really an estimate of a parameter, the rate of substitution between a pair of amino acids, rather than a random quantity. However, we can fit a polynomial (6th order) by the method of least squares to help our eye pick out the main trend in the rate estimates. Examination of the polynomial shows that Kimura's exponential fit to the data does not apply with the improved rate estimates.

---

*The rates are expressed in units of PAMs (accepted point mutations, inverted) which are amino acid substitutions per 100 residues per 100 million years of separation (or 200 million years of actual evolution). To convert from PAMs to actual rates in units of substitutions per site per year multiply the PAMs by 0.5×10^{-10}.

Our data represents average properties taken from a large number of proteins and species. As such, there are many opportunities for biases that could obscure the true relationship. For example, the more rapidly evolving pairs may reflect a tendency for such pairs to be located in regions of proteins far away from ligand binding sites rather than reflecting their chemical differences. Much more work is needed before we can feel confident with this phenomenology.

The final property of amino acid substitution rates that should be mentioned concerns the variation in rates between sites within a protein. Very few proteins have been sequenced in enough species to allow a precise description of the rates for each site. Holmquist et al. [133] examined five proteins—α-crystalline A chains, myoglobin, α and β hemoglobin, and cytochrome c—for which enough sequences were available and showed that the site-specific rates, viewed as random quantities, fit a negative binomial distribution. In some cases the estimated parameters were such that a geometric distribution, which is a special case of the negative binomial, fit the data adequately. If every site evolved at the same rate and if substitutions occurred at exponentially distributed intervals of time, the data would be expected to fit a Poisson distribution rather than a negative binomial.

Holmquist et al. concluded that the rate of substitution varies across sites in a significant fashion. The qualitative part of this conclusion was not new. The earliest studies showed that certain sites were conserved in evolution, for example, those in active sites, whereas others evolved at a much faster rate. The quantitative part was an extension of an earlier observation by Uzzell and Corbin [284].

The negative binomial distribution is not the only one to have been proposed as a description of variation in rates between sites. Many years ago Fitch [77] introduced a model that placed sites into two rate-categories: those that evolve and those that do not. The sites that do evolve were called covarions. He went on to argue that the set of sites that are evolving changes slowly over time. The Holmquist at al. study shows that the covarion model is too restrictive and should be abandoned in favor of models with a greater range of rates.

The main point of this short section is to try to abate, if even slightly, the tendency to equate rates of evolution with functional importance. This idea so permeates our thinking that one commonly reads that some region of a sequence is not important because it is evolving rapidly or that some other region is important because it is evolving slowly. In many instances, this may be the correct interpretation. In others, some interesting phenomena might be missed.

1.3   Electrophoretic surveys

The aim of this section is to provide a statistical description of protein variation in natural populations. We need to know the properties of this variation before we can hope to understand why it is there. The traditional tool for such studies is electrophoresis. Modern DNA techniques have not made a significant inroad because the most widely used techniques—based on restriction enzymes—do not distinguish between nucleotide changes that alter amino acid sequences and those that do not. Even with the limitations of electrophoresis, there are a number of important generalities that have emerged over the years. These will be the focus of this section.

How much protein variation?

Summarizing 25 years of estimates of electrophoretic variation is no small task. We must all be eternally grateful to Nevo and his colleagues who have spent countless hours doing exactly this. Their most comprehensive study is a 200-page tome that summarizes data from 1111 species from all walks of life [220]. This paper will be the source of many of the generalities that appear in this section.

The three most commonly used measures of genetic variation are the fraction of polymorphic loci, the mean number of segregating alleles, and the average heterozygosity. Of the three, only the average heterozygosity is relatively free of sample size effects. It is also the most useful statistic for estimating parameters that appear in theoretical models. For this reason, it will be used as our favored summarizing statistic.

Consider a sample from a particular locus containing K different alleles. Let p_i be the frequency of the ith allele in the sample. The heterozygosity for this locus, call it the jth locus, is defined to be

$$\mathcal{H}_j = 1 - \sum_{i=1}^{K} p_i^2.$$

If the species happens to mate at random, this may be viewed as an estimator for the fraction of individuals that are heterozygous at this locus in the population. Otherwise, the heterozygosity has no biological significance other than as a measure of the level of variation.

The average heterozygosity, $\bar{\mathcal{H}}$, is simply the average of the heterozygosities across loci within a species. Again, for randomly mating species this may be interpreted as the fraction of loci that are heterozygous in the population. Similarly, it may be used to estimate the fraction of loci that are heterozygous in a randomly drawn individual. It is important to note that these interpretations are not meant to extrapolate to the entire genome, but only to those loci that appear in a particular study.

Average heterozygosities from major taxonomic groups are given in Figure 1.13. They range from about 0.04 for mammals to about 0.14 for mollusks. This is only about a 3.5-fold spread over a very diverse set of taxa. The average heterozygosity for all invertebrates is 0.1 and for all vertebrates is 0.054. While these differences are statistically significant, they are not large enough to dispel the impression that there is a remarkable uniformity across taxa.

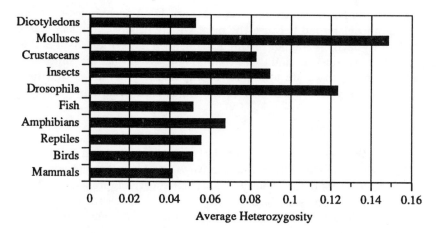

Figure 1.13. The average heterozygosities for various taxa. Parthenogenetic lizards have been excluded from the reptiles and *Drosophila* have been plotted separately from the other insects. Data are from [220].

Average heterozygosities can be misleading. They mask the variation of heterozygosity between species and between loci. For example, Figure 1.14 gives histograms of average heterozygosities for mammals and *Drosophila*. These two groups were chosen because they represent two extremes. Among mammals, the most common heterozygosity class is 0 to 0.01. Included in this class are such disparate groups as the weasels, genus *Mustela*, the pocket gophers, genus *Pappogeomys*, and the black bear, *Ursus americanus*. There are some highly variable mammals as well. For example, two bats of the genus *Myotis* have heterozygosities of 0.126 and 0.144. By contrast, the modal *Drosophila* heterozygosity is in the range 0.09 to 0.12, much higher than in mammals. Interestingly, the most heterozygous *Drosophila* is not much more variable than the most heterozygous mammal. This could represent a biologically imposed limit to variability or a technical limit imposed by electrophoresis.

For several years it was thought that the average heterozygosities of all species fall in the narrow range 0.056 to 0.185 [188, Fig. 18]. It is clear even from our mammal histogram that this is not the case. A histogram of all 1111 species in the Nevo et al. review [220, Fig. 2c] has a mode at zero and decreases monotonically with increasing heterozygosity. This may reflect an overrepresentation of mammals, but does make the point that the lower limit of 0.056 was very misleading. The upper limit of around 0.30 is more intriguing. To understand the nature of this limit—whether it is due mainly to the presence of monomorphic loci or not—we must descend one more step to an examination of the variation of heterozygosities among loci within species.

The most complete analysis of electrophoretic variation within a species other than our own is surely Singh and Rhomberg's recent work on *Droso-*

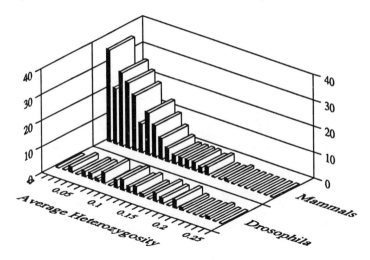

Figure 1.14. Histograms of average heterozygosities for *Drosophila* and mammals. Data are from [220].

phila melanogaster [263]. This study examined 80 to 117 loci at 15 localities world wide. Fifty-six out of the 117 loci (48%) were completely monomorphic. This figure is typical for *Drosophila* species generally. The percent of loci polymorphic in mammals is somewhat lower, 20%, while for vertebrates as a whole it is 23%. Invertebrates are higher at 37%, with the highest percentage among major taxonomic groups being the echinoderms with 55% polymorphic*. This shows that the limit on heterozygosity reflects, in the main, a low percentage of polymorphic loci.

A histogram of heterozygosities for the 61 polymorphic loci of *D. melanogaster* is given in the back part of Figure 1.15. This study included samples from several localities and as allele frequencies generally vary from one locality to another, some form of averaging must be used as an estimate of the heterozygosity of a locus. The one chosen for the figure is based on allele frequencies for the species as a whole. It is called H_T by Singh and Rhomberg. There is an apparent bimodality in the distribution of heterozygosities among polymorphic loci. This is because one group of polymorphic loci tends to have a single allele in fairly high frequency with a group of lesser alleles hovering around (the left mode) and a second group has two or three alleles each of which is in fairly high frequency (the right mode). This feature appears to be fairly general in *Drosophila* [189].

These few observations allow us to answer an aspect of the title question of this section: for those loci that have been examined, roughly 20 to 50% are polymorphic and the average heterozygosity ranges from about 0.04 to 0.15 when the data are averaged by major taxonomic groups. The issue

---

*A locus is arbitrarily called polymorphic if the frequency of the most frequent allele is less than 99% [220].

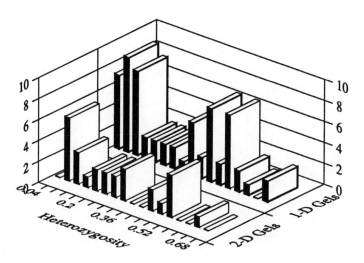

Figure 1.15. Histograms of heterozygosities for polymorphic loci from *Drosophila melanogaster* based on one- and two-dimensional electrophoresis. Data are from [43,263].

that must now be faced is whether or not these figures are representative of the genome as a whole.

This question has captured the imaginations of population geneticists ever since electrophoretic surveys first appeared in the mid 1960s. Beyond our perverse fascination with variation, the ability to assess levels of variation in the genome is critical to our understanding of the mechanisms that maintain variation. Fifteen years ago, the general feeling was definitely in favor of viewing electrophoretic data as being representative of the entire genome [188]. In the past few years, however, a number of observations call this into question. What makes this issue difficult is that there is evidence for both upward and downward biases.

The downward bias is due to the inability of electrophoresis to detect all of the protein variation in a sample. This effect has been carefully studied and can be corrected. More difficult is a bias due to the particular loci being studied. There is convincing evidence for a strong locus-specific effect on levels of variation. Certain groups of loci tend to be highly polymorphic while others are almost always monomorphic. If the proteins used in surveys were chosen at random from these groups there would be no problem. Unfortunately, current evidence suggests that they may be chosen from a group with above average variability.

The first suggestion that there was a locus-specific effect on variability involved a comparison of one group of enzymes loosely defined as having only a single intracellularly generated substrate (Group I enzymes) with a second group with multiple—possibly extracellular in origin—substrates (Group II enzymes) [98,173]. The Group I enzymes were mostly glycolytic

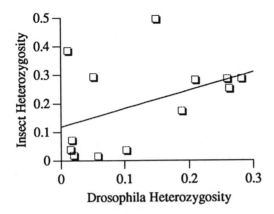

Figure 1.16. A locus-by-locus comparison of heterozygosities for *Drosophila* and other insects. Data are from [253].

and citric acid cycle enzymes. The Group II enzymes were nonspecific esterases, phosphatases, dehydrogenases, and the like. In these studies, the average heterozygosity of *Drosophila* Group II enzymes (0.23) was about 5 times larger than that of Group I enzymes (0.04). Subsequent observations have generally supported this difference and extended the number of species that exhibit it [102,253]. While the reason for the difference remains a mystery, the grouping clearly points out that our genomic extrapolations will vary considerably depending on our judgment about the appropriate mix of Group I and II enzymes that best reflects the genome.

Selander strengthened the case for locus-specific effects on variation by seeking a correlation of heterozygosity between species. He uncovered an effect by comparing *Drosophila* to other species of insects as illustrated in Figure 1.16. The correlation coefficient is 0.6, which is significant at the 1% level. There was, however, no significant correlation between insects and rodents.

A third source of evidence for locus-specific effects comes from studies on the correlation between protein structure and variability. The first evidence of this sort was a study by Harris and his colleagues showing that monomeric enzymes in humans have higher heterozygosities (0.096) than do dimeric (.071), trimeric (0.015), or tetrameric enzymes (0.050) [117]. There is also a positive correlation between the molecular weight of monomers and dimers and the number of alleles in a sample [170] although not with heterozygosity. In *Drosophila*, primates, rodents, reptiles, and fishes, on the other hand, there is a positive correlation between subunit molecular weight and heterozygosity [26,170,217].

The final evidence for locus-specific effects is more far-reaching in its implications, but is also more controversial. When abundant proteins are examined by two-dimensional (O'Farrell gel) electrophoresis, very little variation is detected as was first observed by Brown and Langley [25] in a study of 54 autosomal loci in *Drosophila melanogaster*. Of the 54, only 6 (11%) were polymorphic. The average heterozygosity was a mere 0.04, essentially the same as seen in Group I enzymes in *melanogaster*. A more recent study of male reproductive-tract proteins reveled only 27 polymorphic loci out of 307 (8.7%) [43]. *Drosophila* are not the only creatures with this affliction; mammals also show very low levels of variation when two-dimensional gels are employed [265].

The controversy grows out of the lower resolving power of two-dimensional gels when compared with the traditional one-dimensional techniques. Attempts to compare the two have produced estimates that two-dimensional gels detect from 50 to 90% of the variation detected by one-dimensional gels [43]. Even if the lower number is accepted, this is not sufficient to account for the reduction in levels of variation in abundant proteins.

Coulthart and Singh have presented two other sorts of evidence that two-dimensional gels are reasonably sensitive. The first concerns the distributions of heterozygosities among those loci that are polymorphic. As shown in Figure 1.15, these are similar whether measured by one- or two-dimensional techniques. The numbers of alleles per polymorphic locus are also similar. (In both cases, it must be stressed that these are just impressions.)

The second bit of evidence involves the results of sequential one-dimensional electrophoretic techniques designed to uncover cryptic alleles. These studies have generally shown that loci that are judged to be monomorphic by standard one-dimensional techniques usually remain monomorphic when examined under a variety of one-dimensional experimental conditions [189]. Polymorphic loci, on the other hand, often pour forth a cornucopia of new alleles.

For example, xanthine dehydrogenase in *D. pseudoobscura* reveals 8 alleles by standard one-dimensional electrophoresis and 27 alleles by sequential electrophoresis [262]. Esterase-5 jumps from 12 alleles to 41 alleles [150]. If the loci that are judged monomorphic by one-dimensional techniques remain so under the scrutiny of fancy electrophoresis, then the argument must be that those seen to be monomorphic by two-dimensional techniques are likely to remain so as well. These three observations make a strong enough case for two-dimensional techniques that we must seriously entertain the possibility that abundant proteins are substantially less polymorphic than are soluble enzymes.

Even within two-dimensional surveys there is evidence for locus-specific effects. In yet another study from Singh's prolific laboratory, Coulthart and Singh compared variation detected by two-dimensional electrophoresis in two different organs, testes and male accessory glands, in both *D. melanogaster* and *D. simulans* [44]. In both species, the accessory gland proteins are more polymorphic than are the testes specific proteins which in turn are more polymorphic than the proteins found in both organs. For *melanogaster* the percentages of polymorphic loci for the three classes of proteins are 23.1%, 12.2%, and 7.3%, respectively. For *D. simulans* they are

32.0%, 10.3%, and 4.6%. While not all of these differences are statistically significant, the elevated levels for the accessory proteins are significant in both species. This study is particularly interesting as some of the accessory gland proteins are presumably part of the ejaculate and thus may affect fertility in a way that is open to direct experimental investigation.

The evidence for locus-specific effects is compelling: levels of variation depend on the size, abundance, tissue location, and functional role of proteins. Given this, is there any evidence to suggest that those proteins most commonly used in electrophoretic surveys are a random sample of all proteins? The best evidence suggests the opposite. For example, Singh and Rhomberg showed that there is a highly significant negative correlation between estimates of average heterozygosities and the number of loci used in a study [263]. A tongue-in-cheek extrapolation of the straight line in their Figure 8 shows that a *Drosophila* study using 165 loci should reveal no variation at all. The important point is that electrophoretic studies have favored proteins that tend to be polymorphic. While this is part of the folklore of the field, there is yet to be a serious study to make amends. The best way around the problem is to use modern DNA techniques to pick the closest open reading frame to random positions in the genome and use these reading frames for population surveys. Until this is done, it is difficult to assess the accuracy of the claim that electrophoretic surveys may be extrapolated to the entire genome.

I would like to take this issue one step farther and claim that the entire enterprise of estimating levels of variation for the entire genome is somewhat misplaced. Consider, by way of analogy, the situation with rates of protein evolution. A table in the *Atlas of Protein Sequence and Structure* lists the rates of evolution of 60 proteins. As far as I am aware, no one has ever used this table to estimate an "average rate of protein evolution."* The reason is simple: when we look at the table what captures our attention is that rates of evolution vary by more than two orders of magnitude. Moreover, a comparison of the slowest evolving proteins, histones and ubiquitin, with those that evolve most rapidly, immunoglobulins, immediately suggests various hypotheses to explain the variation in their rates. Explaining this variation is a fundamental and important biological problem. Explaining why the average rate of evolution of these 60 proteins is 1.6×10^{-9} amino acid substitutions per site per year seems much less important.

Similarly, an important problem is to explain why malic enzyme, for example, is almost always monomorphic in *Drosophila* while some esterases are almost always polymorphic. It seems much less important to explain why the average heterozygosity of *Drosophila melanogaster* is 0.1 for the proteins that happen to be used in a particular study.

---

*Naturally, this must have been done by someone. Let us say that this average plays no role in general theories of protein evolution.

Population size and ecological correlates

Grand taxonomic summaries of average heterozygosities are too crude to provide significant insights into the mechanisms responsible for the maintenance of protein variation. We might expect, however, that insights could be gained by clever comparisons of groups of species that differ in some aspects of their ecology. The groupings must necessarily be motivated by a priori notions about the forces acting on genetic variation. Of the comparisons that come to mind, none is more important than that based on population size.

Mechanisms that maintain genetic variation differ dramatically in their dependency on the effective size of a population. They range from essentially no dependence for models of strong balancing selection with constant fitnesses, through weak dependency for models with mildly deleterious alleles, to strong dependency for strictly neutral models. We begin, therefore, with an investigation of the correlation of population size with average heterozygosity.

There are two sufficiently large studies that I am aware of that attempt to correlate the total number of individuals in a species with the average heterozygosity. The first is the study by Nevo et al. [220] mentioned earlier. The overall goal of their project was to find ecological and demographical correlates with heterozygosities. Most published surveys do not report enough information in a sufficiently uniform fashion to allow such a study, so Nevo et al. sent out questionaires to the authors asking for a description of the life histories of their species. For population size, the questionaire asked whether the size was small (thousands), medium (hundreds of thousands), large (millions), or very large (billions). While this is a very crude measure of the effective size of a population, the fact that the categories span six orders of magnitude gives us some confidence that a strong dependency on population size, at least, should be detectable.

When all species are considered, the effect of population size was significant at the 1% level. Moreover, the differences were in the expected direction: small with an average heterozygosity of 0.053, medium at 0.066, large at 0.077, and very large at 0.090. What might not have been expected is that the average difference between the two extremes is only 1.7-fold even though the population sizes are judged to differ by six orders of magnitude! Thus, our initial impression must be that the dependency of average heterozygosity on population size is very weak. The picture gets confusing when the data are subdivided. For example, vertebrates as a group show a significant dependency on population size while invertebrates do not. Within vertebrates, mammals and fish show a highly significant effect but birds, reptiles and amphibians show no effect.

The other study, by Nei and Graur [218], is based on 77 species, most of which presumably appeared in the Nevo et al. study as well. For 20 species, actual estimates of the population size were available. For the remainder, a rough estimate was obtained by multiplying a guess of species density by

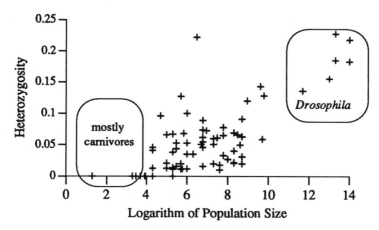

Figure 1.17. The correlation of average heterozygosity with population size. Data are from [218, Table 1].

its range. The relationship of average heterozygosity and population size for 76 of the 77 species is shown in Figure 1.17. The 77th species, *E. coli*, is just too different from the others to include. The figure shows that there is a significant correlation. However, when the species that contribute to the correlation are examined, an interesting pattern appears.

The six species with high heterozygosities and population sizes above 10^{11} are all *Drosophila*. As will be discussed below, high heterozygosities in *Drosophila* appears to be characteristic of the genus for reasons other than the large population sizes of its member species. The group of species with population sizes less than 10^4 and very low heterozygosities are mostly carnivores. (The species at the far left is the elephant seal.) The low heterozygosity of carnivores is a main contributor to the population-size effect seen in mammals in the Nevo et al. study as well. The group of species that lie between these two extremes exhibit no significant correlation of heterozygosity with population size.

Thus, the Nei and Graur study supports the impression that population size and average heterozygosities are only weakly correlated at best. It also points out the intriguing possibility that carnivores may have dramatically reduced heterozygosities because of their comparatively small population sizes.

The most celebrated evidence against a correlation between population size and heterozygosity comes from the endemic Hawaiian *Drosophila*. Most of these species are found on only one of the islands. Many are restricted to a small region within an island. These species are rare even within their ranges, although this impression comes in part from the difficulty of attracting them to baits (Alan Templeton, pers. com.). There can be little question that the population sizes of these species are orders of magnitude smaller than those of such widespread species as *melanogas-*

ter, simulans, pseudoobscura, or *willistoni.* Yet, as a group, the Hawaiian *Drosophila* exhibit heterozygosities that are not very different from their widespread counterparts (see examples in [218]). This is the evidence that high heterozygosities are characteristic of the genus for reasons other than population size effects.

If current population sizes are generally not indicative of the long-term average population sizes of species, then population-size effects would be obscured. For example, one could argue that population sizes of many species were reduced during the last glaciation causing a reduction in levels of variability with a consequent restriction in the total range of heterozygosities. It is easy to imagine that such events, superimposed on asynchronous population expansions as the glaciers receded, could play havoc with searches for population-size effects.

Another approach to finding population-size effects is Coyne's [48] study of the correlation between rates of chromosome evolution and heterozygosity. A correlation might be expected if the fixation of chromosomal mutations occurs most often in small populations as would be the case if chromosomal mutations have deleterious effects when heterozygous. A significant effect was, in fact, uncovered. If the generally held view that deleterious effects of heterozygous chromosomal mutations are large, then those species experiencing rapid rates of evolution would most likely have very small effective populations sizes. Of course, we must consider the possibility that the reduction in heterozygosity may be for entirely different reasons. For example, it could be that chromosomal substitutions are due to meiotic drive and the reduction in heterozygosity to hitchhiking. This, too, will lead to the correlation seen in Coyne's study.

Beyond these large-scale studies, there are anecdotal studies of species with unusually small population sizes with greatly reduced variation. A striking example is a comparison of cave fish in Mexico with their close surface relatives [8]. The heterozygosity of the surface species, *Astyanax mexicanus,* is 0.11, a relatively high figure. Three troglobitic populations of *Astyanax* have average heterozygosities of 0.0, 0.032, and 0.077 for the same set of loci. Unfortunately, we do not know the sizes of the cave populations. Avise and Selander argue that they are currently very small, but were possibly larger in the recent past. Such studies are important in that they suggest that there are populations small enough to exhibit reduced levels of variation. Were we in possession of estimates of the effective sizes of these populations, we would be in a strong position to place bounds on the mutation rate or strength of selection, depending on our preferred mechanism for the maintenance of variation.

If the evidence is taken at face value, our conclusion must be that protein heterozygosity is essentially independent of population size for species whose population sizes exceed about 10^4 individuals. Species with population sizes in the thousands, on the other hand, exhibit markedly lower heterozygosities.

The success rate for finding other ecological correlates with heterozygosity is not much better. An early paper that cast a pall on such studies was a survey of deep sea creatures that were imagined to live in a simpler, less variable environment than surface creatures [10]. The heterozygosities of the deep sea creatures turned out to be not unlike those of other groups.

In their extensive statistical study, Nevo et al. were only able to account for about 20% of the variation in heterozygosity by ecological factors. There was a suggestion that species living in a "broader environmental spectra" have higher heterozygosities but the effect was fairly small. While this finding might be used as evidence that variable environments influence levels of variation, the unexplained 80% of the variation in heterozygosities tells us that a statistical approach that lumps loci is, in the end, uninformative.

Heterozygosity and substitution rates

An empirical question of considerable interest concerns the correlation between heterozygosity and rate of evolution among loci. While this would seem like a rather straightforward question, it has received remarkably little attention. The most important studies are two by Skibinski and Ward [264,292]. These papers explore the correlation between heterozygosity and genetic distance as determined by electrophoretic studies. In the earlier paper, data from 31 loci in mammals were used to show that the correlation of the average heterozygosity and the average genetic distance was 0.759 (P < 0.001) [264].

The subsequent paper extended the analysis to more loci and to other major taxonomic groups and obtained correlation coefficients ranging from 0.46 to 0.71. In all cases, the correlation coefficients were significantly greater than zero. The conclusion that more polymorphic loci evolve more rapidly seems inescapable.

There are some qualifications that must accompany our interpretation of these papers. The most obvious concern is whether the more heterozygous and diverged proteins are simply the ones that electrophoresis is best able to detect amino acid changes in, thus leading to a spurious correlation. Skibinski and Ward successfully defused this objection by examining the correlation between heterozygosity and rate of amino acid substitution for six loci for which substitution rates were available from amino acid sequence studies. The results are illustrated in Figure 1.18.

We clearly need more work on this point. One aspect of the correlation that should be investigated is the extent to which variation in the subunit molecular weight can account for the correlation between the average heterozygosity and genetic distance. We already know that heterozygosity is affected by molecular weight so it is reasonable to suppose that genetic distance is as well. Since Figure 1.18 uses the substitution rate per site rather than per protein, it is clear that subunit molecular weight cannot account for the entire correlation.

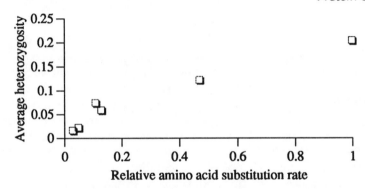

Figure 1.18. The relationship between average rate of amino acid substitution per site and heterozygosity for six loci from mammals. The rates have been scaled such that the most rapidly evolving locus has a rate of one. Data are from [264, Table 2].

Allele frequencies

In this section we will review some of the studies that use allele frequency data directly without collapsing them into heterozygosities. The additional information contained in allele frequencies might tell us considerably more about the mechanisms responsible for maintaining variation. We will consider three sorts of studies. The first examines samples from single populations, the second examines geographic patterns of allele frequencies, and the third looks at null alleles.

When considering a sample from a single population, it is not at all clear what properties of the sample are of interest. Without some guidance from theory, we can do little of substance. The usual approach has been to compare the frequencies of alleles to that expected under the neutral allele theory, as provided by the celebrated *Ewens sampling distribution* (ESD). To do that here might be viewed as a departure from our general aim of divorcing descriptions of data from models. But our compromise is modest: The Ewens sampling distribution applies not only to the neutral model but to certain models of selection in a random environment as well. Thus, we will hope to conclude only that data does or does not fit the distribution and perhaps note the direction of its departure; we do not attempt to attribute mechanism at this juncture.

Consider a sample of n haploid genomes that contains k electrophoretically distinguishable alleles. As the labeling of alleles in the sample is arbitrary, we consider only the configuration of the alleles. A configuration is an unordered set of numbers representing the number of copies of each of the k alleles. For example, if a sample of $n = 5$ genes contains $k = 3$ alleles there are two configurations, $\{1, 1, 3\}$ and $\{1, 2, 2\}$. In the first instance, the sample contains one copy of each of two alleles and three copies of one allele. The second has one copy of one allele and two copies of each of the other two. More generally, let the number of copies of the ith allele be n_i

Table 1.5. Tests for agreement with the Ewens sampling distribution for the esterase-2 locus in four species of *Drosophila*. The exact probability that the homozygosity is more extreme than the expected value is given by P and the probability as determined by simulation is given by Psim. Analysis is from [68, Tables 9.1 and 9.2].

Species	n	k	$\hat{F}$	$E\{\hat{F} \mid k\}$	P	Psim
willistoni	582	7	0.9230	0.4777	0.007	0.009
tropicalis	298	7	0.6475	0.4434	0.130	0.134
equinoxalis	376	5	0.9222	0.5654	0.036	0.044
simulans	308	7	0.2356	0.4452		0.044

so that

$$n_1 + n_2 + \ldots + n_k = n.$$

The Ewens sampling distribution tells us that the probability of observing this configuration, given that there are k alleles in the sample, is

$$\frac{n!}{k! |S_n^{(k)}| \prod_i^k n_i},$$

where $S_n^{(k)}$ is a Stirling number of first kind,* defined as the coefficient of x^k in the product

$$x(x - 1)(x - 2) \ldots (x - n + 1).$$

It must be kept in mind that this distribution is defined over the space of allelic configurations when using it for hypothesis testing.

A simple way to test for agreement of a sample with the ESD is to calculate the sample homozygosity, $\hat{F}$, and to compare it to the critical values appropriate for the number of alleles in the sample using one of the published tables [68,203]. This form of the test is due to Watterson [299] and is called (inaccurately) the *homozygosity test of neutrality*. An example of its use is given in Table 1.5 for the esterase-2 locus in four species of *Drosophila*. This data has been analyzed many times, beginning with Watterson [298]. Three of the four species show a significant departure from the ESD null hypothesis. Of these, the sample homozygosity is too large in two cases and too small in the third. A greater than expected homozygosity may be due to the most frequent allele being more abundant than expected or, equivalently, to the less frequent alleles being rarer than expected. A common description of this situation is that there are "too many rare alleles." In the case of *simulans*, the allele frequencies are more uniform than expected.

The use of the homozygosity test for neutrality to infer mechanism is compromised by the failure of electrophoresis to detect all of the mutations

---

*Abramowitz and Stegun [1, Table 24.3] has an extensive table of Stirling numbers.

at a locus. Thus, with the introduction of sequential electrophoretic techniques in the late 1970s to uncover previously hidden variation, the time was ripe for an informative application of the method.

Watterson [300] analyzed allelic configurations from two published surveys. In the first, Coyne found 18 alleles present in one copy each, one allele present in 32 copies and 4 alleles with intermediate frequencies from 60 xanthine dehydrogenase genes sampled from three *D. persimilis* populations [47]. The probability of observing this or a more extreme configuration under the ESD null hypothesis was determined by Watterson to be 5.9×10^{-7}. Significant deviations in the same direction were obtained when the samples were analyzed from the separate populations. Singh et al. found 10 singletons and one allele present in 68 copies among 27 distinct alleles in a sample of 146 genes [262]. Watterson showed that the probability associated with this configuration was 2.3×10^{-9}. Keith's study of esterase-5 in *D. pseudoobscura* also exhibited an $\hat{F}$ that was too large given the observed number of alleles [150].

Ever since Ohta [227] first pointed out that there were too many rare alleles, it has been commonly accepted that this is, indeed, the case. Our observations thus far appear to support this phenomenon. Unfortunately, the generality of the excess is open to question, not because of any observations to the contrary, but because of the lack of adequate tests.

As most polymorphic loci have only 2 or 3 alleles, the ESD lacks sufficient power to detect significant deviations in the direction of too many rare alleles. Most of the attempts to uncover excesses of rare alleles have examined the frequency spectrum of alleles combined from several loci within a species. In Ohta's analysis, she assumed that the same parameter, $4Nu$ in the case of the neutral model, applies to each locus. While the population size for each locus is obviously the same, the neutral mutation rate clearly is not, calling her conclusion into question.

Chakraborty et al. [38] attempted to circumvent the problem by assuming that the mutation rate is gamma distributed (among loci). They also claim to have found an excess of rare alleles in about one-quarter of the populations. But we could equally well conclude that the gamma distribution does not correctly capture the variation in $4Nu$ among loci.

We seem to be left with the conclusion that the three loci with vast numbers of alleles, *Xdh* in *D. pseudoobscura* and *D. persimilis* and esterase-5 in *D. pseudoobscura* exhibit an excess of rare alleles but for the remaining loci we have no convincing evidence for an excess. Given the power limitations, we cannot feel confident that there is not an excess for most loci, not a happy situation.

Observations of allele frequencies are enriched considerably when they come from distinct geographic localities. Unfortunately, it is impossible to do justice to 25 years of electrophoretic studies reporting geographic patterns in allele frequencies. I find the literature too daunting to even attempt any sort of generalization. Here, I will only mention a few studies that I find particularly provocative.

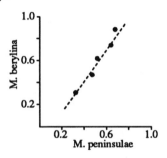

Figure 1.19. The frequencies of phosphohexose isomerase-A alleles in two sympatric species of *Menidia*. The frequencies for each dot were determined at the same locality. Redrawn from [143, Fig. 5].

One of the problems that has plagued the use of geographic patterns to help in our understanding of the forces maintaining variation is the fact that most patterns may be accounted for by both neutral and selection models. It is only when we see extraordinary coincidences that we begin to think that forces in addition to drift and migration are at work. One such coincidence is parallel clines of the same alleles in sibling species. One of the first reported cases was in the closely related minnows, *Menidia beryllina* and *M. peninsulae* which are sympatric from eastern Florida to southern Texas. Johnson [143] examined several enzymes in the two species and discovered one case where what was judged to be the same allele of phosphohexose isomerase-A in both species showed the parallel clines illustrated in Figure 1.19. Other enzymes did not exhibit such a striking parallelism, suggesting that the phenomenon cannot be attributed to gene flow through local hybridization.

A similar parallelism was recently reported by Anderson and Oakeshott [3] for esterase-6 in the sibling species *Drosophila melanogaster* and *D. simulans*. Both species are cosmopolitan with almost identical ranges and habitats. At least 10 alleles have been found in *D. melanogaster*, three of which, Est6-100, -110, and -125, appear to be shared by *D. simulans*. Est6-100 in both species increases with latitude in both the northern and southern hemispheres. By contrast, shared alleles at the phosphoglucomutase locus do not show any significant geographic clines. Whatever forces are responsible for the Est6 clines, they appear to change systematically with latitude in a manner that is shared by both species. Temperature is an obvious, but unproven factor.

Borowsky [22] undertook a much larger study aimed at detecting parallel clinal variation in sympatric species with shared alleles. He found 26 loci with shared alleles scattered over four *Drosophila* and one butterfly species pairs. A randomization test uncovered significant associations at only three loci of the 26. It is difficult to assess the significance of this result. On one hand it could indicate that parallel clines in shared alleles are rare and that either common modes of selection are not operating on the alleles or that selection is dominated by drift and migration. Alternatively, it could be that the alleles that appear to be the same really aren't due to the poor resolving power of electrophoresis. In this regard, it should be noted that the shared esterase-6 alleles in the Anderson and Oakeshott study were examined by a variety of techniques to led credence to their assertion that the shared alleles were really the same.

Oakeshott and his co-workers have documented a number of other world-wide clines in *D. melanogaster*. Of particular interest is the number of cases of parallel latitudinal clines in the northern and southern hemispheres. Three of four Group II (variable-substrate) enzymes and three out of seven Group I enzymes show parallel latitudinal clines in the two hemispheres [223]. Faced with such data, it is tempting to suggest that clines in wide-ranging species should generally be viewed as reflecting the action of some force in addition to mutation and drift, although we cannot rule out the possibility that the clines represent historical effects.

Null alleles represent a class of electrophoretically detectable variants that provide unique insights into the strength of selection operating at enzyme loci because of the generally held view that they are maintained in populations by mutation–selection balance. This assumption, coupled with laboratory measurements of mutation rates and field estimates of the null allele frequencies, should yield rough estimates of the strength of selection against null heterozygotes. Langley, Voelker and their colleagues have gathered the appropriate data with some remarkable results [184,288].

In their first study they estimated the frequencies of null alleles at 25 enzyme loci from a North Carolina population of *D. melanogaster*. They found 39 nulls among the 20 autosomal loci and no nulls from the five X-linked loci. The average frequency of nulls for the autosomes was $\bar{q} = 0.0025$ and unpublished results provided an average mutation rate to null alleles of $\bar{u} = 3.86 \times 10^{-6}$. Assuming that the frequency of nulls is roughly $\bar{q} = \bar{u}/\bar{h}s$, the average selection against heterozygotes is $\bar{h}s = 1.5 \times 10^{-3}$. It is hard to imagine that the strength of selection acting on two nonnull alleles would be stronger than this, leading us to the conviction that if selection is responsible for the maintenance of enzyme variation, the strength of selection is probably less than 10^{-3}. For me, this is one of the most compelling conclusions to emerge from allozyme surveys.

Langley and his colleagues have made a number of other observations related to their null study.

- Thirteen of the 20 autosomal loci had at least one null allele. Of these, only *Pgi* is lethal when homozygous even though most of the loci are from intermediary metabolism. Presumably, the numerous alternative pathways that characterize intermediary metabolism have sufficient redundancy to overcome a blockage in some pathways.

- There was no significant correlation between the heterozygosity and null allele frequency among loci or between molecular weight and null allele frequency. Both are surprising if we hold the view that both nulls and neutral mutations should be most abundant at those loci experiencing the weakest selection or have the highest locus mutation rate.

- The failure to find any nulls at the 5 X-linked loci could be due to the fact that selection is more effective at eliminating deleterious alleles that appear in the hemizygous state.

- Saturation mapping suggests that 80% of all loci are lethal mutable, yet for autosomal enzyme loci no more than 8 of 20 (40%) are lethal mutable. The enzyme loci used in electrophoretic studies may be more weakly selected than most other loci, a conclusion that is concordant with their higher heterozygosities relative to loci with abundant products as examined by two-dimensional electrophoretic surveys.

- The average frequency of visible mutations in natural populations, 0.0028, is remarkably close to that of null mutations suggesting that both sorts are under similar selective pressures.

- The null allele frequencies from a sample from Great Britain are similar to those from North Carolina. In both populations there was significant interlocus variation in null frequencies yet there was no heterogeneity between the populations. The same loci that tended to harbor null alleles in North Carolina also harbored them in Great Britain.

On being heterozygous

The most enigmatic phenomenon uncovered by electrophoretic studies is the correlation between the number of heterozygous loci in an individual, among those examined, and some property of its development, morphology or fitness. Significant correlations have been observed in enough independent systems that we cannot dismiss the phenomenon out of hand, even though there are theoretical reasons why we might wish to do so.

A large proportion of the studies have focused on marine bivalves, a group that seems to enjoy being heterozygous more than most. The results of a typical study by Koehn et al. [169] based on 15 polymorphic enzymes in the coot clam, *Mulinia lateralis*, is illustrated in Figure 1.20. The initial shell lengths of 1906 recently settled clams were measured and regressed on the number of heterozygous loci as determined by electrophoresis. The regression ($r = 0.255$) is highly significant, although heterozygosity accounts for only about 6% of the variation in shell length, a typical value for these studies. Similar results were obtained for the initial growth rate measured in the laboratory. The three enzymes making the greatest contribution to the effect were enolase and two nonspecific aminopeptidases.

In a large study of 42 loci in three species of trout, Leary et al. [185] discovered that more heterozygous individuals were less asymmetric for

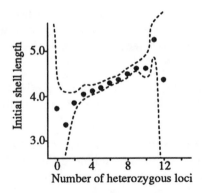

Figure 1.20. Shell length as a function of the number of heterozygous loci in the coot clam. The dashed lines are the 95% confident limits. Redrawn from [169, Fig. 1].

traits that appear on both sides of the body. They conclude, based on this and previous studies, that the reduction of *fluctuating asymmetry* in more heterozygous individuals is a general property of salmonid fishes.

These two studies are typical of many others; the reader is referred to one of the many reviews of the phenomenon [316] for more information.

Our reaction to these studies cannot help but to be one of extreme skepticism. Consider, for example, that a correlation of heterozygosity with some trait is often recorded with as few as 5 loci. It stretches our credulity that 5 loci chosen from tens to hundreds of thousands—not for some a priori expectation that they will have a large effect, but because histochemical stains for them happen to be available—could account for 5% of the variation in a trait that is closely associated with fitness. One obvious explanation is that the loci used in a particular study do not have any direct effect on the measured trait but rather should be viewed as an index of the genome-wide heterozygosity of the individual. If very homozygous individuals suffer some sort of inbreeding depression, then the phenomenon could be explained without having to attribute direct effects to the loci under scrutiny. Unfortunately, Chakraborty [37] concluded that the number of heterozygous loci among a handful is very weakly correlated with that of the genome, assuming no linkage disequilibrium, thus ruling out this explanation. No surprise here, it could hardly be otherwise. Smouse [266], in a particularly insightful discussion, concluded that a likely explanation is that the enzyme loci are in linkage disequilibrium with chunks of the chromosome, making the phenomenon attributable to the direct effects of many loci. This explanation is particularly attractive as it provides a ready interpretation for the failure to observe the phenomena every time it is looked for.

Koehn et al. [169] favor an entirely different explanation. They note that the loci that contribute the bulk of the phenomenon are found in important metabolic pathways or in protein catabolism and, as such, are likely to have a large direct effect. They back up their hypothesis with citations to a number of studies showing physiological and metabolic correlates with the number of heterozygous loci.

I find these studies to be both provocative and frustrating. Provocative because the repeated observations of phenotypic correlations with the number of heterozygous loci suggests that some of the enzyme loci used in electrophoretic studies may have a much larger effect than we have been willing to accept in the past. If so, this could be related to our emerging view that soluble enzymes are more polymorphic than other loci, such as those for abundant proteins. Frustrating because the literature bearing on this question is often contradictory. But this is what would be expected for a phenomenon that accounts for, at best, 5% of the variation in a trait.

What have we learned?

It is stunning how little we have learned from statistical studies of electrophoretically detectable protein variation after 25 years of work. Innumerable attempts to find patterns that give insights into the mechanisms responsible for variation have been almost entirely uninformative. Why is this so? One obvious factor is that electrophoresis itself is an imperfect technique. Within an electrophoretic allele may lurk several cryptic alleles whose patterns, could they be observed, might lead us to the truth.

But I feel that there is much more conspiring against us. The null allele study argues that selection must be very weak, less than 10^{-3}. With this level of selection the time scale of allele frequency change is thousands to tens of thousands of years. It is even longer if the alleles are neutral. If the equilibrium models that we apply to our data are valid, we have to assume that populations have been stable for periods of time that greatly exceed the time scale of frequency change. Species must maintain their population sizes, migration rates, mutation rates and, most distressingly, not experience any strong selection events at loci linked to those used in our enzyme studies. Otherwise, the populations will not be in equilibrium. This is precisely what I feel is going on. The frequencies of polymorphic alleles generally reflect the history of a population far from equilibrium.

2

DNA evolution

As we have seen, our interest in the evolution of protein sequences tends to be focused on locus-specific examples. The evolution of insulin in the hystricomorph rodents, for example, has little in common with the evolution of hemoglobin in Rüppell's griffon. We can discuss one without making reference to the other. By contrast, when discussing the evolution of DNA, we tend to focus on properties that hold for much or all of the genome. The distinction will be evident in the contrasting approaches of this chapter and the previous one. Implicit in our new approach is a belief that most nucleotide substitutions that do not change amino acids (silent substitutions) are the product of similar evolutionary processes no matter which locus is involved. Many workers believe, for example, that the evolution of silent sites and noncoding DNA is driven solely by the interaction of drift and mutation.

We begin by recording some basic observations on rates of silent substitutions. Two bits of information are required to estimate a rate: the number of nucleotide substitutions separating a pair of species and the time back to their common ancestor. The former is obtained by using one of the many algorithms that correct for multiple substitutions. The latter comes from the fossil record. For consistency, all of the rate estimates come from Wen-Hsiung Li and his many collaborators who have worked at the Center for Demographic and Population Genetics in Houston. They all use the same correction algorithm [196] and the same interpretation of the fossil evidence.

Figure 2.1 presents average rates of silent substitutions for exons from a variety of taxa. "Fast" and "slow" for the *Drosophila* rates refer to a group of loci that exhibit, respectively, low and high codon biases.

I do not want to leave the impression that these rate estimates are accurate. They are subject to two sources of error of unknown magnitude. The first involves the corrections for multiple substitutions. To make corrections, one must have a stochastic model of molecular evolution that is compatible with the data. Most available models have obvious deficiencies [92]. For example, most assume that the frequencies of the four bases—A, G, C, and T—are stationary through time. Within mammals the base frequencies

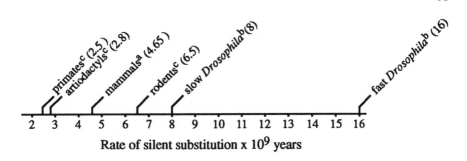

Rate of silent substitution x 10^9 years

Figure 2.1. Average rates of silent substitutions. The superscripts refer the to sources of the rates: a, [196]; b, [256]; c, [194].

are not, in fact, stationary [91,179,280] making the use of these correction algorithms suspect.

Correction formulae also assume that the rate of substitution is homogeneous throughout the locus and that the substitutions at a particular site are independent of those at other sites. Both assumptions are demonstrably false. Little is known about the bias created by these violations.

The second source of bias comes from the interpretation of the fossil record. In many cases, for example, within the genus *Drosophila*, the split times are based on the slimmest of evidence. Even the mammalian fossil record is far too sparse for our purposes. Although the rates presented here appear to be generally accepted, prudence dictates that we keep in mind that in 5 or 10 years we may be staring at very different numbers.

There is a weak correlation between silent and replacement rates as illustated in Figure 2.2. The correlation has been observed in both mammals [108,192] and prokaryotes [255]. The reason for the coupling is unknown. It could be due to common mutation rates, epistatic selection between sites, or some other factor.

Having seen some rates of silent substituton, we now turn to some of the factors that determine the rates and to the nature of the substitutions.

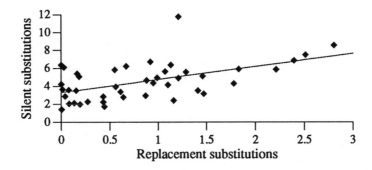

Figure 2.2. The relationship between silent and relacement substitution rates for 43 loci in mammals. Data are from [192, Table III].

We begin by asking whether or not the mutation rate limits the rate of substitution.

2.1 Is mutation limiting?

A demonstration that the mutation rate limits the rate of molecular evolution must rely on a model to connect the two rates. The model need not be very precise. In fact, the most commonly employed model is embodied in the simple assumption that the rate of molecular evolution is proportional to the mutation rate,

$$k \propto u. \tag{2.1}$$

Here, k is the substitution rate and u is the mutation rate.

This model so permeates our thinking about molecular evolution that many writers use the terms "mutation" and "substitution" interchangeably. For example, one often reads about the rate of mutation when, in fact, it is the rate of substitution that is being discussed. For some mechanistic models of molecular evolution, the substitution rate is proportional to the mutation rate. Among these are neutral models, models of mildly deleterious alleles and models where all of the substitutions are due to the fixation of selectively favored alleles. This provides some justification for assuming that $k \propto u$. At the same time, it emphasizes that a demonstration that the rate of substitution is proportional to the mutation rate may limit the set of compatible mechanistic models, but cannot be used to choose among them.

There is a conspicuous ambiguity in equation 2.1: should the rates be expressed as events per year or per generation? When working with sequence data, the convention is to express all rates as events per year,

$$k_y \propto u_y.$$

This is forced on us as the generation times of the ancestors of extant species cannot be known. By contrast, mechanistic models of molecular evolution, such as neutral models, express the rates in units of events per generation,

$$k_g \propto u_g.$$

If g is the generation time of a species measured in years, then the rates per year and per generation are connected by

$$k_y = k_g/g \propto u_g/g = u_y.$$

This immediately suggests a test of the assumption that mutation rates are limiting: the rate of substitution should be higher in creatures with shorter generation times; assuming, of course, that the mutation rate per generation, u_g, is the same for all of the creatures under study. Such a relationship has been described, as will be seen very shortly, and is referred to as the *generation-time effect*.

Table 2.1. Rates of silent evolution. The silent rates are given relative to the average artiodactyl rate, which is estimated to be 2.8×10^{-9} substitutions per site per year. The time to origin column begins with the time used for the rate calculations followed by a range of times that are compatible with the fossil record. Data are from [194].

Comparison or Taxon	Silent Rate	Time to Origin (my.)
Artiodactyls	1.00	80
Primates	0.89	75
Rodents	2.32	75
Human vs. chimpanzee	0.46	7 (5–10)
Human vs. orangutan	0.71	12 (10–16)
Human vs. OW monkeys	0.78	25 (20–30)
Cow vs. goat	1.50	17 (12–25)
Cow/sheep vs. pig	1.25	55 (45–65)
Mouse vs. rat	2.82	15 (10–30)

The generation-time effect

At the time of this writing, the case for the generation-time effect is suggestive, but not totally convincing. The main problem is the lack of diverse taxa with different generation times, adequate fossil record, and a sufficient number of sequences. With time, the appropriate data will become available and the issue will be settled. For now, the case is as follows.

The first suggestions of a generation-time effect came from early observations of the apparent slowdown in the rate of DNA evolution in primates and the speed-up in rodents when compared with other groups of mammals [172,178]. These comparisons were based on DNA hybridization studies and as such were thought to apply mostly to noncoding regions of the genome as these make up the bulk of mammalian DNA. By contrast, the effect was generally absent or greatly reduced in proteins, although it was detected in hemoglobins [105] at about the same time as in the hybridization studies. These initial observations have withstood the test of time remarkably well. The most complete reexaminations are those of Li, Tanimura and Sharp [194] and Britten [24].

The Li et al. study [194] is the most satisfactory as it uses DNA sequences rather than DNA hybridization, thus avoiding the pitfalls of the latter approach. The first half of their investigation compares the rates of silent and replacement substitutions in 21 loci that have been sequenced in representatives of primates, rodents, and artiodactyls. The rates were determined by dividing the inferred number of substitutions separating pairs of species by the time of separation as provided by paleontologists. The number of substitutions are obtained via an algorithm, developed by Li et al. [196], that corrects for multiple substitutions. The results are summarized in Table 2.1 and Figure 2.1.

Using artiodactyls as a point of reference, it appears that the silent rate for rodents is accelerated about 2.3 fold while the primate rate is reduced to 0.9 times the artiodactyl rate. By contrast, the replacement rate for rodents was only 1.8 times that in the artiodactyls whereas the primate rate was equal to the artiodactyl rate. These observations are consistent with those of earlier studies. They are suggestive of a generation-time effect if, as is commonly argued, the average generation times of these taxa over their histories are in the order

primates > artiodactyls > rodents.

One concern with these comparisons is that they represent averages of rates that extend over tens of millions of years. If the differences are due to generation-time effects, they will be diluted by the similar generation times that most likely occurred on the lineages during the time immediately following their separation. Li et al. argued that the primate slowdown, in particular, should be more pronounced in the apes, due to their longer generation time, and most pronounced in humans. This prediction is born out in the three comparisons of humans versus other primates shown in the second section of Table 2.1. The rate for human–chimpanzee is the most disparate, being one-half of the artiodactyl rate. The human–orangutan and human-Old World monkey rates are each larger than the previous, in line with the typical generation times of these groups. Within rodents, the rate obtained from a comparison of mice and rats is seen to be faster than for rodents as a whole.

Data from pseudogenes, as given in Table 2.2, also exhibit the primate slowdown, but gives a different rank-ordering within the primates. The fastest rate is still found in the Old World monkeys, but the slowest now comes from the human–orangutan comparison.

One of the main criticisms of the use of these observations to support the generation-time effect is their dependency on the accuracy of the paleontological data. In an effort to circumvent this limitation, Li et al. examined the rate of divergence of paralogous loci: loci that duplicated before a pair of lineages split. In four such comparisons, three β-like globin gene pairs and one aldolase pair, the average ratio of the silent rates for rodents compared with humans was 1.4. (The equivalent replacement rate ratio was 1.2.) This is considerably less than the value $(2.32/0.89 = 2.61)$ predicted from Table 2.1. The discrepancy would be expected if the duplications occurred well before the rodent–human split, if there were gene conversion, or if the dates used in Table 2.1 were incorrect.

A second way around this problem is to use relative rate tests. Consider a lineage made up of three species, numbered 1 to 3. Call species 3 the outgroup, make humans species 2, and let species 1 be either a monkey or an ape. The difference between the number of substitutions separating the outgroup and species 2 and the outgroup and species 3, $K_{13} - K_{23}$, is a measure of the rate differences leading to the human and ape or monkey lineages. If the difference is positive, then the evolution has proceeded more

Table 2.2. Rates of substitution in pseudogenes. The rates are given relative to the average artiodactyl rate as in Table 2.1. Data are from [194].

Comparison	Substitution Rate	Time to Origin (my.)
Human vs. chimpanzee	0.61	7 (5–10)
Human vs. orangutan	0.36	12 (10–16)
Human vs. rhesus	0.54	25 (20–30)
Human vs. owl monkey	0.57	35 (25–45)
Rhesus vs. owl monkey	0.68	35 (25–45)
Cow vs. goat	0.96	17 (12–25)

slowly on the human lineage. Note that this conclusion does not depend on any information about the times of separation.

Li et al. performed 44 of these relative rate tests; 36 (81%) of them were positive indicating a slower silent rate on the human lineage than on the ape, New World or Old World monkey lineages. Taken together, these observations present a fairly consistent case for a generation-time effect.

There is more support for the primate slowdown and the rodent speedup. Britten [24] reviewed both DNA hybridization and sequence data and concluded that the two kinds of data were consistent and both support a fivefold increase in the silent rates of rodents over those in higher primates. His study included creatures other than mammals, which led to some similarities that prove awkward for the generation-time hypothesis. For example, rodents, *Drosophila*, and sea urchins all appear to evolve at about the same rate even though the generation time of sea urchins is much longer than that of *Drosophila*. Birds, including passerines, evolve at about the same rate as the higher primates even though they have shorter generation times.

A more recent study by Catzeflis et al. [35] using DNA hybridization suggests that the rodent rate may be as much as 10 times higher than the primate rate. While these additional studies support the qualitative pattern in rodents and primates, the fact that three separate studies give ratios of 2.8, 5, and 10 for the rodent to human rates cannot help but make us uncomfortable. The disparity is most likely due to differences between DNA hybridization and sequence data, although Britten's arguments to the contrary are difficult to refute.

There are some scattered counterexamples to the generation-time effect as well. In a study of Phalangeriform marsupials, for example, Springer and Kirsch [270] noted a slowdown in the burramyid lineage even though this group has a short generation time relative to others in the study. A note of caution has been expressed by Cockburn et al. [42] who question the accuracy of the generation time determinations. It has also been suggested that the lemurs have a lower rate of substitution than other primates with similar generation times [20,118].

The real challenge to the generation-time effect has come not from the

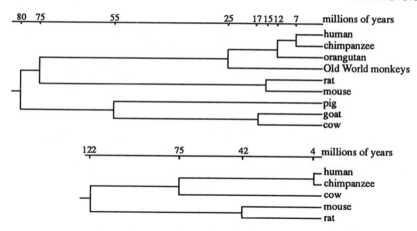

Figure 2.3. The upper tree is the one used by Li et al. [194] for the rate calculations given in Table 2.1. The lower tree eliminates the generation-time effect.

odd counterexample, but rather on two main fronts. The first, and most persistent, has been to attack the topology and split times used in the rate calculations [62,250]. Figure 2.3 shows the topology used by Li et al. to calculate the rates given in Table 2.1. A large bite can be taken out of the generation-time effect by simply changing the order of the three main branches—allow the rodents to split off first—and adjusting the split times.

Assume, for example, that the primate–artiodactyl split occurred 75 million years ago. If the rodents split off from the primate–artiodactyl lineage 122 million years ago, the generation-time effect disappears entirely for these taxa. A further bit of fiddling places the human–ape split at 4 million years and the rat–mouse split at 42 million years. (See the tree in the bottom half of Figure 2.3.) This removes the generation-time effect from within the primate and rodent lineages as well.

Among these changes, those involving the rodents are in sharpest conflict with the conventional reading of the fossil record. Pushing the origins of the rodent lineage back to 122 million years is difficult to justify [197], although the fragmentary nature of the fossil record does not allow it to be ruled out entirely. Placing the rat–mouse split at 42 million years goes against recent interpretations of the record that support moving the split in the other direction, to 10 million years [35]. Given the difficulty in working with rodent fossils, it is quite possible to turn a blind eye to this evidence and use our new tree to argue against the existence of a generation-time effect.

A great deal has been written on both sides of this issue and it seems unlikely to be resolved anytime soon. It is clear that the data are consistent with the generation-time effect as there is no compelling reason to reject the tree given in the top of Figure 2.3. Moreover, the paralogous gene comparisons and the relative rate tests from the Li at al. paper support the rodent speedup and primate slowdown by an argument that is independent of the tree. At the same time, we must recognize that the fossil record is not dependable, and may at some future time change our views on the generation-time effect.

The second challenge involves an eclectic group of biological issues. Foremost among these is the possibility that the variation in rates is not due to a generation-time effect, but rather to different mutation rates in different lineages. This is the explanation favored by Britten [24] who cites as evidence the fact that the DNA repair system of primates differs in some ways from that of rodents. Britten assumes, in effect, that u_g/g is lineage specific. By implication, each new observation—an average rate of substitution on a lineage—yields only an estimate of u_g/g with no degrees of freedom left over to test whether or not the fundamental model given by equation 2.1 is correct. This is a very different situation than before when we implicitly assumed that u_g was similar between species (say, less than twofold variation) and that we had independent estimates of the generation times, g. As a result, we could look directly for a generation-time effect. If we follow Britten's lead and assume that u_g varies considerably, then we must abandon any attempt to answer the title question of this section until comparative information on the nucleotide mutation rates from different mammals becomes available. Only then will we have independent estimates of u_g/g to compare to substitution rates.

Variation in DNA repair mechanisms is but one of several mechanisms that could lead to variation in per generation mutation rates. It is easy to imagine, for example, that the mutation rate per cell generation is relatively constant among mammals, but that the number of cell generations preceding the production of gametes varies considerably. If creatures with longer generation times had more cell generations, this would reduce the magnitude of the generation time effect. If the average number of cell generations preceding the production of a gamete is α, then the rate of substitution becomes

$$k_g \propto \alpha u_g/g.$$

This is the explanation that is most commonly employed to account for the fact that the silent substitution rate in rodents is only 2.8 times that in primates, even though the average generation time in rodents is arguably much greater than 2.8 times that in primates. In fact, this argument points out the futility of becoming obsessed with a precise quantitative investigation of the generation-time effect.

Male-driven molecular evolution

Miyata and his colleagues [212,213] have made a simple but compelling observation that supports the hypothesis that the rate of silent substitution is mutation limited. They exploited the fact that in mammals the number of germ cell divisions in males is much larger than in females. As a consequence, the rate of substitution should be higher in autosomal loci than in those on the X chromosomes. The argument goes as follows. Let u_g be the per generation mutation rate in females. Suppose that males have α times as many germ cell divisions as females. This implies that the per generation mutation rate for males is αu_g ($\alpha > 1$). Consider, now, the average mutation rate for a particular locus on an autosome. In a single generation a randomly chosen autosome is equally likely to be found in a male or a female. Thus, its average mutation rate is

$$\frac{1}{2}u_g + \frac{1}{2}\alpha u_g \approx \frac{1}{2}\alpha u_g.$$

The approximation applies if α is large, say 10 or greater. An X chromosome, on the other hand, is twice as likely to be found in a female as in a male. The average mutation rate for an X chromosome is thus

$$\frac{2}{3}u_g + \frac{1}{3}\alpha u_g \approx \frac{1}{3}\alpha u_g.$$

If α is large, the ratio of the X chromosome mutation rate to the autosome mutation rate is simply 2/3. A similar argument leads to the conclusion that the rate of mutation on the Y chromosome should be twice that on an autosome.

If mutation rates are limiting, we would predict that the rate of silent substitution for X-linked loci should be two-thirds that of autosomal loci. In the most complete study to date, Miyata et al. [213] compared the number of silent substitutions separating rat or mouse and humans for 41 autosomal loci and six X-linked loci and found the ratio to be 0.58. This is significantly less than one but not significantly different than the predicted value, 0.67.

No Y-linked sequences from humans and rodents were available to Miyata et al. so a similar comparison was not possible for this chromosome. However, they argued that the human argininosuccinate synthetase (AS) gene has spawned a pair of pseudogenes in a manner that does allow a meaningful test of the Y chromosome prediction. One pseudogene, ASψ-7, is found on the seventh chromosome; the other, ASψ-Y, is on the Y chromosome. Remarkably, one of these pseudogenes was apparently spawned by the other as evidenced by a shared ALU sequence that is not found in the original functional gene. A comparison of the corrected number of substitutions between the two pseudogenes and the functional genes allows a calculation of the relative rate of substitution. The ratio of the Y-linked to autosomal rates turns out to be 2.2, very close the predicted value of two.

Male-driven molecular evolution is clearly consistent with mutation-limited evolution of silent sites and provides much cleaner evidence than does the generation-time effect. Some additional experimental observations would shore up the case considerably. For example, it would be desirable to have direct evidence that the per generation nucleotide mutation rate in males is much higher than in females and that the per germ cell division mutation rate is the same in the two sexes. Such evidence will be difficult to obtain in the near future.

Miyata has made the more promising suggestion that an examination of rates of substitution in a ZW female/ZZ male system, where the Z chromosomal loci should evolve at 4/3 the rate of the autosomal loci, may provide the most convincing evidence and will also help to rule out the possibility that the slower rate of evolution in X-linked loci is due to a form of selection that produces fewer substitutions at loci that find themselves in the haploid state in one of the sexes.

Fast viruses

Certain RNA viruses evolve at a rate that has been estimated to be roughly 6 orders of magnitude faster than typical nuclear genes of the creatures they infect. One explanation for this astonishing observation is that the mutation rates in these viruses are 6 orders of magnitude higher as well [120, 249]. This would appear to add dramatic support for the model captured in equation 2.1. The influenza and HIV-1 (AIDS) viruses, which have been studied in the greatest detail, will be briefly examined in this subsection.

The influenza viruses are RNA viruses that have been classified into three types: A, B, and C. The types are identified by the antigenic properties of their nucleo- and matrix proteins as determined by serological tests. The A type is responsible for such major epidemics as the "swine" outbreak of 1918, the "Asian" outbreak of 1956, and the "Hong Kong" outbreak of 1968 [233]. The viruses that cause each these epidemics differ antigenically from one another leading to their classification into different subtypes. The proteins used for this classification are the membrane proteins hemagglutinin and neuraminidase.

The evolution leading to different subtypes is called *Antigenic shift*; the evolution that produces variation within subtypes is called *antigenic drift*. Rapid antigenic drift is apparently a major factor that allows A type influenza viruses to reinfect individuals in the course of an epidemic. Antigenic shift has led to the identification of at least 13 different subtypes based on the antigenic properties of hemagglutinin and nine subtypes based on neuraminidase [249]. Interestingly, the B and C types have not evolved into subtypes. Thus, antigenic shifts appears to be a property that is unique to the A type viruses. Antigenic drift occurs in the B strain, although more slowly than in the A strain, and is slower still in the C strain [233].

The rate of nucleotide substitution within a particular subtype of A viruses has been examined by Hayashida et al. [120] and by Saitou and Nei [249]. The main technical problem in these studies is achieving a suitable time scale for evolution. The usual solution is to use the time at which

Table 2.3. Rates of evolution of influenza virus type A loci. The rates are given for the third site in units of substitutions per site per 100 years. Also given is the ratio of the first plus second site rates to the third site rates. Data are from [249, Table 2].

Locus	3rd Rate	(1st+2nd Rate)/3rd Rate
Signal peptide	1.18	0.58
Hemagglutinin 1	1.02	0.40
Neuraminidase	0.63	0.48
Nonstructural protein 1	0.44	0.39
Matrix protein	0.37	0.14

subtypes first appear in collections as the time of their origin. With this approach, it is a simple matter to obtain rates of substitution. Saitou and Nei refined this method by using parsimony to construct the phylogeny of strains and to assign substitutions to each branch. In this way, they were able to calculate a rate for each branch.

A plot of branch length versus number of substitutions reveals that substitutions accumulate approximately linearly with time. The rates of accumulation are summarized in Table 2.3. Of immediate interest in this table is the fact that the rate of substitution at the third position of codons— a measure of the silent rate—is about one substitution per 100 to 1000 years. This is roughly 6 orders of magnitude higher than the typical silent substitution rate for mammalian nuclear genes! The second important observation is that the rate of replacement substitution is about one-half the silent rate, as measured by a comparison of the rate of substitution at the first two positions with that at the third position. The results of Hayashida et al. [120] are similar.

The fact that the replacement rate is smaller than the silent rate suggests that molecular evolution in these viruses may be mechanistically similar to that in more conventional organisms. They just seem to be doing it faster. A simple explanation for the speedup is the generation-time effect since viruses clearly have much shorter generation times than mammals. Accordingly, we might ask: what generation time would be required to account for the rapid evolution if the virus mutation rate per generation were the same as humans? Assuming that the generation time of humans is 20 years (or 2.63×10^7 seconds), the virus generation time would have to be one-millionth of this, or about 26 seconds. This is unrealistically short, so we must entertain the possibility that the mutation rate is higher in type A viruses than in humans.

In fact, the mutation rate in the nonstructural gene has been estimated to be about 1.5×10^{-5} per nucleotide per generation [235] or roughly 3 to 4 orders of magnitude higher than the oft-quoted but never measured rate in mammals. With this estimate in hand, the generation-time effect is now needed to account for only two or three orders of magnitude out of the six that separate the human and virus substitution rates. To bring the two rates into line, the generation time for the virus would have to be from roughly 7 to 70 hours long. While we cannot know the true generation time, these figures do not appear to be too outrageous. An important lesson in this numerology is that under the mutation-limited view, a proper assessment of relative rates of evolution needs to take into account both the variation in mutation rates and generation times.

A second biological issues that needs to be better understood concerns the lower rates of evolution of type B and C viruses. If the rapid evolution of A type is attributed to a higher mutation rate, then we must accept a lower mutation rate for types B and C. As an alternative, it may be that the high rate of evolution of type A viruses is due to Darwinian selection constantly changing the antigenic properties of surface proteins, hemagglutinin and neuraminidase, to avoid being neutralized by the immune system of an infected host. This is supported by the observation that antigenic drift allows recurring infections. To complete this model, we need to postulate that the fast evolution of other proteins is a coevolutionary response to the changes in the surface proteins and that the silent changes are needed to adjust codon usage and the secondary structure and nucleoprotein binding properties of RNA that are disrupted by the replacement changes.

The rate of evolution of the AIDS virus, human immunodeficiency virus type 1 (HIV1), is also very fast. In a study of 10 loci, or parts thereof, in two strains of HIV1, Li et al. [195] found the average silent rate to be 10.3×10^{-3} substitutions per site per year and the average replacement rate to be 3.9×10^{-3}. The fastest silent rate is about 2.4 times the slowest; the fastest replacement rate is about 8.2 times the slowest. There is nothing in these features, other than the fast overall rate, that is at variance with the evolutionary pattern that would be expected for 10 nuclear loci drawn at random from a mammal. Thus, as with the influenza virus, there is nothing to suggest that the mechanism of molecular evolution is different from that in other organisms. Mutation rates have been estimated in several retroviruses. The rate of mutation is similar to that of the influenza virus, about 2×10^{-5}. The high rate appears to be due, in the main, to the infidelity of reverse transcriptase and RNA polymerase [246].

Redundancy

The redundancy of the genetic code is structured such that there is variation in the number of codons assigned to each amino acid. Some amino acids have fourfold degenerate third sites. For these, changing the base at the third site does not alter the amino acid specified by the codon. Other amino acids have twofold degenerate third sites. For these, transversions—purine to pyrimidine or pyrimidine to purine—do alter the amino acid. If the nucleotide mutation rate is u and if the probability of mutating to each of the other bases is equal, then the mutation rate to codons that do not alter the amino acid is u for fourfold degenerate sites but only $u/3$ for twofold degenerate sites. If silent evolution were mutation limited and evolution were such that most replacement substitutions are not allowed, then we would predict that the rate of silent substitution at fourfold degenerate sites should be three times faster than that at twofold degenerate sites.

In their survey of rates of molecular evolution, Li et al. [192] estimated that the average rate of substitution at fourfold degenerate sites was 4.18×10^{-9} while the twofold degenerate rate was 2.26×10^{-9}. Thus, the fourfold rate is larger than the twofold rate, but only by about 1.8 times rather than three times as predicted. However, the real situation is more complex than this simple comparison suggests. Within the fourfold degenerate sites, the rate of transition substitutions (2.5×10^{-9}) is higher than the rate of transversion substitutions (1.7×10^{-9}) despite the fact that there are two opportunities for a transversion to only one opportunity for a transition. The standard explanation for this difference is that substitutions mirror a mutational bias favoring transitions. Thus, the failure to achieve the predicted threefold increase in rates at the fourfold degenerate sites is attributed to the low rate of transversion mutations. That the rate of substitution at twofold degenerate sites is indistinguishable from the rate of transition substitutions at fourfold degenerate sites lends credence to this explanation.

The use of redundancy to argue for mutation-limited evolution is more suspect than some of the other cases. Had the result been negative—equal rates for twofold and fourfold degenerate sites—we could have used that to argue against the hypothesis. Our positive result, on the other hand, could be due to the greater opportunity for evolution provided by fourfold degenerate sites in a model that is not mutation limited.

2.2   The substitutional sieve

Molecular evolution may be thought of as a sieve. New variants pumped into the population each generation by the genetic machinery are the input to the sieve; those that ultimately attain a substantial frequency in the population are the output. In principle, the sieve may be characterized experimentally by determining its input and its output without any knowledge of the evolutionary mechanisms that determine the sieve's behavior. Currently, we know much more about the output of the sieve than about its input. Studies of variation within and between populations are much farther along than are studies of, for example, the spontaneous mutational spectrum.

If a region of the genome were under no selective forces whatsoever, each variant would be equally likely to pass through the sieve. We will call this the *transparent* substitutional sieve. There is a tendency to postulate this sieve when examining, for example, the evolution of pseudogenes. For the transparent sieve, the output—fixations in the context of species comparisons—will reflect the input. Thus, the problem may be turned on its head and fixed variants may be used to make inferences about the

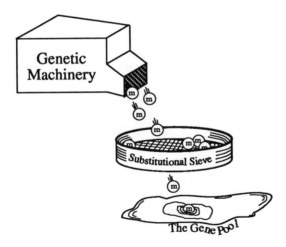

Figure 2.4. A fanciful representation of the substitutional sieve.

mutational process.

In this section, we will review some of the efforts in this area. Such studies are particularly valuable in a comparative sense. A comparison of the output for the substitutional sieve operating in a coding region to one operating in a noncoding region will give insights into the underlying mechanisms of evolution. As a trivial example, fixations of small deletions are fairly common in pseudogenes. On the other hand, they are relatively rare in coding regions. The reason is easy to understand in a mechanistic sense: deletions cause frame shifts that inactivate proteins leading to strong selection against them. Other differences in the sieves for pseudogenes and coding regions are less easily understood. For many of the differences we must be content at this point to provide only the characterization and defer the underlying mechanistic explanation for the future.

Pseudogenes

> Because, with few exceptions, all pseudogenes lack function, one can assume that all mutations occurring in pseudogenes are free from selective constraints, and thus, may be randomly fixed in populations. Therefore, the pattern and rate of substitution in pseudogenes should reflect the pattern and rate of spontaneous mutation [109, Page 279].

This quote is a clear statement of the assumption that pseudogenes evolve through a completely transparent sieve. The evidence in support of this assumption is suggestive, but not complete enough at this time to be totally convincing. We will begin our discussion with some background information on the rates of evolution of pseudogenes followed by an examination of the output and inputs to the sieve.

Published estimates of the average rate of nucleotide substitution in pseudogenes have changed over the years. Earlier studies suggested that pseudogenes evolved faster than silent sites within coding regions. For example, Li et al. [192] found the average rate to be 4.85×10^{-9}. This is about twice the average rate for twofold degenerate sites (2.26×10^{-9}) obtained in the same study, but only slightly higher than the fourfold degenerate rate (4.18×10^{-9}). These early studies included pseudogenes produced by duplications of their parent genes. Thus, part of the procedure for estimating rates involved finding the time at which the duplicate gene is disabled by a frameshift or stop codon.

More recent work has focused on processed pseudogenes since they are almost never functional at the time of insertion. In a recent study, Wolfe et al. [311] failed to find any significant difference in the rate of evolution of processed pseudogenes and the fourfold degenerate rate in comparisons of humans and Old World monkeys. Thus, at the present time there is no compelling evidence to suggest that pseudogene rates of evolution are any different from silent rates. This is somewhat surprising since silent sites do play a role in codon usage, transcription rates, the secondary structure of mRNA, and other functions that are not relevant to the evolution of pseudogenes.

While the rates of substitution in pseudogenes may not differ appreciably from those of fourfold degenerate silent sites, the nature of the substitutions do. The most striking difference involves the substitutions of small deletions and insertions. Figure 2.5 gives histograms of the sizes of deletions and insertions for 22 human and 30 rodent processed pseudogenes from a study by Graur et al. [109]. About half of the insertions and deletions involve single bases; the overwhelming majority are smaller than four bases. Note the unexpected mode at three bases for both deletions and insertions. Deletions outnumber insertions by 7:1 in humans and 3:1 in rodents.

On average, human processed-pseudogenes have had 1.2% of their length deleted and 0.1% inserted. The figures for rodents are 2.3% and 1.1%. Thus, the evolution of pseudogenes is characterized by a gradual shortening, this process being farther along in rodents than in humans. This may reflect the nature of a mutational process that favors deletions over insertions, as Wolfe et al. claim. Alternatively, it may reflect the action of weak selection counterbalancing the lengthening of the genome that accompanies the propagation of pseudogenes.

A rough estimate of the relative rates of nucleotide substitutions to indel (insertion and deletion) substitutions for processed pseudogenes may be obtained even though the time of origin of each pseudogene is unknown. In the Graur et al. study there were about 1747 base-pair substitutions separating all of the processed pseudogenes from their functional parental genes. This number is obtained by applying the Jukes-Cantor correction formula to the fraction of sites that differ between the pseudogene and its parent. As such, it is only a crude estimate since the assumption of equal substitution rates to all bases is not met by pseudogenes. Assuming that

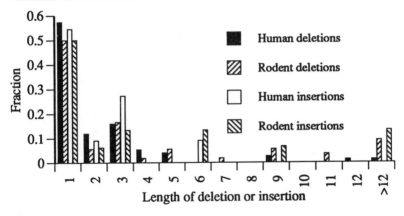

Figure 2.5. A histogram of the lengths of deletions and insertions in 22 human and 30 rodent processed pseudogenes. Data are from [109].

1/4 of the sites in the functional parent gene are silent, and that silent sites and pseudogenes evolve at the same rate, we infer that $(4/5)1747 = 1397.6$ base-pair substitutions have occurred in the pseudogenes, the remaining substitutions having occurred in the parental gene. We can assume that all of the 86 indel substitutions that separate the pseudogenes from their parents occurred in the pseudogenes, since indels are rare in coding regions. Thus, indels make up about 5.6% of the substitutions recorded in the Graur et al. study. The remainder are base-pair substitutions. For the mouse, there were about 915 total base-pair substitutions and 70 indels, implying that about 8.7% of the substitutions are indels.

An intriguing aspect of these results concerns the differences between rodents and humans. Humans experience about twice as many deletions per insertion (7:1) as do rodents (3:1), yet the total fraction of rodent pseudogenes that have been deleted is higher. Does this reflect a difference in the input to the sieve or to the output?

There have been a number of studies describing patterns of base substitutions in pseudogenes [27,103,198]. Since these studies are based on a common pool of pseudogene sequences, their conclusions are in general agreement. The discussion here is based mainly on Bulmer's work as it, being the most recent, uses the largest number of pseudogenes.

Table 2.4 gives the relative frequencies of base substitutions averaged over 14 pseudogenes. From this table and from other observations in these papers we are led to the following generalizations:

- *No strand effects*: The patterns and numbers of substitutions appear to be the same for both (original) sense and antisense strands. Tests designed to detect differences have failed to identify any [27,198]. This could not be predicted a priori since the leading and lagging strands are replicated and repaired by slightly different mechanisms, which could cause different mutational spectra. Some studies, including

Table 2.4. Base substitutions in 14 pseudogenes. The numbers are the percent of the total number of substitutions that occurred in each category. Data are from [27, Table 2].

Base in functional gene	Base in pseudogene				Total
	A	C	G	T	
A	—	3.8	8.5	2.9	15.2
C	6.4	—	5.6	22.8	34.8
G	22.8	5.6	—	6.4	34.8
T	2.9	8.5	3.8	—	15.2
Total	32.1	17.9	17.9	32.1	

Bulmer's, use the absence of a strand effect to collapse the data into equivalent substitutional classes. For example, A→C substitutions are combined with T→G substitutions. This leads to the symmetries evident in Table 2.4.

- *Homogeneity*: There is, at present, no evidence that the substitutional process is different in different pseudogenes. Li et al. [198] conjectured that there is no significant heterogeneity between eight pseudogenes. Bulmer checked for heterogeneity in his data and also failed to find any. Further work may uncover differences. This is particularly likely if a pseudogene is studied that has been inserted into a GC-rich isochore. Such pseudogenes may not exhibit the evolution toward higher AT seen in pseudogenes studied to date.

- *Transitions outnumber transversions*: Of all of the substitutions recorded in Table 2.4, 62.6% are transitions. This is twice what would be expected (33%) were the probabilities of substitutions to all three bases equal. Note that a big contributor to this effect are the two substitutions C→T and G→A. The reason for this will be discussed below.

- *AT content increases*: The right hand column in Table 2.4 shows that C and G are about twice as likely to experience a substitution as are A and T. The bottom row shows that A and T are twice as likely to be the bases that replace the original base when a substitution does occur. Together, this implies that the AT content of pseudogenes should be increasing. This may be examined quantitatively by comparing the AT% in the functional genes, 0.47, to that of the pseudogenes, 0.51. (Both figures may be obtained from Table 2.4.) The comparison may be continued to the AT% predicted by an equilibrium analysis of the substitutional pattern. The equilibrium calculation that Bulmer provides [27, Table 4] goes beyond what is possible using Table 2.4 alone in that it uses dinucleotide substitution patterns. He concludes that the equilibrium AT% will be 0.624, or about 50% higher than in functional genes. As with the previous item, the C→T and G→A substitutions are big contributors to the increase in AT.

- *Deficiency of CpG:* Since at least 1961 we have known that species with heavily methylated DNA exhibit a deficiency in CpG doublets over that expected in the absence of neighbor effects [17]. In humans, for example, there are about one-fifth as many CpG doublets as expected. The deficiency is attributed to the fact that cytosine in CpG doublets is often methylated, which, in turn, elevates the mutation rate from cytosine to thymidine. Thus, the deficiency of CpG is accompanied by an excess in the frequency of TG and CA. Part of the evidence in support of this explanation is the striking correlation between the level of methylation of a genome and the extent of its deficiency of CpG [17]. Bulmer's analysis of substitutions in pseudogenes shows that a large fraction of C→T and G→A substitutions evident in Table 2.4 are due to substitutions in CpG doublets. His equilibrium projection based on dinucleotide substitution patterns predicts that the frequency of CpG in noncoding DNA should be about one-fifth that predicted in the absence of neighbor effects, in remarkable agreement with the observed deficiency. Bulmer detected other neighbor effects in his study, but none are as striking as the CpG pattern.

Our view of pseudogene evolution will undoubtedly change over the next few years. The observations summarized here are mostly from papers that were written before the isochore structure of the mammalian genome was understood. (Isochores will be covered in a later section.) Both GC% and levels of methylation vary throughout the mammalian genome; presumably, the evolutionary dynamics of pseudogenes vary as well. Future work should focus on the variation in dynamics rather than average properties.

The mutational spectrum

To judge whether or not the substitutional sieve for pseudogenes is transparent we need to compare its output, the substitutions summarized in the previous section, to its input, the mutational spectrum for mammalian gametes. Work on mutagenesis in mammals is in its infancy, making the appropriate comparison impossible at the present time. There are, however, some aspects of mutagenesis that are remarkably concordant with the substitutional pattern.

The extraordinarily low spontaneous mutation rates in eukaryotes—10^{-10} to 10^{-12} errors per base pair per cell generation [289]—suggests that DNA replication, repair, and recombination all conspire to assure the fidelity of DNA transmission. Our understanding of these processes in mammals comes mainly from two approaches. The first examines replication in vitro using purified polymerases or replication complexes. The second

Table 2.5. Fidelity of mammalian polymerases. Data are from [175, Table II].

	Error rate	
Error Category	Human Pol α	Rat Pol β
Base substitutions	3.23×10^{-4}	7.69×10^{-4}
Frameshifts		
Overall average	1.28×10^{-4}	9.09×10^{-4}
Plus-one-base	9.09×10^{-6}	1.11×10^{-5}
Minus-one-base	1.18×10^{-4}	9.09×10^{-4}

examines spontaneous mutations in mammalian cell cultures using various selection schemes.

In mammals, it is thought that α polymerase is the primary enzyme for DNA replication and β polymerase is used mainly for repair. Neither of these polymerases have any proofreading activity. The results of an in vitro study of purified polymerases by Kunkel and Bebenek [175] is given in Table 2.5. The error ratesattributable to polymerization is obviously quite high, indicating that fidelity is due to proofreading and other processes that occur on elements of the replicative complex that are not purified along with the polymerase. Note, however, that the rank ordering of relative error rates mirrors that of substitutions in processed pseudogenes. Base changes* occur more frequently than indels; within indels, deletions occur more often than insertions. However, the quantitative relationships between these classes of mutations do not agree very well with the substitution patterns. If the sieve is transparent, then proofreading and repair must operate differentially on the three types of mutations.

Recent work on replication complexes using HeLa cell extracts and simian virus 40 (SV40) have lowered the in vitro mutation rate to 1 error per 150,000 nucleotides incorporated [245]. (Compare this to 1 per 5000 in the purified α polymerase system.) The α polymerase replication complexes from HeLa cells have been shown to have $3' \rightarrow 5'$ exonuclease activity, which is thought to contribute to the increased fidelity. However, these studies are not advanced enough to allow a direct comparison with the polymerase results in Table 2.5.

Studies using the polymerase chain reaction technique and DNA sequencing for in vivo estimates of mutation rates in mammalian cell cultures are just beginning, but hold promise as a valuable source of information on mutational spectra. A recent study [281] using the bacterial *gpt* gene in Chinese hamster ovary cells produced results that are at variance with both the substitution pattern in pseudogenes and the in vitro studies. Of 62 spontaneous mutations, 49 (79%) were deletions. This high percent-

---

*Substitution is used in mutagenesis studies to refer to mutational rather than populational events.

age may reflect a selection scheme that is not sufficiently sensitive to point mutations. Nineteen of the 49 deletions were 3-base deletions. Again, this fraction is high relative to the other studies, yet is intriguing when measured against the 3-base mode seen in Figure 2.5 for substitutions.

The 3-base deletions were not scattered randomly over the *gpi* gene, but were concentrated in a small 6-base region. This same region was removed by a single 7-base deletion. The occurrences of such mutational hot spots is a constant feature of all mutagenesis studies. They are due to *contextual effects*, local properties of the DNA that cause dramatic alterations in the mutation frequency. The high rate of transition from methylated CpG doublets is another example of a contextual effect. Kunkel and his colleagues, among others, have found contextual effects from in vitro studies that elevate mutation rates by as much as 2 orders of magnitude at specific sites. His explanation, based on a mechanism called *transient misalignment* [176], rests heavily on local sequence patterns in DNA.

If contextual effects can alter local mutation rates by 1 or 2 orders of magnitude, then we should probably be rethinking our general approach to the study of the evolution of pseudogenes. Rather than aiming toward summary statistics that average events across several pseudogenes, we should be trying to identify specific "substitutional hot spots" by comparing site by site processed pseudogenes from a single parent gene. Once a substitutional hot spot is identified, its local sequence may be used in an in vitro study to determine if it is a mutational hot spot. Should this be so, then we will have yet more evidence for the transparence of the pseudogene substitutional sieve.

2.3   CG% and codon usage

The previous sections dealt with rates and patterns of substitutions without paying attention to their biological significance. In this section we turn to the evolution of two aspects of the genome whose biological significance cannot be ignored: the GC content and codon usage. These aspects are so intertwined that they are most profitably considered together even though they are frequently uncoupled in the literature. The presentation has been constructed to support the unorthodox view that the GC% of the genome is molded by a force—perhaps natural selection—whose strength is sufficient to be a major determinant of codon usage in many organisms. The argument in support of this view will coalesce as the relevant observations are described.

The GC/AT pressure

Among the eubacteria, there is remarkable variation in the genomic GC content. The GC% varies from about 25%, as in some *Mycoplasm*, to 75%, as in *Micrococcus luteus* [230]. The genomic GC% is correlated with the GC content of the four major classes of DNA: coding regions, tRNA loci, rRNA

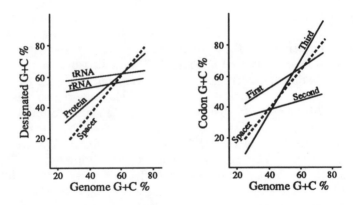

Figure 2.6. The dependency of various regions of DNA on the genomic percent of G plus C. Redrawn from [230, Figs. 1 and 2].

loci, and spacer as illustrated in Figure 2.6. The correlation is weakest for tRNA and rRNA loci, which make up less than 1% of the total DNA, somewhat stronger for coding regions (70-80% of the DNA), and strongest for spacer DNA (20-30%) [230]. This is as would be expected were there some force—call it the *GC/AT pressure* [230]—that pushes the GC% to a particular value.

The GC/AT pressure is opposed by selection for the functions performed by the products of the various loci. Transfer and ribosomal loci are presumably under direct sequence selection and as such oppose the GC/AT pressure to the greatest extent. In coding regions selection acts, in part, on the proteins and thus not directly on properties of DNA. The redundancy of the code allows some flexibility for DNA sequence evolution in response to the GC/AT pressure. This leads to a stronger correlation with genomic GC% than seen in the RNA loci. Finally, spacer DNA is generally considered to be under the fewest constraints and as such is most susceptible to the GC/AT pressure.

The variation in GC% among bacteria suggests that a nontrivial fraction of molecular evolution may be in response to the GC/AT pressure. The fact that even relatively closely related bacteria can have very different GC percentages (e.g., within *Mycoplasma* or *Clostridium* [310]) suggests that the rate of evolution under the GC/AT pressure may be high. What, then, is the nature of the GC/AT pressure?

Many years ago, Sueoka proposed that the GC/AT pressure is due almost entirely to mutational bias [274,275]. That is, in some species the spontaneous mutational spectrum favors A and T over G and C, whereas in others it is the opposite. If the majority of mutations were nearly neutral, then this explanation would nicely account for the observed patterns. In fact, this is the only explanation for the GC/AT pressure that appears to be seriously entertained in the literature [230].

As an historical sidelight, Sueoka's theory appears to be one of the first neutral theories of DNA evolution. It explicitly assumes that natural selection plays no role in the dynamics of allele frequencies. However, as it does not incorporate genetic drift, it cannot describe the fixation of nucleotides. This aspect of the theory had to wait six more years for the publication of the papers by Kimura [155] and King and Jukes [164].

There is, of course, another explanation for the GC/AT pressure: The GC content of DNA might be under direct natural selection toward an optimal value. If selection toward this optimum were stronger than the mutational bias, then the genomic GC% should be essentially independent of the mutational bias.

Although these two mechanistic explanations for the GC/AT pressure are very different, they make essentially the same predictions about the correlations between the GC% of the genome and that of the various loci. It is impossible to choose one over the other based only on the observations presented thus far. There is, however, a new observation that seems to provide one argument in favor of the selection-based hypothesis. This is illustrated in the right-hand graph in Figure 2.6 showing the relationship between the GC% of the entire genome and that of the three positions of codons. As expected, the second position is only weakly dependent on genomic GC% whereas the third position is strongly dependent. Note, however, that the slope for the third position is even steeper than that of spacer DNA. We would imagine that spacer DNA, being the least constrained, reflects most faithfully the value toward which the GC/AT pressure is pushing. If the GC/AT pressure were due to a mutational bias, we would expect the slope for the third position to lie between that of the second position and the spacer. On the other hand, if the pressure were due to selection for an optimum, then constraints on selection at the first and second positions that generally weaken the correspondence between the optimum and local GC% can be compensated by making the GC% at the third position even more extreme. This provides a very natural explanation for the patterns seen in the graph.

The explanation for the steeper slope of third positions given by Osawa et al. [230] involves the influence of tRNA abundances. They argue that the GC% should be viewed as the sum of two pressures: the mutational bias and the influence of tRNA abundances. Thus, bacteria with very high (low) GC percentages also have tRNAs that favor codons with an even higher (lower) GC%. What remains obscure in this explanation is the reason why the particular tRNAs that cause this pattern are the most abundant. This point will be taken up again after we explore codon usage in more detail.

Unicellular codon usage

The degenerate genetic code provides more than one codon for most amino acids. Leucine, serine, and arginine lead the pack with six codons each. Five other amino acids (pro, ala, val, gly, and thr) have four codons each.

The four in each case differ only in the third position. For example, valine is encoded by GUU, GUC, GUA, and GUG. In general, these eight amino acids require more than one tRNA to handle all of their codons. Nine amino acids (phe, tyr, his, gln, asn, lys, asp, glu and cys) have two codons each with twofold degenerate third positions. The two bases in the third position are always either purines (A or G) or pyrimidines (U or C) for each amino acid. These amino acids require only a single tRNA each. Tryptophan and methionine have only one codon each while isoleucine is unique in having three codons and two isoaccepting tRNAs (in *E. coli*, at least).

It has been known for some time that the codons for each amino acid are not used with equal frequencies. This raises the important issue as to whether the departures from equality are due to mutational biases acting on mostly neutral traits (the different codons of each amino acid) or whether natural selection is somehow involved. There can be no simple answer since the patterns of codon usage vary dramatically between taxonomic groups. To further complicate the picture, codon usage is confounded with the evolution of GC% in the genome.

In unicellular organisms with extreme GC contents, where there is little latitude for codon usage, we would expect the usage to be dictated almost entirely by the GC%. This appears to be true in the few cases that have been reported. Winkler and Wood [310], for example, examined a number of AT-rich bacteria and discovered that they used A or U almost exclusively in the two- and fourfold degenerate third positions of codons. Moreover, in the sextets (amino acids with six codons), the codons with the maximal number of U and A were used most often. For example, UUA is used for leucine much more frequently than is UUG or any of the codons of the form CUN. Among the latter group, CUA and CUU are used more frequently than CUG or CUC. Winkler and Wood conclude from their study of five clostridial genes, five mycoplasmal genes and three rickettsial genes that the use of A and U in these AT-rich bacteria is very close to the maximum possible.

Unicellular organisms with intermediate GC%, on the other hand, are free to evolve more complex patterns of codon usage. The yeast *Saccharomyces cerevisiae* and the bacterium *Escherichia coli* are remarkable in that they share a simple pattern of codon usage that lends itself to a straightforward evolutionary interpretation. The main features of the *E. coli*-yeast pattern are as follows.

- The **direction** of the codon bias is species specific rather than locus specific. Thus, all *E. coli* loci exhibit a bias in a direction that differs from all loci of yeast. Grantham et al. [107] were among the first to note the species-specific bias and referred to it as the *genome hypothesis*. Figure 2.7 illustrates the bias for proline and alanine for two loci in the two species. A more complete comparison may be found in Ikemura's review [139, Table 1].

- The **degree** of codon bias varies among loci with the most highly ex-

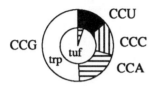 

Figure 2.7. Pie diagrams illustrating the codon bias for proline in *E. coli* on the left and yeast on the right. The inner pies are for highly expressed genes, the outer are for lowly expressed genes. Data are from [139].

pressed loci showing the greatest bias. Ikemura [138] and Grantham et al. [106] are the names associated with the first description of this correlation although many others noted it at about the same time [139]. Figure 2.7 illustrates this property for proline for the highly expressed *trp* and CYC 1,7 loci and the lowly expressed *tuf* and G3PDH loci in *E. coli* and yeast, respectively. The correlation between the frequency of use of the "optimal codon" (see below) and the number of protein molecules per cell for *E. coli* is shown in Figure 2.8

The direction of the bias in *coli* and yeast is determined by four empirical "rules." The first of these applies to the nine amino acids with three or more codons and more than one isoaccepting tRNA. The three remaining rules apply only to the twofold degenerate amino acids with a single tRNA each.

- *Rule 1*: The frequency of use of a particular codon is correlated with the abundance of its isoaccepting tRNA for the nine amino acids with three or more codons [138]. (The abundances of isoaccepting tRNAs differ between *coli* and yeast, contributing to the genome effect.)

- *Rule 2*: If the wobble U (the first position in the anticodon) is modified to thiolated or 5-carboxymethyl uridine, then A-terminated codons (the proper Watson-Crick partner) are preferred over G-terminated codons. (Modifications of the wobble U often differ between *E. coli* and yeast contributing to the genome effect.)

- *Rule 3*: Inosine—a close chemical relative of adenine—at the wobble position prefers U- and C-terminated codons over A-terminated codons.

- *Rule 4*: A codon of the form A/U-A/U-pyrimidine favors a C in the third position over U. Since the A-U pairing is weaker than the G-C pairing, the feeling is that C is needed to raise the bond energy for these codons. Conversely, codons of the form G/C-G/C-pyrimidine prefer U to C in the third position.

These rules lead to unambiguous choices of "optimal" codons for most amino acids [139, Table 1]. For certain amino acids, the rules imply that

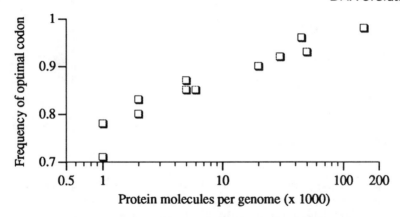

Figure 2.8. The relationship between the frequency of use of the "optimal" codon and the concentration of the protein for loci from *E. coli*. Data are from [139, Table 4].

there will be more than one optimal codon. The frequency of use of optimal codons, F_{op} in Ikemura's terminology [139], is strongly correlated with the level of expression of a locus. This striking phenomenon is illustrated in Figure 2.8.

Bulmer [30] has reexamined the validity of these rules by using a much larger number of loci than was available when the rules were originally stated. He concluded that Rule 1 fits the data quite well. The remaining rules, which apply to codon sets that use only a single tRNA, are more variable in their success. Yeast conform reasonably well to Rules 2, 3, and 4 while *E. coli* follows only Rule 3 with convincing fidelity.

The match between frequently used codons and the abundance of the corresponding isoacceptor tRNAs, particularly for highly expressed loci, immediately suggests that this is an adaptation for efficient protein synthesis. In fact, it has been demonstrated experimentally that if a codon corresponding to a rare tRNA is substituted in a highly expressed gene, the rate of translation is lowered [287]. What remains enigmatic is the driving force behind the correlation. Are tRNA abundances set by some—as yet uncovered—strong evolutionary force with codon frequencies weakly evolving to match? Or is the converse true: some strong force, also unknown, dictates codon usage with tRNA abundances evolving to match? Michael Bulmer [28] views the problem as coevolutionary, with both codon usage and tRNA abundances evolving to maximize the rate of protein synthesis.

The degree of codon bias in *E. coli* is inversely correlated with the rate of silent evolution [139,255]. The effect can be impressive. For example, the rate of silent substitution for the highly expressed and biased *rpsU* locus is 44 times less than that of the lowly expressed *trpA* locus [255, Table 1]. The rates in this case are determined by comparing *E. coli* to its close relative, *Salmonella typhimurium*. More typically, highly biased loci evolve about four times more slowly than less biased ones.

Not all unicellular organisms with intermediate GC percentages have such extreme biases in codon usage. The first major study of codon bias in the bacterium *Bacillus subtilis*, for example, resulted in a paper entitled "Markedly unbiased codon usage in *Bacillus subtilis*" [225]. There is little doubt when examining the codon usage table for the 21 loci examined in this paper that the striking biases observed in *E. coli* and yeast are not evident. In fact, the average usage across all 21 loci looks remarkably even.

Shields and Sharp [258] followed this original study with a second that involved more loci, 56, and a more sophisticated statistical quest for evidence of a bias of the sort seen in *E. coli* and yeast. They used a multivariate statistical technique called *correspondence analysis* that had been used successfully in the past to uncover hidden patterns of codon usage. The technique is similar to principle component analysis in that it finds a transformation that maximizes the dispersion of codon usage between loci.

When applied to *Bacillus*, correspondence analysis produced an axis along which a group of six loci emerged as having a shared pattern of codon bias that differed substantially from the others. Three of these turned out to be ribosomal protein loci and three were for small, acid-soluble spore proteins. All six are thought to be highly expressed. Moreover, at the opposite end of the first axis were a number of sporulation loci that are thought not to be highly expressed. Thus, there is some similarity with the *E. coli*-yeast pattern in that the degree of bias appears to be correlated with the degree of expression. Unfortunately, there is not sufficient information on the abundances of isoaccepting tRNAs to check whether or not Rule 1 applies. The agreement with Rule 4, however, increases with the level of expression.

Among unicellular organisms, we have seen evidence for two different forces that operate directly on the DNA sequence. One affects the GC% of the entire genome, the other affects codon usage within coding regions. Of the two, the GC/AT pressure appears to be the stronger. Two observations support this. One is the maximal use of A and U in the third positions of AT-rich bacteria. The other is the steeper slope for the third position GC% versus the genomic GC% than the spacer GC%. In the case of *E. coli*, the fact that the adherence to Rule 1 increased with the level of expression led us to conclude that selection was responsible for codon usage. Thus, the GC/AT pressure is generally stronger than the force of natural selection acting on codon bias.

Drosophila

Codon usage in multicellular organisms is likely to be more complex than that in unicellular organisms due to that added complication of adapting to various differentiated cell types with different tRNA populations [139]. The experience with unicellular organisms suggests that progress will only come from studies that include three critical observations: codon bias, level of expression, and rate of substitution. I have been unable to find any studies of "lower" multicellular organisms with all three except for the Shields at al. [259] examination of *Drosophila*. The *Drosophila* story has many elements in common with the unicellulars. Mammals, on the other hand, exhibit a strikingly different pattern. They will be relegated to the next section.

Shields at al. [259] tabulated codon usage for 91 loci in *D. melanogaster* and made the following observations:

- Codon usage varies between loci mainly due to variation in the frequency of GC in the third position. The variation exceeds that attributable to binomial sampling.

- The first axis in a correspondence analysis ranked the loci in such a way that the most highly biased loci were at one extreme and the least biased at the other. The most highly biased loci tend to have G or C in the third position. The increase in GC is due almost entirely to an increase in C rather than G.

- The average GC content for loci with little bias is about 60%, that for highly biased loci is about 80%. These are higher than the average for introns ($\approx$ 37%) or the entire genome ($\approx$ 40%).

- There is no correlation among loci in the GC content of silent and replacement sites or in the GC content of introns and silent sites as there is in mammals (as we will document in the next section).

- For those few loci for which it could be examined, it appears that the more highly expressed loci have a greater codon bias than lowly expressed loci.

- The rate of silent substitution at highly biased loci is lower than at less biased loci as illustrated in Figure 2.9.

- There is a very tenuous suggestion that the tRNAs may mirror codon usage.

In broad outline, this pattern is remarkably similar to that for *E. coli* and yeast. The conspicuous difference being that the highly biased loci all share the same pattern of bias: an increase in the use of C in the third position. One explanation for the difference is that the bias does not represent an interaction with tRNA pools, but reflects some property of mRNA, such as secondary structure, that is relevant to translation or message stability. Unfortunately, not enough is known about the tRNA population to discover whether or not the favored codons match the most abundant tRNA species.

As was pointed out by Shields et al., it seems extraordinarily unlikely that a bias in codon usage due to an increase in the C content could be due to a local mutation effect. Were this so, we would expect to see a correlation of silent site GC% and intron GC%. They suggest that some as yet unknown evolutionary force favors higher GC% for coding regions generally, and that

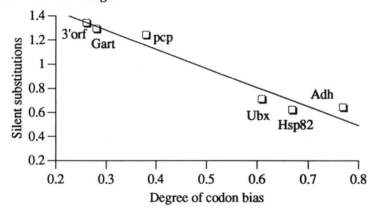

Figure 2.9. The relationship between the degree of codon bias and the number of silent substitutions for loci from *D. melanogaster* and *D. pseudoobscura*. The names of the loci are given next to each point. Data are from [259, Table 3].

the force is stronger in more highly expressed loci. Whatever this force is, it must run counter to the genome-wide GC/AT pressure. It is suggestive, but not statistically significant, that the intron GC% is lower than that of the entire genome, as if it is compensating for the elevated GC% of the exons.

Riley [244] compared the DNA sequences of *Xdh* (xanthine dehydrogenase) from *D. melanogaster* and *D. pseudoobscura* and observed that the codons used at this locus, whose bias is at the low end for *Drosophila*, are significantly different between the two species. By contrast, the same statistical procedure failed to find a significant difference in the codon usage in *Adh*, a highly biased locus. Were this pattern repeatable across loci, it would suggest that there is a temporally fluctuating force altering the usage of codons and that the force is opposed by the codon-usage rules. The rules themselves also appear to change. Starmer and Sullivan [271] noted that there are significant differences in codon usage in *Adh* when species from the two subgenera, *Drosophila* and *Sophophora* are compared.

Isochores

The genomes of mammals and birds are compartmentalized into *isochores*, stretches of DNA several hundred kilobases in length that are relatively homogeneous in their GC content. The GC% of different isochores are often quite disparate, but within an isochore there is remarkably little variation. Three different lines of research pointed to the existence of isochores: CsCl density gradient centrifugation, chromosome banding, and replication-time fractionation. Although many workers have contributed to our understanding of isochores, Giorgio Bernardi, who coined the term, was among the first to realize their importance and has been a major force in isochore research. Bernardi's [13] and Holmquist's [132] reviews are excellent sources for in-

Table 2.6. Properties of isochores.

GC-Rich Isochores	AT-Rich Isochores
GC% > 50%	GC% < 50%
In R bands	In G bands
Early replicating	Late replicating
C_pG rich islands	Few C_pG rich islands
Codon usage favors G and C	Codon usage favors A and T
Genes relatively common	Depauperate in genes
Housekeeping genes	Mostly tissue-specific genes

formation about isochores.

Our interest in isochores is tied up with their influence on codon usage. As we shall see, the bases used in the third position of most mammalian codons are chosen to bring the GC% of the coding regions into agreement with that of their local isochore. Before documenting this, it is important that we spend some time describing more about isochores since our final judgment about the mechanisms responsible for the patterns of codon usage depend on our understanding of the forces maintaining the homogeneous base composition of isochores.

Mammalian isochores may be lumped into two major classes: GC-rich (GC content greater than 50%) and AT-rich (GC less than 50%). The AT-rich isochores may often be seen under the light microscope in G-bands (Giemsa dark) and GC-rich isochores as R-bands (reverse bands). The AT-rich isochores are associated with late-replicating regions of the genome, the GC-rich isochores with early replicating regions. These and other facts about isochores are summarized in Table 2.6.

Genes are not placed randomly in isochores. GC-rich isochores, which are a minor fraction of the total DNA, appear to have a much higher density of genes than do AT-rich isochores. In fact, the majority of loci that have been sequenced fall into GC-rich isochores. The current interpretation of the data is that housekeeping genes, genes that are expressed in most tissues, tend to be found in GC-rich isochores whereas tissue-specific genes tend to occur more often in AT-rich isochores.

A peculiarity of GC-rich isochores is the presence of *CpG islands*. Recall that CpG doublets are generally under-represented in creatures with methylated cytosine because the methylated cytosines in CpG doublets have an elevated mutation rate to T. Surprisingly, while CpG doublets are under-represented in AT-rich isochores, they occur at about the expected frequency in GC-rich isochores. Moreover, they often occur in short regions of DNA with very high GC%, clustered unmethylated CpG doublets, G/C boxes, and a number of other high-GC motifs. Such stretches are called CpG islands. As might be expected, the levels of methylation in GC-rich isochores is very low.

As the first evidence for isochores appeared, it was immediately apparent that codon usage in mammals is strongly correlated with the local isochore GC%. A particularly easy way to document this is by plotting, say, intron GC% against third-position GC%. Alternatively, one could use 3' or 5' flanking DNA in place of intron DNA. Whichever is used, a highly significant correlation inevitably results [4,14,29]. An example from humans is illustrated in Figure 2.10. This pattern of codon usage differs from that of unicellular organisms and *Drosophila* in that there are marked differences in the codons preferred by different loci (depending on the isochore they find themselves in). It is not clear at this time whether there is any correlation in the level of expression of a gene and its bias.

Superimposed on this gross pattern of codon usage are various refinements. The most striking of these is the tendency for the GC% of third positions to be higher than that of the surrounding isochore [74,140]. The effect is particularly dramatic in the two α-globin loci in humans as illustrated on the right-hand side of Figure 2.11 which was redrawn (with some smoothing) from a paper by Ikemura and Aota [140]. The effect is less striking, but still present, for most of the β-globin loci as illustrated on the left side of the figure. The figures were prepared by sliding a 2001 base-pair window along a DNA sequence and plotting the GC% for the window as a function of its position.

A rough indication of the amount of fluctuation that would be expected from binomial sampling in the absence of any systematic effects is given by the standard deviation of GC%. Were the nucleotides thrown down at random with 50% GC, the standard deviation would be about 1%. Given that the fluctuations in Figure 2.11 are much larger than that, it is apparent that there is a great deal of statistically significant fluctuation around the mean of the isochore, at least some of which is due to the presence of coding regions. In the high GC content regions, this is reminiscent of a similar phenomena in bacteria as we illustrated on the right-hand side of Figure 2.6. Whether there is a common mechanism operating is, of course,

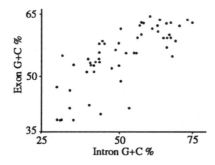

Figure 2.10. The correlation of exon GC% and intron GC% for 56 human loci. Redrawn from [29, Fig. 1].

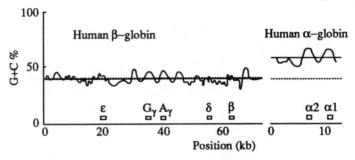

Figure 2.11. The GC% as calculated from a 2001-base window moved along the human α- and β-globin complexes. Redrawn from [140, Fig. 3].

a complete mystery. Note that the α-globin loci are located in a GC-rich isochore whereas the β-globin loci are in an AT-rich isochore. Such a distribution would not be expected were codon usage keyed to tRNA populations.

Bernardi et al. [15] have made a number of interesting observations about the evolution of isochores. They begin by pointing out some of the differences in isochores among vertebrates. Generally, isochores are limited to the warm-blooded vertebrates, birds and mammals. Within mammals, there appears to be two compositional patterns: the "murid" pattern found in three families of rodents—murids (rats and mice), cricetids (hamsters), spalacids (mole rats)—and the "general" pattern found in most of the remaining mammals. If one looks only at third positions within coding regions, murids have a lower average and a narrower distribution of GC%. The distribution of GC% in fractionated DNA is narrower as well, but the mean is slightly higher than that of other mammals. These differences do not involve changes in the gross GC content of homologous isochores; loci in GC-rich isochores in humans are also found in GC-rich isochores in rodents. By contrast, since GC-rich isochores are not found in most cold-blooded vertebrates, the emergence of GC-rich isochores in mammals and birds is accompanied by dramatic increases in the GC content of third positions and, less so, in first and second positions.

Bernardi et al. recognize two modes of isochore evolution: the "conservative" mode whereby evolution proceeds without major shifts in GC content and the "compositional shift" mode such as occurred in the evolution of warm-blooded vertebrates. Wolfe et al. [311] have shown that silent substitution rates in the conservative mode (they used rats and mice) are highest in isochores with an intermediate GC content and drops off as the GC% approaches zero or one. Such a pattern would be expected under almost any mechanistic model since a highly skewed GC% reduces by one-half the number of nucleotides that can occupy a site when compared with a site with 50% GC.

There is little agreement as to the forces responsible for isochores.

Table 2.7. Properties of codon biases in three groups of organisms.

Bias	E. coli/yeast	Drosophila	mammals
Direction locus-specific	no	yes	yes
Matches tRNA abundances	yes	?	?
Matches local GC%	NA	no	yes
Inverse of substitution rate	yes	yes	no

Bernardi et al. [15] argue that the compositional shift to GC-rich isochores may well have been in response to the increase in body temperature in birds and mammals. If so, this parallels similar increases seen in bacteria that live in hot environments. In the conservative mode, they argue that stabilizing selection is acting on GC% much as it would on any other quantitative trait. They recognize that selection on individual nucleotides could be extraordinarily weak, yet the GC% of an isochore could be held within fairly narrow limits. Such a model allows for essentially neutral substitutions to occur even if the phenotype is under strong selection.

The opposite view is that the high GC content of GC-rich isochores is a neutral by-product of the differences in replication times of the two types of isochores. Wolfe et al. [311] argue that the early-replicating GC-rich isochores deplete the nucleotide pools of G and C and thus alter the mutational bias of late-replicating isochores to favor A and T. Filipski [73], on the other hand, has argued that different polymerases with different mutational biases may be used in early and late replication and this may lead to different GC contents in the two classes of isochores. Both of these hypotheses attach no special biological significance to the GC content of isochores. Rather, the GC% is a neutral phenotype.

It is worth pointing out that it is possible for a large region of DNA to be under fairly strong stabilizing selection for its GC%, yet the dynamics of individual nucleotides be nearly neutral. Thus, the question of whether or not the GC% viewed as a *phenotype* is neutral may be partially decoupled from the question of whether or not the silent substitutions are neutral.

A summary of some of the major features of codon usage is given in Table 2.7. But this table does not capture what I find the most intriguing aspects of the interaction of codon usage and GC%. Patterns such as the increase in GC% in exons seen in both mammals and *Drosophila* suggest that either mutational processes vary on a small scale, or that other forces are molding the genome for reasons that are, at this point, completely obscure.

2.4   DNA polymorphisms

Two techniques are commonly employed to measure variation in DNA. The older of the two uses restriction enzymes to cut DNA at specific four or six base sequences. Variation in the occurrence of these sequences among chromosomes is measured by variation in the length of cut fragments as determined by electrophoresis. Such studies are called restriction fragment length polymorphism (RFLP) studies or, if the DNA sequence of the region is available, restriction map variation studies. The second technique uses DNA sequencing. Historically, the amount of labor required for cloning and sequencing has prohibited its widespread use for population studies. Fortunately, a radical change is underway with the advent of the polymerase chain reaction (PCR) which removes the cloning step. Unfortunately, at the time of this writing, the anticipated explosion of sequence studies has yet to appear.

There is a marked disparity in the usefulness of restriction map and sequence data for understanding the mechanisms of molecular evolution and polymorphism. One of the threads winding through this book, for example, is the contrast in the dynamics of silent and replacement mutations. Since restriction map studies cannot distinguish these two types of mutations, they cannot contribute to our description of the contrast. Similarly, they offer nothing to nourish our interest in codon usage or GC%. For this reason, our emphasis will be on sequencing studies.

Statistics

There are some interesting—and largely unresolved—problems that appear when we try to provide summary statistics for DNA polymorphism data. If we have a set of sequences, each several kilobases in length, then it is entirely possible that no two sequences are exactly the same. If this occurs in a sample of n sequences, for example, the allelic heterozygosity is $1 - 1/n \approx 1$, a rather uninspiring statistic for such rich data. Clearly, we must abandon this venerable measure that carried us through many years of electrophoretic studies.

The obvious replacement for the allelic heterozygosity is the nucleotide site heterozygosity. Let the frequency of each of the four bases at the ith out of m sites in the population in the tth generation be $p_{ij}(t), j = A, C, G, T$. The heterozygosity at this site is

$$h_i(t) = 1 - p_{iA}(t)^2 - p_{iC}(t)^2 - p_{iG}(t)^2 - p_{iT}(t)^2$$

and the sum of the heterozygosities across all sites is

$$S_h(t) = \sum_{i=1}^{m} h_i(t).$$

Finally, the average heterozygosity per site, site heterozygosity for short, is

$$\hat{\pi} = S_h(t)/m.$$

Note that $ES_h(t)$ has the interpretation of being the average number of nucleotide differences between a randomly drawn pair of alleles. This has prompted the use of the average number of nucleotide differences between alleles in a sample, $\hat{k}$, as an estimator of $S_h(t)$.

On the surface, everything looks fairly standard: we imagine a population parameter called the mean site heterozygosity, $Eh_i(t)$, and expect that, as $m \to \infty$, $S_h(t)/m$ will converge to it. We might also expect that we would be able to calculate the sampling variance of $S_h(t)/m$ and use it to place confidence limits on our estimate of the site heterozygosity. Unfortunately, things are not quite this simple. Two factors cloud the picture.

- The site heterozygosities, $h_i(t)$, are stochastic processes that are not, in general, independent across sites even for the neutral allele model. For that model, the covariance of site heterozygosities is known only under the very restrictive condition that the population is in equilibrium.

- The expected values of the site heterozygosities, $Eh_i(t)$, will, in general, vary from site to site. For example, silent and replacement sites tend to have different heterozygosities. Even within each of these categories there will, in general, be regions with different mean site heterozygosities. For example, under the neutral model it is frequently claimed that the mutation rates vary in different regions of a locus.

Were it known that separate loci are independent replicates of each other with respect to S_h, we could circumvent these problems by averaging across loci. Unfortunately, there are ample theoretical and empirical reasons for not treating separate loci as independent replicates.

There is a second summary statistic in common usage:

$$\hat{\theta} = \frac{S_s}{m[1 + 1/2 + 1/3 + \ldots + 1/(n-1)]}$$

where S_s is the number of segregating sites in a sample of size n. The statistic is called $\hat{\theta}$ because $E\hat{\theta} = \theta$ under the equilibrium neutral model, where θ is four times the effective population size times the neutral mutation rate. The popularity of this statistic is unfortunate. We have no guarantee that $\hat{\theta}$ converges as $n \to \infty$ except under the neutral model. Should it converge, it is not at all clear what property of the population is captured by its limiting value (except, again, under the equilibrium neutral model).

It is easy to illustrate the problems with $\hat{\theta}$ with an extreme example. Consider a locus without recombination with $m-1$ neutral sites and one site that is held polymorphic by balancing selection that is so strong as to keep the frequency of the two selected nucleotides fixed at one-half. Assume, in addition, that there is no further mutation at the selected site. If the population has been evolving for a very long time, then a reasonably sized sample will contain at least one chromosome with one of the two selected nucleotides and one with the other. The expected number of segregating sites, assuming that each nucleotide mutates to the other with equal frequency, will be greater than $3m/4$ and $\hat{\theta}$ will be greater than about

$3/(4 \log(n - 1))$. This value has nothing to do with θ or anything else of much biological interest. While this example may seem extreme, it is not out of line with what might be expected were, say, 1 out of every 10 nucleotide polymorphisms selected. The important point is that the example bares the extreme model-dependence of $\hat{\theta}$ and should caution us against its use.

There is an interesting contrast in the asymptotic properties of $\hat{\pi}$ and $\hat{\theta}$ under the neutral model as the sample size increases. Note first that the expected values of both of these estimators is θ. Curiously, the average site heterozygosity, $\hat{\pi}$, approaches the *random* quantity $S_h(t)/m$ as $n \to \infty$ while $\hat{\theta}$ approaches the constant (nonrandom) θ. Were we absolutely certain that all of the variation at a site is neutral and that the population is in equilibrium (ruling out recent linked substitutions, balancing selection and bottlenecks), then $\hat{\theta}$ would be the preferred estimator of θ. However, equilibrium neutrality may seldom occur at any locus, making $\hat{\pi}$ more attractive as we know what biological quantity it is estimating irrespective of the underlying model.

I belabor this point to emphasize that we really have no satisfactory way to place any confidence in our estimates of nucleotide diversity. I could follow convention and use the neutral confidence limits around $\hat{\theta}$ and $\hat{\pi}$, but I feel strongly that this is wholly unjustified and terribly misleading for the reasons mentioned above. Beyond this, there is a problem with many of the published studies that use samples from widely spaced locations, quite possibly in violation of the panmixia assumptions used to place confidence limits on estimates within the framework of neutral models. To be consistent with my skepticism, I will refer to my summary of the nucleotide diversity as *quantitative natural history*, a phrase coined by Monty Slatkin when faced with an equally untenable statistical setting. I will, however, quote the statistical conclusions of others who have felt comfortable enough with the equilibrium neutral model to use it as a basis for hypothesis testing.

Drosophila

The alcohol dehydrogenase (ADH) locus in *Drosophila melanogaster* has probably been the subject of more variation studies than any other locus in any species. It is fitting that our discussion begins with ADH. From earlier protein studies we know that there are at least two ADH alleles with different electrophoretic mobilities: the F (fast) and S (slow) alleles. The gross pattern of sequence variation around the locus was first described in 1982 by Langley et al. [183] using six-cutter restriction enzymes. This study was expanded in 1986 by Aquadro et al. [6]. The latter paper will form the basis of our initial observations on the ADH locus.

The Aquadro et al. study examined a 13-kb region around the ADH locus in 48 second chromosome lines from four eastern U. S. populations and one Japanese population. Extensive variation was discovered in both restriction sites and sequence length. The locations of the variants are illustrated in Figure 2.12.

Sequence length variation was determined to be due to small deletions (21 to 200 base pairs in length) and two categories of insertions: transposable elements and small insertions (31 to 34 base pairs) of apparently unique DNA. Eighty percent of the lines had at least one insertion or deletion, the large insertions (all transposable elements) occurring at a density of 0.018 per kilobase. The figure clearly shows that the insertion sites of transposable elements are not uniform throughout the region but are concentrated in a region 3′ to the ADH locus.

The frequency of a particular transposable element at a particular site is so low that in a sample one seldom finds the same element in the same site in multiple chromosomes. Charlesworth and Langley [40] have reviewed the various explanations for this and other patterns. As this topic is tangential to the main theme of the book, I refer the readers to their review for more details on the fascinating topic.

Restriction site variation allows a crude estimate to made of the nucleotide diversity. For the ADH study, the average site heterozygosity was estimated to be $\hat{\pi} = 0.006$; $\hat{\theta} = 0.006$ as well. This implies that about 1 nucleotide out of every 166 will differ between randomly drawn chromosomes. Since this estimate comes from restriction site data, we have no way of knowing the biological role of the nucleotides that vary.

The frequency distribution for the ADH region is illustrated in Figure 2.13. A frequency distribution is obtained by first rank-ordering each variant by frequency, from highest to lowest, on the horizontal axis and then raising a bar to its frequency on the vertical axis. The distribution suggests that there is a tendency for restriction site variation to dominate the left or most abundant part of the spectrum and for transposable elements to dominate the right part. This pattern tends to repeat itself for other loci in *Drosophila* [180].

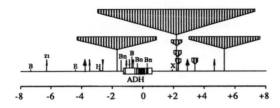

Figure 2.12. Variation in a 13-kb region around the ADH locus in $D.\ melanogaster$ as uncovered by restriction enzyme analysis. Downward-pointing polygons indicate insertions; those shaped grey are transposable elements, those that are black are unique copy DNA. Upward-pointing polygons are deletions. The letters above the lines are variable restriction sites. The blocks indicate the location of the ADH gene. Redrawn from [6].

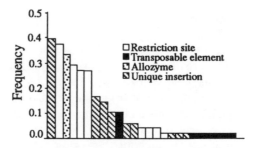

Figure 2.13. Frequency spectrum for variation in a 13-kb region around the ADH locus in *D. melanogaster* as uncovered by restriction map analysis. Redrawn from [6].

The 26 different variants were distributed over only 29 different haplotypes among the 48 sampled chromosomes, suggesting that significant nonrandom associations between variants must occur. A complete pairwise disequilibrium analysis showed that within the F-bearing chromosomes there were much higher levels of disequilibrium than within the S-bearing chromosomes. A haplotype genealogy suggested that the F- and S-bearing chromosomes fall on opposite sides of a deep split within the genealogy. The F-bearing chromosomes were also shown to have a lower haplotype diversity* (0.419) than S-bearing chromosomes (0.819) for restriction sites although not when all variation was considered. These and other observations have led to the suggestion that the F mutation entered *Drosophila* populations relatively recently [174].

Four- and six-cutter analyses from other *D. melanogaster* loci exhibit patterns of variation that are remarkably similar to that of ADH as is evident in Table 2.8 which is reproduced from Langley's recent review [180] of molecular variation in *Drosophila*. The one anomaly is the apparent reduction in variability in regions of low recombination. Should this observation hold up as more loci are examined under higher resolution, it may provide evidence that variation is reduced by "hitchhiiking" on linked positively selected mutations on their way to fixation [180].

There has been much less work on other species of *Drosophila*. In a recent survey Aquadro [5] used all of the available resticiton enzyme data from loci that have been examined in two or more of the four species: *D. melanogaster, D. simulans, D. ananassae,* and *D. pseudoobscura*. His Table 3 is reproduced in Table 2.9. The most striking pattern in the table is the fact that *D. melanogaster* is distinctly less polymorphic than the other three species. Its site heterozygosity is only about 20% that of *D. pseudoobscura* and 28% that of its sibling species, *D. simulans*. Aquadro has called attention to the latter comparison because it stands in sharp contrast to an older observation that allozyme heterozygosity is significantly lower

---

*Haplotype diversity is defined as $n(1 - \sum x_i^2)/(n - 1)$ where x_i is the frequency of the ith haplotype.

Table 2.8. Molecular variation found in natural populations of *Drosophila melanogaster* as summarized by Langley [180, Table 5-1].

Locus	kb	n	Restriction sites $\hat{\theta}$	Restriction sites $\hat{\pi}$	Large insertions density	Large insertions freq.
X chromosome						
forked	25	64	0.004	0.002	0.002	0.02
vermilion	24	64	0.006	0.003	0.002	0.02
white	45	64	0.007	0.009	0.011	0.03
zeste-tko	20	64	0.004	0.004	0.006	0.02
Autosomes						
Amy	15	85	0.006	0.008	0.001	0.01
Adh	13	48	0.006	0.006	0.018	0.02
Ddc	65	46	0.004	0.005	0.003	0.02
rosy	40	60	0.003	0.003	0.002	0.02
Low recombination						
su(f)	24	64	0.000	0.000	0.004	0.02
Zw	13	64	0.002	0.001	0.007	0.19
y-ac-sc	104	64	0.001	0.0003	0.003	0.01

in *D. simulans* than in *D. melanogaster*. The possible explanations for this disparity will be taken up in the Chapter 6. Here we will point out that this is one of several instances where there is a contrast between the dynamics of silent (assuming that most of the restriction site variants lie in noncoding regions) and replacement mutations.

The first published study of DNA variation based on sequencing is Kreitman's survey of the ADH locus in *Drosophila melanogaster* [174]. In that study, he sequenced 2721 base pairs in the ADH region of 11 chromosomes sampled from 5 geographic regions. The ADH locus is composed of four exons, the first two of which participate in an alternative splicing scheme that uses exon 1 as the leader sequence in the adult and the first portion of exon 2 as the leader sequence in the larva. The translated portions of the gene are found in exons 2 through 4. The fourth exon also contains a sizeable 3′ untranslated region. The average site heterozygosities for the translated portions of exons 2 through 4 are illustrated in Figure 2.14. The average site heterozygosity for the all of the exons, both the translated and untranslated regions, is 0.006 in agreement with the earlier six-cutter study [183].

Figure 2.14 also presents the separate site heterozygosities for the F- and S-bearing chromosomes. The reduction in variation within the F chromosomes is seen here, just as it was in the restriction-site data. Of perhaps more interest is the elevated F+S site heterozygosity in the 4th exon, indicating that there is extensive disequilibrium within the exon with certain mutations being restricted to F-chromosomes and others to S-chromosomes.

Table 2.9. Site heterozygosities ($\hat{\pi}$) for four species of *Drosophila* as determined by restriction enzyme analyses. The *vermilion* locus in *D. ananassae* was not used in the averages because it is in a region of reduced recombination. The table is from Aquadro [5]

	D. melan.	*D. sim.*	*D. anan.*	*D. pseudo.*
X chromosome				
per	0.001	0.007		
forked	0.004		0.010	
Om(1D)			0.009	
vermilion	0.006		0.003	
Autosome				
Adh	0.006	0.015		0.026
Amy	0.008			0.019
rosy	0.005	0.018		0.013
Average	0.004	0.014	0.010	0.022

From this it seems likely that the F/S variation is probably not maintained by the same mechanism that is maintaining the remainder of the variation. Were it otherwise, the pattern of variation in the F- and S-bearing chromosomes would be similar. More evidence comes from Kreitman's observation that there is more silent variation (6.7% of silent sites are polymorphic) than amino acid variation (0.17% of replacement sites are polymorphic). These figures would be more similar if both sorts of mutations were following similar dynamics. We will include both of these contrasts among those suggesting that the dynamics of replacement and silent mutations are different.

Very recently, McDonald and Kreitman (unpublished) have extended the sequencing of ADH to the *D. melanogaster* sibling species *D. simulans* and *D. yakuba*. They discovered that, among replacement sites, 7 are fixed between species but only 2 are polymorphic within the three species. By contrast, 17 silent sites have fixed differences between the species and 42 are polymorphic within the species. Said another way, there are 3.5 times more fixed than polymorphic replacement sites compared with 0.4 times more fixed than polymorphic silent sites. Within these species, is appears that protein evolution is proceeding in a mode that emphasizes substitutions over polymorphisms, while silent DNA evolution is the reverse.

In Chapter 1 we reviewed work of Skibinski and Ward showing that the protein heterozygosity at a locus is correlated with its genetic distance between species. It would be of considerable interest to know if the same relationship holds for silent variation. Aquadro [5] examined a 100-kb region around the *rosy* locus in *D. melanogaster* and *D. simulans* by restriction map analysis and plotted the ratio of the heterozygosity within a species over the divergence between the two species in a 5-kb sliding window. Al-

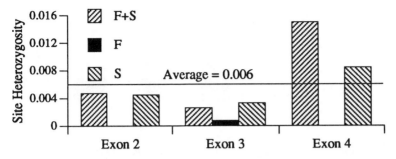

Figure 2.14. Average site heterozygosities for the translated portions of three exons of the ADH locus in *D. melanogaster*. The site heterozygosities for the S- and F-bearing chromosomes are also displayed. Data are from [174].

though no statistical tests were performed, the wild fluctuations in the ratio suggest that there is no simple relationship between polymorphism and substitutions between species.

Hudson et al. [135] used the equilibrium neutral allele theory as a null hypothesis to test for compatability in the level of polymorphism and diverence between two regions of the *Adh* locus in *D. melanogaster* and *D. sechellia*. They were able to reject the null hypothesis due to the extraordinary divergence between the two species in the relatively monomorphic 5′ flanking region compared with the low level of divergence and extensive polymorphism in the *Adh* locus itself. These two studies are the first hints that patterns of polymorphism and divergence may be very complex, perhaps reflecting historical factors more than anything else.

Humans

The only other organism for which sequence data on DNA polymorphisms are available is humans. Although there do not appear to be any studies designed specifically to measure variation, there are instances of multiple sequences in the GenBank database that were collected for other purposes. There is a danger in using such sequences for estimates of DNA variation because there are no guarantees that the sequencing was performed with the level of precision required of polymorphism studies. Li and Sadler [193] has recently used this data to estimate $\hat{\pi}$, but only after a check to assure that each variable nucleotide had been carefully verified by the laboratory reporting it. He was able to find 49 loci with more than one published allele that passed his criteria of rigor. His results are illustrated in Figure 2.15.

It is clear that the average site heterozygosities are low, roughly one-twentieth those in *Drosophila*. As pointed out by Li and Sadler, such a large difference is in striking contrast to the figures for protein heterozygosities, which differ by no more than a factor of two. This contrast is reminiscent of the *D. simulans–D. melanogaster* comparison made by Aquadro and presents yet another instance where silent and replacement mutations

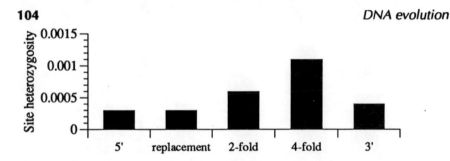

Figure 2.15. Average site heterozygosities for 49 human loci reported separately for the 5′ and 3′ untranslated regions of the coding sequence, the replacement sites, and 2- and 4-fold degenerate silent sites. Data are from Li [193].

behave differently. The higher heterozygosities for silent vs. replacement sites observed in *Drosophila* are also apparent in the human data. Li has placed the silent variation into two categories: twofold and fourfold redundant sites with the latter exhibiting greater diversity. This mirrors the higher rate of substitution seen in fourfold degenerate sites.

This ends our short description of DNA polymorphism. Hopefully, the story will become much clearer in the next few years as sequencing studies appear in the literature.

3

The molecular clock

The molecular clock is an abstraction of the common observation that the number of amino acid or nucleotide substitutions separating a pair of species is roughly proportional to the time back to their common ancestor. For example, Figure 3.1 shows the number of amino acid substitutions in α globin that have occurred on the lineages separating humans from a variety of other species. The figure illustrates two important aspects of the clock. The first is the linear increase in the number of substitutions with time; the second is the variation around the line: the clock is erratic.

The "ticks" of the molecular clock correspond to substitutions of mutations. They do not occur at regular intervals as do the ticks of more conventional clocks, but rather at random points in time. As a consequence, characterizations of the clock must use *point processes*, statistical models that describe events occurring at random times. One goal of this chapter is to obtain point processes that are compatible with data like that illustrated in Figure 3.1.

The molecular clock has generated controversy since it was first described in 1962 by Zuckerkandl and Pauling [317]. The original clock was embodied in the simplest of point processes, the *Poisson process*. Let $\mathcal{N}(t)$ be the total number of amino acid substitutions at a particular locus over a period of t years. The original clock assumes that $\mathcal{N}(t)$ is Poisson distributed with mean λt. That is,

$$\text{Prob.}\{\mathcal{N}(t) = i\} = \frac{e^{-\lambda t}(\lambda t)^i}{i!}.$$

The parameter λ is the mean rate of substitution for the locus under study in units of substitutions per locus per year.

The average rate of substitution under the Zuckerkandl and Pauling clock is constant per unit time—no matter what. The constancy has been the center of the controversy. Were it generally true, then the molecular clock would provide a time scale for evolution. It would also provide direction in our choice of mechanistic models of nucleotide substitutions. Thus, there are both practical and scientific reasons to look closely at the stochastic behavior of the clock.

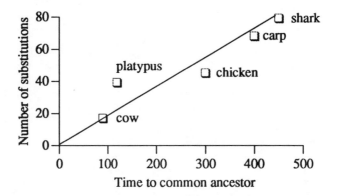

Figure 3.1. The molecular clock for α globin. Each point represents the number of amino acid substitutions separating the indicated animal from humans. Time is measured in units of millions of years. Data are from [54, Table 3.3].

The molecular clock violates the assumptions of a Poisson process in two fundamental ways. The first, called *lineage effects*, involves variation in average rates across lineages. The generation-time effect is an example. The second involves the possibility that average rates are constant, say within a restricted set of lineages, but that the substitutions do not follow a Poisson process. A simple measure of departure from a Poisson process is the *index of dispersion*,

$$I(t) = \frac{\text{Var}\mathcal{N}(t)}{E\mathcal{N}(t)},$$

where E means "expectation of" and Var, "variance of." As the mean and variance of a Poisson process are equal, the index of dispersion for the Zuckerkandl and Pauling clock is exactly one. For more general point processes, the index of dispersion can range from zero to infinity.

There is ample evidence for both lineage effects and indices of dispersion that are not equal to one as will be described in the following sections. The development begins with some of my favorite examples of rate variation. These will motivate and make real some of the more abstract statistical work that follows.

3.1   Examples of rate variation

We have already encountered several examples of variation in the rate of substitution. The most dramatic was the speedup in the rate of replacement substitution in the insulin gene of hystricomorph rodents. As we saw, the rates varied by as much as 30-fold. The acceleration was apparently due to adaptive changes as part of a general evolution of the gastroenteropancreatic hormonal system. Less dramatic was the 2.5-fold acceleration in the

Table 3.1. The ratio of the number of replacement to silent substitutions in α hemoglobins from various pairs of species. Data are from [257, Table 2]

Comparison	$\dfrac{\text{Replacement}}{\text{silent}}$
Human–orangutan	0.43
Human–rhesus	1.00
Human–mouse	0.47
Human–baboon	2.54
Rhesus–baboon	25.0

rate of replacement substitution in the lysozyme of langurs that was associated with the recruitment of lysozyme to digest bacteria in the stomach.

Both of these examples show clearly that the accelerations were due to adaptive changes. The temptation is to generalize and to suggest that whenever we observe an acceleration we attribute it to a greater environmental challenge. However, in general we cannot make this leap as the causes of most of the accelerations described in this section are unknown.

Baboon hemoglobin

The baboons separated from the rhesus macaques 5 to 7 million years ago. During the subsequent evolution of α globin in the baboons there was a burst of amino acid substitutions approximately 10 times greater than that in the rhesus lineage [257]. Significantly, there was no accompanying acceleration in the rate of silent substitution. The data supporting this conclusion are presented, in part, in Table 3.1. The table gives only the ratio of replacement to silent substitutions as this is the best index of the strange events in the baboon lineage.

The substitutions do not appear to be random in any sense. For example, there are 13 nucleotide differences in the coding regions between the baboon and the rhesus monkey. In 10 of these, a C or G in the rhesus corresponds to an A in the baboon. These 10 are concentrated in only 6 codons. In one instance, GGC (gly) in the rhesus monkey corresponds to AAA (lys) in the baboon. The occurrence of three substitutions in one codon is highly nonrandom and could be due to the fixation of a single complex mutational event or to a burst of two or three sequential substitutions. In the latter case, each of the substitutions will be a replacement substitution.

The amino acid substitutions in the baboon lineage are not chemically conservative. The substitution of lysine for glycine just mentioned would have to be called chemically radical. In two cases, alanine is replaced by aspartic acid; in another case, glycine is replaced by glutamic acid. Although we do not know the forces responsible for this evolution, the nonconservative nature of the amino acid substitutions suggests that baboon and rhesus

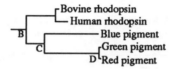

Figure 3.2. The phylogeny of the visual pigments. Redrawn from [314, Fig. 19.1].

globins are functionally different.

Visual pigment genes

There are four major visual pigments in humans: rhodopsin along with the red-, green-, and blue-sensitive pigments. They are members of a family of receptors that includes the G-protein-coupled receptors. Yokoyama and Yokoyama [314] have reconstructed the phylogeny of these receptors, the visual pigment portion being reproduced in Figure 3.2. The substitutions generally follow the familiar pattern of replacement rates being lower than silent rates.

In the evolution preceding the emergence of the three color pigments, some interesting anomalies occur. In two branches the rate of replacement substitution exceeds the silent rate. One is on the branch labeled B-C in Figure 3.2, the other is on the short branch from D to the red-sensitive pigment. The former difference is statistically significant, the latter is not. Assuming that the silent rate has been relatively constant throughout the evolution of pigment genes, the Yokoyamas interpret this as an acceleration in the replacement rate leading to a shift in the absorption spectrum.

The pattern of substitutions in the color pigments themselves also suggests evolution for absorption characteristics, although these are not accompanied by a measurable acceleration in the rate of substitution.

Human cytochromes

There is an remarkable story of a coordinated acceleration in two of the electron transport enzymes, cytochrome c and cytochrome oxidase II. The former is a nuclear-encoded locus; the latter is coded in the mitochondria. It has been known for a number of years that cytochrome c, usually a slowly evolving enzyme, experienced a burst of amino acid substitutions in the primate lineage. More recently, it was discovered that the replacement rate of cytochrome oxidase II accelerated in the primate lineage as well [34]. A summary of these events is given in Figure 3.3.

The burst of evolution in the primate cytochrome c has left a trail in the human genome. Cytochrome c seems to enjoy spawning processed pseudogenes. In some mammals, as many as 35 copies have been identified [65]. In humans, the processed pseudogenes fall into two groups. One group (HS) was spawned before the burst of substitutions, the other (HC) af-

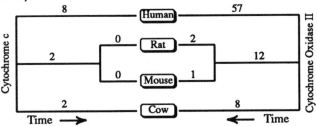

Figure 3.3. The numbers of amino acid substitutions on the lineages leading to four species of mammals in cytochrome c and cytochrome oxidase II. Redrawn from [34, Fig. 19.1].

ter. The amino acid sequence that would be produced by the first group, were they functional, is nearly identical to the nonprimate cytochrome c. That produced by the latter group is nearly identical to the sequence of the functional human enzyme.

Using these pseudogenes, Evans and Scarpulla have arrived at the following reconstruction. Assuming that the nucleotide substitution rate in the pseudogenes is 1.3×10^{-9} per site per year, they calculated that the HC pseudogenes appeared about 15 million years ago and the youngest of the HS pseudogenes appeared about 30 million years ago. This implies that the nine amino acid replacements occurred in the relatively short span of 15 million years. By contrast, the rodent lineage accumulated two amino acid substitutions in 85 million years. Thus, the burst of substitutions within the primates yields a rate that is about 25 times higher than that in the rodent lineage.

In fact, the rate differential may have been even higher. As the rhesus and human functional cytochrome c's are nearly identical, and the common ancestor of these two primates occurred about 30 million years ago (recall that this is the age of the youngest HS pseudogene), all of the substitutions may have been concentrated in an interval that is instantaneous on a time scale of millions of years.

The coevolution of cytochrome c and cytochrome oxidase in primates has produced enzymes that function more efficiently with each other than with those from other nonprimate mammals [231] suggesting that this episodic evolution was adaptive.

3.2 Statistical analyses

Ohta and Kimura [229], in 1971, were the first to examine the constancy of evolutionary rates in a proper statistical setting. Their null hypothesis was the Zuckerkandl and Pauling clock: the rate of substitution, λ, is constant across lineages and the number of substitutions on a given lineage of length t years is Poisson distributed with mean λt.

They examined three loci for which a sufficient number of protein se-

Table 3.2. Ohta and Kimura's [229] analysis of rate variation in three proteins.

Comparison	$\bar{k} \times 10^9$	$s \times 10^9$	$\sigma \times 10^9$	s/σ
β globin	1.526	0.610	0.298	2.05
α globin	0.973	0.409	0.299	1.37
Cytochrome c	0.281	0.208	0.114	1.82

quences were available, α globin, β globin, and cytochrome c. For each pair of species within a locus they estimated k_{aa}, the mean number of amino acid substitutions per site per year. For example, in α globin $\hat{k}_{aa} = 0.699 \times 10^{-9}$ when human and dog are compared (the hat indicates that this is an estimator of k_{aa}), 0.290×10^{-9} when kangaroo and horse are compared, and so forth.

The variance of the estimators under the Poisson assumption had been derived several times by 1971, so it was a simple matter to compare the standard deviations of the estimates, s, to the expected standard deviations, σ. The results are given in Table 3.2 where $\bar{k}$ is the average rate of substitution, s is the observed standard deviation in the estimates of k_{aa}, and σ is the expected standard deviation under the Poisson clock. An F-test (based on $F = s^2/\sigma^2$) indicates that the variance in rates for β globin and cytochrome c are significantly greater than expected under the Poisson clock.

Ohta and Kimura concluded "that the variations in evolutionary rates among highly evolved animals are larger than expected by chance." Although their analysis has some rough edges, their conclusion remains valid. Most subsequent studies have also identified β globin and cytochrome c as proteins that deviate from the Poisson clock and α globin as one that exhibits a remarkably constant rate.

Two years later, Langley and Fitch [181,182] completed a much larger study that addressed some of the weaknesses of the Ohta and Kimura paper. Rather than using rate estimates for species considered two at a time, they reconstructed the entire substitutional history of each locus using parsimony techniques. In so doing, they avoided the correlations between pair-wise rate estimates induced by shared phylogenies that weakened the Ohta and Kimura study.

The inputs to the Langley and Fitch analysis were sequences of four proteins (α and β globins, cytochrome c, and fibrinopeptide A) from a variety of species and the phylogenetic tree for these same species as inferred from the fossil record. The null hypothesis was the Poisson clock with constant rates for each protein. In the first step of the analysis, substitutions were assigned to each branch of the tree using the maximum parsimony technique developed earlier by Fitch [77]. In the second step, maximum likelihood was used to estimate the average rate of substitution for each of

Table 3.3. Langley and Fitch's [229] analysis of rate variation in four proteins.

Comparison	Uncorrected			Corrected		
	χ^2	df	Prob.	χ^2	df	Prob.
Lineage effects	63.0	26	$< 10^{-4}$	48.7	24	< 0.002
Residual effects	102.7	62	$< 10^{-3}$	102.7	62	$< 10^{-3}$
Total	165.7	88	$< 10^{-5}$	151.4	86	$< 10^{-4}$

the four proteins and the length of each branch on the tree. Finally, the null hypothesis was examined by a likelihood ratio test.

The model that forms the basis of the likelihood analysis assumes that the number of substitutions (as determined by parsimony) at the mth locus on the ith branch is Poisson distributed with mean $\lambda_m T_i$. These parameters were defined such that λ_m is the relative rather than the absolute rate of substitution at the mth locus, $\sum \lambda_m = 1$. The length of the ith branch, T_i, is measured in units of substitutions rather than in units of real time. Together, these assumptions imply that the likelihood (or probability) of observing $x_{m,i}$ substitutions is

$$L(m, i) = \frac{e^{-\lambda_m T_i} (\lambda_m T_i)^{x_{m,i}}}{x_{m,i}!}.$$

From here to the final likelihood ratio test is a well-trodden path. Langley and Fitch did add a few twists to end up with the tests that are summarized in Table 3.3. Note first that the probability of observing the data if the Poisson clock applies is less than 10^{-5}, a severe blow to the Poisson clock. It was not unexpected given that two of the four proteins had already been shown by Ohta and Kimura to be incompatible with the Poisson clock.

The other tests in Table 3.3 come from a partitioning of the likelihood ratio into lineage effects and residual effects. The test for lineage effects assumes that the relative rates of substitution are constant and looks for variation in the total number of substitutions on different branches beyond that predicted by the Poisson clock. The generation-time effect, for example, could lead to significant lineage effects. From Table 3.3 we see that these effects are significant.

Residual effects occur when the relative rates of substitution vary across branches. For example, β globin might evolve more rapidly relative to cytochrome c on certain branches than would be expected given their average rates over all branches. This effect is also significant. As there is only one observation per protein per branch, the residual effects are analogous to locus-by-lineage interactions or to the error variance.

A third test for locus effects could have been performed, but the differences in average substitution rates between loci are so large that statistical evidence is superfluous.

The partitioning into two effects represents a major advance over the Ohta and Kimura study since it uncovers a new source of variability in rates. The variation seen by Ohta and Kimura could be dismissed as being due entirely to generation-time effects and/or inaccurate dating of lineages. Both of these contributions are incorporated into lineage effects in the Langley and Fitch study. The residual effects, on the other hand, are a new phenomenon that demands a mechanistic explanation.

There are some problems with the Langley and Fitch study. Perhaps the most enigmatic is the error introduced by the parsimonious assignment of substitutions to branches. Parsimony assigns the fewest possible substitutions, and thus is at variance with the Poisson clock. Langley and Fitch made some attempt to correct this by augmenting the number of substitutions on long branches by an empirically derived procedure. The results are given on the right half of Table 3.3. The levels of significance are lowered somewhat, as would be expected.

The second problem concerns the tree. From a statistical point of view, the tree was not part of the analysis. No effort was made to find another tree that might make the data compatible with the Poisson clock. The branching pattern is generally accepted today except for the placement of the lagomorph branch. Langley and Fitch made rodents and lagomorphs sister groups whereas today the lagomorphs are more commonly placed as a sister group to the primates. It is impossible to say how the results would change with another tree without repeating the entire analysis.

Wilson et al. [308] summarized a number of other studies of rate variation from the early and mid-seventies. Their general conclusion about the stochastic nature of the molecular clock is nicely summarized in the following quote.

> Whereas the expected standard deviation for radioactive decay equals $(counts)^{1/2}$, the standard deviation for the evolutionary clock appears to be approximately $(2 \times number of substitutions)^{1/2}$. [308, p. 608]

Said another way, the variance in the number of substitutions is about two times the Poisson expectation. This quote represents a subtle but important shift in the description of the molecular clock. My reading of the literature prior to the Wilson et al. paper suggested that the most common alternative to the Poisson clock is a model with a fixed parameter for each rate on each branch but with the number of substitutions on a particular branch still Poisson distributed. This view is similar to a fixed-effect model in the analysis of variance. Lineage effects fall naturally into this framework but residual effects do not.

By contrast, Wilson et al. seem to be gravitating toward a stochastic clock that is more complex than the Poisson clock yet preserves the overall constancy of rates. This is well suited to residual effects, but not for lineage effects. This distinction will become clear in the next two sections when we look at the properties of more general point processes.

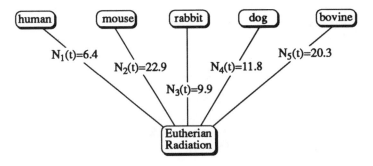

Figure 3.4. The star phylogeny for β globin. The numbers of substitutions on each lineage are from Kimura's least squares method [160].

Kimura returned to the problem in his 1983 book on the neutral theory [159]. Here he made an important shift from hypothesis testing, the focus of his earlier paper with Ohta, to estimation. His method exploits *star phylogenies*, radiations that occur in a relatively short span of time relative to the time back to the time of the radiation. Kimura used the late Mesozoic radiation leading to the modern orders of mammals most often. Figure 3.4 illustrates this phylogeny for β globin. The numbers of substitutions on the n lineages are viewed as a set of independent, identically distributed random variables, $\{\mathcal{N}_i(t)\}$. The mean, variance and index of dispersion,

$$I(t) = \frac{\operatorname{Var}\mathcal{N}_i(t)}{E\mathcal{N}_i(t)},$$

of these random variables are the quantities to be estimated.

Kimura's procedure begins with a matrix of amino acid differences between pairs of species from a star phylogeny. The first step corrects for multiple substitutions. The fraction of amino acids that differs between typical proteins from different orders of mammals is so small that this step has only a minor effect on the final answer.

The next step entails a simple calculation of the mean and variance of all of the corrected pair-wise distances. Kimura calls these estimators $\overline{D}$ and V_D. The estimate for the mean of $\mathcal{N}_i(t)$ is just

$$M = \overline{D}/2;$$

the estimator for the variance is

$$S^2 = \frac{(n+1)V_D}{2(n-1)}.$$

Both of these estimators are unbiased as is easily seen once the hidden assumption that the corrected number of substitutions separating species i and j is equal to $\mathcal{N}_i(t) + \mathcal{N}_j(t)$ is recognized.

Table 3.4. Estimates of $R(t)$ from Kimura's book [159]. The starred estimates are incompatible with a Poisson clock.

Locus	Radiation	M	S^2	R
α globin	Eutherian	12.67	15.97	1.3
β globin	Eutherian	14.95	46.33	3.1*
Myoglobin	Eutherian	12.35	20.97	1.7
Cytochrome c	Reptilian	8.26	27.25	3.3*
Ribonuclease	Eutherian	20.57	48.45	2.4

Finally, the estimator for $I(t)$ is

$$R = \frac{S^2}{M}. \tag{3.1}$$

Unlike the others, this is not an unbiased estimator as it is a ratio of random quantitities. It tends to underestimate the true value of $I(t)$ by about 10% [94].

There is an additional complication in using R—or as we will often call it, $R(t)$—as an estimator for the index of dispersion of $\mathcal{N}_i(t)$. Because of polymorphism, the relationship between $R(t)$ and $I(t)$ is model dependent. If t is very large, the error is insignificant so we will ignore this for now. We will return to it in Chapter 6.

Kimura used these estimators to examine five proteins. The results are listed in Table 3.4. The indices of dispersion for two of the five proteins are incompatible with a Poisson distribution of substitutions. The average value for R is 2.36. Kimura concluded that:

> These results suggest that although the strict constancy may not hold,
> yet a rough constancy of the evolutionary rate for each molecule among
> the various lineages is a rule rather than an exception. [159, p. 79]

Kimura makes the important point that hypothesis testing may not be the whole story. Even though protein evolution is statistically incompatible with the Poisson clock, the magnitude of the deviation may be small and unimportant. Recall that Kimura was using the Poisson clock as an argument in favor of the neutral allele theory for which $R(t) \approx 1$. He is, in effect, claiming that the observed values of $R(t)$ are so close to one—they are not equal to 1000, for example—that we may assume that $2.36 \approx 1$. This view will be challenged in the next two sections.

The estimation of $R(t)$ via star phylogenies compounds a number of problems that we have seen before. Foremost among these is the possibility that the fossil record was read improperly and that the true phylogeny is not at all star-like. While this cannot be ruled out, it should be noted that the heterogeneity of estimates of $R(t)$ suggests that no one phylogeny can make all five estimates of $R(t)$ compatible with the Poisson clock. By using

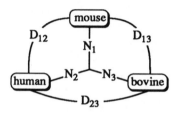

Figure 3.5. The three-species unrooted tree used in estimating the index of dispersion complete with the appropriate notation.

the correct phylogeny we can hope to learn which loci have erratic clocks, but we should not be able to change our view that the clock is erratic for some loci.

The other problem with star phylogenies, or more correctly with Kimura's analysis of them, is that lineage and residual effects are compounded. In this sense, Kimura's analysis is a step backward from that of Langley and Fitch. The biological interpretation of the high values of $R(t)$ depends critically on the relative contributions of residual and lineage effects. Without some effort to partition R, we are limited in what we can conclude from the analysis.

Despite these problems, a number of studies have used star phylogenies to estimate $R(t)$ (see [92] for a summary). Rather than reviewing these here, we will end this section with an approach based on only three species that seems to provide a more satisfying method for estimating the index of dispersion.

There is only one unrooted tree when three species are used. This frees us, at last, from the tyranny of the fossil record. Moreover, with three species, the number of substitutions on each branch can, in principle, be known exactly from the number of substitutions separating each pair of species. Let D_{ij} be the number of substitutions separating species i and j and let $\mathcal{N}_i$ be the number of substitutions on the ith branch as illustrated in Figure 3.5. As

$$D_{ij} = \mathcal{N}_i + \mathcal{N}_j$$

it is easy to see that the numbers of substitutions on each branch, as a function of the observables D_{ij}, are

$$\mathcal{N}_1 = (D_{12} + D_{13} - D_{23})/2 \tag{3.2}$$
$$\mathcal{N}_2 = (D_{12} + D_{23} - D_{13})/2 \tag{3.3}$$
$$\mathcal{N}_3 = (D_{13} + D_{23} - D_{12})/2. \tag{3.4}$$

In what follows, the $\mathcal{N}_i$ will be viewed as primary observations that may be used to estimate parameters. We are turning a blind eye to the fact that the real observables are the D_{ij} and that the $\mathcal{N}_i$ are obtained only after correcting the D_{ij} for multiple substitutions. The errors introduced by these corrections will be discussed later.

The main goal of the procedure that we are about to describe is to remove lineage effects and to focus on residual effects. Lineage effects will be viewed as fixed constants reflecting the length of the lineage and/or the species-specific average rate of evolution. They will be estimated by combining data from a large number of loci. The variation in rates that is left over after removing lineage effects will be attributed to residual effects.

Let the number of substitutions at the mth locus on the ith lineage be $\mathcal{N}_{m,i}$. Assuming that the $\mathcal{N}_{m,i}$ are independent random variables—the sample—we will write their moments in a form that allows the removal of lineage effects. For the mean, write

$$E\mathcal{N}_{m,i} = w_i \mu_m.$$

With this notation, we are capturing the lineage effects in the weighting factor w_i. The average value of the weighting factors will be constrained to equal one,

$$\frac{1}{3}\sum_{i=1}^{3} w_i = 1.$$

As will been seen shortly, this guarantees that the adjustments for lineage effects do not alter the estimates of the average rate of substitution for a locus, μ_m. Note also that if there are no lineage effects, then $w_i = 1$.

The variance of $\mathcal{N}_{m,i}$ will be written

$$\mathrm{Var}\mathcal{N}_{m,i} = w_i \sigma_m^2.$$

With this notation, the mean and variance of $\mathcal{N}_{m,i}$ will depend on the lineage effects but their ratio,

$$R_m = \frac{\mathrm{Var}\mathcal{N}_{m,i}}{E\mathcal{N}_{m,i}} = \frac{\sigma_m^2}{\mu_m},$$

will not. The index of dispersion is no longer written as a function of time because we cannot know whether lineage effects reflect variation in the average rate of substitution for a species or the length of the branches.

With these moment definitions, the natural estimator for the locus-specific mean number of substitutions is

$$\hat{\mu}_m = \frac{1}{3}\sum_{i=1}^{3} \frac{\mathcal{N}_{m,i}}{w_i}.$$

This is unbiased as

$$E\hat{\mu}_m = \frac{1}{3}\sum_{i=1}^{3} \frac{E\mathcal{N}_{m,i}}{w_i} = \mu_m.$$

An unbiased estimator for the variance is

$$\hat{\sigma}_m^2 = \frac{9}{2}(\sum_{i=1}^{3} 1/w_i)^{-1}\left[\frac{1}{3}\sum_{i=1}^{3}(\mathcal{N}_{m,i}/w_i)^2 - \hat{\mu}_m^2\right].$$

A biased estimator for $I(t)$ is

$$\hat{R}_m = \frac{\hat{\sigma}_m^2}{\hat{\mu}_m}.$$

The bias is not serious for typical proteins from different orders of mammals. One could correct the bias analytically, but the effort is hardly worth while because the sampling error far exceeds the bias.

To apply these estimators we require three species for which sequences are available from a fairly large number of loci. Human, mouse, and cow are obvious choices. The number of loci is increased somewhat if we use instead human, rodent (mouse or rat), and artiodactyl. In doing this, we are assuming that the lineage effects are homogeneous within the latter two orders. Our job is made considerably easier because the D_{ij}, corrected for multiple substitutions by the method of Li, Wu, and Luo [196], for 21 loci from these three orders have been published by Li et al. [194, Table 1]. It is a simple matter to adapt this table to our purposes.

There are two distinct stages in the analysis: the determination of the weights and the estimation of R for individual loci. The first may be done in a variety of ways. We will use three:

- *Equal weights*: For this trivial case we set each of the weights equal to one,

$$w_p = 1.0, \ w_r = 1.0, \ w_a = 1.0.$$

  The subscripts p, r, and a refer to primate, rodent, and artiodactyl. This case corresponds to the assumption of a star phylogeny without lineage effects as used in previous studies.

- *Silent weights*: In the Li et al. study, the average numbers of silent substitutions per 100 silent sites are 19.75 for primates, 50.77 for rodents, and 24.05 for artiodactyls, yielding the weights

$$w_p = 3 \times \frac{19.75}{19.75 + 50.77 + 24.05} = 0.627, \ w_r = 1.611, \ w_a = 0.762.$$

- *Replacement weights*: The numbers of replacement substitutions per 100 replacement sites are 5.50 for primates, 8.42 for rodents, and 5.83 for artiodactyls, yielding the weights

$$w_p = 0.830, \ w_r = 1.279, \ w_a = 0.885.$$

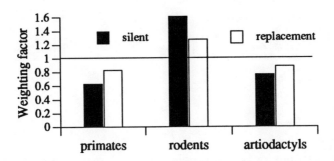

Figure 3.6. The weighting factors for three orders of mammals for silent and replacement substitutions.

These weights are viewed as constants rather than as estimates of parameters. In particular, variation in these numbers will play no role in hypothesis testing.

Figure 3.6 shows that the spread in the w_i is larger for silent substitutions than for replacement substitutions. This agrees with our previous discussion of the generation-time effect.

In the second stage of the analysis, the corrected distances are used to calculate the numbers of substitutions and the sample index of dispersion. As an example, the first entry in Table 1 of the Li et al. study is prolactin for which

$$D_{p,r} = 25.1, \ D_{p,a} = 14.5, \ D_{r,a} = 30.8$$

for replacement substitutions. From these we obtain, using equation 3.2,

$$N_p = 4.4, \ N_r = 20.7, \ N_a = 10.1.$$

These figures are scaled to units of numbers of substitutions per 100 replacement sites. Prolactin has, on average, 462 replacement sites, implying that the inferred total number of substitutions on the three lineages are

$$N_p = (462/100) \times 4.4 = 20.33, \ N_r = 95.63, \ N_a = 46.66.$$

To estimate the parameters we must decide on which weights to use. For purposes of illustration, we will use the silent weights. The estimate for the mean number of substitutions is now

$$\hat{\mu} = \frac{1}{3} \left(\frac{20.33}{0.627} + \frac{95.63}{1.611} + \frac{46.66}{0.762} \right) = 51.0.$$

The estimate for the variance in the number of substitutions is $\hat{\sigma}^2 = 220.14$, and for R_m, $(220.14/51) = 4.32$.

This procedure must be repeated for each locus and each set of weights. The results are given in Table 3.5 for 20 of the 21 loci. The anomalous locus, endozepine, was not included because it gave a negative estimate for one

Table 3.5. Estimates of the index of dispersion for 20 loci. The subscripts e, r, and s refer to equal, replacement, and silent weights. One star represents rejection of the Poisson clock at the 5% level, two stars at the 1% level. Data are from [94, Table 1].

Locus	Replacement $R_e(t)$	$R_r(t)$	$R_s(t)$	Silent $R_e(t)$	$R_s(t)$
Prolactin	26.94	12.21**	4.32	10.33	1.02
Parathyroid	8.03	3.47*	1.04	16.96	4.58
Proenkephalin	8.57	3.73*	2.18	30.34	9.05*
Proglucagon	1.58	2.13	2.82	16.99	9.39*
α globin	0.23	0.32	1.62	18.21	4.68
β globin	7.30	3.41*	1.78	4.72	0.73
Thyrotropin, B	2.80	2.26	2.31	6.77	4.89
POMC	15.10	6.44**	2.14	9.84	1.46
Growth hormone	32.22	43.82**	60.25	3.45	17.10**
GPHA	22.43	27.74**	34.67	1.00	2.52
Luteinizing, B	3.21	6.55**	12.85	11.74	2.16
Relaxin	3.38	0.13	3.29	13.08	0.28
Interleukin-2	12.80	8.85**	8.84	57.45	17.19**
Signal peptides	9.98	3.25*	0.82	18.11	7.52*
CCK	2.36	0.31	0.21	5.00	1.20
ACHRG	1.52	0.61	2.20	13.40	3.71
UPA	0.01	5.11**	19.64	21.38	0.25
ANF	1.94	1.64	2.53	10.05	2.17
β crystallin	1.38	2.50	4.39	5.40	0.36
Na,K-ATPase	3.49	4.46*	5.50	13.95	2.48
Average	8.26	6.95	8.67	14.41	4.64

of the $\mathcal{N}_i$, presumably because of an error in sequencing or reporting. The table also indicates which values of R are significantly above the Poisson expectation. The details for these tests will be given after our discussion of the results.

Table 3.5 shows that the correction for lineage effects does not have a particularly large effect on the estimation of R for replacement substitutions, but does have a large effect for silent substitutions. The average value of R for replacement substitutions is lowered from 8.26 to 6.95 when replacement weights are used, but is raised to 8.67 with silent weights. In either case, we are faced with an average value of R that is considerably higher than those from previous studies. This is remarkable when one considers that in those other studies lineage effects were compounded into the estimates of R. The higher average is due to the increased number of loci with high Rs. Interestingly, most of these are hormones.

The average value of R for silent substitutions is lowered dramatically when silent weights are used: from 14.4 to 4.6. It is lowered even more

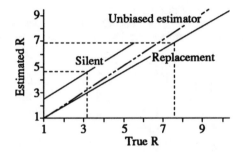

Figure 3.7. The results of a simulation study of the biases in the estimation of R. Redrawn from [94].

when an adjustment is made for the upward bias that accompanies the correction for multiple substitutions [31]. Figure 3.7 presents the results of a computer simulation designed to mimic the entire estimation procedure for R. The simulation differs from the procedure used to produce Table 3.5 in that substitutions to different bases are assumed to be equally likely and that the Jukes-Cantor formula is used to correct for multiple substitutions. This simulation was also used for the significance measures in Table 3.5. The tests were only performed on replacement Rs with replacement weights and silent Rs with silent weights as these are the most conservative tests.

There are two opposing biases that effect the estimation of R. The first is a downward bias that comes from the fact that the estimator for R is a ratio of the estimators for the variance and mean numbers of substitutions. The expected value of a ratio of two random quantities does not equal the ratio of expectations; therefore, the estimator for R must necessarily be biased. As it happens, this bias is downward as seen in the line for replacement substitutions in Figure 3.7.

The second bias, that due to corrections for multiple substitutions, has little effect on the estimation of R for replacement substitutions since the frequency of these is so low. We can use Figure 3.7 to conclude that the average R for replacement substitutions is about 7.8.

Silent substitutions, on the other hand, are much more frequent and do lead to a significant upward bias. Note that were the true R equal to one, then the estimated R would be about 2.5. Thus, correcting for multiple substitutions raises the value of R by about 1.5 for silent sites.

The temptation is to conclude from Figure 3.7 that the average R for silent sites is about 3.3. However, since this average is based on a correction formula that posits an incorrect model of molecular evolution (one, for example, that assumes that the frequencies of the four bases do not change), we should view it with great skepticism. In particular, we can have no confidence in the statistical tests that lead to the rejection of the Poisson clock.

There are two important conclusions from our brief history of the estimation of R. The first is that any effort to estimate R must first remove lineage effects. In saying this, I am adopting the view that if we are to understand the mechanisms of molecular evolution we must study lineage effects and residual effects separately. I am also taking the somewhat arrogant position that past efforts to estimate R have often mistakenly compounded the two effects and I am usurping the latter for residual effects alone.

The second conclusion is that the average $R(t)$ for replacement substitutions is 7.8 and that there is ample evidence that the Poisson clock is incompatible with protein evolution. By contrast, the average $R(t)$ for silent substitutions is probably much lower, perhaps around 3.3, and we have no compelling reason to reject the Poisson clock for silent substitutions. The contrast between silent and replacement substitutions is very important as it suggests that the two processes may be driven by different mechanisms.

3.3 Point processes

To understand the biological significance of the high values of $R(t)$, we require some results from the theory of point processes. These play such a key role in our unfolding view of molecular evolution that they will be incorporated into the flow of the book rather than banished to an appendix. The presentation will be intuitive rather than rigorous, with ample references to the secondary literature where more details may be found. The books by Cox and Isham [46] and Daley and Vere-Jones [50] are excellent sources for additional information.

Basic definitions

A point processes may be described in three ways, as illustrated in Figure 3.8:

- As a collection of the times when events occur. The times are written as a random sequence, $\{\ldots, T_{-1}, T_0, T_1, T_2, \ldots\}$, where one event is arbitrarily chosen to be the zeroth event. In our discussion this will be the last event before time zero.

- As the intervals of time between events. If $X_i = T_i - T_{i-1}$, the sequence of intervals $\{\ldots, X_{-1}, X_0, X_1, X_2, \ldots\}$ provides an alternative description of the process.

- As the cumulative number of events. Suppose we begin observing the process at time zero and let $\mathcal{N}(t)$ be the total number of events in the interval $(0, t)$. $\mathcal{N}(t)$ will equal k if $T_1 \ldots T_k$ are less than t and $T_{k+1} > t$.

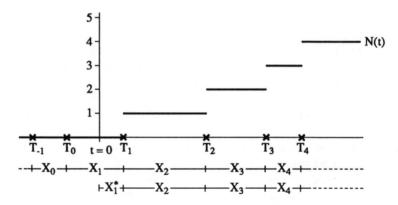

Figure 3.8. The three methods of describing point processes.

The most important class of point processes for our purposes are stationary point processes. These may be thought of as processes with properties that are the same no matter when we begin observing the process. Our interest in stationary processes reflects the common view that molecular evolution is homogeneous over large blocks of time.

The technical definition of stationarity involves the idea of invariance with translation in time. For example, the distribution of the number of events in the interval $(0, t)$ is the same as in the translated interval $(\tau, \tau + t)$. More generally, the joint distribution of the number of events in a set of nonoverlapping intervals will remain the same if all of the intervals are translated by the same amount.

The most important parameters of stationary point processes are those reflecting the rate of occurrence of events. The simplest of these is called the intensity or rate of the process, ρ.* It is defined as

$$\rho = \lim_{\delta \to 0+} \frac{E\mathcal{N}(\delta)}{\delta},$$

where $\delta \to 0+$ means that δ approaches zero from the positive direction. If the process is such that no more than one event will occur in a small interval of time, $\rho\delta$ is an approximation to the probability that an event will occur in an interval of length δ.

There are measures of the intensity of a process that depend on local events. The most informative of these is the intensity given that an event occurred at a specified time in the past. This rate is called the *conditional intensity function.* It is defined as

$$h(t) = \lim_{\delta_1, \delta_2 \to 0+} \frac{Pr\{\mathcal{N}(t, t + \delta_2) > 0 \mid \mathcal{N}(-\delta_1, 0) > 0\}}{\delta_2}.$$

---

*The notation in this section will follow Cox and Isham [46].

When the deltas are small, this definition implies that the probability that an event will occur in an interval of length δ, separated from a previous event by a period of time t, is $h(t)\delta$. If events tend to be clustered, $h(t)$ will be larger than ρ for small values of t.

These two definitions suggest that a point process can have a constant rate yet appear to be clumped. There is no reason to suppose that a clumped process needs to have a variable rate. A measure of the clumpedness of a process is the *index of dispersion*,

$$I(t) = \frac{\text{Var}\mathcal{N}(t)}{E\mathcal{N}(t)}.$$

This is closely related to $R(t)$. The distinction is meaningful only in the context of the neutral allele theory where the method of observation does not allow a direct measurement of the index of dispersion.

Examples of point processes

The *Poisson process* is both the simplest and most important point process. Its role in the theory of point processes is analogous to that of the normal distribution in the theory of random variables. It is called a Poisson process because the cumulative number of events in an interval of length t is Poisson distributed with mean ρt,

$$\Pr\{\mathcal{N}(t) = i\} = \frac{e^{-\rho t}(\rho t)^i}{i!}.$$

The intensity and the conditional intensity of the process are both equal to ρ. Thus, the occurrence of an event at one point in time has no influence on the occurrences at other times. As the mean and variance of the Poisson distribution are both equal to ρt, the index of dispersion is equal to one for all t. Note also that both moments increase linearly with time.

The intervals between events, the X_i, are independent exponentially distributed random variables with density $\rho \exp(-\rho x)$ and moments

$$EX_i = 1/\rho, \ \text{Var}X_i = 1/\rho^2.$$

Renewal processes are a class of point processes that generalize the Poisson process by dropping the assumption that the times between events are exponentially distributed. Instead, assume that the set of intervals, $\{X_i\}$, are independent, identically distributed, positive random variables. They might be, for example, gamma or negative-binomially distributed. This seemingly innocuous change wreaks havoc with the mathematics. For example, the distribution of $\mathcal{N}(t)$ can only be written as a messy sum of convolutions of the distribution of X_i.

There is an ambiguity in our description of renewal processes that is relevant to their use for modeling molecular evolution. We could imagine two ways to start the process. We could start at $t = 0$ with an event and follow the evolution of the process using the intervals $X_1, X_2, \ldots$. This means setting $T_0 = 0$ in Figure 3.8. Alternatively, we could assume that the process has been renewing for an infinite period of time before $t = 0$. In this case, the time until the first event, X_1^*, will have a distribution that is different from that of the remaining X_i. This process is called an equilibrium renewal process and is the appropriate starting scheme for a stationary point process.

Another casualty of the generalization to renewal processes is the ability to write down simple expressions for the moments of $\mathcal{N}(t)$. For large t, it is known that $\mathcal{N}(t)$ approaches a normal distribution with mean

$$E\mathcal{N}(t) \sim t/\mu_x$$

and variance

$$\mathrm{Var}\mathcal{N}(t) \sim t\sigma_x^2/\mu_x^3,$$

where $\mu_x = EX_i$ is the mean time between events and σ_x^2 is the variance in the time [46, p. 53]. The index of dispersion for large t is

$$\lim_{t\to\infty} I(t) = \sigma_x^2/\mu_x^2.$$

The index of dispersion can be greater or less than one, depending on the magnitude of the variance relative to the square of the mean. In the former case we say that the process is *underdispersed*; in the latter, *overdispersed*. Note that as the variance of an exponential distribution is equal to the square of the mean, we have a second way to show that the index of dispersion of the Poisson process is one.

The intensity or rate of an equilibrium renewal process is just the reciprocal of the mean time between events, $\rho = 1/\mu_x$. If t is small enough to ignore multiple events, the probability of an event in the interval $(0, t)$ is approximately t/μ_x. The mean number of events in $(0, t)$ is t/μ_x while the variance is

$$t/\mu_x(1 - t/\mu_x) \approx t/\mu_x.$$

Thus, for small t, the index of dispersion approaches one as illustrated in Figure 3.9. Should a large number of replicate renewal processes be watched for a short period of time, they will be judged to be close to a Poisson process.

As models of molecular evolution, renewal processes introduce a new wrinkle. They show that there is no single number that reflects the index of dispersion as there is for a Poisson process. Rather, the index of dispersion will be close to one for studies of closely related species and will grow as more distantly related species are examined. They are also the first instance of a recurring theme: there are many aspects of point processes as applied to molecular evolution that make them appear more Poisson-like than they should.

The next process, the *compound Poisson process*, is one that pops up frequently in molecular evolution. Like renewal processes, it is a simple

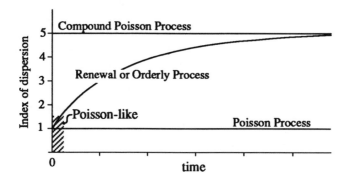

Figure 3.9. The index of dispersion, $I(t)$, for three point processes.

extension of the Poisson process. A compound Poisson process is constructed by starting with a Poisson process, called the generating process, and allowing a random number of events at each event of the generating process. Such a process is used to model rapid bursts of substitutions or substitutions of mutational events that change more than one nucleotide.

There is a particularly simple representation for compound Poisson processes. Call the generating process $M(t)$ and let its rate be ρ. Let $Z_1, Z_2, \ldots$ be a sequence of independent, positive, integer-valued random variables. The total number of events may now be written as

$$\mathcal{N}(t) = Z_1 + Z_2 + \cdots + Z_{M(t)}.$$

As $\mathcal{N}(t)$ is a random sum of random variables, it is said to have a compound distribution.

The moments of $\mathcal{N}(t)$ may be derived using generating functions as explained in Feller's book [70, page 286]. They are

$$E\mathcal{N}(t) = EM(t)EZ_i = \rho t \mu_z, \tag{3.5}$$

and

$$\mathrm{Var}\mathcal{N}(t) = EM(t)\mathrm{Var}Z_i + \mathrm{Var}M(t)(EZ_i)^2 = \rho t(\sigma_z^2 + \mu_z^2). \tag{3.6}$$

As with the Poisson process, both the mean and the variance increase linearly with time. As a consequence, the index of dispersion,

$$I(t) = \mu_z + \frac{\sigma_z^2}{\mu_z}, \tag{3.7}$$

will be independent of time. If Z_i is always greater than one, as when these processes are used to model molecular evolution, then the index of dispersion is always greater than one.

The final process is called the *doubly stochastic Poisson process*—Cox process for short. This process is yet another generalization of the Poisson process obtained in this instance by allowing the rate of the process to change at random through time. The key observation that allows the Cox process to be analyzed is that the distribution of $\mathcal{N}(t)$, given a particular trajectory of the rate, is Poisson with mean

$$Z(t) = \int_0^t \Lambda(s)ds,$$

where $\Lambda(t)$ is the random process representing the rate as a function of time. That is,

$$\Pr\{\mathcal{N}(t) = i \mid \Lambda(s), 0 < s < t\} = \frac{e^{-Z(t)}Z(t)^i}{i!}.$$

If we knew the distribution of the integral $Z(t)$, it would be a simple matter to write down the full (unconditional) distribution of $\mathcal{N}(t)$. Unfortunately, there are very few nonnegative stochastic processes for which the distribution of the integral is known. The moments of $\mathcal{N}(t)$, on the other hand, are simple functions of the moments of $\Lambda(t)$.

For $\mathcal{N}(t)$ to be a stationary point process, the rate process $\Lambda(t)$ must be a stationary process as well. Stationarity of $\Lambda(t)$, like that of $\mathcal{N}(t)$, means that the process is invariant with translations in time. As a consequence, the moments of $\Lambda(t)$ do not depend on time. For the mean, let

$$E\Lambda(t) = \mu_\lambda.$$

The second order moments of $\Lambda(t)$ are described by the autocovariance function

$$r_\lambda(x) = \text{Cov}[\Lambda(t), \Lambda(t+x)].$$

The autocovariance is a measure of the similarity of the process when observed at two points separated by a lag of x units of time. The variance of $\Lambda(t)$ is the autocovariance function with lag zero, $r_\lambda(0)$.

With the moments of $\Lambda(t)$ in hand, we can obtain those for $Z(t)$ and $\mathcal{N}(t)$ in short order. The mean of $Z(t)$ is just

$$EZ(t) = \int_0^t E\Lambda(s)ds = \mu_\lambda t.$$

The variance is

$$\begin{aligned}
\text{Var}Z(t) &= E[Z(t) - \mu_\lambda t]^2 \\
&= E\int_0^t \int_0^t [Z(x) - \mu_\lambda][Z(y) - \mu_\lambda]dxdy \\
&= \int_0^t \int_0^t r_\lambda(x - y)dxdy \\
&= 2\int_0^t (t - x)r_\lambda(x)dx.
\end{aligned}$$

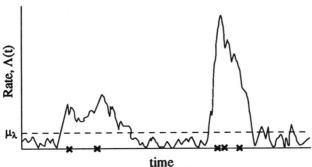

Figure 3.10. A realization of the doubly stochastic Poisson process.

The last step comes through a change of variables setting, say, $u = x - y$ and $v = x$.

We are finally in a position to write down the moments of $\mathcal{N}(t)$. For a given $Z(t)$, $\mathcal{N}(t)$ is Poisson distributed; thus, we can obtain the moments of $\mathcal{N}(t)$ by using the standard partitioning of moments. For the mean we have

$$E\mathcal{N}(t) = E_Z E[\mathcal{N}(t) \mid Z(t)] = E_Z Z(t) = \mu_\lambda t.$$

The variance is obtained from the following steps:

$$\begin{aligned} \text{Var}\mathcal{N}(t) &= E_Z \text{Var}[\mathcal{N}(t) \mid Z(t)] + \text{Var}_Z E[\mathcal{N}(t) \mid Z(t)] \\ &= E_z Z(t) + \text{Var}_Z Z(t) \\ &= \mu_\lambda t + 2 \int_0^t (t - x) r_\lambda(x) dx. \end{aligned}$$

The index of dispersion for the Cox process,

$$I(t) = 1 + \frac{2 \int_0^t (1 - x/t) r_\lambda(x) dx}{\mu_\lambda}, \tag{3.8}$$

is always greater than one.

In applications we will often be interested in the asymptotic value of the index of dispersion as $t \to \infty$. Notice in equation 3.8 that the value of x/t will approach zero as t grows and x remains fixed, while $r_\lambda(x)$ will approach zero as x gets large. Together, these observations show that

$$\lim_{t \to \infty} I(t) = 1 + \frac{2 \int_0^\infty r_\lambda(x) dx}{\mu_\lambda}. \tag{3.9}$$

Figure 3.10 illustrates the essential features of the Cox process. The high index of dispersion reflects the tendency for points to cluster during those times when the rate of the process is higher than average.

3.4   Biological significance

Having documented the existence of significant residual effects and laid a
foundation in point process theory, we must now combine the two for a
discussion of the biological significance of residual effects. This is the first
of two places that this discussion will take place. Here we will be concerned
only with the implications of residual effects on the dynamics of molecular
evolution. In Chapters 6 and 7 we will discuss their impact on our views
of the mechanisms of molecular evolution.

The distinction between dynamics and mechanism is important and follows the general effort in this book to separate the description of variation
from its mechanistic interpretation. In this case, we will be mirroring an extensive literature that provides empirically motivated stochastic models of
molecular evolution without addressing the evolutionary mechanisms that
lead to substitutions.

I hope to make two main points in this section. The first is that residual
effects imply that the substitutions at individual sites within loci are not
independent. As the vast majority of models of molecular evolution assume
independence between sites, this conclusion has profound effects on our view
of molecular evolution. The second point is that if we adopt a model of
variable rates of evolution, then we are almost surely led to the view that
molecular evolution is episodic, with bursts of substitutions separated by
periods of quiescence. This is a significant departure from the conventional
view of molecular evolution as well.

Independence of sites

In the 1940s, studies of the times at which connections were made or broken
at large telephone switchboards were shown to look very much like a Poisson
process. This was a strange observation as the switching times should be
Poisson only if the times between the arrival of new calls and the durations
of individual calls are exponentially distributed. It was known that neither
property held. (Few of us use an exponential random number generator
to govern the length of our phone calls.) Thus, there is something about
the way this point process was observed that made it appear Poisson-like
when, in fact, it wasn't.

There are two key conspirators in this deception: the independence of
calls and the short period of observation. Essentially no one regulates the
length of their conversation by events on other phone lines. Thus it is
natural to assume that calls are independent. At a large switchboard there
are so many lines that by watching for only a short time relative to the
length of a typical call it is possible to accumulate enough data to test for
agreement with a Poisson process. These are the two ingredients that lead
to the Poisson character of the observations. Figure 3.11 illustrates the
structure of the problem.

What does this have to do with molecular evolution? The physical

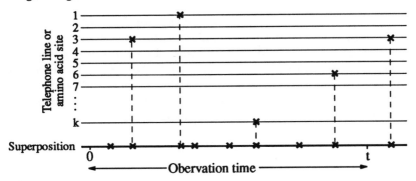

Figure 3.11. An illustration of the superposition of k processes to form a single process.

analogy is as follows: amino acid or nucleotide sites are like telephone lines and substitutions are the same as made or broken connections. A typical site experiences a substitution about once every billion years, yet a typical study examines species that have been separated for only tens of millions of years. Thus, the observation time is short relative to the time scale of events at individual sites just as for the telephone switchboard. Finally, if the sites are independent, the substitution process for the entire protein should appear to be a Poisson process.

In fact, amino acid substitutions for the entire protein are not Poisson distributed. The obvious conclusion is that the substitutions at different sites are not independent. To make this more rigorous, we need to spend some time examining the quantitative aspects of this problem.

The adding together of point processes is called superpositioning. The summed process is called the superposition. Imagine that we have k independent point processes, $\mathcal{N}_i(t)$. The superposition is written

$$\mathcal{N}(t) = \mathcal{N}_1(t) + \mathcal{N}_2(t) + \cdots + \mathcal{N}_k(t). \tag{3.10}$$

The claim is that the superposition will appear Poisson-like if observed for a short period of time relative to the time scale of substitution for single amino acid sites. If we do what comes naturally and look at the index of dispersion for the superposition we get

$$I_k(t) = \frac{\text{Var}[\mathcal{N}_1(t) + \cdots + \mathcal{N}_k(t)]}{E[\mathcal{N}_1(t) + \cdots + \mathcal{N}_k(t)]} = \frac{k\text{Var}\mathcal{N}_i(t)}{kE\mathcal{N}_i(t)} = I(t),$$

where $I(t)$ is the index of dispersion for the component processes. Clearly, this is of no help as the index of dispersion for the superposition is the same as for the individual processes.

We could look at the problem another way. Suppose we increase the number of component processes while lowering their intensities in such a way that the intensity of the superposition remains constant. That is, let the intensity of the superposition be ρ and that of each of the component processes be ρ/k. Now let k increase. The rate for each of the component processes will decrease until the probability of an event occurring at a specified process during the period of observation, time 0 to t, is approximately $\rho t/k$. We now find ourselves in a setting that is often used to define the Poisson distribution. There are a large number of independent trials with the probability of success at any one trial low, but the average number of successes fixed. In particular, we must conclude that

$$\lim_{k \to \infty} I_k(t) = 1$$

for any fixed t. On the surface, this conflicts with our previous conclusion that $I_k(t) = I(t) \neq 1$.

The difference between these two approaches rests with the assumptions about the change of the intensity of the individual processes as k increases. In the first case the intensity was kept fixed, in the second case it approached zero. This suggests that to understand the Poisson character of the superposition we must understand the significance of the low intensities of the component processes in the second case.

Any point process that is orderly, that is, has no more than one event at a single point in time, will "look" like a Poisson process if watched for a short enough period of time. If the intensity is ρ and if ρt is very small, then only two outcomes during the fixed period of time t are likely to occur: zero or one events. They occur with approximate probabilities $1 - \rho t$ and ρt, respectively. Likewise, if the mean of a Poisson distribution is very small only two outcomes are likely: zero or one. If the mean of the Poisson is written ρt, then the probabilities of these two outcomes are approximately the same as for the point process. Thus, the point process is approximately Poisson when observed for a short enough period of time.

One consequence of the Poisson nature of orderly point processes over short periods of time is that

$$\lim_{t \to 0} I(t) = 1.$$

Thus, the index of dispersion illustrated in Figure 3.9 for a renewal process applies more generally with regard to its behavior near $t = 0$. Note that the compound Poisson process illustrated in the same figure is not orderly since more than one event can occur at a single instant in time. This is why it fails to approach one at $t \to 0$.

Our discussion of the convergence to a Poisson process at k increases has been casual. I have attempted to motivate rather than prove the result that is often called the Palm-Khintchine theorem. A very readable proof may be found in Cox and Isham's book [46, Section 4.5]. They also provide a useful approximation for the index of dispersion of the superposition,

$$I_k(t) = 1 + \frac{t}{k}(h_0 - \rho) + \frac{t^2 h_1}{3k^2} + O\left(\frac{1}{k^3}\right),$$

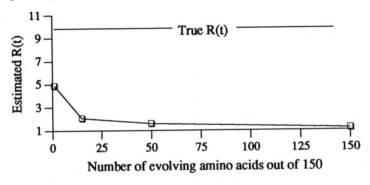

Figure 3.12. Simulation results illustrating the Palm-Khintchine effect. Simulation results are from [87, Table 2].

where h_0 and h_1 are the leading terms of the Taylor series expansion of the conditional intensity,

$$h(u) = h_0 + h_1 u + \cdots,$$

and O means "of the same order of magnitude as." This approximation shows that the convergence to the Poisson process goes as $1/k$.

Figure 3.12 illustrates the Palm-Khintchine effect as it might apply to a protein with evolutionary properties similar those of β globin. It is based on a simulation of a protein composed of 150 independently evolving amino acids sites in six species from a star phylogeny. Each site is governed by a renewal process with log-normally distributed intervals and an asymptotic index of dispersion of 10 ($I(\infty) = 10$). The intensity of the process was chosen so that a pair of species will be separated by 15 substitutions on average. $R(t)$ was estimated by Kimura's method as given in equation 3.1.

The simulation concentrated all of the substitutions—the average number is held fixed—onto 1, 15, 50, or 150 amino acid sites. As is evident, the estimated index of dispersion drops rapidly toward one as the number of amino acid sites experiencing substitutions increases. Note also that even when all of the substitutions are concentrated at a single site, the asymptotic index of dispersion is still substantially underestimated. For this renewal process, more than 15 events are required, on average, before the estimated index of dispersion will be close to the asymptotic value.

To further illustrate the dramatic consequences of the Palm-Khintchine effect we could ask: how large would the true index of dispersion have to be to observe the value of 3.4 estimated by Kimura for β globin? The answer, again obtained from a simulation, is $I(\infty) \approx 1000$ [87].

These simulations clearly illustrated that, if sites evolve independently, the true index of dispersion for replacement substitutions must be very large indeed. Observing an average index of dispersion of seven, for example, would indicate that the dynamics of substitutions at individual sites are not at all like a Poisson process. They also should warn us that our failure to find convincing evidence for an elevated index of dispersion for silent sites may not necessarily be evidence for a more Poisson-like dynamic at individual sites, but rather that the evolution of silent sites are more nearly independent of one another than are replacement sites.

My own conclusion from these simulations is that amino acid sites do not evolve independently. Rather, the occurrence of a substitution at one site increases the likelihood of substitutions at other sites. If the average index of dispersion for silent sites remains significant upon further analysis, then the same conclusion must hold for them as well.

This view is in sharp contrast to the prevailing one. Most models of sequence evolution postulate independent Markov chains for each site. All such models are incompatible with high values of the index of dispersion and thus do not provide faithful mimics of molecular evolution.

Once this conclusion is accepted, it becomes necessary to construct models for the evolution of the entire sequence rather than for individual sites. One such model will be described in the next subsection.

Episodic evolution

The usual conclusion from studies that reject the Poisson clock is that rates of substitution are variable. The simplest model that incorporates fluctuating rates is the doubly stochastic Poisson process or, as we will refer to it here, the Cox process. However, before the Cox process can be used we need to choose a stochastic process for the rate, call it $\Lambda(t)$. Since the set of possible processes is unbounded, there is no obvious way to proceed.

One way out of this impasse is to recognize that there is a time scale problem that must be addressed along with the choice of rate processes: how fast does the rate of evolution itself change? That question is not tied down very well. A better question is: how fast does the rate of evolution change relative to the mean rate of substitution? It is this relative form of the question that is most informative.

Many proteins, like the globins, experience a substitution about once every 10 million years. Thus, the time scale of protein evolution is frequently on the order of tens of millions of years. Should we also assume that this is the natural time scale of change of the rate of evolution? This depends on our view about the causes of the changes in the rate of evolution. If we feel that the changes are due to fluctuations in the environment, then it seems extraordinarily unlikely that environmental changes would occur on a time scale as long as tens of millions of years. Recall that the ice ages, for example, occur on a time scale of tens of thousands of years or about three orders of magnitude faster than the time scale of molecular evolution. Ice ages occur on a rather long time scale for climatic processes. Others occur on scales of tens (sun spot driven) or hundreds (e.g., the "little ice ages") of years.

If we accept that the time scale of change of the rate of molecular evolution is very fast relative to the time scale of molecular evolution itself, and if we use the Cox process to model evolution, then we must conclude that evolution is episodic, with bursts of substitutions separated by periods of quiescence. The route to this conclusion will concern us for much of this section.

As we saw in the previous section, the number of substitutions under the Cox process depends on the integral of the rate, $\int^t \Lambda(s)ds$. Integration is a smoothing operation, so we should expect that variations in the rate will be hidden to some extent. The faster that the rate changes, the greater will be the smoothing effect. To see this, look at the variance in the number of substitutions,

$$\operatorname{Var}\mathcal{N}(t) = \mu_\lambda t + 2r_\lambda(0) \int_0^t (t-x)\frac{r_\lambda(x)}{r_\lambda(0)}dx. \tag{3.11}$$

In rewriting this from equation 3.8 we have brought the variance in the rate, $r_\lambda(0)$, outside the integral and replaced the autocovariance function of the integrand with the autocorrelation function, $r_\lambda(x)/r_\lambda(0)$.

A rapidly changing environment is one with a low autocorrelation. As the autocorrelation gets smaller, so does the integral in equation 3.11. If the environment changes very fast, the autocorrelation becomes vanishingly small and the variance of $\mathcal{N}(t)$ approaches its mean, $\mu_\lambda t$. At the same time, the index of dispersion approaches one. We argued above that environmentally driven changes in the rate might be occurring on time scales that are at least three orders of magnitude faster than the time scale of molecular evolution. If this were so, how can we account for a high index of dispersion?

The only viable answer is that the variance in the rate, $r_\lambda(0)$, is large. This, in turn, leads to an interesting problem. The distribution of the rate, $\Lambda(t)$, for a fixed t must have three properties:

1. The rate must be greater than or equal to zero, $\Lambda(t) \geq 0$.

2. The mean of the rate must be very small, $E\Lambda(t) \approx 10^{-7}$ for typical proteins.

3. The variance in the rate must be large enough to elevate the variance of $\mathcal{N}(t)$ sufficiently to account for a high index of dispersion.

To accommodate all three, the distribution of $\Lambda(t)$ must be such that most of the probability mass is very close to zero to preserve the small mean, yet there must be a very long tail to elevate the variance. The process, $\Lambda(t)$, will spend most of its time near zero where it prevents substitutions from occurring, yet will make rare excursions to high values that will lead to a burst of substitutions.

If our intuition is correct, we should be able to write the substitution process as the compound Poisson process

$$\mathcal{N}(t) = X_1 + X_2 + \cdots + X_{M(t)}, \tag{3.12}$$

where the X_i are independent, positive, random variables and $M(t)$ is a Poisson process. The process, $M(t)$ represents the times when bursts of substitutions occur. The random variable X_i represents the number of substitutions that occurred on the ith burst.

Let the mean burst size be $EX_i = \mu_b$ and the episodic rate be ρ_e. Using equation 3.5 we can write the mean number of substitutions as

$$EN(t) = EX_i EM(t) = \mu_b \rho_e t. \tag{3.13}$$

That is, the mean rate of substitution is just the episodic rate times the mean number of substitutions per episode. From equation 3.6 we see that the variance is

$$\text{Var}N(t) = EM(t)\text{Var}X_i + \text{Var}M(t)E^2 X_i = \rho_e t E(X_i^2) \tag{3.14}$$

We have reached an impasse: the equations for the mean and variance of $N(t)$ use three parameters—$\rho_e t$, μ_b, and $\mu_2 = E(X^2)$—while we currently have only two estimates, those for the mean and the index of dispersion of $N(t)$. There are two obvious ways to proceed. We could estimate a higher order moment of $N(t)$ giving us three estimators and three parameters or we could specialize the model in such a way as to reduce the number of parameters by one. Of the two, the latter appears to hold more promise.

A suggestive observation that moves us in the right direction is that the index of dispersion depends only on the properties of the bursts,

$$I(t) = \frac{E(X_i^2)}{EX_i}.$$

If we use a one-parameter distribution for X_i, say a geometric distribution, we could estimate that parameter using an estimate of $I(t)$ and have, as a consequence, an estimate of the mean burst size, μ_b. This could be used, in turn, to estimate the mean number of episodes, $\rho_e t$.

There is nothing wrong with this approach from a statistical point of view. From a scientific perspective there is something unsatisfying about pulling a one-parameter distribution out of the air without connecting it in any way with a fluctuating rate of evolution. In what follows we will make the connection, although via an equally *ad hoc* assumption about the nature of the clock. However, the approach that we will use does generalize, which allows us to conclude that, in general, a rapidly changing clock leads to an episodic pattern of substitutions.

Figure 3.13 illustrates the stochastic rate function, $\Lambda(t)$, that will be used for the clock. We will call this rate function the gamma clock. The rate spends an exponentially distributed time at zero before jumping to a gamma distributed value where it stays for a fixed time, ϵ^2, before returning to zero. This alternation is repeated with independently chosen exponential and gamma random variables. The mean of the exponential distribution is ϵ/ρ_c, so ρ_c/ϵ is also the rate of change of the clock. The gamma distribution has mean $1/\epsilon$ and variance v/ϵ^3.

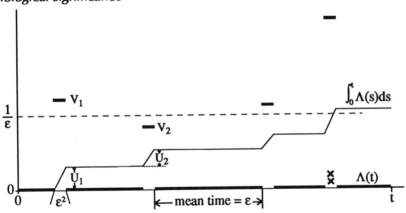

Figure 3.13. The gamma clock.

This form of the clock was chosen for its behavior as $\epsilon \to 0$. As ϵ gets smaller, several important things happen. Note first that the *relative* time spent in the intervals where $\Lambda(t) > 0$ approaches zero. As a consequence, the times that the rate jumps from zero to a positive value approaches a Poisson process with rate ρ_c/ϵ.

Substitutions can only occur when $\Lambda(t) > 0$. Let $\Lambda(t) = V_i$ in the ith interval where this condition holds (see Fig. 3.13). The V_i are independent identically distributed gamma random variables. Given V_i, the number of substitutions within the ith interval will be Poisson distributed with mean $U_i = V_i \epsilon^2$. Thus, the unconditional mean number of substitutions is

$$EU_i = \epsilon^2 EV_i = \epsilon.$$

As $\epsilon \to 0$, the mean number of substitutions that occurs in any particular interval where $\Lambda(t) > 0$ goes to zero. Note that, since a constant times a gamma random variable is also gamma distributed, the U_i are independent gamma random variables as well.

Consider the full distribution of the number of substitutions in the ith interval. We have seen that, given U_i, the number of substitutions is Poisson distributed. Thus, to find the full distribution we need only randomize a Poisson distribution by a gamma distribution with mean ϵ and variance

$$\mathrm{Var}U_i = \epsilon^4 \mathrm{Var}V_i = \epsilon v.$$

This particular randomized Poisson is known to have a negative binomial distribution.* The mean of the resulting negative binomial is ϵ and the variance is $\epsilon(1 + v)$.

---

*One source for this result is the book on discrete distributions by Johnson and Kotz [145, Section 5.4]. Their book will be the source for all of the results from probability theory needed in this section.

As expected, the mean and variance get small as $\epsilon \to 0$. Our interest naturally turns to those intervals where there are one or more substitutions. The negative binomial distribution, conditioned on at least one event occurring, approaches a logarithmic series distribution as $\epsilon \to 0$ [145, Section 7.2]. That is, if k has the negative binomial distribution just described, then

$$\lim_{\epsilon \to 0} \Pr\{k \mid k > 0\} = \frac{1}{\ln(1+v)} \left(\frac{v}{1+v}\right)^k \frac{1}{k}.$$

Call the log-series distributed random variable for the ith interval for which at least one substitution occurs X_i. The mean of X_i is the mean burst size,

$$\mu_b = EX_i = \frac{v}{\ln(1+v)}. \tag{3.15}$$

This completes the description of the positive random variables describing the number of substitutions in each burst, X_i in equation 3.12.

The only remaining task is to find the rate of occurrence of episodes. This is given by the rate of occurrence of positive values of $\Lambda(t)$, ρ_c/ϵ, times the fraction of positive values that produce at least one substitution. The latter may be found from the negative binomial probability

$$\Pr\{k = 0\} = \left(1 - \frac{v}{1+v}\right)^{\epsilon/v} \sim 1 - \frac{\epsilon}{v} \ln(1+v).$$

From this we get the episodic rate

$$\rho_e = \frac{\rho_c}{\epsilon} \times \frac{\epsilon}{v} \ln(1+v) = \frac{\rho_c \ln(1+v)}{v}.$$

Thus, the number of episodes in a period of time t is Poisson distributed with mean $\rho_e t$.

We are now back to our representation of the total number of substitutions,

$$\mathcal{N}(t) = X_1 + X_2 + \cdots + X_{M(t)}$$

from equation 3.12. As $\mathcal{N}(t)$ is a Poisson sum of log-series random variables, it has a negative binomial distribution [145, Section 5.4] with mean

$$E\mathcal{N}(t) = \mu_b \rho_e t$$

and, using equation 3.14, variance

$$\mathrm{Var}\mathcal{N}(t) = \mu_b(1+v)\rho_e t.$$

Although this looks like a three-parameter distribution, μ_b and v are related through equation 3.15.

To estimate the mean burst size and the episodic rate we need relationships between these quantities and the index of dispersion

$$I(t) = \frac{\mathrm{Var}\mathcal{N}(t)}{E\mathcal{N}(t)} = 1 + v.$$

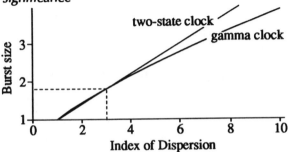

Figure 3.14. The burst size for the gamma and two-state clocks as a function of the index of dispersion. The dotted line shows the median index of dispersion for the replacement substitutions in Table 3.5.

From this and equation 3.15 we have

$$\mu_b = \frac{I(t) - 1}{\ln I(t)},$$

which shows that the mean burst size is a function of the index of dispersion alone and that $\mu_b \to 1$ as $I(t) \to 1$. Figure 3.14 illustrates the dependency of the burst size on the index of dispersion. The median R_r from Table 3.5 is about three, which corresponds to a mean burst size of 1.8.

The mean number of episodes is given by

$$\rho_e t = E\mathcal{N}(t)\frac{\ln I(t)}{I(t) - 1},$$

which is the mean number of substitutions divided by the burst size, as we saw before. Thus, if we have estimates of $I(t)$ and $E\mathcal{N}(t)$, we can estimate the mean burst size and the mean number of episodes.

There is a second example of a clock that also allows a direct calculation. This is called the two-state clock because $\Lambda(t)$ jumps back and forth between zero and a fixed positive value, remaining at each state for an exponentially distributed length of time. A limiting argument similar to that for the gamma clock shows that the X_i are geometrically distributed,

$$\frac{1}{\mu_b}\left(\frac{\mu_b - 1}{\mu_b}\right)^k \quad k = 1, 2, \ldots,$$

with mean μ_b and $E(X_i^2) = 2\mu_b^2 - \mu_b$ [94]. Using these moments and equation 3.14 we can express the mean burst size as a function of the index of dispersion,

$$\mu_b = \frac{1 + I(t)}{2},$$

and the mean number of episodes as

$$\rho_e t = \frac{2E\mathcal{N}(t)}{1 + I(t)}.$$

Table 3.6. Estimates of the mean burst size and the mean number of episodes for two clocks based on the data from Table 3.5.

Locus	$R_s(t)$	μ	Gamma clock		Two-state clock	
			$\hat{\mu}_b$	$\hat{\rho}_e t$	$\hat{\mu}_b$	$\hat{\rho}_e t$
Prolactin	4.32	51.00	2.27	22.49	2.66	19.18
β globin	1.78	1.78	1.35	14.94	1.39	14.54
Thyrotropin, B	2.31	8.77	1.56	5.61	1.65	5.30
Relaxin	3.29	64.14	1.92	33.36	2.14	29.91
Interlukin-2	8.84	54.35	3.60	15.11	4.92	11.05
β crystallin	4.39	7.64	2.29	3.34	2.69	2.84
Na,K-ATPase	5.50	15.13	2.64	5.73	3.25	4.66

Figure 3.14 compares the dependence of the mean burst size on the index of dispersion to that of the gamma clock. As is apparent, the two clocks have similar properties in the region of the data.

Table 3.6 presents some estimates of the mean burst size and the mean number of episodes for some representative loci from Table 3.5. It is interesting that the estimated mean burst sizes are generally fairly small, typically smaller than three. This implies that evolution does not, in general, go on long excursions with copious substitutions. Mechanistic models must somehow account for this fact. A second point of interest is that the two clocks give very similar estimates of the parameters suggesting that the two representative clocks may reflect the properties of a much broader class of clocks.

We have accomplished our two main goals: we have shown how to obtain the representation for $\mathcal{N}(t)$ given by equation 3.10 and how to estimate the mean burst size and episodic rate for two clocks. These results rely explicitly on the details of the two clocks. It is natural to worry about their generality, particularly as both clocks are "episodic": they jump between zero and positive values. In fact, it has been shown that the representation as a Poisson sum of positive random variables (equation 3.12) holds generally[*] when the autocorrelation of the clock approaches zero and the variance goes to infinity [94]. In particular, there is no requirement that a clock spend time at zero to yield episodic dynamics. The details of the general argument are technical and will not be repeated here. The essential obstacle to a simple demonstration is that there is no satisfactory way to describe the distribution of the integral of the rate function, $\int^t \Lambda(s)ds$. The two clocks were chosen as simple cases where the distribution could be found, at least approximately. This allowed us to proceed using a direct argument.

The general approach also shows that there is no restriction on the

---

[*]There is, in fact, a gap in the proof of the general result [94, p. 146]. I was unable to find conditions on $\Lambda(t)$ that made the limiting form of its integral a process with independent rather than orthogonal increments.

distribution of burst sizes. Any positive random variable may be used, including ones with two or more parameters. At the present time, there have been no attempts to choose between various burst size distributions. It is unlikely that there would be enough power for such a test.

3.5 Is there a clock?

There are two distinct reasons why one might be concerned with the molecular clock: as a device to estimate the times of divergence of lineages and for its implications about the mechanisms of molecular evolution. They differ dramatically in the importance that we attach to the acceptance of a clock.

The first concern is for the establishment of a "time scale for evolution." For this, we only care that the clock's intrinsic error be known and incorporated into the confidence limits placed around the estimates. There are some difficulties even with this seemly straightforward program. If, for example, the variability in the clock is due to lineage effects, and if lineage effects are set for each lineage by some deterministic mechanism, then knowledge of the variability of the clock for one set of lineages will not help to assess its variability on another. Had we calibrated the insulin clock using primates, artiodactyls, and carnivores and used it to estimate the split times for hystricomorph rodents, we would have been off by an order of magnitude. There is no obvious way around this problem. We could base estimates of split times on a large number of loci, but even here such phenomena as the general slowdown of primate evolution will cause problems.

For the second concern, we must be much more suspicious than we are when judging the clock's utility as a time scale for evolution. A bit of erraticism in the clock may inject only a small error in estimates of split times. It may, by contrast, alter dramatically our choice of models of molecular evolution.

The contrast between these two concerns is brought into focus by a defense of the clock's use as a time scale of evolution by Allan Wilson and his colleagues:

> Biochemists can agree with naturalists that every nucleotide position has a unique history, as does every atom of a gas. But, they also recognize that the universal gas law ($PV = nRT$) was not discovered by detailed analysis of the behavior of individual atoms. Bringing together molecular biology and natural history in the search for general laws of evolution requires, as many naturalists now recognize, a willingness to transcend 'microscopic' analysis. [309]

Two points should be made at the risk of belaboring the obvious. The first is that the clock is not as easily verified as were Boyle's and Charles' laws. We cannot be sure at this time that we even have a "law." The second is that $PV = nRT$ may be derived from the laws of statistical mechanics of large numbers of molecules. The molecular clock—in its strict incarnation with a constant rate over all lineages—cannot be derived from a mechanistic model of evolution. Thus, while the quote is wistful, it deflects the important scientific problems presented by the molecular clock.

Since our interest here is entirely with the scientific implications of the clock, I will take the stronger position that the clock does not exist. That is, there is adequate evidence that there is variation in the rate of substitution—lineage effects—beyond that attributable to residual effects.

There appear to be at least two different dynamics of allele substitutions, neither of which is strictly clock-like:

- *Silent dynamics*: Within coding regions silent substitutions show strong lineage effects and weak residual effects. The lineage effects appear to be due, in the main, to the generation-time effect.

- *Replacement dynamics*: These are the opposite: weak lineage effects and large residual effects. The weak lineage effects are in the same direction as those for silent substitutions, suggesting that they too are due to the generation-time effect, although a considerably weaker one.

The simplest explanation for this pattern is that silent substitutions are mostly mutation limited while replacement substitutions are not.

In an effort to find clock-like behavior, it may be profitable to consider substitutions as a stationary point process within a set of lineages where lineage effects have been removed. In our study of residual effects with three species this is precisely what we did. Even though the existence of lineage effects rules out a clock, there may still exist a substitution process that is common to all lineages once mean effects are removed.

This is treacherous ground. We seem to be giving special meaning to the lineages that appear in our studies even though they were chosen simply because sequences from them happen to be available in the GenBank or EMBL databases. They were not chosen because they were thought to be somehow homogeneous with respect to molecular evolution. In our analysis of sequences from orders of mammals, we implicitly assume that lineage effects are constant within each of the orders. Yet, we have seen that within primates at least, there is a progressive slowdown in the silent substitution rate as we move toward the apes.

In light of this, it is tempting to suggest that the rate of substitution evolves along lineages. Daughter lineages might inherit their initial rate from their parental lineage and evolve new rates independently. The evolution of rates is conceptually similar to that of morphological traits. Can such a model account for both lineage effects and residual effects?

The answer is a highly qualified yes [87]. The qualification is that the rate of evolution of rates must be similar to the time scale of molecular evolution. If it were much faster, we would require an episodic model to account for the high values of $R(t)$, thus moving us back to a model with stationary residual effects. Were the rate much slower, it would induce a correlation of rates between lineages that would make it very difficult to account for the high values of $R(t)$ [87].

If we were to entertain the idea that the rate of evolution of the rate of molecular evolution were similar to the time scale of evolution, we would need a biologically plausible reason why this extraordinary coincidence should hold. An obvious explanation is that the substitutions themselves alter the rate of evolution. This assumption is the basis of Takahata's "fluctuating neutral space" model [277]. We will examine the underlying assumptions of this model in Chapter 6.

Much remains to be done to sort out these issues. For the remainder of this book, I will adhere closely to the view that both lineage and residual effects are commonplace for replacement substitutions, but only lineage effects are established for silent substitutions. When present, residual effects may be adequately modeled by a stationary compound Poisson process. This view may well change as more data become available.

4

Selection in a fluctuating environment

In this chapter we will explore some mathematical aspects of natural selection in a temporally and spatially fluctuating environment. This is an area of population genetics that has received relatively little attention over the years. The reasons for this are complex, but a lack of relevance is certainly not one of them. Population genetics theory is concerned with the evolutionary consequences of fitness differences between genotypes. The fitness of a genotype is a measure of its success in the natural environment. It is clear to even the most casual observer that the environment is in a constant state of flux. It must be the case that fitness differences between genotypes are also in a constant state of flux. Thus, models of selection in a fluctuating environment should be central to that part of population genetics theory that is concerned with natural selection.

There are two formidable obstacles to the development of a satisfactory mathematical theory of selection in a fluctuating environment. The first is the problem of specification: there are simply too many models. Consider, by way of contrast, the simple world of the one-locus k-allele diploid model of selection in a constant environment. This model is completely specified by $k(k + 1)/2$ parameters reflecting the fitnesses of the distinct genotypes. There is no disagreement on the merit of the model and any new results on its dynamics are welcomed.

When we move the constant fitness model into a fluctuating environment, we are immediately faced with a plethora of questions. Should the environment fluctuate in time or space or both? If there are temporal fluctuations, should they be stochastic or periodic? If stochastic, what sort of stochastic process should be used for the fitness of a particular genotype? Should it be autocorrelated, stationary, Markovian, or something less orthodox? If there are spatial fluctuations, how many subdivisions should there be? Should there be restricted or free migration? Should selection be hard, soft, or something in between? What should be the relationships between the fitnesses of the different genotypes? Unlike the constant fitness case, there is no consensus about the merits of any particular choice among the many that present themselves. We quickly find ourselves in the strange position of feeling that work on constant fitness models is very general, whereas work on selection in a fluctuating environment is very specific, and somehow less worthy. This is the stifling effect of the problem of specification.

The second obstacle is the mathematical difficulties presented by the models themselves; they are extraordinarily difficult to analyze. This has unquestionably, and unjustifiably, steered them away from the central position they should occupy in population genetics theory.

Given these problems, how should we proceed to develop a compelling mathematical theory? The first step must be to consider the goal of the theory: what biological phenomena will the theory help us to understand? As this book is primarily concerned with molecular evolution and polymorphism, the mathematics to be developed will be geared to our understanding of molecular phenomenon. This immediately suggests that the fitness differences between genotypes should be very small. There are three important consequences of this assumption. The first, a purely technical consequence, is that we will be able to make use of diffusion approximations. The second is that very small primary effects make the use of nearly additive models of gene action biologically reasonable. The third is that the details of the environmental variations often don't matter; many different situations give rise to the same diffusion model. Thus, the problems of specification are, to some extent, resolved. The technical difficulties remain, although they are lessened considerably by the ability to use diffusion theory.

Diploid models of nearly additive gene action are based on an underlying additive scale which is mapped into fitness by a continuous function called the fitness function. They are very similar to haploid models. The similarity is so important that our development of the theory we will begin with an examination of haploid models, which are relatively simple, before moving on the the more complicated diploid models. In fact, we will introduce a fiction, the c-haploid model, which is a bridge between haploid and diploid models. The approximate dynamics of c-haploid models are the same as those of diploid models, but the model itself is divorced of the complexities that plague diploid models. The sequence of models—haploid, c-haploid, diploid—appears to be the most natural way to develop the theory and is the sequence that will be followed in this chapter.

This is the first time that this theory has been presented in a cohesive fashion. Anyone who has attempted to extract the theory from the literature has undoubtedly been frustrated by inconsistent notation, terse derivations, and many tangents that make the central thread of the theory difficult to follow. I am more guilty than most for these problems. Hopefully, this chapter will make the theory accessible to anyone who is interested. More importantly, it may provide a platform for future work. There are a number of important mathematical questions that have yet to be answered. The theory should represent a cornucopia of problems for population geneticists and mathematicians alike.

4.1 Overview

Those readers who do not wish to slog through 100 pages of mathematics will find the most important conclusions from this chapter summarized in this section.

The chapter begins with a discussion of haploid selection in a temporally fluctuating environment. The most important biological conclusions are that the genotype with the largest geometric mean fitness ultimately wins out over all others and that all variation is eventually driven from the population, even if all genotypes have the same geometric mean fitness. The real purpose of this chapter, however, is the derivation of the diffusion model for haploid selection in a temporally fluctuating environment as given by equation 4.8. This diffusion forms the basis of our subsequent analysis of diploid models. The complete transient solution of the diffusion is easily found because the transformation given by equation 4.2 carries the haploid diffusion into Brownian motion.

The transition from haploid to diploid models is made via a new model called the c-haploid model that is the focus of the next section. Past experience has shown that a large class of diploid models share a common diffusion approximation. The parameters of the diffusion reflect the relative contributions of three aspect of diploids: the dominance relationships between alleles, the amount of spatial subdivision of the population, and temporal autocorrelations of the environment. As the mathematics that connect each of these factors to the parameters of the diffusion can be lengthy, I have chosen to investigate the dynamics of the diffusion first and make the connections with the biology later, hence, the somewhat abstract incarnation of the c-haploid model.

The c-haploid model is obtained from a haploid model by simply multiplying the single generation change in the allele frequency by the constant c. This leads immediately to the diffusion process given by equation 4.12. Three aspects of this diffusion are described: its stationary distribution, its hitting probabilities, and its waiting time properties.

The stationary distribution for the c-haploid model is a Dirichlet distribution as given by equation 4.19. The fact that a stationary distribution exists implies that the stable coexistance of alleles due to temporal fluctuations in the environment is possible under the c-haploid model, a significant departure from the haploid result. Various special cases of the Dirichlet distribution are investigated. The most important of these is a symmetric case with an infinite number of alleles. The distribution in this case is the same as that for the neutral allele model. From this we are lead to the unfortunate conclusion that samples from a single population cannot be used to distinguish between neutral models and models of selection in a fluctuating environment.

As the c-haploid model does not incorporate genetic drift, alleles cannot leave the population in a finite period of time. To investigate sample path properties we must impose artificial boundaries that are hit by alleles whose frequencies achieve a small value ϵ. These sample path properties turn out to be precisely what is needed to understand the role of genetic drift in diploid populations.

The dynamics of k-allele models may be split into two regions. Rare alleles, those with frequencies close to ϵ, live in a boundary layer where the time scale of change is very long. Common alleles, those with frequencies much larger than ϵ, live in the interior where the time scale of change is much faster than that of rare alleles. As $\epsilon \to 0$, the difference in time scales in the two regions magnifies, allowing a standard asymptotic approach to finding sample path properties. The most important of these is the mean time to lose the first of k alleles from the interior as given by equation 4.45 and illustrated by Figure 4.7. The figure shows that the time to lose alleles from the interior drops precipitously if the number of interior alleles exceeds some critical value.

The next section adapts the c-halploid results to a class of diploid models called SAS-CFF models. SAS-CFF models are diploid models with two components reflecting gene action:

- *Stochastic additive scale (SAS)*: Alleles contribute an amount to a stochastic additve scale that depends on the state of a randomly fluctuating environment.

- *Concave fitness function (CFF)*: The additive scale is mapped into fitness by a concave function called the *fitness function*.

The SAS-CFF model clearly shares much in common with standard quantitative genetics models with genotype environment interaction.

There are three components of SAS-CFF models that determine the main features of their dynamics:

- *Dominance*: The degree of dominance is reflected in the curvature of the fitness function. Greater curvature implies greater dominance and, as shown in the section on SAS-CFF models, more polymorphic alleles and higher heterozygosity.

- *Spatial subdivision*: The contribution of spatial subdivision to heterozygosity is complex. For soft selection, where subdivisions contribute a fixed fraction of individuals to a random mating pool each generation, increasing the amount of subdivision increases the level of polymorphism. For hard selection, where subdivisions contribute a fraction of individuals that is proportional to the mean fitness of the subdivision, increasing the amount of subdivision decreases the level of polymorphism.

- *Temporal autocorrelation*: Increasing the temporal autocorrelation of the environment always decreases the level of polymorphism.

Table 4.1 summarizes the mathematical formulae that lead to these conclusions. Biologically, these results show that flucutations in the environment can be a powerful force for the maintenance of genetic variation.

When drift and mutation are added to SAS-CFF models, the mathematics become horrendous. All of our results come from an asymptotic approach that assumes strong selection and weak mutation (SSWM for short). Under SSWM assumptions, we show that a symmetric k-allele SAS-CFF model collapses to a one-dimensional Markov chain whose state space is the number of interior alleles. Thus, we are able to describe the state of a population in terms of the times that alleles enter or leave the population. This is a powerful appraoch that allows a us to ignore many of the detailed dynamics and to concentrated on just those properties of populations that are most easily observed.

4.2 Haploids

Although haploid population genetics is not our main concern, several important properties of selection in a temporally fluctuating environment that are shared by haploid and diploid models may be investigated more easily in haploid models. Moreover, the diffusion approximation for the haploid model is almost identical to that of the additive diploid model. In certain cases, the diffusions are the same. The time spent investigating simple haploid models will prepare us for the less intuitive diploid models that lie ahead.

The haploid under scrutiny is a creature with one locus, k segregating alleles, separate generations, and an effectively infinite population size. The fitness of the ith allele in the tth generation will be written $w_i(t)$; its relative frequency in the population, $x_i(t)$, where $\sum_{i=1}^{k} x_i(t) = 1$. The change in the frequency of the ith allele in a single generation is given by

$$\Delta x_i(t) = x_i(t+1) - x_i(t) = \frac{x_i(t)[w_i(t) - \overline{w}(t)]}{\overline{w}(t)}, \qquad (4.1)$$

where

$$\overline{w}(t) = \sum_{i=1}^{k} x_i(t)w_i(t)$$

is the mean fitness of the population. The transformation

$$y_i(t) = \ln[x_i(t)/x_k(t)] \qquad (4.2)$$

takes the nonlinear difference equation 4.1 into the $k-1$ dimensional linear difference equation

$$\Delta y_i(t) = \ln[w_i(t)/w_k(t)], \quad i = 1, \ldots, k-1. \qquad (4.3)$$

Herein lies the secret to the haploid model's simplicity in the theory of selection in a temporally fluctuating environment. If the fitnesses happen to fluctuate at random, the transformed version is a random walk, a particularly simple stochastic processes. (No such transformation is known for diploid models.) Known results about random walks may be used to write down the distribution of the vector of allele frequencies at any generation. Alternatively, the solution to the diffusion equation may be used to the same end. Before following the latter course, some simple but fundamental properties of the two-allele case will be presented.

For the two-allele haploid model, it is sufficient to follow the frequency of the first allele, which we will call simply $x(t)$, and its transformed version,

$$y(t) = \ln[x(t)/(1 - x(t)]. \tag{4.4}$$

If the initial state is at $t = 0$, then the value of y at generation t, using equation 4.3, is

$$y(t) = y(0) + \sum_{i=0}^{t-1} \ln[w_1(i)/w_2(i)]. \tag{4.5}$$

Since $x(t)$ is a monotonically increasing function of $y(t)$,

$$x(t) = (1 + e^{-y})^{-1}, \tag{4.6}$$

its value depends monotonically on the sum in equation 4.5 which may be rewritten as

$$
\begin{aligned}
S(t) &= \sum_{i=0}^{t-1} \ln(w_1(i)/w_2(i)) \\
&= \ln\left[\prod_{i=0}^{t-1} \frac{w_1(i)}{w_2(i)}\right] \\
&= t\ln\left[\frac{\left(\prod_{i=0}^{t-1} w_1(i)\right)^{1/t}}{\left(\prod_{i=0}^{t-1} w_2(i)\right)^{1/t}}\right].
\end{aligned}
$$

The argument of the logarithm will be recognized as the ratio of the geometric mean fitnesses of the two alleles averaged across generations. For a particular sequence of environments, the frequency of the allele with the larger geometric mean fitness will increase. The geometric mean plays this central role due to the multiplicative nature of reproduction.

So far, the two-allele model has no probabilistic content. The sequence of fitnesses is known with certainty; as a consequence, so is the sequence of allele frequencies. There are many ways to add randomness; the simplest assumes that the collections $\{w_1(t)\}$ and $\{w_2(t)\}$, $t = 0, 1, \ldots$, each contain independent identically distributed (IID) random variables. In more biological terms, the environment in any particular generation is independent of all those in past generations. As a consequence of this assumption, $S(t)$ is random walk—a sum of IID random variables—making the wealth of results on random walks immediately available for our purposes.

The question of immediate interest concerns the eventual state of the population. Since the variance of $S(t)$ grows linearly with time,

$$\text{Var } S(t) = t \text{Var} \ln[w_1(t)/w_2(t)],$$

it is clear that the population will eventually be composed almost entirely of one allele or the other. Since the mean of $S(t)$ also changes linearly with time,

$$ES(t) = tE \ln[w_1(t)/w_2(t)],$$

it is also clear that the allele with the larger mean log fitness will eventually dominate the population,

$$\lim_{t \to \infty} x(t) = \begin{cases} 1 & \text{if } E \ln w_1(t) > E \ln w_2(t) \\ 0 & \text{if } E \ln w_1(t) < E \ln w_2(t) \ . \end{cases}$$

The geometric mean fitness of an allele is e raised to the power of the expected value of the logarithm of its fitness. Thus, the allele with the largest geometric mean fitness will eventually dominate in the population. This observation, due to Dempster [53], is the most important property of haploid selection in a random environment. Note that it carries with it the corollary that temporal fluctuations in fitness will not maintain a stable polymorphism when the two alleles have different geometric mean fitnesses.

The two-allele case with equal geometric means is particularly interesting. Because of the symmetry and the linear increase of the variance of $S(t)$ with time, it seems likely that $x(t)$ will be very close to zero or very close to one if t is sufficiently large. Similarly, if the population is examined at widely separated points in time, it seems likely that $x(t)$ will sometimes be near zero and sometimes near one, though almost never far away from one or the other. This suggests that the allele frequency will occasionally flip relatively rapidly across the intermediate frequencies. If these flips were to occur at a constant rate, the haploid model might provide a basis for an interesting model of continuing evolution without polymorphism. Sadly, this is not the case.

The easiest way to investigate the evolutionary aspects of the haploid model is to use the classical random walk as a model of the environment. Let

$$\ln[w_1(t)/w_2(t)] = \begin{cases} +s & \text{with probability } 1/2 \\ -s & \text{with probability } 1/2 \end{cases},$$

making $S(t)$ a random walk on a lattice with points at integer multiples of s.

Whenever $x(t)$ flips from near one to near zero, $S(t)$ will change from a very large positive value to a very large negative value, crossing zero in the process. A flip in allele frequency may be equated with the random walk crossing zero. The probability that $S(t)$ equals zero is the probability that the number of jumps in the positive direction exactly equals the number in the negative direction, which can only occur when t is an even number.

Since the direction of the jumps are independent from one generation to the next, the probability that there are t out of $2t$ in the positive direction is the binomial probability

$$\binom{2t}{t}\left(\frac{1}{2}\right)^{2t} \sim \frac{1}{\sqrt{\pi t}},$$

where the asymptotic form for large t uses Stirling's approximation. We conclude that the rate of crossing is inversely proportional to the square root of time* and thus that the simple haploid model cannot provide a model of continuing evolution.

The contrast between the symmetrical and asymmetrical cases is worth emphasizing. When the geometric mean fitnesses of the two alleles are not equal, the allele frequency will cross one-half a finite number of times. Such processes are called *transient* in probability theory [23, Section 3.7]. By contrast, when the geometric means are equal, the allele frequency will cross one-half infinitely often, although the interval between crossings increases with time. These processes are called *recurrent*. While this distinction is mainly of mathematical interest, it does suggest that the symmetrical case may exhibit some interesting properties if a small amount of mutation is added.

The distribution of $x(t)$ may be derived if some additional assumptions are entertained. For example, suppose the random variables

$$\ln[w_1(t)/w_2(t)]$$

are normally distributed with moments

$$\begin{aligned} E\ln[w_1(t)/w_2(t)] &= \mu \\ \operatorname{Var}\ln[w_1(t)/w_2(t)] &= \sigma^2. \end{aligned}$$

As a sum of normal random variables is also normal, $y(t)$ will be normally distributed with mean $y(0) + \mu t$ and variance $\sigma^2 t$. Its density is given by

$$\frac{1}{\sqrt{2\pi\sigma^2 t}}\exp\left[-\frac{(y - y(0) - \mu t)^2}{2\sigma^2 t}\right].$$

The density for $x(t)$ may be obtained by transforming the normal distribution with equation 4.6,

$$\frac{1}{\sqrt{2\pi\sigma^2 t}\,x(1-x)}\exp\left[-\frac{(\ln\frac{x(1-x(0))}{(1-x)x(0)} - \mu t)^2}{2\sigma^2 t}\right].$$

Direct examination of this density† shows that the probability mass will pile up near one if μ is positive, near zero if μ is negative, or at both end

---

*This and other facts about random walks may be found in Chapter 3 of Feller's book [70].

†This inelegant density has been dubbed the S_B distribution [144]. There are no simple expressions for any of its moments.

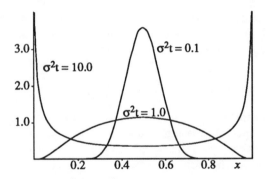

Figure 4.1. The transient density of the symmetrical haploid model.

points if μ is zero. The allele frequency will never actually equal zero or one because of our assumption that the population size is infinite. For this reason the boundaries are said to be *inaccessible*. Kimura [152] coined the term *quasi-fixation* to distinguish this behavior from the loss of variation through the fixation of alleles by genetic drift. An example of the change in the density with time is given in Figure 4.1.

The multiple-allele case could be investigated in an entirely analogous fashion using a $k-1$ dimensional random walk. However, the route to the diploid case will be made clearer if we forgo this approach in favor of one based on diffusion approximations. To obtain the approximating diffusion process for the multiple-allele case, we need the mean and covariance of the changes in the allele frequencies and some conditions to assure that these moments are small.

Selection will change things slowly if the fitnesses remain close to one. To emphasize this restriction, write

$$w_i(t) = 1 + Y_i(t),$$

where $Y_i(t)$ must remain near zero. Assume that $\{Y_i(t)\}$ is a collection of IID random variables with moments

$$EY_i(t) = \mu_i$$
$$\text{Cov}(Y_i(t), Y_j(t)) = \sigma_{ij}.$$

Assume further that the μ_i and σ_{ij} are small and of similar orders of magnitude and that all higher order moments of $Y_i(t)$ are of smaller orders of magnitude. This is a loaded assumption, one with important biological and mathematical ramifications. The former will be taken up later in the book; of the latter, note for now that this assumption permits us to write, for example,

$$EY_i(t)^2 = \sigma_{ii} + \mu_i^2 \approx \sigma_{ii}$$

because the first- and second-order moments are both small and of the same order of magnitude, implying that the square of the mean will be of a smaller order of magnitude. Similarly, $EY_i(t)^3$ is assumed to be so much smaller than $EY_i(t)^2$ that it may be ignored in all moment calculations, and so forth.

Using these assumptions, the mean change in the frequency of the ith allele may be approximated by

$$
\begin{aligned}
E\Delta x_i &= E\frac{x_i\left(Y_i - \sum_{j=1}^k x_j Y_j\right)}{1 + \sum_{j=1}^k x_j Y_j} &&(4.7)\\
&\approx x_i E(Y_i - \sum_{j=1}^k x_j Y_j)(1 - \sum_{j=1}^k x_j Y_j)\\
&= x_i E(Y_i - \sum_{j=1}^k x_j Y_j - \sum_{j=1}^k x_j Y_i Y_j + \sum_{i=1}^k \sum_{j=1}^k x_i x_j Y_i Y_j)\\
&\approx x_i(\mu_i - \sum_{i=1}^k x_i \mu_i - \sum_{j=1}^k x_j \sigma_{ij} + \sum_{i=1}^k \sum_{j=1}^k x_i x_j \sigma_{ij})\\
&= x_i(\mu_i - \bar{\mu} + \bar{\sigma} - \bar{\sigma}_i),
\end{aligned}
$$

where

$$
\bar{\mu} = \sum_{i=1}^k x_i \mu_i, \quad \bar{\sigma}_i = \sum_{j=1}^k x_j \sigma_{ij}, \quad \bar{\sigma} = \sum_{i=1}^k x_i \bar{\sigma}_i.
$$

This series of steps uses the familiar small ϵ approximation for the sum of a geometric series, $1/(1+\epsilon) \approx 1 - \epsilon$.

The second-order moments for the changes in allele frequencies are approximated by

$$
\begin{aligned}
E\Delta x_i \Delta x_j &\approx x_i x_j E(Y_i - \sum_{l=1}^k x_l Y_l)(Y_j - \sum_{l=1}^k x_l Y_l)\\
&\approx x_i x_j [\sigma_{ij} - \sum_{l=1}^k x_l(\sigma_{il} + \sigma_{jl}) + \sum_{i=1}^k \sum_{j=1}^k x_i x_j \sigma_{ij}]\\
&= x_i x_j(\sigma_{ij} + \bar{\sigma} - \bar{\sigma}_i - \bar{\sigma}_j).
\end{aligned}
$$

For all practical purposes, this completes the derivation of the diffusion. We have approximations for the mean and covariance of the change of allele frequencies that completely characterize the diffusion process. Using the notation of stochastic differential equations, the approximating diffusion may be written

$$
\begin{aligned}
E dx_i &= x_i(\mu_i - \bar{\mu} + \bar{\sigma} - \bar{\sigma}_i)dt &&(4.8)\\
E dx_i dx_j &= x_i x_j(\sigma_{ij} + \bar{\sigma} - \bar{\sigma}_i - \bar{\sigma}_j)dt,
\end{aligned}
$$

where we understand that time is now continuous, but is still measured in units of generations.

The derivation can be made more rigorous. The usual approach introduces a scaling parameter, say ϵ, and guarantees the order of magnitude assumptions on the moments by writing them as

$$
\begin{aligned}
EY_i(t) &= \mu_i \epsilon \\
E(Y_i(t)Y_j(t)) &= \sigma_{ij}\epsilon \\
EY_i(t)^m Y_j(t)^n &= o(\epsilon), m+n > 2.
\end{aligned}
$$

The final ingredient is a sequence of continuous time processes, indexed by ϵ,

$$
x_i^{(\epsilon)}(t) \equiv x_i([t/\epsilon]_{\text{GIF}}),
$$

where $[\cdot]_{\text{GIF}}$ is the greatest integer function. As ϵ approaches zero, the sequence of processes, $x_i^{(\epsilon)}(t)$ converges to equation 4.8. The only distinction involves the measurement of time. In the casual derivation time is measured in units of generations. In the rigorous approach, each unit of time corresponds to $1/\epsilon$ generation. The scalings on the moments guarantee that the two approaches give the same answer for any particular model.

For a thorough discussion of convergence as it applies to population genetics see the book by Ethier and Kurtz [64]. Issues of rigor are not of great concern for the haploid model because it is a transformed version of Brownian motion. The extensive literature on the convergence of random walks to Brownian motion gives us confidence that we are on firm footing.

The obvious route to the full transient solution of the haploid diffusion is to transform it into Brownian motion using equation 4.2, obtain the transient solution of the Brownian motion, then transform it back to the space of allele frequencies using the inverse of equation 4.2. Fortunately, most of the work has already been done, so we are spared what would otherwise be a lengthy calculation.

Instead of transforming the diffusion, it is easier to achieve the same end by deriving the diffusion approximation of the transformed difference equation 4.3. Use the small ϵ expansion,

$$
\ln(1+\epsilon) \sim \epsilon - \frac{1}{2}\epsilon^2,
$$

to get

$$
\begin{aligned}
E\ln[w_i(t)/w_k(t)] &= E\ln[1 + Y_i(t)] - E\ln[1 + Y_k(t)] \\
&\approx \gamma_i - \gamma_k,
\end{aligned}
$$

and

$$
E[\ln \frac{w_i(t)}{w_k(t)} \ln \frac{w_j(t)}{w_k(t}] \approx c_{ij},
$$

where

$$
\gamma_i = \mu_i - \frac{1}{2}\sigma_{ii} \tag{4.9}
$$

$$
c_{ij} = \text{Cov}[(Y_i - Y_k),(Y_j - Y_k)] = \sigma_{ij} - \sigma_{ik} - \sigma_{jk} + \sigma_{kk}. \tag{4.10}
$$

The quantities γ_i and c_{ij} appear frequently in the theory of selection in a random environment, so the reader should commit them to memory. The parameter γ_i is approximately the geometric mean fitness minus one; c_{ij} is the covariance of the fitness differentials.

The diffusion for the transformed process is thus the Brownian motion

$$E dy_i = (\gamma_i - \gamma_k) dt$$
$$E dy_i dy_j = c_{ij} dt.$$

The transient behavior of this process is described by a Gaussian distribution of the vector $\mathbf{y} = (y_1, \ldots, y_{k-1})$,

$$(2\pi)^{-\frac{1}{2}(k-1)} \mid \mathbf{C} \mid^{-\frac{1}{2}} e^{-\frac{1}{2}(\mathbf{y}-\mathbf{b})'\mathbf{C}^{-1}(\mathbf{y}-\mathbf{b})},$$

with mean vector

$$[\mathbf{b}]_i = y(0) + (\gamma_i - \gamma_k)t,$$

and covariance matrix

$$[\mathbf{C}]_{ij} = c_{ij} t.$$

To transform this into the distribution of allele frequencies, express $\mathbf{y}$ in terms of allele frequencies using equation 4.2,

$$\mathbf{y} = \left(\log \frac{x_1}{x_k}, \ldots, \log \frac{x_{k-1}}{x_k} \right),$$

use

$$y_i(0) = \ln[x_i(0)/x_k(0)]$$

in $\mathbf{b}$, and multiply the resulting function by the absolute value of the determinant of the Jacobian of the transformation,

$$\begin{vmatrix} \frac{1}{x_1} + \frac{1}{x_k} & \frac{1}{x_k} & \cdots & \frac{1}{x_k} \\ \frac{1}{x_k} & \frac{1}{x_2} + \frac{1}{x_k} & \cdots & \frac{1}{x_k} \\ \vdots & \vdots & \ddots & \vdots \\ \frac{1}{x_k} & \frac{1}{x_k} & \cdots & \frac{1}{x_{k-1}} + \frac{1}{x_k} \end{vmatrix} = (x_1 x_2 \cdots x_k)^{-1}. \qquad (4.11)$$

Direct examination of the solution shows that nothing much has changed from the two-allele case. The second-order moments of the transformed process still increase linearly with time, and the allele with the largest geometric mean fitness still wins.

Our transformation of the multiple-allele model conferred special status to the kth allele even though nothing about this allele sets it apart from the others. The transformation actually destroys some of the natural geometry of the process. This is seen in the diffusion for $\mathbf{y}$, which has moments of Y_k appearing in all of the drift and diffusion coefficients. There is a device for preserving the natural geometry when transforming to Brownian motion that was introduced by Notohara et al. [221]. Rather than following allele frequencies, they follow the logarithms of the total numbers of alleles. Let $z_i(t)$ be the logarithm of the total numbers of the ith allele. The difference equation for $z_i(t)$, viewing $w_i(t)$ as the total number of offspring of an allele, is

$$\Delta z_i(t) = \ln w_i(t) = \ln[1 + Y_i(t)].$$

The k-dimensional diffusion process for the logarithms of the total number of alleles is

$$E dz_i = \gamma_i dt$$
$$E dz_i dz_j = \sigma_{ij} dt.$$

The transient density of this Brownian motion is Gaussian with mean

$$[\mathbf{b}]_i = z(0) + \gamma_i t,$$

and covariance matrix

$$[\Sigma]_{ij} = \sigma_{ij} t.$$

This is certainly a more pleasing geometry than before.

   A price is extracted for this elegance when we attempt to transform the Gaussian process back to the space of allele frequencies. The Brownian motion is a k-dimensional process, while the space of allele frequencies lives in $k - 1$ dimensions. Thus, some device must be used to make the transformation one-to-one. One method adds an extra dimension—call it x_k—in the transformation, and then obtains the marginal distribution of the first $k - 1$ dimensions after the transformation is completed. The appropriate transformation is

$$x_i = \frac{e^{z_i}}{\sum_{j=1}^{k} e^{z_j}}, \quad i = 1, \ldots, k - 1$$

$$x_k = \sum_{j=1}^{k} e^{z_j}.$$

When the dust settles, the final result is the same as we obtained from the previous approach.

4.3   The c-haploid model

When we turn our attention to diploids, all of the niceties of haploid models evaporate. It is not simply the increase in parameters—roughly k^2 in one-locus haploid models compared with k^4 in diploid models—but also that the parameters do not enter in a symmetrical fashion. Real progress in multiple-allele models can only come by specializing to highly simplified versions of the general diploid model. Hopefully, the simplifications will be guided by biological rather than mathematical considerations. In the best of all worlds, the most convincing biological simplifications will also lead to the most tractable mathematics. This has been the case for a class of diploid models, affectionately known as SAS-CFF* models, which are closely related to haploid models. The biological motivation for these models rests on an assumption that the biochemical differences between alleles are very small and additive, heterozygotes being intermediate between their associated homozygotes. Mathematically, this underlying additivity allows SAS-CFF models to be developed as extensions of the haploid model.

The full range of SAS-CFF models includes such effects as dominance, temporal autocorrelations in the environment, and spatial subdivision. The analysis of each of these effects can be computationally exhausting, but experience has shown that the diffusion approximations that come out the other end are always of the same form, differing only in the interpretations placed on the parameters. In light of this experience, it now seems that the most natural way to develop the theory of SAS-CFF models is through an artificial model, called the c-haploid model, whose diffusion approximation exhibits the full dynamic behavior of SAS-CFF diffusions, yet is divorced of the computational nightmares.

The simplest example of a c-haploid model is a diploid model with the fitness of a heterozygote being exactly intermediate between that of the two associated homozygotes. That is, let the fitness of the $A_i A_j$ genotype be

$$w_{ij}(t) = 1 + [Y_i(t) + Y_j(t)]/2.$$

This is what we mean by no dominance or, equivalently, additive alleles. The change in the frequency of the ith allele in a single generation is

$$\Delta x_i = \frac{1}{2} \frac{x_i \left(Y_i - \sum_{j=1}^{k} x_j Y_j \right)}{1 + \sum_{j=1}^{k} x_j Y_j},$$

which is one-half the change in a haploid model with the fitness of the ith haploid allele set equal to the fitness of the $A_i A_i$ homozygote (compare to equation 4.7). The mean change, $E\Delta x_i$, is one-half the mean change of the haploid model, while $E\Delta x_i \Delta x_j$ is one-quarter the haploid value. The unexpected consequence of this factor of one-half is that the diffusion has a stationary solution, implying that the diploid model leads to stable polymorphism, as will be shown shortly.

The fact that the difference equation for the additive diploid model differs from that of the haploid model only in the factor of one-half suggests that a class of models worthy of consideration would be those with a general multiplier of the haploid model difference equation. If the multiplier is called c, we have the c-haploid model defined by the difference equation

$$\Delta x_i = c \frac{x_i \left(Y_i - \sum_{j=1}^{k} x_j Y_j \right)}{1 + \sum_{j=1}^{k} x_j Y_j}.$$

---

*Stochastic Additive Scale-Concave Fitness Function

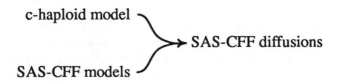

Figure 4.2. The relationships between models.

Life is made easier if we also assume that $\{Y_i(t)\}_{i=0}^{\infty}$ are collections of IID random variables.

The rich variety of dynamic behavior that results from multiplying the difference operator of the haploid model by the constant, c, is remarkable. In fact, the diffusion approximation to any diploid SAS-CFF model corresponds to that of a c-haploid model if the parameters of the c-haploid model are chosen appropriately. It must be stressed, however, that for most values of c, the c-haploid model does not correspond to any known diploid model. (An exception occurs when $c = 1/2$, which corresponds to the additive model.) Only when we allow the first- and second-order moments of $Y_i(t)$ to approach zero is the resulting diffusion the same as the diffusion of a more complex SAS-CFF model. Our strategy is clear: have fun studying the dynamics of the c-haploid model now, figure out how the parameters of the c-haploid model depend on assumptions about dominance and environmental fluctuations in real diploid models later.

The diffusion approximation to the c-haploid model is obtained by multiplying the drift coefficient of the haploid model (see equation 4.8) by c, and the diffusion coefficient by c^2,

$$\begin{aligned} Edx_i &= cx_i(\mu_i - \bar{\mu} + \bar{\sigma} - \bar{\sigma}_i)dt \qquad\qquad (4.12) \\ Edx_i dx_j &= c^2 x_i x_j(\sigma_{ij} + \bar{\sigma} - \bar{\sigma}_i - \bar{\sigma}_j)dt. \end{aligned}$$

For all of the diploid models that will be considered in the next section, c is less than or equal to one as will be assumed in all that follows.

At present, the only exact result that is known for the k-allele version of the diffusion equation 4.12 is the stationary distribution. This will be derived in the next subsection. Beyond this, the important results concerning the mean times and probabilities for alleles to become rare or common are only known through asymptotic expansions. These will be given in subsequent subsections.

The stationary distribution

The method of choice for finding the stationary distribution of a $(k - 1)$-dimensional diffusion process was introduced into population genetics by Kimura [154]. The basic idea is to assume that (at stationarity) there is no net flow of probability mass from one region of the state space to another. The flow in a specified direction is called the *probability flux* in that direction. Let the probability density for the process at time t be $\Psi(\mathbf{x}, t)$. The flux in the direction of the ith coordinate is

$$J_i(\mathbf{x}, t) = b_i(\mathbf{x})\Psi(\mathbf{x}, t) - \frac{1}{2}\sum_{j=1}^{k-1}\frac{\partial}{\partial x_j}[a_{ij}(\mathbf{x})\Psi(\mathbf{x}, t)]$$

for a diffusion with drift and diffusion coefficients

$$\begin{aligned}
Edx_i &= b_i(\mathbf{x})dt \\
Edx_i dx_j &= a_{ij}(\mathbf{x})dt.
\end{aligned}$$

Kimura's approach to finding the stationary distribution is to set the flux in each orthogonal direction equal to zero,

$$J_i(\mathbf{x}, t) = 0, \ i = 1, 2, \ldots, k-1, \tag{4.13}$$

and to solve the resulting system of first-order partial differential equations for the stationary distribution $\Psi(\mathbf{x})$, which is independent of t.

For the c-haploid model, solving this system of partial differential equations is a daunting task. It works, but a much easier method, due to Seno and Shiga [254], is to transform the diffusion into a more malleable form, get the stationary distribution for the transformed process, and then transform the distribution back to the original space of allele frequencies. It should come as no surprise that the transformation is the very one that carried the haploid diffusion into Brownian motion,

$$y_i = \log[x_i/x_k].$$

This is not a panacea: the algebra is messy. Fortunately, it is straightforward, and the answer collapses at the end to a very likable diffusion.

The drift coefficient of the transformed process is obtained via the Ito formula for change of variables,[*]

$$Edy_i = (\sum_{j=1}^{k-1}\frac{\partial y_i}{\partial x_j}Edx_j + \frac{1}{2}\sum_{j=1}^{k-1}\sum_{l=1}^{k-1}\frac{\partial^2 y_i}{\partial x_j \partial x_l}Edx_j dx_l)dt.$$

The first step in the calculation, using equation 4.12, is

$$\begin{aligned}
Edy_i = \Bigg[&\sum_{j=1}^{k-1}(\frac{1}{x_k} + \frac{\delta_{ij}}{x_i})cx_j(\mu_j - \bar{\mu} + \bar{\sigma} - \bar{\sigma}_j) \\
&+ \frac{1}{2}\sum_{j=1}^{k-1}\sum_{l=1}^{k-1}(\frac{1}{x_k^2} - \frac{\delta_{ij}\delta_{il}}{x_i^2})c^2 x_j x_l(\sigma_{jl} + \bar{\sigma} - \bar{\sigma}_j - \bar{\sigma}_l) \Bigg] dt,
\end{aligned}$$

---

[*]A discussion of Ito's formula may be found in Gardiner's book [79, p. 95].

where $\delta_{ii} = 1$ and $\delta_{ij} = 0$ for $i \neq j$. From here on everything is pretty routine.

The initial strategy is to express all of the sums from 1 to $k-1$ as sums from 1 to k. This will introduce a lot of overbar terms (like $\bar{\mu}$) that will ultimately cancel. For example, use

$$\sum_{j=1}^{k-1} x_j \sigma_{ij} = \bar{\sigma}_i - x_k \sigma_{ik}.$$

After a few lines you will get to the following:

$$c(\mu_i - \mu_k) - \frac{c^2}{2}(\sigma_{ii} - \sigma_{kk}) - (c - c^2)(\bar{\sigma}_i - \bar{\sigma}_k).$$

At this point the strategy should be reversed, and the two overbar terms should be written as sums from 1 to $k-1$,

$$\bar{\sigma}_i - \bar{\sigma}_k = \sum_{j=1}^{k-1} x_j c_{ij} + \sigma_{ik} - \sigma_{kk},$$

where we have reintroduced the notation (see equation 4.10),

$$c_{ij} = \sigma_{ij} - \sigma_{ik} - \sigma_{jk} + \sigma_{kk}.$$

Finally, we get

$$Edy_i = [c(\gamma_i - \gamma_k) + \frac{1}{2}c^2(B-1)c_{ii} - c^2(B-1)\sum_{j=1}^{k-1} x_j c_{ij}]dt,$$

where

$$\gamma_i = \mu_i - \frac{1}{2}\sigma_{ii}, \ B = c^{-1}.$$

The use of the parameter B may seem redundant, but there are two good reasons for introducing it. The first is that many of the results turn out to be functions of $1/c$ rather than c, so we benefit from streamlined notation. The second is historical: B has a small but enthusiastic following. To use $1/c$ in its place would be unconscionable!

Note that the drift coefficient is written as if it were still a function of x_i; this is done for notational convenience. The x_i are actually functions of the y_i through the inverse transformation,

$$x_i = \frac{e^{y_i}}{1 + \sum_{j=1}^{k-1} e^{y_j}}.$$

The transformed diffusion coefficient may be derived in an entirely analogous manner. The Ito formula in this case is

$$Edy_i dy_j = (\sum_{l=1}^{k-1} \sum_{m=1}^{k-1} \frac{\partial y_i}{\partial x_l} \frac{\partial y_j}{\partial x_m} Edx_l dx_m)dt.$$

The first step is

$$Edy_i dy_j = \sum_{l=1}^{k-1} \sum_{m=1}^{k-1} \left(\frac{1}{x_k^2} + \frac{\delta_{il}}{x_i} + \frac{\delta_{jm}}{x_j} + \frac{\delta_{il}\delta_{jm}}{x_i x_j} \right) c^2 x_l x_m (\sigma_{lm} + \bar{\sigma} - \bar{\sigma}_l - \bar{\sigma}_m) dt.$$

A shorter calculation than that for the drift coefficient yields the diffusion coefficient

$$Edy_i dy_j = c^2 c_{ij} dt.$$

In summary, the transformed diffusion has drift coefficients

$$b_i(\mathbf{y}) = [c(\gamma_i - \gamma_k) + \frac{1}{2}c^2(B-1)c_{ii} - c^2(B-1)\sum_{j=1}^{k-1} x_j c_{ij}] \qquad (4.14)$$

and diffusion coefficients

$$a_{ij}(\mathbf{y}) = c^2 c_{ij}. \qquad (4.15)$$

This process has a clear advantage over the original diffusion in that the diffusion coefficient is constant.

It is now time to find the stationary distribution, $\Psi(\mathbf{y})$, for the transformed diffusion. Following Kimura, we will not work with the stationary distribution directly, but rather with a new function

$$\psi(\mathbf{y}) = \log[\Psi(\mathbf{y})]. \qquad (4.16)$$

When ψ is plugged into the zero probability flux, equation 4.13, and the signs are reversed, we obtain

$$-b_i(\mathbf{y}) + \frac{1}{2}\sum_{j=1}^{k-1} \frac{\partial a_{ij}}{\partial y_j} + \frac{1}{2}\sum_{j=1}^{k-1} a_{ij} \frac{\partial \psi}{\partial y_j} = 0. \qquad (4.17)$$

Here is where all of our hard work pays off. Since a_{ij} is equal to the constant $c^2 c_{ij}$, the first sum in this equation is zero.

From equation 4.14 we get the drift coefficient $b_i(\mathbf{y})$ for equation 4.17, giving

$$\sum_{j=1}^{k-1} c_{ij} \frac{\partial \psi}{\partial y_j} = m_i - 2(B-1)\sum_{j=1}^{k-1} c_{ij} x_j,$$

where

$$m_i = 2B(\gamma_i - \gamma_k) + (B-1)c_{ii}.$$

These equations may be viewed as a system of linear equations in $\partial \psi / \partial y_j$. The system may be written in matrix notation by introducing the matrix $\mathbf{C}$ with components c_{ij}, and the vectors $\mathbf{m}$ with components m_i, $\mathbf{x}$ with components x_i, and ψ with components $\partial \psi / \partial y_j$.

Equation 4.17 now becomes

$$\mathbf{C}\psi = \mathbf{m} - 2(B-1)\mathbf{C}\mathbf{x}.$$

Multiplying both sides by $\mathbf{C}^{-1}$ yields the solution

$$\psi = \beta - 2(B-1)\mathbf{x},$$

where

$$\beta = \mathbf{C}^{-1}\mathbf{m} \qquad (4.18)$$

is a vector with components β_i.

We can write the ith member of the solution as

$$\frac{\partial \psi}{\partial y_i} = \beta_i - 2(B-1)\frac{e^{y_i}}{1+\sum_{j=1}^{k-1} e^{y_j}},$$

which may be integrated to

$$\psi = \text{constant} + \beta_i y_i - 2(B-1)\log(1+\sum_{j=1}^{k-1} e^{y_j}),$$

where the "constant" of integration may depend on $y_j, j \neq i$. In fact, the equivalence of all of the dimensions immediately suggests that the "constant" will be a sum with terms $\beta_j y_j$, giving

$$\psi = C + \sum_{i=1}^{k-1} \beta_i y_i - 2(B-1)\log(1+\sum_{j=1}^{k-1} e^{y_j}),$$

where C is a constant that does not depend on any of the y_i. Raising this to the power e (the inverse of the transformation in equation 4.16) gives the stationary distribution for the transformed process,

$$\Psi(\mathbf{y}) = \frac{C\exp(\sum_{i=1}^{k-1} \beta_i y_i)}{(1+\sum_{j=1}^{k-1} e^{y_j})^{2(B-1)}}.$$

To transform this distribution back to the space of allele frequencies, use

$$y_i = \log(x_i/x_k)$$

and the determinant of the Jacobian of this transformation (4.11),

$$(x_1 x_2 \ldots x_k)^{-1},$$

to get the stationary distribution of allele frequencies,

$$\Psi(\mathbf{x}) = \Gamma(2B-2)\prod_{i=1}^{k} x_i^{\beta_i - 1}/\Gamma(\beta_i), \qquad (4.19)$$

where

$$\beta_k = 2(B-1) - \sum_{i=1}^{k-1} \beta_i. \qquad (4.20)$$

The distribution in equation 4.19 is called the Dirichlet distribution.* The only restrictions on the Dirichlet parameters are that

$$\beta_i > 0, i = 1, \ldots, k. \tag{4.21}$$

These, in turn, impose conditions on the parameters of the c-haploid model that must be met for there to be a stationary distribution with all k alleles segregating. The conditions are only interesting in the context of particular models, so further discussion on them will be deferred until the next section.

The Dirichlet stationary distribution for a c-haploid with symmetric second-order moments was first published by Gillespie [83]. The stationary distribution for models with asymmetric second-order moments (equation 4.19) is due to Turelli [282] who called his model the SOS model (for Son of SAS-CFF).

Nothing in our derivation guarantees that the stationary distribution is unique. That the Dirichlet distribution is the unique stationary distribution that satisfies the zero probability flux condition was proven by Seno and Shiga [254]. Their paper also contains a weak convergence proof showing that our diffusion is a bona fide limit of a discrete SAS-CFF model. There remains the unlikely possibility that a stationary distribution exists that does not satisfy the zero probability flux condition.

Many of the important properties of the Dirichlet distribution may be derived from the marginal distributions of individual alleles. Among these are the mean homozygosity and the frequency spectrum. Note, however, that there is no one-dimensional "marginal diffusion." In this regard the SAS-CFF diffusion differs from its neutral counterpart.

The marginal distribution of the ith allele is obtained by integrating $\Psi(\mathbf{x})$ with respect to x_j for $j = 1, \ldots, k-1$ but $j \neq i$,

$$\Psi_i(x_i) = \frac{\Gamma(2B-2)}{\Gamma(\beta_i)\Gamma(2B-2-\beta_i)} x_i^{\beta_i-1} (1-x_i)^{2(B-1)-\beta_i-1}.$$

This is a beta distribution with moments

$$Ex_i = \frac{\beta_i}{2(B-1)} \tag{4.22}$$

$$\operatorname{Var} x_i = \frac{2(B-1)\beta_i - \beta_i^2}{4(B-1)^2(2B-1)} \tag{4.23}$$

$$Ex_i^2 = \frac{1}{2B-1} Ex_i + \frac{2(B-1)}{2B-1}(Ex_i)^2. \tag{4.24}$$

Using these moments, it is easy to obtain the mean homozygosity,

$$E\mathcal{F}_k = \sum_{i=1}^{k} Ex_i^2 = \frac{1}{2B-1}\left[1 + \frac{1}{2(B-1)}\sum_{i=1}^{k}\beta_i^2\right]. \tag{4.25}$$

*A particularly captivating introduction to the distribution as well as some interesting applications may be found in a paper by Kingman [165].

Similarly, the frequency spectrum, $\zeta(x)$, is

$$\sum_{i=1}^{k} \Psi_i(x) = \Gamma(2B-2)(1-x)^{2(B-1)} \sum_{i=1}^{k} \frac{[x/(1-x)]^{\beta_i-1}}{\Gamma(\beta_i)\Gamma(2B-2-\beta_i)}.$$

Recall that the frequency spectrum has the interpretation that its integral,

$$\int_a^b \zeta(x)dx,$$

is the mean number of alleles found in the interval (a, b). The significance of these general results becomes clear as we now specialize to some symmetrical cases that have proven useful in various applications.

The most important case is a totally symmetrical model defined by $\mu_i = \mu$ and

$$\sigma_{ij} = \begin{cases} (1+r)\sigma^2 & \text{if } i=j \\ r\sigma^2 & \text{otherwise.} \end{cases}$$

This form of the symmetrical moments was chosen to simplify the parameters that appear in the resulting diffusions. The correlation between $Y_i(t)$ and $Y_j(t)$ is given by

$$\rho = \frac{\sigma_{ij}}{\sqrt{\sigma_{ii}\sigma_{jj}}} = \frac{r}{1+r}.$$

In most of the published work on symmetrical SAS-CFF models, the basic parameters are σ^2 and ρ rather than σ^2 and r. The conversion between the two is simple enough, so we will adopt the latter convention for its significant contributions to more elegant answers.

The symmetry assumptions transform the diffusion (4.12) into

$$\begin{aligned} E dx_i &= c^2\sigma^2 Bx_i(\mathcal{F}_k - x_i)dt \\ E dx_i dx_j &= c^2\sigma^2 x_i x_j(\delta_{ij} + \mathcal{F}_k - x_i - x_j)dt \end{aligned} \tag{4.26}$$

with the aid of

$$\begin{aligned} \bar{\sigma} &= \sigma^2 r + \sigma^2 \mathcal{F}_k \\ \bar{\sigma}_i &= \sigma^2 r + \sigma^2 x_i. \end{aligned}$$

The stationary distribution in this case is the Dirichlet

$$\frac{\Gamma(2B-2)}{\Gamma((2B-2)/k)^k} \prod_{i=1}^{k} x_i^{2(B-1)/k-1}. \tag{4.27}$$

In deriving equation 4.27 from equation 4.19 we used

$$\beta_i = 2(B-1)/k.$$

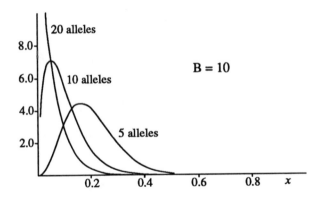

Figure 4.3. Marginal distributions for the symmetrical c-haploid model.

There are two ways to justify this. The first appeals to the symmetry of the model and the fact that the sum of the betas equals $2(B - 1)$. The second uses the definition of β directly. For the symmetrical case, the matrix $\mathbf{C}$ is

$$[\mathbf{C}]_{ij} = \begin{cases} 2\sigma^2 & \text{if } i = j \\ \sigma^2 & \text{otherwise,} \end{cases}$$

with inverse

$$[\mathbf{C}^{-1}]_{ij} = \begin{cases} (k-1)/k\sigma^2 & \text{if } i = j \\ -1/k\sigma^2 & \text{otherwise.} \end{cases}$$

Each component in the vector $\mathbf{m}$ is

$$2(B - 1)\sigma^2,$$

so $\beta = \mathbf{C}^{-1}\mathbf{m}$ is a vector with components $2(B - 1)/k$. The conditions for the existence of the stationary distribution, $\beta_i > 0$, become simply $B > 1$.

Examples of the marginal distribution for $B = 10$ and different numbers of alleles are illustrated in Figure 4.3. As the number of alleles increases, the marginal distribution shifts from one with a mode near $1/k$ to one with a mode at zero. The critical value for the shift is $k = 2(B - 1)$. When there is an interior mode, the distribution approaches zero as $x \to 0$. If k is greater than $2(B - 1)$, the probability mass approaches infinity as $x \to 0$. This difference has a profound effect on the fate of alleles when genetic drift is introduced. In the former case selection retards the loss of variation; in the latter, selection accelerates the loss.

The mean homozygosity for the symmetrical case is, from equation 4.25,

$$E\mathcal{F}_k = \frac{1}{2B - 1} + \frac{2(B - 1)}{k(2B - 1)}. \tag{4.28}$$

As the number of alleles increases to infinity,

$$\lim_{k \to \infty} E\mathcal{F}_k = \frac{1}{2B - 1}. \tag{4.29}$$

The frequency spectrum for finite k is

$$\zeta_k(x) = \frac{\Gamma(2B-2)x^{2(B-1)/k-1}(1-x)^{2(B-1)(k-1)/k+1}}{\Gamma((2B-2)/k)\Gamma((2B-2)(1-1/k))}.$$

As the number of alleles increases,

$$\lim_{k\to\infty} \zeta_k(x) = 2(B-1)x^{-1}(1-x)^{2B-1}.$$

These formulae should have a familiar ring: they are in exactly the same form as the equivalent formulae from the neutral model. A comparison shows that $2(B-1)$ plays the same role in SAS-CFF models as does $4Nu$ in neutral models. In fact, the Dirichlet distribution itself is the stationary distribution of both models. This has the distressing implication that there can be no way to use observations on allele frequencies from a single point in time to distinguish between these two models.

While it seems obvious at this point that the sampling distributions for neutral and SAS-CFF models are the same, the argument has a few twists that should be noted. First among these is that the sameness cannot follow from Ewens' original derivation of his sampling distribution [67] as this was based on the dynamics of neutral alleles. Rather, the sameness follows from a theorem due to Kingman [166].

In an earlier paper, Kingman [165] investigated the limiting form of the k-dimensional Dirichlet distribution as k approaches infinity. This is an interesting problem in its own right since an examination of equation 4.27 shows that something strange happens at the limit: all of the marginal distributions pile up at zero. Thus, the probability that any particular allele is found in a closed interval that does not include zero is zero; yet, the homozygosity of the population is not one. Kingman pointed out that the correct way to describe this peculiar limit is through order statistics. Denote by $x_{(i)}$ the frequency of the ith most common allele. For finite k we have

$$x_{(1)} \geq x_{(2)} \geq \ldots \geq x_{(k)}.$$

As $k \to \infty$, the distribution of these order statistics approaches a non-degenerate limit called the Poisson Dirichlet distribution. Kingman showed that samples from a Poisson Dirichlet distribution conform to the Ewens sampling distribution. Thus, samples from the infinite-allele symmetrical SAS-CFF model will also exhibit the Ewens sampling distribution.

Asymmetries may be introduced in a relatively painless fashion if we relax only our assumption of equal means. The diffusion in this case is

$$\begin{aligned} Edx_i &= x_i[c(\mu_i - \bar{\mu}) + c^2\sigma^2 B(\mathcal{F}_k - x_i)]dt & (4.30)\\ Edx_idx_j &= c^2\sigma^2 x_i x_j(\delta_{ij} + \mathcal{F}_k - x_i - x_j)dt. \end{aligned}$$

The matrix $\mathbf{C}$ is the same as in the symmetrical model, but the ith component of $\mathbf{m}$ becomes

$$2B(\mu_i - \mu_k) + 2(B-1)\sigma^2.$$

The ith component of the product, $C^{-1}m$, is now

$$\beta_i = \frac{2(B-1)}{k} + \frac{2B\sum_{j=1}^{k}(\mu_i - \mu_j)}{k\sigma^2}.$$

For all k alleles to remain in the population we require β_i to be positive (see equation 4.21), or

$$B\sum_{j=1}^{k}(\mu_j - \mu_i) < (B-1)\sigma^2. \tag{4.31}$$

This interesting condition illustrates the tension between mean effects, which tend to eliminate alleles from the population, and variance effects, which tend to promote polymorphism.

For any set of μ_i, it is always possible to find a σ^2 that is large enough to maintain all of the alleles. Conversely, for any σ^2 it is always possible to find an allele with a large enough μ_i to prevent the stable coexistence of the other $k - 1$ alleles. A possible implication of this observation is that species that live in more variable environments (i. e., have a larger σ^2) should have more segregating alleles. However, in the symmetrical model the stationary distribution is independent of σ^2, suggesting that there should be no relationship between the variability in the environment and the genetic variation. The relationship between environmental and genetic variation will be made even less certain when we consider the effects of environmental subdivision.

For the symmetrical neutral and SAS-CFF models, the infinite-allele cases have proven to be the most important in applications. It is natural, therefore, to explore infinite-allele limits for the asymmetrical SAS-CFF model. In doing this, we will be particularly interested in finding limiting distributions other than the Poisson Dirichlet distribution. The relevant theorem is again due to Kingman [165] who provided sufficient conditions for the convergence of a Dirichlet distribution to the Poisson Dirichlet distribution as k approaches infinity,

$$\beta_1 + \beta_2 + \ldots + \beta_k \to \lambda < \infty$$

$$\max(\beta_1, \beta_2, \ldots, \beta_k) \to 0.$$

In our case the sum of the betas is always equal to $2(B - 1)$, so the first of these two conditions is always met. Thus, our search for strange limits has been dealt an initial blow that, while not fatal, must severely restrict the class of inifinite-dimensional distributions that may be reached.

As an initial example, consider the case where all of the mean effects are equally spaced. One way to accomplish this is by setting

$$\mu_i = \frac{2\epsilon i}{k(k-1)}.$$

To satisfy the conditions for polymorphism from equation 4.31 with all k alleles segregating, we need only guarantee that $\beta_1 > 0$ as allele one is, on average, the least fit. This will happen when

$$\epsilon < (B-1)\sigma^2/B.$$

Assuming that ϵ has this property, we may then ask whether the limiting distribution, as k approaches infinity, is Poisson Dirichlet.

Kingman's second condition applies to the largest of the β_i, which for this example is

$$\beta_k = \frac{2(B-1)}{k} + \frac{2B\epsilon}{k\sigma^2}.$$

Clearly, β_k does approach zero so the limiting distribution is, in fact, a Poisson Dirichlet distribution.

Why should such a manifestly asymmetrical model yield a symmetrical limit? The reason follows immediately from the requirement that all k alleles be held in a polymorphic state. It is this condition that forces the spacing between alleles to be inversely proportional to $k(k-1)$, which, in turn, forces the difference, $\mu_k - \mu_1$, to be inversely proportional to k. Thus, as more alleles are entertained, the total spread of their mean values actually shrinks.

If we are to find a more exotic limit, it must come from a case where alleles may be added without having to shrink the total range of their mean values. An obvious candidate is a model where there are a few good alleles, with masses of ordinary alleles. For example, suppose allele one has mean effect $\mu_1 = 0$ while the mean effects of the other $k-1$ alleles are $-\epsilon$. The condition for polymorphism from equation 4.31 in this instance is

$$\epsilon < (B-1)\sigma^2/B.$$

As k increases,

$$\beta_1 \to 2B\epsilon/\sigma^2,$$

while $\beta_i, i > 1$ approaches zero. Thus, Kingman's second condition is not satisfied so we are facing a new infinite-allele stationary distribution.

The marginal distribution for allele one does not degenerate, being a beta distribution with parameters β_1 and $2(B-1) - \beta_1$, where the limiting value for β_1 is used. The marginal distribution of the remaining alleles approaches a Poisson Dirichlet distribution, as is easily verified by integrating the k-allele Dirichlet distribution with respect to x_1 and allowing k to approach infinity. This is an interesting result in several respects. From a biological point of view, we have a case that resembles mutation-selection balance. There is a "good" allele with average frequency

$$\frac{\beta_1}{2(B-1)} = \frac{B\epsilon}{(B-1)\sigma^2}$$

and $k - 1$ "bad" alleles, each with average frequency

$$\frac{\beta_2}{2(B-1)} = \frac{1}{k-1}\left(1 - \frac{B\epsilon}{(B-1)\sigma^2}\right).$$

Not only is the marginal distribution of the $k - 1$ lesser alleles a Poisson Dirichlet, but so is their distribution conditioned on the frequency of the first allele and renormalized to one. In this regard, their distribution is exactly like that of alleles that are held in the population by the balance between mutation and selection. This, coupled with the result from the symmetrical case that the distribution of SAS-CFF alleles is the same as that of neutral alleles, gives support to the view that one sample from a population is not useful for distinguishing between these models.

There is no reason to stop with only one good allele; the same approach will work with a finite set of good alleles, providing that the conditions for polymorphism are met. The infinite-allele distribution, in general, will have a Dirichlet marginal distribution for the good alleles and a Poisson-Dirichlet marginal distribution for the bad alleles. This suggests that the class of all infinite-allele distributions may be limited to those with these marginal properties.

Little is gained by moving to more general models. The models that we examined allow for an independent β_i for each allele. As the stationary distribution depends only on the betas, no new properties can be uncovered by considering more general models. They may be important, however, when one attempts to relate the betas to some underlying biological situation; this will be covered in a later section.

Hitting probabilities

For the study of molecular evolution, we need the probability that an allele enters or exits the population and the mean time required for this to happen. With these in hand, the rate of molecular evolution as well as the number of alleles that are found in the population may be derived. Unfortunately, there are no exact results available for any of these problems. It is a simple matter to write down, for example, the equation satisfied by the mean time to lose an allele from the population. It is another matter entirely to solve it. Thus, as we reluctantly turn away from stationary distributions, we leave behind the only known exact results for the multiple-allele c-haploid model. From here on, it is a world dominated by approximations. Our main task is to develop an approach for approximating the probabilities that interesting things happen and for the mean times until they do.

The approach that will be used is a slight variant on the technique introduced by Matkowsky and Schuss [204], which is suited to systems that exhibit boundary layer dynamics. For the c-haploid model, the mean and variance of the change in the frequencies of rare alleles are much smaller than that of common alleles. This is evident in the fact that the drift coefficient of a particular allele is proportional to its frequency and the diffusion coefficient is proportional to the square of its frequency. The time scale of change of rare alleles is thus much longer than that of common alleles.

The identification of different time scales is a key ingredient in the approximation of many processes in the physical sciences. An example that is not unlike our own is called the adiabatic elimination of fast variables.* In our case, the fast variables are the common alleles and the slow variables are the rare alleles. This differs from the more usual case in which the speed of variables is dictated by parameters rather than the values of the variables themselves. It will emerge that the difference in time scales is necessary but not sufficient for the existence of a boundary layer. In addition, we will discover that the diffusion process must be stationary.

In this section we will be examining hitting probabilities: the probability that a particular allele is the first to leave the interior of the population. In subsequent sections we will take up the mean time for this to occur and the entry probabilities and times. As the method is new to population genetics, the approach will be leisurely—almost pedagogical. It will begin with the two-allele case where everything is elementary, then proceed to three alleles where things begin to get hairy. The only cases that will be considered are those with symmetrical second-order moments. This restriction is done solely for convenience; the approach should work—albeit tediously—for asymmetrical moments as well. To date, no one has taken on the more general cases.

Consider the two-allele version of the c-haploid model with symmetrical second-order moments and unequal means. We will follow the first allele and shorten the symbol for its frequency to x. The drift coefficient in this case is, from equation 4.30,

$$b(x) = x[c(\mu_1 - \overline{\mu}) + c^2\sigma^2 B(\mathcal{F}_2 - x)].$$

Writing the coefficient in this form preserves its origins but is an obstacle to performing some of the calculations. Replacing all occurrences of x_2 with $1 - x$ and performing a modicum of algebra changes the drift coefficient into the more manageable

$$b(x) = x(1 - x)[c(\mu_1 - \mu_2) + c^2\sigma^2 B(1 - 2x)].$$

Similarly, the diffusion coefficient becomes

$$a(x) = 2c^2\sigma^2 x^2(1 - x)^2.$$

The hitting problem that we are interested in is the probability that allele one, with initial frequency x, hits the small frequency ϵ before allele two does. That is, we want to know the probability that x leaves the interval

---

*Gardiner's book [79] is an excellent source for this and many other applications of diffusion processes.

$(\epsilon, 1 - \epsilon)$ for the first time via the left end point. Call this probability $u_1(x)$, the subscript one reminding us that we are following allele one. The probability satisfies the differential equation

$$\frac{1}{2}a(x)u_1''(x) + b(x)u_1'(x) = 0 \qquad (4.32)$$

with boundary conditions $u_1(\epsilon) = 1$ and $u_1(1 - \epsilon) = 0$. The solution is*

$$u_1(x) = \frac{\int_x^{1-\epsilon} \psi(y)dy}{\int_\epsilon^{1-\epsilon} \psi(y)dy},$$

where

$$\psi(y) = \exp\left(-2\int^y \frac{b(z)}{a(z)}dz\right).$$

For our case

$$\psi(y) = y^{-B(\mu_1-\mu_2)/\sigma^2 - B}(1 - y)^{B(\mu_1-\mu_2)/\sigma^2 - B}.$$

This brings us face to face with a problem that plagues the theory of selection in a random environment: the integral of $\psi(y)$ cannot be expressed as a finite number of elementary functions, hence the need for approximations.

Usually, approximations are obtained through an asymptotic analysis of the integral of ψ. This works quite well in the two-allele case, but will not generalize to more than two alleles where the exact solution to the differential equation is not available. There is no multiple-allele integral to explore with asymptotic techniques. Thus, if we expect to find an approach that will work with any number of alleles, it must be based on the differential equation rather than on its solution.

Consider the case where the parameters are such that a stationary distribution exits. If ϵ is very small, it will take a long time for an allele to reach the end point of the interval. Before it gets there, it will have moved around the interior, passing through most of the points many times. This suggests that the probability that it hits ϵ before $1 - \epsilon$ will be fairly insensitive to the initial frequency of the allele. In fact, as ϵ approaches zero, the probability should become independent of the initial frequency. Suddenly things look promising: rather than trying to find a function, $u_1(x)$, we are now interested in a number, call it C_0. If, in a fit of naiveté, we set $u_1(x) = C_0$ and plug it into the differential equation, we see that, by chance, it satisfies the equation. However, we cannot fit the boundary conditions: a constant cannot equal both zero and one.

We arrived at this impasse by assuming that $u_1(x)$ is independent of x. The argument that we used made sense for common alleles, but what about rare alleles? If the initial frequency is very close to ϵ, then it no longer

---

*The derivation and solution of this equation may be found in any treatment of exit probabilities for diffusions, including the books by Gardiner [79, p. 143] and Ewens [68, p. 119].

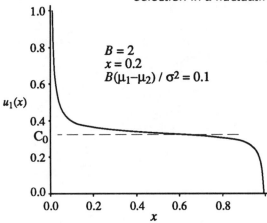

Figure 4.4. The hitting probability for the two-allele c-haploid model.

seems reasonable that the hitting probability is independent of x. However, consider the fate of an allele that does begin close to ϵ. Two things could happen: either it hits ϵ before becoming common or it doesn't. In the latter case, its probability of hitting ϵ is once again C_0 as it has returned to the interior. In the former case, the probability of hitting ϵ will surely depend on its initial frequency. But, as all of its activity is in the boundary layer, we could hope to approximate its dynamics in this tiny portion of the state space with some simpler process. Should we succeed, and also be able to repeat the analysis when x is close to $1-\epsilon$, we will have removed the problem of meeting the boundary conditions by providing one set of approximations for $u_1(x)$ near the boundaries and a different approximation in the interior. An example of $u_1(x)$ is shown in Figure 4.4 for the case $\epsilon = 0.01$, along with a horizontal line that represents C_0. The figure illustrates our intuition rather well.

Turning this intuition into mathematics involves a trick that, in effect, forces most of the action into the boundary layer. It is easier to show how this is done by using the general one-dimensional diffusion process rather than the particular case of the c-haploid diffusion. It also helps to introduce a notation based on forward and backward operators that allows most of the ideas from the derivation to be extended immediately to higher dimensions. Using this concise notation, equation 4.32 satisfied by the hitting probability, u, may be written

$$L[u(x)] = 0, \tag{4.33}$$

where L is the backward operator,

$$L = \frac{1}{2}a(x)\frac{d^2}{dx^2} + b(x)\frac{d}{dx}.$$

We will also make use of the solution to the equation

$$L^*[v(x)] = 0,$$

where L^* is the forward operator—the adjoint of L,

$$L^*[v(x)] = \frac{1}{2}\frac{d^2}{dx^2}[a(x)v(x)] - \frac{d}{dx}[b(x)v(x)].$$

Should the diffusion have a stationary density, the density will satisfy $L^*[v] = 0$, as we saw in the previous section. So will any function formed by multiplying this density by a constant. In our modification of the Matkowsky and Schuss technique, it will be assumed throughout that the diffusion process does have a stationary distribution, and that it satisfies the zero probability flux condition

$$\frac{1}{2}\frac{d}{dx}[a(x)v(x)] - b(x)v(x) = 0.$$

However, the $v(x)$ that we use will not, in general, be a density since it will not be normalized.

The first step of the Matkowsky and Schuss approach multiplies both sides of the equation $L[u] = 0$ by v, and integrates over the interval $(\epsilon, 1-\epsilon)$:

$$\int_{\epsilon}^{1-\epsilon} v(x)L[u(x)]dx = 0.$$

The integrand, $vL[u]$, may be modified by adding and subtracting the term

$$\frac{1}{2}\frac{d}{dx}[a(x)v(x)]\frac{du(x)}{dx}$$

to give

$$
\begin{aligned}
v(x)L[u(x)] &= \frac{1}{2}\left[a(x)v(x)\frac{d^2u(x)}{dx^2} + \frac{d}{dx}[a(x)v(x)]\frac{du(x)}{dx}\right] \\
&\quad - \frac{du(x)}{dx}\left[\frac{1}{2}\frac{d}{dx}[a(x)v(x)] - b(x)v(x)\right].
\end{aligned}
$$

The assumption that v satisfies the zero probability flux condition means that the second term in square brackets will be zero. The first term in square brackets will be recognized as the derivative of a product, giving

$$v(x)L[u(x)] = \frac{1}{2}\frac{d}{dx}\left[a(x)v(x)\frac{du(x)}{dx}\right].$$

Thus, by the simple trick of multiplying $L[u]$ by v, we put the integrand into a form where it is readily integrated:

$$\int_{\epsilon}^{1-\epsilon} v(x)L[u(x)]dx = \frac{1}{2}a(1-\epsilon)v(1-\epsilon)\frac{du(1-\epsilon)}{dx} - \frac{1}{2}a(\epsilon)v(\epsilon)\frac{du(\epsilon)}{dx}.$$

The equation 4.33, which is satisfied by the hitting probability, is now

$$a(1-\epsilon)v(1-\epsilon)\frac{du(1-\epsilon)}{dx} - a(\epsilon)v(\epsilon)\frac{du(\epsilon)}{dx} = 0. \qquad (4.34)$$

This remarkable series of calculations has done exactly what we had hoped: the equation to solve is now written entirely in terms of the values of functions evaluated at the two boundaries of the process. The action has certainly been concentrated where we want it! Notice that the only unknowns are the derivatives of the hitting probabilities evaluated at the end points. We should be able to use some sort of boundary layer expansion to discover the behavior of u in the region of the end points. Before doing this, a somewhat more abstract observation about what we have accomplished should be made as it is the foundation of our ability to extend this approach to higher dimensions.

By multiplying $L[u]$ by v, we were able to write the product $vL[u]$ as the derivative of the function avu' and thus were able to write the integral of $vL[u]$ in terms of the values of avu' at the two end points. Said another way, we are able to write the integral over a one-dimensional region in terms of objects evaluated at its bounding zero-dimensional points. Exactly the same thing will happen when we move up to higher dimensions. For example, in the three-allele case the integral of $vL[u]$ over a two-dimensional region will be expressed in terms of a path integral over the one-dimensional curve that bounds the region. The calculations may be daunting, but the basic idea is exactly the same as in the two-allele case.

Although symbols have been flying about, we have really only rearranged the equation to be solved. We now turn to the solution itself. In doing so we will return to the c-haploid diffusion. To solve equation 4.34 we require the derivatives of the hitting probability, $u_1(x)$, evaluated at ϵ and $1 - \epsilon$. These may be obtained by using a standard boundary layer expansion near these points.

Consider the left point first. A common way of obtaining the boundary layer expansion of $u_1(x)$ near ϵ is to work with the stretched variable

$$y = x/\epsilon.$$

We will view y as a transformed diffusion with mean change

$$Edy = \frac{1}{\epsilon}Edx = y[c(\mu_1 - \mu_2) + c^2\sigma^2 B][1 + O(\epsilon)]dt,$$

where terms of order of magnitude ϵ have been dumped into the symbol $O(\epsilon)$. As ϵ approaches zero, the drift coefficient for y becomes

$$y[c(\mu_1 - \mu_2) + c^2\sigma^2 B].$$

Similarly, the diffusion coefficient becomes

$$2c^2\sigma^2 y^2.$$

There is nothing magical about the use of stretched variables: we would get the same result by simply retaining only the lowest order power of x in the drift and diffusion coefficients of the original process. By using stretched variables we place ourselves firmly in the traditional approach to asymptotics as well as providing a recipe that protects us from leaving out a term that we should not.

The hitting probability, u_1, when written as a function of y near the left end point, will be called $U_1(y)$ to emphasize that it is a boundary layer expansion for allele one and satisfies the backward equation

$$c^2\sigma^2 y^2 U_1''(y) + y[c(\mu_1 - \mu_2) + c^2\sigma^2 B]U_1'(y) = 0, \qquad (4.35)$$

with boundary conditions

$$U_1(1) = 1, \ U_1(\infty) = C_0.$$

Obviously, the boundary conditions will need a little explanation.

Recall that $u_1(x)$ is the probability that the allele frequency will hit ϵ before $1 - \epsilon$. This being the case, $u_1(\epsilon) = 1$. Because $y = x/\epsilon$, this furnishes the left boundary condition for U_1.

The right boundary condition is given at infinity because ϵ is approaching zero. For any value of x that is not of order ϵ, the corresponding value of y will approach infinity. In a sense, this provides a measure of the size of the boundary layer. If an allele leaves the boundary layer, that is, attains a frequency of larger order of magnitude than ϵ, then the probability that it ever hits ϵ is the same as for an allele that begins outside of the boundary layer, namely, C_0.

The boundary layer equation, equation 4.35, is a particularly simple first-order linear differential equation whose solution is

$$U_1(y) = C_0 + (1 - C_0)y^{-\beta_1},$$

where

$$\beta_1 = B - 1 + B(\mu_1 - \mu_2)/\sigma^2$$

is the same parameter that appears in the stationary distribution. For equation 4.34 we need the derivative of U_1,

$$\frac{d}{dx}U_1(x/\epsilon) = -(1 - C_0)\beta_1(x/\epsilon)^{-\beta_1 - 1}\epsilon^{-1},$$

evaluated at ϵ:

$$\frac{du_1(\epsilon)}{dx} \sim \frac{dU_1(1)}{dx} = -(1 - C_0)\beta_1\epsilon^{-1}.$$

The right boundary is attacked in the same way. The stretched variable is

$$y = (1 - x)/\epsilon,$$

and the equation to solve is

$$c^2\sigma^2 y^2 U_2''(y) + y[-c(\mu_1 - \mu_2) + c^2\sigma^2 B]U_2'(y) = 0,$$

with boundary conditions,

$$U_2(1) = 0, \ U_2(\infty) = C_0.$$

The solution is

$$U_2(y) = C_0(1 - y^{-\beta_2}),$$

where

$$\beta_2 = B - 1 - B(\mu_1 - \mu_2)/\sigma^2.$$

The derivative of $u_1(x)$ evaluated at $1 - \epsilon$ is, asymptotically,

$$\frac{du_1(1 - \epsilon)}{dx} \sim \frac{dU_2(1)}{dx} = -C_0\beta_2\epsilon^{-1}.$$

The two boundary-layer approximations are only valid if β_1 and β_2 are greater than zero. Otherwise, the right boundary condition could not be met. The existence of a stationary distribution also requires that the betas be positive. From this we learn that a proper boundary layer will only exist if there is a stationary distribution.

All of the components that appear in equation 4.34 are now in hand. For $v(x)$, we will use

$$v(x) = x^{\beta_1 - 1}(1 - x)^{\beta_2 - 1},$$

which is the stationary distribution without the normalizing constant. Putting the various pieces into equation 4.34 and solving for C_0 gives

$$u_1(x) \sim C_0 = \frac{\beta_1\epsilon^{\beta_1}}{\beta_1\epsilon^{\beta_1} + \beta_2\epsilon^{\beta_2}}.$$

The limiting behavior of this approximation may be summarized as follows:

$$\lim_{\epsilon \to 0} u_1(x) = \begin{cases} 0 & \text{if } \beta_1 > \beta_2 \\ 1/2 & \text{if } \beta_1 = \beta_2 \\ 1 & \text{if } \beta_1 < \beta_2 \end{cases}.$$

The accuracy of the approximation and the rate of convergence may be judged by examining Figure 4.5. The "true" values for $u_1(x)$ in the figure were obtained by numerical integration of the exact solution. The asymptotic solution is substantially below the true solution until ϵ is less than about 0.01. The asymptotic solution is lower because the initial condition, 0.2, is close to ϵ. In this example $\beta_1 > \beta_2$ so $u_1(x)$ approaches zero as ϵ approaches zero.

The extension to three alleles has a few new ideas, but is remarkably like the two-allele case. The equation to solve is

$$L[u(x)] = 0 \text{ in } \Omega_\epsilon \tag{4.36}$$

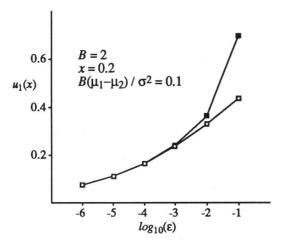

The plot shows $u_1(x)$ on the vertical axis with values 0.2, 0.4, 0.6, and $log_{10}(\varepsilon)$ on the horizontal axis with values -6, -5, -4, -3, -2, -1. Annotations: $B = 2$, $x = 0.2$, $B(\mu_1-\mu_2)/\sigma^2 = 0.1$.

Figure 4.5. The asymptotic (open squares) and true (closed squares) values of the hitting probability.

with boundary condition

$$u(\mathbf{x}) = f(\mathbf{x}) \text{ on } \partial\Omega_\epsilon, \tag{4.37}$$

where $\mathbf{x}$ is now a vector of allele frequencies, L is the partial differential operator

$$L = \frac{1}{2}\sum_i \sum_j a_{ij}(\mathbf{x})\frac{\partial^2}{\partial x_i \partial x_j} + \sum_i b_i(\mathbf{x})\frac{\partial}{\partial x_i},$$

Ω_ϵ is the region in which the diffusion unfolds, $\partial\Omega_\epsilon$ is the boundary of that region, and f is a function that specifies the region of the boundary that, if hit, will be scored as the loss of the allele of interest.

In the one-dimensional case, the equation $L[u] = 0$ held inside the interval $[\epsilon, 1-\epsilon]$. This interval may be viewed as a region in one-dimensional space that depends on the parameter ϵ with the property that as ϵ approaches zero, the region approaches the unit interval. In higher dimensions, we will be constructing a similar region, called Ω_ϵ, that will approach the unit simplex

$$\sum_{i=1}^{k-1} x_i \leq 1,$$

as ϵ approaches zero. The region will have a boundary, $\partial\Omega_\epsilon$, that corresponds to the two points ϵ and $1 - \epsilon$ in the one-dimensional case.

The regions will be set up such that the boundary can only be hit by rare alleles. A hitting probability in this case is the probability that the boundary is hit for the first time in some specified region. The function f in the boundary condition, equation 4.37, may be used to specify the region by setting it equal to one in the region and to zero everywhere else. Again, this is completely analogous to setting $u_1(x)$ equal to one when $x = \epsilon$ and zero when $x = 1 - \epsilon$ in the one-dimensional case.

The first step in the transmutation of equation 4.36 into a form that concentrates the action at the boundary requires a function $v(\mathbf{x})$ that satisfies the equation

$$L^*[v(\mathbf{x})] = 0,$$

where the multidimensional form of the forward operator L^* is defined by

$$L^*[v(\mathbf{x})] = \frac{1}{2} \sum_i \sum_j \frac{\partial^2}{\partial x_i \partial x_j} [a_{ij}(\mathbf{x})v(\mathbf{x})] - \sum_i \frac{\partial}{\partial x_i} [b_i(\mathbf{x})v(\mathbf{x})].$$

As before, we assume that v satisfies the zero probability flux condition in each dimension,

$$\frac{1}{2} \sum_j \frac{\partial}{\partial x_j} [a_{ij}(\mathbf{x})v(\mathbf{x})] - b_i(\mathbf{x})v(\mathbf{x}) = 0.$$

With v in hand, the differential equation 4.36 is converted to the integral equation

$$\int_{\Omega_\epsilon} v(\mathbf{x})L[u(\mathbf{x})]d\mathbf{x} = 0.$$

The product $vL[u]$ may be simplified by adding and subtracting the term

$$\frac{1}{2} \sum_i \sum_j \frac{\partial}{\partial x_j} [a_{ij}(\mathbf{x})v(\mathbf{x})] \frac{\partial u(\mathbf{x})}{\partial x_i}$$

to get

$$
\begin{aligned}
v(\mathbf{x})L[u(\mathbf{x})] =\ & \sum_j \frac{\partial}{\partial x_j} \left(\frac{1}{2} \sum_i a_{ij}(\mathbf{x})v(\mathbf{x}) \frac{\partial u(\mathbf{x})}{\partial x_i} \right) \\
& - \sum_i \frac{\partial u(\mathbf{x})}{\partial x_i} \left\{ \frac{1}{2} \sum_j \frac{\partial}{\partial x_j} [a_{ij}(\mathbf{x})v(\mathbf{x})] - b_i(\mathbf{x})v(\mathbf{x}) \right\}.
\end{aligned}
$$

The second term on the right side is a sum of probability fluxes, hence equal to zero. The first term on the right side is a sum of partial derivatives of the functions:

$$P_j(\mathbf{x}) = \frac{1}{2} \sum_i a_{ij}(\mathbf{x})v(\mathbf{x}) \frac{\partial u(\mathbf{x})}{\partial x_i}. \tag{4.38}$$

Equation 4.36 now takes on the simple form

$$\int_{\Omega_\epsilon} \sum_j \frac{\partial}{\partial x_j} P_j(\mathbf{x}) = 0. \tag{4.39}$$

At the comparable point in the one-dimensional development, we were in the enviable position of having to integrate the derivative of a function. Although it may not be obvious, we are in exactly the same position in the general case. To avoid introducing ideas and notation from vector analysis at this point, we will specialize to the three-allele case that lives in two dimensions. The two-dimensional form of equation 4.39 is

$$\iint_{\Omega_\epsilon} \left[\frac{\partial P_1(x_1, x_2)}{\partial x_1} + \frac{\partial P_2(x_1, x_2)}{\partial x_2} \right] dx_1 dx_2 = 0,$$

where the integrand is in the form required of *Gauss's Theorem*—the two-dimensional equivalent of the fundamental theorem of calculus that we used in the one-dimensional case.

Gauss's theorem shows that an area integral over a region may be expressed in terms of a line integral along its boundary.* The line integral must be oriented such that the region is always to the left. Using Gauss's theorem, the equation becomes

$$\int_{+\partial\Omega_\epsilon} [P_1(x_1, x_2) dx_2 - P_2(x_1, x_2) dx_1] = 0,$$

where the plus sign indicates the positive direction of the line integral. Expanding fully using equation 4.38, we have

$$\int_{+\partial\Omega_\epsilon} \left[(a_{11}v\frac{\partial u}{\partial x_1} + a_{12}v\frac{\partial u}{\partial x_2}) dx_2 - (a_{12}v\frac{\partial u}{\partial x_1} + a_{22}v\frac{\partial u}{\partial x_2}) dx_1 \right] = 0,$$

where the arguments to the functions have been suppressed for clarity.

To proceed with the boundary layer expansion, we need to define the region Ω_ϵ and the boundary conditions on $\partial\Omega_\epsilon$. There is a great deal of freedom in choosing the region; the one that will be used was chosen to allow a simple evaluation of the line integral. It is the simplex defined by

$$\epsilon \leq x_i \leq 1 - 2\epsilon, \quad x_1 + x_2 \leq 1 - \epsilon$$

and is illustrated in Figure 4.6. The boundary condition that will be used is

$$u_1(x_1, x_2) = \begin{cases} 1 & \text{if } x_1 = \epsilon \text{ and } (x_1, x_2) \text{ is on } \partial\Omega_\epsilon \\ 0 & \text{if } x_1 \neq \epsilon \text{ and } (x_1, x_2) \text{ is on } \partial\Omega_\epsilon. \end{cases}$$

That is, we are seeking the probability that the process leaves the region Ω_ϵ for the first time on the edge where $x_1 = \epsilon$.

The drift and diffusion coefficients for the three-allele c-haploid model are, from equation 4.30,

$$b_i(x_1, x_2) = x_i[c(\mu_i - \bar{\mu}) + c^2\sigma^2 B(\mathcal{F}_3 - x_i)]$$
$$a_{ij}(x_1, x_2) = c^2\sigma^2 x_i x_j(\delta_{ij} + \mathcal{F}_3 - x_i - x_j)$$

---

*A very readable account of Gauss's theorem may be found in Chapter 5 of the textbook by Courant and John [45].

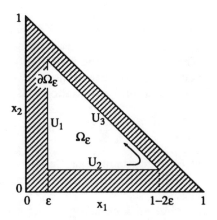

Figure 4.6. The region of integration showing the direction of integration of the line integral and the areas where the three boundary-layer expansions apply.

for $i, j = 1, 2$. These are used for the boundary layer expansion by introducing stretched variables just as was done in the one-dimensional case.

Consider first the region where allele one is rare. The stretched variable for allele one is

$$y = x_1/\epsilon.$$

As ϵ approaches zero, the drift coefficient for the stretched process approaches

$$y\{c[\mu_1 - x_2\mu_2 - (1 - x_2)\mu_3] + c^2\sigma^2 B[x_2^2 + (1 - x_2)^2]\}, \qquad (4.40)$$

and the diffusion coefficient approaches

$$c^2\sigma^2 y^2[1 + x_2^2 + (1 - x_2)^2].$$

Were we to follow slavishly the one-dimensional example, we would use these coefficients in the appropriate differential equation and solve for the boundary layer function U_1. However, this would not make a lot of sense since the variable x_2 that appears in the drift and diffusion coefficients is actually a random variable. Its appearance as a parameter in U_1 would definitely be bizarre.

An appeal to the difference in time scales in the boundary layer versus the interior appears to provide a natural escape from this impasse. As the rate of change of x_1 in the boundary layer is ϵ times that of x_2 in the interior, x_2 will realize most of its dynamics before x_1 changes appreciably. As a consequence, it seems reasonable that the drift and diffusion coefficients for y should be averaged over the stationary distribution for x_2 in the absence of x_1. This represents a departure from the usual Matkowsky and Schuss approach reflecting the fact, mentioned earlier, that the asymptotics in our case are generated not by a shrinking parameter, but rather by different time scales for rare and common alleles.

There is an analogous approach that appears in the theory of the adiabatic elimination of fast variables mentioned earlier. In that theory, when one dimension appears in another through a simple averaging as we did above, the fast variable is called a *silent slave* [79, p. 225]. When the fast variable alters the form of the slower process, it's called a *noisy slave*. The alteration comes from the fact that the fast variable is autocorrelated and that the autocorrelation can affect the drift coefficient just as it does in the Stratonovich approach to stochastic differential equations. This dichotomy is mentioned as a warning that there are other possibilities than the one that we have adopted. At the present time there is no rigorous justification for our approach, although the averaging of the dynamics of rare alleles over those of common alleles has been used successfully in other genetic contexts [283].

To avoid doing any calculations until absolutely necessary, define the (mean) drift coefficient for y to be $M_1 y$ where

$$M_1 = E\{c[\mu_1 - x_2\mu_2 - (1 - x_2)\mu_3] + c^2\sigma^2 B[x_2^2 + (1 - x_2)^2]\},$$

as obtained by averaging equation 4.40 with respect to the stationary density of alleles two and three, pretending that allele one does not exist:

$$\frac{\Gamma(2B - 2)}{\Gamma(\beta_2')\Gamma(\beta_3')} x_2^{\beta_2'-1}(1 - x_2)^{\beta_3'-1}.$$

The betas have been primed as a reminder that they will be different from the corresponding (nonprimed) betas when all three alleles are part of the model. Similarly, the diffusion coefficient will be written $V_1 y^2$, where

$$V_1 = E\{c^2\sigma^2[1 + x_2^2 + (1 - x_2)^2]\}.$$

The boundary layer expansion for u_1, when allele one is rare, satisfies the backward equation

$$\frac{1}{2}V_1 y^2 U_1'' + M_1 y U_1' = 0$$

with boundary conditions

$$U_1(1) = 1, \ U_1(\infty) = C_0.$$

The solution is just as it was in the two-allele case,

$$U_1(y) = C_0 + (1 - C_0)y^{1-2M_1/V_1}.$$

The partial derivative, which will be needed in the line integral, is

$$\frac{\partial U_1(y)}{\partial x_1} = (1 - C_0)(1 - 2M_1/V_1)\epsilon^{-1}(x_1/\epsilon)^{-2M_1/V_1}.$$

The expansion along the horizontal line applies to allele two when rare. The boundary conditions for this expansion are

$$U_2(1) = 0, \ U_2(\infty) = C_0.$$

As in the other cases, we easily get the required partial derivative:

$$\frac{\partial U_2(y)}{\partial x_2} = -C_0(1 - 2M_2/V_2)\epsilon^{-1}(x_2/\epsilon)^{-2M_2/V_2}.$$

The next expansion should be for the case where allele three is rare, giving U_3. The expansion is slightly trickier, since the stretched variable is $(1 - x_1 - x_2)/\epsilon$. However, it is really not necessary to do the third case since, by symmetry, it will be exactly like that for allele two with the obvious parameter changes.

The line integral along the horizontal segment of $\partial\Omega_\epsilon$ has $x_2 = \epsilon$ and $dx_2 = 0$. Thus, the integral along this segment is the garden variety integral

$$-\int_\epsilon^{1-2\epsilon} a_{22}(x_1, \epsilon)v(x_1, \epsilon)\frac{\partial U_2(1)}{\partial x_2}dx_1$$

that approaches

$$c^2\sigma^2 C_0(1 - \frac{2M_2}{V_2})\int_0^1 [1 + x^2 + (1 - x)^2]x^{\beta_1 - 1}(1 - x)^{\beta_3 - 1}dx\epsilon^{\beta_2}.$$

Let

$$A_2 = (1 - \frac{2M_2}{V_2})\int_0^1 [1 + x^2 + (1 - x)^2]x^{\beta_1 - 1}(1 - x)^{\beta_3 - 1}dx$$

so that we can write the integral along this segment in the less intimidating form

$$c^2\sigma^2 C_0 A_2\epsilon^{\beta_2}.$$

The value of the integral along the hypotenuse will be in exactly the same form since the labeling of alleles is arbitrary. Simply switch all of the twos and threes to get the condensed form

$$c^2\sigma^2 C_0 A_3\epsilon^{\beta_3}.$$

Along the vertical segment, $dx_1 = 0$ and $x_1 = \epsilon$. The integral along this segment approaches

$$c^2\sigma^2(C_0 - 1)A_1\epsilon^{\beta_1},$$

where

$$A_1 = (1 - \frac{2M_1}{V_1})\int_0^1 [1 + x^2 + (1 - x)^2]x^{\beta_2 - 1}(1 - x)^{\beta_3 - 1}dx.$$

Be sure, when verifying this, to adjust the sign of the integral to take into account that the path integral moves down rather than up the vertical segment.

The line integral around the edge of the simplex equals zero,

$$c^2\sigma^2(C_0 - 1)A_1\epsilon^{\beta_1} + c^2\sigma^2 C_0 A_2\epsilon^{\beta_2} + c^2\sigma^2 C_0 A_3\epsilon^{\beta_3} = 0,$$

which provides the final asymptotic expression for the hitting probability for allele one:

$$u_1(\mathbf{x}) \sim C_0 = \frac{A_1\epsilon^{\beta_1}}{A_1\epsilon^{\beta_1} + A_2\epsilon^{\beta_2} + A_3\epsilon^{\beta_3}}.$$

This answer is a rather straightforward extension of the two-allele case, although the constant multipliers of the powers of ϵ are in a much less appealing form. The limiting form of the hitting probability is

$$\lim_{\epsilon \to 0} u_1(x) = \begin{cases} 0 & \text{if } \beta_1 > \min(\beta_2, \beta_3) \\ 1/3 & \text{if } \beta_1 = \beta_2 = \beta_3 \\ 1 & \text{if } \beta_1 < \min(\beta_2, \beta_3) \end{cases}.$$

Recalling that the mean frequency of an allele is $\beta_i/2(B - 1)$ (see equation 4.22), we see that an allele's mean frequency determines whether or not it will be the first allele to leave the interior. The probability that the allele with the smallest mean frequency will leave first approaches one as ϵ approaches zero. Tracing back through the calculation, it is clear that the power of ϵ comes from the stationary distribution. Thus, this aspect of the result should also hold for c-haploid models with asymmetrical second-order moments. The constant multipliers, on the other hand, will depend on other aspects of the parameters than those summarized in the betas.

The fact that the probability that the allele with the smallest beta hits ϵ first approaches one means that there is a kind of determinism to the outcome as long as the boundary layer is small enough. It is as if all of the randomness gets ironed out and the mean effects are left to determine the final outcome.

As a final point, note that the boundary layer expansions are only valid if the quantities

$$1 - 2M_i/V_i = (V_i - 2M_i)/V_i, \ i = 1, 2, 3$$

are negative. Otherwise the right boundary condition, $U_i(\infty) = C_0$ could not be met. Since V_i is always positive, the sign of this expression is determined by $V_i - 2M_i$, which, after some painful algebra, may be written

$$-\frac{3\beta_i}{2\sigma^2 B^2}.$$

These will be negative only if the three betas are positive, which is precisely the condition for the existence of a stationary distribution. Thus, as in the two-allele case, the boundary layer only appears for those models that possess a stationary distribution.

Waiting times

In the previous section we learned where alleles go; in this section we learn how long it takes them to get there. This section will continue the trend toward symmetry; in fact, it will deal exclusively with symmetrical models. As before, we will begin with the two-allele case to illustrate the main principles, then move to the three-allele case, and end up with k alleles. We will be finding the mean time for a common allele to become rare. More precisely, we will be seeking an asymptotic expression for the mean time for one of the interior alleles to hit a barrier at ϵ. Fortunately, this time may be found by an almost trivial modification of the hitting probability solution from the previous section. Moreover, we will be able to establish that the time to hit ϵ is (asymptotically) exponentially distributed in the two-allele case and conjecture that this holds also for the k-allele case.

Consider the symmetrical two-allele case with drift coefficient

$$b(x) = c^2\sigma^2 Bx(1-x)(1-2x)$$

and diffusion coefficient

$$a(x) = 2c^2\sigma^2 x^2(1-x)^2.$$

Let $\bar{t}(x)$ be the mean time until either allele one or allele two hits ϵ, or, equivalently, the mean time until x leaves the internval $(\epsilon, 1-\epsilon)$. The mean time satisfies the differential equation

$$L[\bar{t}(x)] = -1 \tag{4.41}$$

with boundary conditions

$$\bar{t}(\epsilon) = \bar{t}(1-\epsilon) = 0.$$

The solution to this equation is known,* but involves a double integral and other debris that makes it totally opaque. Therefore, we will jump immediately into the asymptotic analysis.

As before, assume that v satisfies the forward equation $L^*[v] = 0$. Multiply both sides of equation 4.41 by v and integrate to get

$$\int_\epsilon^{1-\epsilon} v(x)L[\bar{t}(x)]dx = -\int_\epsilon^{1-\epsilon} v(x)dx.$$

Following the same steps used to get the hitting probabilities yields

$$a(1-\epsilon)v(1-\epsilon)\frac{d}{dx}\bar{t}(1-\epsilon) - a(\epsilon)v(\epsilon)\frac{d}{dx}\bar{t}(\epsilon) = -2\int_\epsilon^{1-\epsilon} v(x)dx.$$

---

*The derivation and solution of this equation may be found in any treatment of exit times for diffusions, including the books by Gardiner [79, p. 136] and Ewens [68, p. 120].

This equation concentrates the action at the boundaries, leading into the boundary layer expansion for each of the alleles when rare.

To explore the boundary layer expansion of $\bar{t}(x)$ when x is close to ϵ, we introduce the stretched variable $y = x/\epsilon$ and the function $T_1(y)$ that approximates $\bar{t}$. The function $T_1(x)$ satisfies the equation

$$c^2\sigma^2 y^2 T_1''(y) + y c^2 \sigma^2 B T_1'(y) = 0$$

with boundary conditions

$$T_1(1) = 0, \ T_1(\infty) = C_0,$$

where C_0 is now the asymptotic mean time to hit the boundary. There is clearly something very odd here: why should the equation to solve be $L[T] = 0$ rather than $L[T] = -1$? What follows is a summary of the full explanation contained in the Matkowsky and Schuss paper [204].

Using the maximum principle for differential equations, a lower bound on the mean time to hit the barrier for interior alleles may be found and used to rescale time. When this is done, the -1 term becomes an order-one term divided by the bound, and hence approaches zero as ϵ approaches zero. The time spent in the boundary layer is insignificant compared with the time spent in the interior. Recall that the width of the boundary layer is only of order ϵ, as is the rate of change in x. Thus, the time spent in the boundary layer should be an order one quantity, even as ϵ approaches zero. The time spent in the interior, on the other hand, grows to infinity as ϵ approaches zero. Moreover, the time spent in the interior does not depend on the initial value of the process.

If we translate these ideas into a representation of the mean time it looks like

$$\bar{t}(x) \sim u(x)(0) + [1 - u(x)]C_0 = [1 - u(x)]C_0,$$

where $u(x)$ is the probability of hitting ϵ before entering the interior. If we now multiply the second derivative of $\bar{t}(x)$ by one-half the diffusion coefficient and the first derivative by the drift coefficient we get

$$\frac{a(x)}{2}\bar{t}''(x) + b(x)\bar{t}'(x) = -C_0[\frac{a(x)}{2}u''(x) + b(x)u'(x)] = 0,$$

which is the correct form for the boundary layer equation.

The solution to the boundary layer equation is

$$T_1(y) = C_0(1 - y^{1-B}).$$

Note that this solution will meet the right boundary condition only if B is greater than one, which is also the condition for the existence of the stationary distribution.

The derivative of T_1 with respect to x at ϵ is

$$- C_0(1 - B)\epsilon^{-1}. \tag{4.42}$$

Similarly, the derivative of the expansion near one evaluated at $1 - \epsilon$ is

$$C_0(1 - B)\epsilon^{-1}.$$

The remaining ingredient required for C_0 is

$$-2 \int_\epsilon^{1-\epsilon} v(x)dx \sim -2\frac{\Gamma(B - 1)^2}{\Gamma(2B - 2)},$$

where we have used

$$v(x) = x^{B-2}(1 - x)^{B-2}.$$

Putting all of this together yields

$$\bar{t}(x) \sim C_0 = \frac{\Gamma(B - 1)^2}{2c^2\sigma^2(B - 1)\Gamma(2B - 2)}\epsilon^{-(B-1)}. \tag{4.43}$$

As expected, the mean time to hit the barrier at ϵ increases as ϵ approaches zero. The rate of increase is larger for larger values of B because larger values of B cause a stronger push of allele frequencies toward the interior, making it harder for them to hit a barrier that is near the end points.

Much more is known about the time to hit the barrier thanks to a remarkable theorem due to Mandl [202, p. 109], which shows that the time to hit a barrier near the boundary of a one-dimensional diffusion with inaccessible boundaries is asymptotically exponentially distributed with the same mean that we derived above. The only condition that must be placed on the diffusion—other than the inaccessibility of the boundaries—is that it have a stationary distribution, as ours does. The two-allele c-haploid diffusion also has inaccessible boundaries at zero and one. This is easy to verify using the standard criteria for the classification of the boundaries of diffusions.* To say that a boundary is inaccessible simply means that it will not be hit in a finite length of time. Since the c-haploid model in its present incarnation assumes that the population is made up of an infinite number of individuals, there is no genetic drift to propel an allele to fixation or loss once it approaches a boundary. Thus, Mandl's theorem applies to the c-haploid model and shows that the time for an allele to hit a barrier that is near a boundary approaches an exponential distribution.

Why an exponential distribution? There are many answers, some analytic, some probabilistic. Of the latter, one should be mentioned as it forms the basis of a conjecture that the exponentiality applies to models with more than two alleles. It is based on the property of exponential distributions that they "lack memory." If a waiting time is exponentially distributed and if you have been waiting patiently for an event to occur, then the time that you must continue to wait is independent of the time that you have already waited. This property actually characterizes an exponential distribution [11, Chapter 1.1]. The fact that the asymptotic form of the waiting

---

*Discussions of the classification of boundaries for one-dimensional diffusions may be found in the books by Ewens [68, p. 131] and Gardiner [79, p. 123].

time to hit a boundary for the c-haploid model is independent of the initial frequency of an interior allele is an instance of this lack of memory property. If the process has failed to hit a barrier during a certain interval of time, then knowing its state at the end of this interval will add no information about the distribution of the subsequent time until the barrier is hit.

The k-allele extension is based on the symmetrical c-haploid diffusion with drift coefficient

$$b_i(\mathbf{x}) = c^2\sigma^2 B x_i(\mathcal{F}_k - x_i)$$

and diffusion coefficient

$$a_{ij}(\mathbf{x}) = c^2\sigma^2 x_i x_j(\delta_{ij} + \mathcal{F}_k - x_i - x_j).$$

The first step in the solution of the problem is, as before: multiply both sides of the equation $L[\bar{t}] = -1$ by the solution of the equation $L^*[v] = 0$ and integrate over the region Ω_ϵ to get

$$\int_{\Omega_\epsilon} v L[\bar{t}(\mathbf{x})]d\mathbf{x} = -\int_{\Omega_\epsilon} v(\mathbf{x})d\mathbf{x}.$$

Specializing to three alleles and using Gauss's theorem, this equation becomes

$$\int_{+\partial\Omega_\epsilon} \left[(a_{11}v\frac{\partial\bar{t}}{\partial x_1} + a_{12}v\frac{\partial\bar{t}}{\partial x_2})dx_2 - (a_{12}v\frac{\partial\bar{t}}{\partial x_1} + a_{22}v\frac{\partial\bar{t}}{\partial x_2})dx_1\right]$$
$$= -2\int_{\Omega_\epsilon} v(\mathbf{x})d\mathbf{x}.$$

There are two differences from the hitting probability problem. First, all three, not just two, boundary layer expansions use the same boundary conditions:

$$T_i(1) = 0, \ T_i(\infty) = C_0,.$$

Second, the right hand side of the equation, which was zero for the hitting probability, is now

$$-2\int_{\Omega_\epsilon} v(\mathbf{x})d\mathbf{x} \sim -2\frac{\Gamma(2(B-1)/3)^3}{\Gamma(2B-2)}$$

when we use

$$v = [x_1 x_2(1 - x_1 - x_2)]^{2(B-1)/3-1}.$$

Because of the symmetry assumptions, it is possible to write down explicit results with very little effort. The first place where the symmetries impart this advantage is in the mean of the drift coefficient for the allele in the boundary layer, $M_i y$, where

$$M_i = c^2\sigma^2 BE\mathcal{F}_2.$$

From equation 4.28 we have

$$E\mathcal{F}_2 = \frac{B}{2B-1},$$

giving

$$M_i = c^2\sigma^2 B^2/(2B-1).$$

The diffusion coefficient is $V_i y^2$, where

$$V_i = c^2\sigma^2(1 + E\mathcal{F}_2) = c^2\sigma^2(3B-1)/(2B-1).$$

These are combined in the boundary layer solution,

$$1 - \frac{2M_i}{V_i} = -\frac{(B-1)(2B-1)}{3B-1},$$

to give

$$T_i(y) = C_0[1 - y^{-(B-1)(2B-1)/(3B-1)}].$$

Thus, the derivative of the boundary layer expansion with respect to x_i, evaluated at ϵ, is

$$\frac{\partial T_i(y)}{\partial x_i} = \frac{C_0(B-1)(2B-1)}{3B-1}\epsilon^{-1}. \tag{4.44}$$

All of the pieces are now in hand to solve for C_0. As each of the segments along the three edges of the curve $\partial\Omega_\epsilon$ will contribute the same value to the line integral, it is only necessary to evaluate the integral along one of the edges. For example, along the horizontal edge $x_2 = \epsilon$ and $dx_2 = 0$ so the line integral along this edge is

$$-C_0 c^2\sigma^2\frac{(B-1)(2B-1)}{3B-1}\int_\epsilon^{1-2\epsilon}[1+x^2+(1-x)^2]x^{\beta-1}(1-x)^{\beta-1}dx\,\epsilon^\beta,$$

where

$$\beta = 2(B-1)/3.$$

As ϵ approaches zero, this expression approaches

$$-C_0 c^2\sigma^2\frac{6B(B-1)(2B-1)\Gamma(\beta)^2}{(3B-1)(4B-1)\Gamma(2\beta)}\epsilon^\beta.$$

There are three such terms in the line integral, so if this is multiplied by three and set equal to the right hand side of the equation being solved, we get

$$\bar{t}_3(\mathbf{x}) \sim C_0 = A_3\epsilon^{-2(B-1)/3},$$

where

$$A_3 = \frac{(3B-1)(4B-1)\Gamma(2(B-1)/3)\Gamma(4(B-1)/3)}{c^2\sigma^2 9B(B-1)(2B-1)\Gamma(2B-2)}.$$

The extension to k alleles is straightforward. In the boundary layer,

$$1 - \frac{2M_i}{V_i} = -\frac{(B-1)(2B-1)}{kB-1}.$$

This may be used to obtain the derivative of T_i at the boundary:

$$\frac{\partial T_i(y)}{\partial x_i} = \frac{C_0(B-1)(2B-1)}{kB-1}\epsilon^{-1}.$$

In higher dimensions, the line integral becomes an oriented surface integral that is composed of the k sides of the simplex Ω_ϵ. Because of the symmetries, we need only multiply the integral over one of the sides by k to obtain the integral over the entire surface, $\partial\Omega_\epsilon$. By analogy to the three-allele case, it seems clear that the integral over one of the sides of the simplex approaches

$$-C_0 c^2 \sigma^2 \frac{(B-1)(2B-1)}{kB-1} \int \left(1+\sum_{i=1}^{k-1} y_i^2\right) \prod_{i=1}^{k-1} y_i^{\beta_k-1} dy \, \epsilon^{\beta_k},$$

where

$$\beta_k = 2(B-1)/k$$

and

$$y_{k-1} = 1 - y_1 \cdots - y_{k-2}.$$

The integral is over the entire $k-1$ dimensional unit simplex and evaluates to

$$\frac{2Bk\Gamma(\beta_k)^{k-1}}{[2(B-1)(k-1)+k]\Gamma(\beta_k(k-1))}.$$

The right hand side of the equation is given by

$$-2\int_{\Omega_\epsilon} v(\mathbf{x})d\mathbf{x} \sim -2\frac{\Gamma(\beta_k)^k}{\Gamma(2B-2)}.$$

Putting all this together we get the general result

$$\bar{t}_k(\mathbf{x}) \sim C_0 = A_k \epsilon^{-2(B-1)/k}, \tag{4.45}$$

where

$$A_k = \frac{(kB-1)[2(B-1)(k-1)+k]\Gamma(2(B-1)/k)\Gamma(2(B-1)(k-1)/k)}{c^2\sigma^2 k^2 B(B-1)(2B-1)\Gamma(2B-2)}.$$

A quick check shows that this answer does, in fact, specialize to the two- and three-allele cases. The constant, A_k, differs slightly from the one that I published earlier [90]. In that paper I was too cavalier about setting $\mathcal{F}_i$ equal to its expectation. Fortunately, the two constants differ only by about 2% for reasonable values of B and k.

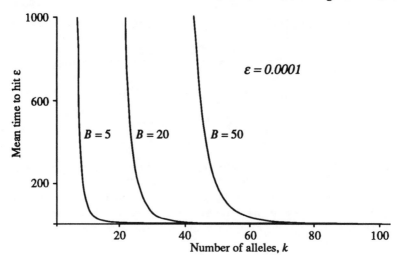

Figure 4.7. The mean time for the first interior allele to hit the boundary.

Figure 4.7 illustrates the behavior of $\bar{t}_k(\mathbf{x})$ as a function of B and k. A striking property of the mean is the sharp rise that occurs when the number of alleles is below some critical value that depends on B. When the number of alleles is above this value, the mean time for an allele to become rare is relatively short. When the number is below this value, alleles tend to remain in the interior a very long time before becoming rare. It is easy to imagine that this property will place an upper bound on the number of interior alleles in a finite population, even though the number in an infinite population is unbounded.

The asymptotic expansions presented in this section have not been verified by any rigorous mathematical treatment. The approach differs sufficiently from that of Matkowsky and Schuss that the proof of their method given by Kamin [148] is probably not applicable. This would appear to be a fertile area for additional work. We need to know if the mean time given here is, in fact, the leading term in the asymptotic expansion as $\epsilon \to 0$, if the distribution of the time is asymptotically exponential, and the rate of convergence to the asymptotic form. There are two steps in our approach that are of particular concern. The first is the assumption that the behavior in the boundary layer may be viewed as a one-dimensional process by averaging over the interior. The second is the fact that we ignored all of the corners. That is, there is a hidden assumption that alleles always leave the interior one at a time. While both of these assumptions appeal to intuition, they cry out for mathematical justification.

To assess the accuracy of the approximations, a series of computer simulations were performed. The results are given in Figure 4.8. The agreement is quite good, although the logarithmic scale on the vertical axes hides the

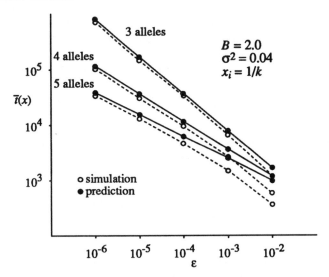

Figure 4.8. A comparison of simulation results with the asymptotic expression for the mean time for the first interior allele to hit the boundary.

fact that the asymptotic approximation is higher than the simulated value by about 10%. Other simulations have suggested that this error is attributable, at least in part, to the triangular distribution that was used in the simulations for the values of $Y_i(t)$ and to the fact that σ was a rather large 0.2.

4.4 SAS-CFF models

The diploid models to be introduced in this section share an underlying additive structure that makes their approximating diffusion processes the same as those of the c-haploid model. Let Y_i be the contribution of the ith allele to the underlying additive scale. The contribution of the genotype $A_i A_j$ to the additive scale is just $(Y_i + Y_j)/2$. The values of the Y_i will, by assumption, depend on the state of the environment. The models to be examined include both temporal and spatial components to the variation in the environment, so the Y_i should be viewed as random variables that change in both time and space. In certain cases, the additive scale may correspond to some measurable biological object. For example, in the Ur SAS-CFF model [84] the additive scale represented the activity of an enzyme. At the other extreme, it could be a morphological trait such as those studied by quantitative geneticists. In this case, the dependence of the allelic contributions on the state of the environment is what quantitative geneticists call genotype-environment interaction.

The additive scale could be fitness itself, but more often it is mapped into fitness by a function called the fitness function, ϕ. If the fitness function is nonlinear, this induces dominance in fitness. In the Ur SAS-CFF model the fitness function was concave, birthing the abbreviation SAS-CFF for Stochastic Additive Scale-Concave Fitness Function.* Using all of these assumptions, the fitness of the genotype $A_i A_j$ in a particular environment may be written

$$w_{ij} = \phi \left(a + \frac{Y_i + Y_j}{2} \right),$$

where the constant a represents the value of the additive scale to which the ith and jth alleles contribute. In the Ur SAS-CFF model $a = 1$, but it may take on other values as well. The fitness function, when evaluated at a, will always equal one.

As the lead off member of the parade of models, consider an additive locus—one without dominance—in a diploid species experiencing nonauto-correlated temporal fluctuations in the environment. In this case,

$$\phi(y) = 1 + y$$

so the fitness of the genotype $A_i A_j$ is

$$w_{ij}(t) = 1 + \frac{Y_i(t) + Y_j(t)}{2}. \tag{4.46}$$

Plugging this into the standard diploid recursion equation yields

$$\Delta x_i = \frac{1}{2} \frac{x_i \left(Y_i - \sum_{j=1}^{k} x_j Y_j \right)}{1 + \sum_{j=1}^{k} x_j Y_j}$$

for the change in the allele frequency in a single generation. This will be immediately recognized as a c-haploid model with $c = 1/2$ or, equivalently, $B = 2$. Thus, we already know a tremendous amount about the dynamics of this diploid model.

For example, if the first- and second-order moments of the Y_i are the same for all alleles, then, from equation 4.27, the stationary distribution is the Dirichlet distribution

$$\frac{1}{\Gamma(2/k)} \prod_{i=1}^{k} x_i^{2/k-1}.$$

In the two-allele case, this is just a uniform density. The biological message is that the diploid model that is most nearly equivalent to a haploid model differs from the haploid model in being able to support a balanced polymorphism in a temporally fluctuating environment. This is a profound difference. However, before running to the field to document the higher levels of variation in diploids, the experimentally inclined reader should

---

*SAS-CFF is not the Celtic word for truth and beauty as is commonly believed.

Table 4.1. The parameters of the c-haploid models that correspond to various forms of SAS-CFF models. To construct a c-haploid model, simply set each of the three c-haploid parameters from the top row equal to the corresponding entry from the SAS-CFF model of interest.

Model	$B = 1/c$	c-haploid σ_{ij}	c-haploid μ_i
Additive	2	σ_{ij}	μ_i
Dominance	$2 - \frac{\phi''}{\phi'^2}$	$(\frac{\phi' B}{2})^2 \sigma_{ij}$	$B(\frac{\phi' \mu_i}{2} + \frac{\phi'' \sigma_{ii}}{8})$
Subdivision:			
Soft selection	$\frac{2}{1-\kappa(1-\rho)}$	$\frac{1}{1-\kappa(1-\rho)}\sigma_{ij}$	$\frac{B}{2}\mu_i$
Hard selection	2	$[1 - \kappa(1 - \rho)]\sigma_{ij}$	μ_i
Mushy selection	$\frac{2[1-p\kappa(1-\rho)]}{1-\kappa(1-\rho)}$	$\frac{[1-p\kappa(1-\rho)]^2}{1-\kappa(1-\rho)}\sigma_{ij}$	$\frac{B}{2}\mu_i$
Autocorrelation:			
Weak	$\frac{1+\eta^2}{\eta^2}$	$\frac{(1+\eta^2)^2}{4\eta^2}\sigma_{ij}$	$B(\frac{\mu_i}{2} + \frac{\eta^2-1}{8}\sigma_{ii})$
Moderate	1	$\frac{\eta^2}{4}\sigma_{ij}$	$\frac{\mu_i}{2} + \frac{\eta^2}{8}\sigma_{ii}$

read on to learn that spatial variation superimposed on temporal variation allows plenty of variation in both haploids and diploids.

The additive model will be used as a benchmark to assess the effects of dominance, spatial subdivision, and temporal autocorrelations. Each of these will be injected separately into the model so their effects may be understood in isolation, without any compounding from the others. For each case, the approximating diffusion will be derived, and the correspondences between this diffusion and that of the c-haploid model will be written in Table 4.1. For the additive case this is trivial, but is nonetheless given as the first entry in the table.

Dominance

Dominance in fitness may be included by mapping the additive scale into fitness with a nonlinear function, ϕ. Since the additive contributions of alleles are small, the fitness of the genotype $A_i A_j$ may be approximated by

$$w_{ij}(t) = \phi\left(a + \frac{Y_i + Y_j}{2}\right) \approx 1 + \phi'(a)\frac{Y_i + Y_j}{2} + \frac{1}{2}\phi''(a)\left(\frac{Y_i + Y_j}{2}\right)^2.$$

These fitnesses may be plugged into the general diploid recurrence equation

$$\Delta x_i = \frac{x_i(\bar{w}_i - \bar{w})}{\bar{w}}$$

to obtain the means of Δx_i and $(\Delta x_i)^2$ as required in the diffusion approximation. The calculation of these moments is a bit of a grunt, but uses the same approach as was used for the haploid model. When the dust settles, we have a diffusion process with mean differential

$$Edx_i = x_i[(\frac{\phi'\mu_i}{2} + \frac{\phi''\sigma_{ii}}{8} - \frac{\phi'\bar{\mu}}{2} - \frac{\phi''}{8}\sum_{j=1}^{k}x_j\sigma_{jj}) + (\frac{\phi'^2}{2} - \frac{\phi''}{4})(\bar{\sigma} - \bar{\sigma}_i)]dt$$

and mean squared differential

$$Edx_idx_j = \frac{\phi'^2}{4}(\sigma_{ij} - \bar{\sigma}_i - \bar{\sigma}_j + \bar{\sigma})dt.$$

By comparison, recall (from equation 4.12) that the c-haploid diffusion is

$$Edx_i = cx_i(\mu_i^H - \bar{\mu}^H + \bar{\sigma}^H - \bar{\sigma}_i^H)dt$$
$$Edx_idx_j = c^2(\sigma_{ij}^H - \bar{\sigma}_i^H - \bar{\sigma}_j^H + \bar{\sigma}^H)dt,$$

where the superscript Hs are used to differentiate the c-haploid parameters from the diploid parameters.

The easiest way to discover the parameter equivalences is to write all of the c-haploid covariance parameters as a constant, ν, times the diploid covariance parameters

$$\sigma_{ij}^H = \nu\sigma_{ij}.$$

Plugging these into the c-haploid diffusion shows that if

$$c^2\nu = \phi'^2/4$$

the two models will have the same diffusion coefficient. Comparing the coefficient of the $\bar{\sigma} - \bar{\sigma}_i$ in the drift coefficients of two models gives

$$c\nu = (\phi'^2 - \frac{\phi''}{2})/2.$$

Solving this pair of equations shows that the value for B in the c-haploid model should be

$$B = \frac{1}{c} = 2 - \frac{\phi''}{\phi'^2},$$

while the covariance parameter of the c-haploid model should be

$$\sigma_{ij}^H = (\phi'^2/2)^2\sigma_{ij}.$$

A similar approach will yield the equivalence for the mean terms:

$$\mu_i^H = B(\frac{\phi'\mu_i}{2} + \frac{\phi''\sigma_{ii}}{8}).$$

These parameter equivalences are summarized in line 3 of Table 4.1.

We turn now to one of the more intriguing properties of the SAS-CFF model with dominance: the conditions for the existence of a stationary distribution are the same as those for the existence of a stable central equilibrium in a constant fitness model in which the geometric mean fitness of a genotype is used as its constant fitness. There is something about the additive structure of the SAS-CFF model that endows it with this property that, as shown by Turelli [282], does not generalize to other models of selection in a random environment. It is probably best to view the formal similarity of the equilibrium as a coincidence that does not hint at any deeper structure of models of selection in temporally fluctuating environments.

The geometric mean fitness of the genotype $A_i A_j$ is approximately one plus its arithmetic mean fitness,

$$\frac{1}{2}\phi'(\mu_i + \mu_j) + \frac{1}{8}\phi''(\sigma_{ii} + 2\sigma_{ij} + \sigma_{jj}),$$

minus one half its variance in fitness,

$$\frac{1}{2}\phi'^2(\sigma_{ii} + 2\sigma_{ij} + \sigma_{jj}),$$

or

$$1 + \gamma_{ij},$$

where

$$\gamma_{ij} = \frac{1}{2}\phi'(\mu_i + \mu_j) - \frac{1}{8}\phi'^2(B-1)(\sigma_{ii} + 2\sigma_{ij} + \sigma_{jj}).$$

These approximations come from the first three terms of the Taylor series expansion of the fitness, w_{ij}.

If $1 + \gamma_{ij}$ is now viewed as the constant fitness of genotype $A_i A_j$, it is possible to find the equilibrium of the population using standard population genetic arguments. There are two approaches to finding the equilibrium of a multiple-allele model. One, due to Kimura [153], views the problem as living in $k - 1$ dimensions throughout. The other, due to Mandel [201], pretends that the problem lives in k dimensions through most of the calculation, then normalizes at the end to recover allele frequencies that add to one. Kimura's approach is much more convenient for our purposes since the SAS-CFF diffusions are firmly rooted in $k - 1$ dimensions.

Kimura's approach makes use of the fact that the mean fitness of a constant-fitness multiple-allele model is maximized at a stable internal equilibrium. Given this, one way to discover the equilibrium is to find a maximum of the mean fitness with all allele frequencies falling between zero and one. In our case, the mean fitness is the quadratic form

$$\bar{\gamma}(\mathbf{x}) = 1 + \sum_{i=1}^{k}\sum_{j=1}^{k} x_i x_j \gamma_{ij},$$

where

$$x_k = 1 - x_1 \ldots - x_{k-1}.$$

The maximum may be found by solving the set of linear equation obtained by setting each of the $(k-1)$ partial derivatives of $\bar{\gamma}$ equal to zero. The ith equation is given by

$$\sum_{j=1}^{k-1} x_j g_{ij} = \gamma_{kk} - \gamma_{ik}, \qquad (4.47)$$

where

$$g_{ij} = \gamma_{ij} - \gamma_{ik} - \gamma_{jk} + \gamma_{kk}.$$

The g_{ij} are readily found to be

$$g_{ij} = -\frac{1}{4}\phi'^2(B-1)c_{ij},$$

where c_{ij} is the, by now, familiar

$$c_{ij} = \sigma_{ij} - \sigma_{ik} - \sigma_{jk} + \sigma_{kk}.$$

The mean effects are missing from the g_{ij} because they always enter as linear effects that exactly cancel in the pluses and minuses that define g_{ij}.

The term on the right hand side of equation 4.47 may be simplified to

$$-m_i = \frac{1}{2}\phi'(\mu_k - \mu_i) - \frac{1}{4}\phi'^2(B-1)(\sigma_{kk} - \sigma_{ii} + c_{ii}/2).$$

If the vector of the m_i is called $\mathbf{m}$, and the matrix of c_{ij}, $\mathbf{C}$, then equation 4.47 becomes

$$\frac{1}{4}\phi'^2(B-1)\mathbf{C}\mathbf{x} = \mathbf{m}$$

with solution

$$\mathbf{x} = \frac{4\mathbf{C}^{-1}\mathbf{m}}{\phi'^2(B-1)}. \qquad (4.48)$$

This looks a lot like equation 4.18, the formula for the betas that appear in the stationary distribution of the c-haploid model. In fact, this is where the connection between the stochastic model and the constant fitness model will be made.

To make the connection, we need to substitute the appropriate diploid parameters from Table 4.1 into a slightly rearranged equation 4.18,

$$\mathbf{C}^H\beta = \mathbf{m}^H.$$

Some straightforward algebra yields

$$\frac{1}{8}\phi'^2\mathbf{C}\beta = \mathbf{m}$$

as the equation that is satisfied by the betas for the stationary distribution of the diploid model. The solution may be formally written as

$$\beta = \frac{2}{\phi'^2}\mathbf{C}^{-1}\mathbf{m}.$$

A comparison of this to equation 4.48 shows that $\mathbf{x}$ and β are related by

$$\mathbf{x} = \frac{1}{2(B-1)}\beta.$$

Recalling that the sum of the betas is $2(B-1)$, we see immediately that the allele frequencies will, in fact, add to one. As all of the betas must be positive for the stationary distribution to exist, the allele frequencies will all lie between zero and one. Moreover, as the mean frequency of the ith allele at stationarity is $\beta_i/2(B-1)$, we obtain the result that the equilibrium frequency of an allele under the constant fitness model using geometric means is equal to the mean frequency of the allele under the SAS-CFF model. A remarkable result, indeed!

One loose end needs to be tied up. We have shown that the conditions for the existence of a stationary distribution are the same as the conditions for an internal equilibrium of the constant fitness model. However, we have not established that the internal equilibrium is at a maximum rather than a minimum of the mean fitness. Kimura provided a convenient criterion to assure that the equilibrium is at a maximum. It is that

$$(-1)^r T_r > 0, \ r = 1, 2, \cdots, k-1,$$

where

$$T_r = \begin{vmatrix} g_{11} & g_{12} & \cdots & g_{1r} \\ g_{21} & g_{22} & \cdots & g_{2r} \\ \vdots & \vdots & & \vdots \\ g_{r1} & g_{r2} & \cdots & g_{rr} \end{vmatrix}.$$

Recalling that g_{ij} is a negative constant, $-(\phi'^2 - \phi')c_{ij}/4$ times the covariance c_{ij}, and that the determinant of a matrix with a constant multiple of each of its elements is equal to the constant raised to the power of the order of the matrix times the determinant of the matrix without the constant, the determinants may be written

$$T_r = (-1)^r [\phi'^2 (B-1)/4]^r |\mathbf{C}|.$$

As $\mathbf{C}$ is a covariance matrix, its determinant will be positive. The conditions for stationarity require that B is greater than one, as is always true for the SAS-CFF model with a stationary distribution with all k alleles segregating. Thus, the equilibrium point is at a maximum for the mean geometric mean fitness.

The best way to assess the effects of dominance on the conditions for polymorphism is to specialize to a model with symmetrical second-order moments. The condition for polymorphism for the c-haploid model given by equation 4.31 is readily modified using the entries in Table 4.1 to obtain

$$\sum_{j=1}^{k}(\mu_j - \mu_i) < \frac{(B-1)\phi'\sigma^2}{2}. \tag{4.49}$$

Dominance, as measured by ϕ'', appears in these conditions only through its effects on B. Increasing the curvature of a concave ϕ will increase B and lead to higher levels of polymorphism. Increasing the dominance of a concave ϕ will also increase the heterozygosity. Just the opposite will hold if ϕ is convex.

Subdivision

The models that we have examined thus far include only temporal fluctuations in the environment. It would be a strange species, indeed, that could find a niche with such a simple structure. The usual case must be an environment that fluctuates in both time and space. Models that include both temporal and spatial fluctuations fall naturally into two groups: those with free migration and those with restricted migration. By free migration we mean only that migration, as an evolutionary force, dominates selection. In a freely migrating species there will be no geographic differentiation. Differential changes in allele frequencies that occur in particular subpopulations within a generation are swamped out when a round of random mating occurs. Such models are within the scope of the diffusion approach that we have been developing. Models with restricted migration, on the other hand, require new methods.

The simplest structure of a freely migrating species is one that was introduced by Levene [186] that has unfortunately come to be called soft selection [41,290]. Unfortunate because the term soft selection carries little useful information about the structure of the model. The species is assumed to be distributed over n subdivisions. After selection occurs within the subdivisions, each one contributes a fixed fraction of individuals, denoted by a_j, to a round of random mating. The subdivisions are then repopulated from the offspring of the mating, and the cycle begins anew. The essence of the model is captured in the simple expression

$$\Delta x_i(t) = \sum_{j=1}^{n} a_j \Delta x_i(j, t), \qquad (4.50)$$

where $\Delta x_i(j, t)$ represents the change in the frequency of the ith allele in the jth subpopulation in the tth generation and

$$\sum_{j=1}^{n} a_j = 1.$$

The change in the frequency of an allele in the species is a weighted average of its changes across the subdivisions, the weights reflecting the relative contributions of each subdivision to the next generation.

An important feature of the Levene model is that the contribution of each subdivision is independent of the fitnesses of the individuals within the subdivision. It is as if there were strong local regulation of the population size within a subdivision. However, without explicit population size dynamics, one should not take this interpretation too seriously.

Subdivision leads to an explosion of parameters. If fitnesses are assigned at random, there will be n sets of parameters summarizing the moments of fitness within subdivisions and $n(n-1)/2$ sets reflecting correlations in fitnesses across environments. A completely general analysis, while possible, would be too convoluted to be of much biological interest. Things become manageable if we are willing to accept some symmetries. One obvious approach is to assume that the subdivisions all experience the same environmental fluctuations, although at different times.

In equation 4.46, $Y_i(t)$ is the additive component in the tth generation. Now, let $Y_i(t, j)$ be a set of random variables reflecting the state of the environment in the jth patch in the tth generation. Assume, as before, that there are no temporal autocorrelations. Our symmetry assumption is simply that the moments of $Y_i(t, j)$ do not depend on t or j.

We will introduce one new parameter, ρ,

$$\text{Corr}[Y_i(t, l), Y_j(t, m)] = \rho \sigma_{ij}, \ i \neq j$$

that reflects the correlation of the Y_i across patches. Not all values of ρ are acceptable. In applications, it must be checked that ρ is chosen such that the (huge) covariance matrix involving all of the $Y_i(t, j)$ is positive definite.

In accord with the program of adding each effect separately onto the additive model, assume that in the mth patch

$$\Delta x_i(m) = \frac{1}{2} \frac{x_i \left(Y_i(t, m) - \sum_{j=1}^{k} x_j Y_i(t, m) \right)}{1 + \sum_{j=1}^{k} x_j Y_j(t, m)}.$$

Plugging this into equation 4.50 and going through the usual diffusion approximation steps gives the diffusion coefficient

$$E dx_i = \frac{1}{2} x_i (\mu_i - \bar{\mu} + \bar{\sigma} - \bar{\sigma}_i) dt,$$

which is the same as for the additive model without subdivision. This is as it should be since each of the subdivisions has the same mean change in the allele frequency because of the symmetry assumptions.

The diffusion coefficient is more interesting. The first step in its derivation involves changing equation 4.50 to

$$\Delta x_i \Delta x_j = \sum_{u=1}^{n} \sum_{v=1}^{n} a_u a_v \Delta x_i(u) \Delta x_j(v).$$

This may be broken up into a term with cross products from within a patch and one with cross products from between patches:

$$\Delta x_i \Delta x_j = \sum_{u=1}^{n} a_u^2 \Delta x_i(u) \Delta x_j(u) + \sum_{u=1}^{n} \sum_{v=1, \neq u}^{n} a_u a_v \Delta x_i(u) \Delta x_j(v).$$

At this point it should be clear how to derive the squared differential

$$Edx_i dx_j = \frac{1}{4}[1 - \kappa(1 - \rho)]x_i x_j(\sigma_{ij} + \overline{\sigma} - \overline{\sigma}_i - \overline{\sigma}_j)dt,$$

where

$$\kappa = 1 - \sum_{u=1}^{n} a_u^2.$$

Once again, the resulting diffusion is in the same form as a c-haploid model. To find the parameter equivalences we will use the same approach as we did for dominance. Examination of the drift and diffusion coefficient shows that

$$\nu c^2 = 1 - \kappa(1 - \rho)$$

and

$$\nu c = 1/2.$$

From this we see that B in the equivalent c-haploid model is

$$B = \frac{2}{1 - \kappa(1 - \rho)}$$

as recorded in Table 4.1 along with the other equivalences.

Under soft selection, the main effect of environmental subdivision is to increase the value of B, and thus to increase the strength of the balancing component of selection. Both parameters contribute to the effect. If the correlation between patches, ρ, decreases, the degree of environmental subdivision and the magnitude of B will increase. If the number or equality of patches increases, so will the value of κ and with it the magnitude of B. The effect of increases in B on the conditions for polymorphism in the model with symmetrical second-order moments are found using equation 4.31:

$$\sum_{j=1}^{k}(\mu_j - \mu_i) < \frac{(B - 1)\sigma^2}{B}.$$

Clearly increasing B makes polymorphism more likely, supporting the intuition that environmental heterogeneity should be positively correlated with the level of polymorphism. (In this business generalities are hard to come by: the next example of environmental subdivision will show a different relationship.)

An interesting limit occurs if the number of subdivisions increases in such a way that

$$1 - \kappa(1 - \rho) \to 0.$$

This could happen, for example, if the correlation between patches is zero ($\rho = 0$), if all of the patches are the same size ($a_i = 1/n$), and if the number of patches increases to infinity ($n \to \infty$). At the limit, the diffusion coefficient is zero, so the diffusion equation becomes the deterministic system of ordinary differential equations:

$$\frac{dx_i}{dt} = \frac{1}{2}x_i(\mu_i - \bar{\mu} + \bar{\sigma} - \bar{\sigma}_i).$$

This model is widely known as the *random Levene model*. The other variants of SAS-CFF models will yield similar limiting deterministic models if B is allowed to approach infinity. This opens up the strange possibility that deterministic models may be adequate approximations to the dynamics of selection in a fluctuating environment.

Hard selection [41,290] differs from soft selection in that the contribution of each subdivision is made proportional to the size of the subdivision times the mean fitness of the population residing there. It is as if the regulation of the size of the population involved the population as a whole rather than the subdivisions separately. If the mean fitness of the population in the uth patch is written $\bar{w}(u)$, then the contribution of the uth patch to the random mating pool is

$$\frac{a_u \bar{w}(u)}{\sum_{j=1}^n a_j \bar{w}(j)}.$$

Writing the marginal fitness of the ith allele in the uth patch as $w_i(u)$, we can write the change in frequency of the ith allele as

$$\Delta x_i = \sum_{u=1}^n \frac{a_u \bar{w}(u)}{\sum_{j=1}^n a_j \bar{w}(j)} \frac{x_i[w_i(u) - \bar{w}(u)]}{\bar{w}(u)} = \frac{x_i[\sum_u a_u x_i(u) - \sum_u a_u \bar{w}(u)]}{\sum_u a_u \bar{w}(u)}.$$

The latter form shows that the model behaves as if fitnesses were first averaged across environments and then plugged into a standard constant fitness model. Averaging tends to smooth things out, making the effects of environmental fluctuations less pronounced than in the soft selection model.

For the additive model, we can introduce a random variable Z_i for the average of the additive effects,

$$Z_i(t) = \sum_{u=1}^n a_u Y_i(t, u),$$

and use Z_i everywhere that Y_i appears in the additive model with no subdivision. The moments of the Z_i are

$$EZ_i = \mu_i, \quad EZ_i Z_j = [1 - \kappa(1 - \rho)]\sigma_{ij}.$$

Note the reduction in the variance due to the averaging. Using these moments, it is easy to obtain the approximating diffusion

$$
\begin{aligned}
Edx_i &= \frac{1}{2}x_i\{\mu_i - \bar{\mu} + [1 - \kappa(1 - \rho)](\bar{\sigma} - \bar{\sigma}_i)\}dt \\
Edx_i dx_j &= \frac{1}{4}[1 - \kappa(1 - \rho)]x_i x_j(\sigma_{ij} + \bar{\sigma} - \bar{\sigma}_i - \bar{\sigma}_j)dt.
\end{aligned}
$$

For hard selection $B = 2$, being independent of the subdivision entirely. This and the other equivalences for the c-haploid model are given in Table 4.1. The conditions for polymorphism when the second-order moments are symmetrical are, from equation 4.31,

$$\sum_{j=1}^{k}(\mu_j - \mu_i) < \frac{[1 - \kappa(1 - \rho)]\sigma^2}{2}.$$

As the spatial heterogeneity increases, the conditions for polymorphism become more stringent, exactly the opposite of soft selection. The conflicting properties of these two models were originally discovered by Dempster [53] in an analysis of models that lacked the temporal component of the fluctuations. In this context, the comparisons of hard and soft selection can lead to unexpected consequences if the fitnesses within subdivisions are scaled inappropriately as pointed out by Walsh [291].

Hard and soft selection may be viewed as two extremes on a continuum of models. The intermediate models are less likely to fall into a simple metaphor involving population regulation, suggesting that they be termed *mushy selection.* The key to finding the intermediate models is to generalize the contribution of the uth patch to the random mating pool,:

$$\frac{a_u \bar{w}(u)^p}{\sum_{j=1}^{n} a_j \bar{w}(j)^p}.$$

If $p = 0$, the model reduces to soft selection; if $p = 1$ it reduces to hard selection. Using the same approach as in the previous models, we get the diffusion

$$Edx_i = \frac{1}{2}x_i\{\mu_i - \bar{\mu} + [1 - p\kappa(1 - \rho)](\bar{\sigma} - \bar{\sigma}_i)\}dt$$

$$Edx_i dx_j = \frac{1}{4}[1 - \kappa(1 - \rho)]x_i x_j(\sigma_{ij} + \bar{\sigma} - \bar{\sigma}_i - \bar{\sigma}_j)dt.$$

The c-haploid equivalences are given in Table 4.1. The conditions for polymorphism when the second-order moments are symmetrical are

$$\sum_{j=1}^{k}(\mu_j - \mu_i) < [\frac{1}{2} + \kappa(1 - \rho)(\frac{1}{2} - p)]\sigma^2.$$

If $p < 1/2$, the conditions for polymorphism become easier to meet as the spatial heterogeneity increases; if $p > 1/2$ it gets harder to maintain polymorphism as the heterogeneity increases. For the peculiar case where $p = 1/2$, spatial heterogeneity has no effect.

These results cloud any effort to interpret observations on correlations of environmental variability with levels of polymorphism. Positive, negative, and no correlations are all compatible with selection in a temporally and spatially fluctuating environment. A more interesting use of the results may be through comparisons of haploids and diploids. All of the results in this section may be readily adapted to haploid species. When this is done, we discover that soft selection will allow polymorphisms in haploids, but hard selection will not. If it were known that levels of variation in haploids and diploids were similar, then our theory would suggest that soft rather than hard selection is operative in nature.

Temporal autocorrelations

The temporal fluctuations that provide the randomness in our models have the peculiar property that the environment in each generation is independent of the environments in all past generations. It may be that this situation seldom, if ever, holds in nature. If our models are to be taken seriously, they must be modified to include environmental correlations.

From a mathematical point of view, it would appear that autocorrelations require an entirely new approach. Recall that the independence of environments means that the allele frequency process is a Markov process. The state of the process in one generation depends only on its state in the previous generation. Our method of approximation has been through diffusion processes that are also Markov processes. If we were to allow the environment to be autocorrelated, that is, to depend on past states, then we would destroy the Markovian nature of the allele frequency process. It would seem that diffusion approximations would be a casualty as well.

Remarkably, this need not be the case. There is a recent mathematical literature on the approximation of non-Markovian processes by diffusion processes that was motivated, in part, by models of selection in a random environment. Unfortunately, the methods that are used are quite advanced, far beyond the level of mathematics that characterizes this book. Given the importance of this area, it seems appropriate to provide a heuristic derivation of the main results. We will only derive the two-allele result. The extension to k alleles may be readily understood once the two-allele case is in hand.

Consider the stochastic difference equation

$$\Delta x = F(x, \mathbf{Y}(t)) = \frac{1}{2} \frac{x(1-x)[Y_1(t) - Y_2(t)]}{1 + xY_1(t) + (1-x)Y_2(t)},$$

where $\mathbf{Y}(t)$ is a vector with components $Y_1(t)$ and $Y_2(t)$. The function F will be used to hide some of the details of the genetic model.

Because $F(x, \mathbf{0}) = 0$, if the Y_i are small, the change in x is small as well, allowing a diffusion-style approximation. Diffusion approximations are usually obtained by calculating the mean and variance of Δx. If x and $\mathbf{Y}(t)$ are uncorrelated, as when $\mathbf{Y}(t)$ is not autocorrelated, then this calculation is easy, at least in principle. However, when $\mathbf{Y}(t)$ is autocorrelated, x and $\mathbf{Y}(t)$ become correlated with each other. In this case, the calculation of the moments of Δx requires that the correlation between x and $\mathbf{Y}(t)$ be known. The only exact method for obtaining the correlation is by solving the difference equation completely. This is not possible, in general, so we must resort to some trickery.

An approach that has proven successful approximates the nonlinear difference equation with a linear equation that can be solved exactly, thus allowing the calculation of the appropriate moments. If a bunch of linear processes, which are viewed as local approximations to the original process, are patched together, they provide the correct diffusion approximation to the nonlinear process. To suggest such an approach with a straight face without supporting theorems would be outrageous; nevertheless, this was the approach that lead to the original conjecture for the diffusion approximations and provides the motivation for the method of proof.

The first step on the road to the diffusion is the approximation of the nonlinear process with a linear process. Assuming that the original process is initiated at time zero at $x(0)$, we are seeking an approximation of

$$u(t) = x(t) - x(0)$$

that is valid as long as $u(t)$ remains small. Doing what comes naturally, we will use the first two terms of the Taylor series expansion of F around $x(0)$,

$$x(t+1) - x(t) = F[x(0), \mathbf{Y}(t)] + F_x[x(0), \mathbf{Y}(t)][x(t) - x(0)],$$

where the subscript x means the partial derivative of F with respect to x. This expansion provides the difference equation for $u(t)$:

$$u(t+1) = F[x(0), \mathbf{Y}(t)] + \{1 + F_x[x(0), \mathbf{Y}(t)]\}u(t).$$

The most interesting initial condition is $u(0) = 0$, as this is the only one that corresponds to the difference $x(t) - x(0)$. The wisdom of hindsight suggests that this equation should be written in the more convenient form

$$u(t+1) = f[\mathbf{Y}(t)] + \exp\{g[\mathbf{Y}(t)]\}u(t),$$

where

$$\begin{aligned}
f[\mathbf{Y}(t)] &= F[x(0), \mathbf{Y}(t)] \\
g[\mathbf{Y}(t)] &= \ln\{1 + F_x[x(0), \mathbf{Y}(t)]\}.
\end{aligned}$$

The general solution of the linear equation, in terms of a particular realization of the process $\mathbf{Y}(t)$, may be found by writing $u(1)$ in terms of $u(0)$, then $u(2)$ in terms of $u(1)$, and so forth. The result is

$$\begin{aligned}
u(t) &= f[\mathbf{Y}(t-1)] + \sum_{i=0}^{t-2} f[\mathbf{Y}(i)] \exp\left\{\sum_{j=i+1}^{t-1} g[\mathbf{Y}(j)]\right\} \\
&\quad + \exp\left\{\sum_{i=0}^{t-1} g[\mathbf{Y}(i)]\right\} u(0).
\end{aligned}$$

The next step could be to find a limiting form of the solution to the linear equation as $\mathbf{Y}(t)$ approaches zero in some appropriate way. However, for our more narrowly focused drive toward the diffusion approximation, we really do not care about the complete solution; rather, we only need an approximation of the first two moments of $u(t)$ when $u(0) = 0$.

Use

$$f[Y(t)] \approx f_1 Y_1(t) + f_2 Y_2(t) + \frac{1}{2} f_{11} Y_1(t)^2 + f_{12} Y_1(t) Y_2(t) + \frac{1}{2} f_{22} Y_2(t)^2$$

and

$$\exp \left\{ \sum_{i=j}^{t-1} g[\mathbf{Y}(i)] \right\} \approx 1 + g_1 \sum_{i=j}^{t-1} Y_1(i) + g_2 \sum_{i=j}^{t-1} Y_2(i),$$

where the subscripts of f and g are partial derivatives with respect to the corresponding Y_i and all of the partial derivatives are evaluated at zero, with $u(0) = 0$ to obtain

$$
\begin{aligned}
u(t) \quad \approx \quad & f_1 \sum_{i=0}^{t-1} Y_1(i) + f_2 \sum_{i=0}^{t-1} Y_2(i) \qquad\qquad\qquad (4.51) \\
& + \frac{1}{2} f_{11} \sum_{i=0}^{t-1} Y_1(i)^2 + f_{12} \sum_{i=0}^{t-1} Y_1(i) Y_2(i) + \frac{1}{2} f_{22} \sum_{i=0}^{t-1} Y_2(i)^2 \\
& + \sum_{i=0}^{t-2} \sum_{j=i+1}^{t-1} [f_1 g_1 Y_1(i) Y_1(j) + f_1 g_2 Y_1(i) Y_2(j) \\
& + f_2 g_1 Y_2(i) Y_1(j) + f_2 g_2 Y_2(i) Y_2(j)].
\end{aligned}
$$

We will also need an approximation for the square of $u(t)$:

$$
\begin{aligned}
u(t)^2 \quad \approx \quad & f_1^2 \sum_{i=0}^{t-1} \sum_{j=0}^{t-1} Y_1(i) Y_1(j) + 2 f_1 f_2 \sum_{i=0}^{t-1} \sum_{j=0}^{t-1} Y_1(i) Y_2(j) \\
& + f_2^2 \sum_{i=0}^{t-1} \sum_{j=0}^{t-1} Y_2(i) Y_2(j).
\end{aligned}
$$

For the evaluation of the expectations of $u(t)$ and $u(t)^2$, we need to define the moments of $\mathbf{Y}(t)$. At this point, it will be useful to become a bit more formal by writing these moments as explicit functions of a number, ϵ, that will approach zero. For the means and covariances use

$$
\begin{aligned}
EY_i(t) &= \mu_i \epsilon \\
EY_i(t) Y_j(t) &= \sigma_{ij} \epsilon^{1+\delta},
\end{aligned}
$$

where δ is a number from the closed interval $[0, 1]$. Note that this represents a departure from earlier definitions in that the covariances may become much smaller than the means if $0 < \delta$. This is done because the presence of autocorrelations causes an inflation in the effects of the random fluctuations that must be kept under control. Smaller covariances are the obvious way to accomplish this.

Let the autocorrelations be described by the autocorrelation function

$$\text{Corr}(Y_i(t), Y_j(t + \tau)) = \rho(\tau; \epsilon, \delta).$$

We are assuming that the autocorrelation is the same for each of the alleles. This assumption is not necessary for the derivation of the diffusion, but is required for the diffusion to be a c-haploid diffusion. As an example, a Markovian environmental process might have an autocorrelation function of the form

$$\rho(\tau; \epsilon, \delta) = (1 - a\epsilon^\delta)^{|\tau|}, \tag{4.52}$$

which has the property that, if $0 < \delta$, the autocorrelation approaches one as ϵ approaches zero. Otherwise, it is independent of ϵ. We will often adopt this special form of ρ as it will allow a concrete representation of the results.

The limiting forms of the moments of $u(t)$ depend on the value of δ. In fact, there are three limiting forms: one occurs if $\delta = 0$, another if $0 < \delta < 1$, and the third if $\delta = 1$. These limits are sufficiently different from each other that they will be considered separately.

When $\delta = 0$, the environment is said to be *weakly autocorrelated*. In this case the autocorrelation function does not depend on ϵ. As ϵ approaches zero, $u(t)$ slows down, causing it to experience more and more environmental states before changing appreciably. In fact, once it has changed, so many environmental states will have occurred that the current and future environments will be essentially uncorrelated with those that caused x to change. For this reason, the weakly autocorrelated case represents a rather small departure from the nonautocorrelated case that may be approximated with a diffusion process once the expectations of $u(t)$ and $u(t)^2$ are known.

To know $Eu(t)^2$, we require

$$E\sum_{i=0}^{t-1}\sum_{j=0}^{t-1} Y_m(i)Y_n(j) = \sigma_{mn}\epsilon \sum_{i=0}^{t-1}\sum_{j=0}^{t-1} \rho(i - j).$$

A useful relationship for evaluating this sum is

$$\sum_{i=0}^{t-1}\sum_{j=0}^{t-1} \rho(i - j) = t\eta(t)^2,$$

where

$$\eta(t)^2 = 1 + 2\sum_{i=1}^{t-1}(1 - i/t)\rho(i).$$

For the special form of the autocorrelation function given by equation 4.52,

$$\eta(t)^2 = 2/a - 1 - \frac{2(1 - a)[1 - (1 - a)^t]}{ta^2}.$$

By scaling time such that $t = t'/\epsilon$, where t' is a real number, we obtain a continuous time approximation for $Eu(t)^2$. With this scaling, we have

$$\eta^2 = \lim_{\epsilon \to 0} \eta(t'/\epsilon)^2 = 1 + 2\sum_{i=1}^{\infty} \rho(i).$$

There is a hidden assumption that the infinite sum of the autocorrelation function is finite. For the special case, equation 4.52, this does hold, and

$$\eta^2 = 2/a - 1.$$

Putting all this together, the diffusion coefficient for the limiting diffusion process becomes

$$\lim_{t' \to 0} \frac{Eu(t')^2}{t'} = \eta^2 (f_1^2 \sigma_{11} + 2f_1 f_2 \sigma_{12} + f_2^2 \sigma_{22}).$$

For the drift coefficient, we need the following:

$$E\sum_{n=0}^{t-1} Y_i(n) = t\mu_i \epsilon$$

$$E\sum_{n=0}^{t-1} Y_i(n)Y_j(n) = t\sigma_{ij}\epsilon$$

$$E\sum_{n=0}^{t-2}\sum_{m=i+1}^{t-1} Y_i(n)Y_j(m) = t\sigma_{ij}\epsilon(\eta^2(t) - 1)/2.$$

This yields

$$\lim_{t' \to 0} \frac{Eu(t')}{t'} = f_1\mu_1 + f_2\mu_2 + f_{11}\sigma_{11}/2 + f_{12}\sigma_{12} + f_{22}\sigma_{22}/2$$
$$+ (\eta^2 - 1)(f_1 g_1 \sigma_{11} + 2f_1 g_2 \sigma_{12} + f_2 g_2 \sigma_{22})/2.$$

To apply this to the genetic model, use

$$\begin{aligned}
f_1 = -f_2 &= x(1-x)/2 \\
g_1 = -g_2 &= 1/2 - x \\
f_{11} &= -x^2(1-x) \\
f_{12} &= -x(1-x)(1/2 - x) \\
f_{22} &= x(1-x)^2
\end{aligned}$$

to get

$$\begin{aligned}
Edx &= x[\mu_1^* - \bar{\mu}^* + \frac{1+\eta^2}{4}(\bar{\sigma} - \bar{\sigma}_1)]dt \\
Edx^2 &= (\eta^2/4)x^2(\sigma_{11} - 2\bar{\sigma}_1 + \bar{\sigma})dt,
\end{aligned}$$

where

$$\mu_i^* = \mu_i/2 + \sigma_{ii}(\eta^2 - 1)/8.$$

In arriving at this result, in effect, we lumped together the linear approximations of the original process at each point in the domain of $x(t)$. Recall that the linear process focused on the single point $x(0)$. Now we are viewing $x(0)$ not as a fixed numerical argument of F, but rather as the state of the process at time t.

The extension to an arbitrary number of alleles is obvious:

$$Edx_i = x_i[\mu_i^* - \bar{\mu}^* + \frac{1+\eta^2}{4}(\bar{\sigma} - \bar{\sigma}_i)]dt$$

$$Edx_i dx_j = (\eta^2/4)x_i x_j(\sigma_{ij} - \bar{\sigma}_i - \bar{\sigma}_j + \bar{\sigma})dt.$$

From this we see that

$$B = (1 + \eta^2)/\eta^2.$$

The various equivalences for the c-haploid model are given in Table 4.1.

The effects of weak autocorrelations on the level of polymorphism is rather interesting. As B is a decreasing function of the strength of the autocorrelation as measured by η^2, we might expect that the conditions for polymorphism become harder to meet as η^2 increases. That this is not the case may be seen by plugging the c-haploid equivalences from Table 4.1 into the conditions for polymorphism (equation 4.31 for the model with symmetrical second-order moments) to get

$$\sum_{j=1}^{k}(\mu_j - \mu_i) < \frac{(B-1)\sigma^2}{2}.$$

This condition is independent of η^2 and consequently independent of the strength of the autocorrelation. We saw earlier that the conditions for polymorphism may be written in terms of the geometric mean fitness of the genotypes. The geometric mean fitnesses are also independent of the level of autocorrelation. This implies that the geometric mean fitness conditions, which were derived for the case of a nonautocorrelated environment, should apply to an autocorrelated environment as well.

Although weak autocorrelations do not affect the conditions for polymorphism, they do affect the homozygosity of the population. This may be seen in a variety of ways. In the completely symmetrical model, the homozygosity is a decreasing function of B. Since B decreases with the autocorrelation, the homozygosity will increase. As η^2 approaches infinity, the homozygosity approaches one yet the conditions for polymorphism continue to be met. At the limit, the dynamics are the same as for the moderately autocorrelated case, as will be seen shortly.

The heuristic approach for deriving the limiting diffusion that we have just slogged through will work for a large class of stochastic difference equations. The conjecture for the form of the limiting diffusion first appeared in 1978 [97] and was proven for the one-dimensional case by Iizuka and Matsuda[137] and for the k-dimensional case by Kushner and Huang [177]. The fact that the autocorrelation drops off rapidly with time makes this case somewhat easier to investigate than the cases of moderate and strong autocorrelations

Moderately autocorrelated environments occur when $0 < \delta < 1$. In this instance, the autocorrelation must approach one as ϵ approaches zero. However, it must not approach one so fast that the time scale of environmental change is the same or greater than that of the change of $u(t)$. One way to quantify the relationship of the time scales is through the *persistence time* of the environment defined as the time required for the autocorrelation to equal $1/e \approx 0.368$. For the special case of equation 4.52, this is given by

$$\tau_p = -1/\ln(1 - a\epsilon^\delta) \sim 1/a\epsilon^\delta.$$

As ϵ approaches zero, the persistence time increases to infinity as $1/\epsilon^\delta$ whereas the time scale of change of $u(t)$ is $1/\epsilon$. Thus, the environment is changing more rapidly than $u(t)$. This is the property that leads to the diffusion limit.

The route to the limiting diffusion is exactly like the previous case. Begin by noting that, for the special case of equation 4.52,

$$\lim_{\epsilon \to 0} \epsilon^\delta \eta(t'/\epsilon)^2 = 2/a.$$

As before, the special form is really unnecessary, so we will assume only that

$$\lim_{\epsilon \to 0} \epsilon^\delta \eta(t'/\epsilon)^2 = \eta^2 < \infty.$$

A simple but useful consequence is

$$\lim_{\epsilon \to 0} \epsilon^\delta [\eta(t'/\epsilon)^2 - 1]/2 = \eta^2/2.$$

From here it is a simple matter to get the diffusion coefficient of the linear process

$$\lim_{t' \to 0} \frac{Eu(t')^2}{t'} = \eta^2(f_1^2 \sigma_{11} + 2f_1 f_2 \sigma_{12} + f_2^2 \sigma_{22}).$$

This is in exactly the same form as for the weakly autocorrelated environment. By contrast, the drift coefficient,

$$\lim_{t' \to 0} \frac{Eu(t')}{t'} = f_1 \mu_1 + f_2 \mu_2 + (\eta^2/2)(f_1 g_1 \sigma_{11} + 2f_1 g_2 \sigma_{12} + f_2 g_2 \sigma_{22}),$$

lacks terms involving second-order derivatives of f that appeared in the weakly autocorrelated case. Applying these to the genetic case yields the diffusion

$$Edx_i = x_i[\mu_i^* - \bar{\mu}^* + \frac{\eta^2}{4}(\bar{\sigma} - \bar{\sigma}_i)]dt$$

$$Edx_i dx_j = \frac{\eta^2}{4} x_i x_j (\sigma_{ij} - \bar{\sigma}_i - \bar{\sigma}_j + \bar{\sigma})dt,$$

where

$$\mu_i^* = \mu_i/2 + \sigma_{ii}\eta^2/8.$$

The limiting argument is quite delicate due to the increase in the autocorrelation with decreasing ϵ. A formal weak convergence proof has been provided by Iizuka and Matsuda [137] for the two-allele case. The k-allele case has yet to be examined.

The moderately autocorrelated diffusion has $B = 1$, making it formally equivalent to a haploid model. Thus, polymorphism due to balancing selection is impossible. From a biological point of view, this is an important difference between the mildly and strongly autocorrelated cases. If temporal fluctuations in the environment are to be invoked as the cause of polymorphism, then it must be that the fluctuations are weakly autocorrelated.

The final case, that of a *strongly autocorrelated* environment ($\delta = 1$), differs from the other two in that the limit is not a diffusion process. Rather, it is the solution of an ordinary differential equation with a stochastic process appearing as a parameter. This is suggested by the fact that the persistence time,

$$\tau_p \sim 1/a\epsilon,$$

is of the same order of magnitude as the time scale of change of $u(t)$.

The actual form of the differential equation can be inferred from the linear solution, given by equation 4.51. As $\delta = 1$, the variance of $Y_i(t)$ will be of order ϵ^2. A bold move—which happens to be correct—is to use this observation to remove all terms from equation 4.51 that contain the products $Y_i(t)Y_j(t)$. This gives the refreshingly plain

$$u(t) \approx f_1 \sum_{i=0}^{t-1} Y_1(i) + f_2 \sum_{i=0}^{t-1} Y_2(i).$$

One way of guaranteeing the order of magnitude assumptions is to write

$$Y_i(t) = \mu_i\epsilon + \epsilon Z_i(t; \epsilon),$$

where the moments,

$$EZ_i(t; \epsilon) = 0, \quad EZ_i(t; \epsilon)Z_j(t; \epsilon) = \sigma_{ij},$$

are independent of ϵ. The autocorrelation function for $Z_i(t; \epsilon)$, on the other hand, does depend on ϵ, being the same as for $Y_i(t)$. If time is scaled as $t = t'/\epsilon$, then

$$u(t') \approx (f_1\mu_1 + f_2\mu_2)t' + f_1 \sum_{i=0}^{t'/\epsilon} Z_1(i; \epsilon)\epsilon + f_2 \sum_{i=0}^{t'/\epsilon} Z_2(i; \epsilon)\epsilon.$$

The sums that appear in this solution should approach integrals if the processes $Z_i(t; \epsilon)$ approach integrable processes. Assume that this is the case:

$$Z_i(t) = \lim_{\epsilon \to 0} Z_i(t; \epsilon).$$

The solution may then be written

$$u(t') \approx (f_1\mu_1 + f_2\mu_2)t' + f_1 \int_0^{t'} Z_1(t)dt + f_2 \int_0^{t'} Z_2(t)dt,$$

suggesting immediately that

$$\frac{du}{dt} = f_1[\mu_1 + Z_1(t)] + f_2[\mu_2 + Z_2(t)]$$

is the limiting stochastic ordinary differential equation. For the k-allele genetic case this becomes

$$\frac{dx_i}{dt} = \frac{x_i}{2} \sum_{i=1}^{k} x_j[\mu_i + Z_i(t) - \mu_j - Z_j(t)].$$

In producing this result, we assumed that $Z_i(t;\epsilon)$ approaches a continuous stochastic process. To assure that the result is not vacuous, we need an example where the convergence does occur as assumed. One example is a first-order autoregression process,

$$Z_i(t+1;\epsilon) = (1 - a\epsilon)Z_i(t;\epsilon) + \sqrt{1 - (1 - a\epsilon)^2}U_i(t),$$

where $U_i(t)$ is a sequence of independent standardized normal random variables. $Z_i(t;\epsilon)$ is a stationary Markov Gaussian process with mean zero, variance one, and autocorrelation function

$$\rho(t) = (1 - a\epsilon)^{|t|}.$$

When time is scaled by $t = t'/\epsilon$, the autocorrelation function approaches

$$\lim_{\epsilon \to 0}(1 - a\epsilon)^{|t'|/\epsilon} = e^{-a|t'|}.$$

Thus, the limiting process, $Z_i(t')$, is a stationary Gaussian Markov process with an exponential autocorrelation function. In fact, it is an Ornstein Uhlenbeck process, which is a diffusion process with continuous sample paths. As we had hoped, there is at least one process that yields the limiting differential equation; the reader will have no difficulty in producing many others.

Iizuka [136] has provided the weak convergence proof for the strongly autocorrelated case. His proof is very general, covering an arbitrary number of dimensions and having a very general form for the difference operator.

As the limit of the strongly autocorrelated case is not a diffusion, we cannot appeal to any of our previous results to investigate the properties of the model. It shares with the moderately autocorrelated case the fact that the limiting process is in the same form as a haploid model. Thus, the differential equation may be transformed to a linear process just as was done for the haploid diffusion and the general solution displayed. This will not be pursued here. The reader may refer to [80] for the two-allele solution.

The SAS-CFF diffusion

Each of the three modifications of the additive model leads to an approximating diffusion process that is the same as that for a c-haploid model. The equivalent parameters need only be plucked from Table 4.1. This suggests that a diffusion that combines all three elements would be of the same form as well. The derivation would be a herculean task and there seems to be no compelling reason to attempt it. It is clear that the diffusion will be the c-haploid diffusion with parameters reflecting, in a complex way, the relative contributions of dominance, subdivision, and autocorrelation. If we could envision an experimental program that would allow us to estimate the contributions of these three elements, then the combined model might prove to be of value. However, even the most optimistic experimenter will realize that this simply isn't in the cards. To make the needed observations on fitnesses differences that are likely to be smaller than 0.1% is not possible.

Attempts to estimate the parameters that appear in the diffusion models by careful direct observations on fitness differences between genotypes and demographic properties of populations may be called the *microscopic approach*. For example, one outcome of this approach might be the determination that the alleles at a locus exhibit neither dominance nor mean differences, that the fitnesses are not autocorrelated, and that hard selection is operating with parameters ρ and κ whose values have been estimated. In this case we know that

$$B = \frac{2}{1 - \kappa(1 - \rho)}.$$

We could think of B as a macroscopic parameter whose value we just determined by careful microscopic observations combined with theoretical work showing the dependency of B on ρ and κ.

By contrast, we could admit at the outset the impossibility of ever making such observations and attempt to estimate B from allele frequency dynamics. In practice, this will necessitate making some additional assumptions. For example, we may want to begin with the simplest model—the totally symmetrical model—to see how far it can be pushed. In this case, B may be estimated from the observed homozygosity using

$$E\mathcal{F}_k = \frac{1}{2B - 1} + \frac{2(B - 1)}{k(2B - 1)},$$

which we obtained earlier. From this point of view, we really do not care why B exhibits the value that it does. If B were small, for example, we abandon any hope of knowing whether this is due to autocorrelations or hard selection and simply savor the knowledge that it is small. By going through the various models in this section, we have learned that B can range upward from one, and that B may be large or small for a variety of reasons. This gives us confidence that the diffusion corresponds to at least some situations in nature and suggests that it may apply to many other situations that we have not examined.

It is a small extension of this line of reasoning to suggest that the SAS-CFF diffusion model should be viewed as primitive. We know that it applies to some situations in nature and could very likely apply to more. The most convenient parameterization of the SAS-CFF model is that used for the c-haploid model as given in equation 4.12. However, even this model is too general for most applications since it has $i(i+1)/2+i+1$ parameters. At the other extreme, the totally symmetrical version given by equation 4.26 is the most useful since it has only two parameters, B and $c^2\sigma^2$. In the sequel, when the symmetrical SAS-CFF model is used, it will be written

$$
\begin{aligned}
E dx_i &= \sigma^2 B x_i (\mathcal{F}_k - x_i) dt && (4.53)\\
E dx_i dx_j &= \sigma^2 x_i x_j (\delta_{ij} + \mathcal{F}_k - x_i - x_j) dt,
\end{aligned}
$$

where we have lumped the combined c-haploid parameter, $c^2\sigma^2$, in the single SAS-CFF parameter, σ^2. When an asymmetrical version of the SAS-CFF model is needed, we will never go beyond the version that uses the symmetrical second-order moments

$$
\begin{aligned}
E dx_i &= x_i[(\mu_i - \bar{\mu}) + \sigma^2 B(\mathcal{F}_k - x_i)] dt && (4.54)\\
E dx_i dx_j &= \sigma^2 x_i x_j (\delta_{ij} + \mathcal{F}_k - x_i - x_j) dt. && (4.55)
\end{aligned}
$$

Here the same lumping of $c^2\sigma^2$ is used as is a lumping of the c-haploid $c\mu_i$ into the SAS-CFF μ_i. From this point on these two diffusion models will be adopted and a great deal of effort will go into judging their success in accounting for observations on molecular evolution and polymorphism.

4.5 Drift and mutation

Most alleles begin their lives as a single copy and, in their infancy, are subject to the whims of genetic drift. Should they become common, they still face an eventual death at the hands of genetic drift. Thus, models of molecular evolution must include mutation and drift if they are to be faithful to the real world. The most important properties of models with drift and mutation are the mean time to lose a segregating allele and the mean time for an allele to enter the population. Combining these two times allows a description of both the levels of variation in the population and the rate of molecular evolution.

Losing alleles

We will examine the effects of genetic drift first. We hope to find an asymptotic expression for the mean time to lose an interior allele from the population. Based on past experience, it would seem that the Matkowsky-Schuss technique would provide the answer. However, a straightforward application of the technique breaks down due to changes caused by genetic drift near the boundary. Yet, the technique seems particularly well suited to examining boundary and interior dynamics separately, suggesting that, if properly modified, it might still be applicable to models with genetic drift. This appears to be the case, as will be argued in this section. The results, however, must remain suspect until a more rigorous approach can be found.

Consider a diploid population of effective size N. The finiteness of the population adds a new element of randomness that appears in the diffusion coefficient. As genetic drift is due to multinomial sampling of a population, the additional term is

$$x_i(\delta_{ij} - x_j)/2N.$$

When this is added to the symmetrical SAS-CFF diffusion from equation 4.53, we have the new diffusion

$$
\begin{aligned}
Edx_i &= \sigma^2 Bx_i(\mathcal{F}_k - x_i)dt \\
Edx_i dx_j &= [\sigma^2 x_i x_j(\delta_{ij} + \mathcal{F}_k - x_i - x_j) + x_i(\delta_{ij} - x_j)/2N]dt.
\end{aligned}
$$

Population geneticists traditionally scale time so that it is measured in units of $2N$ generations. This has the effect of removing one parameter from the model and helps to focus on inequalitites in the magnitudes of parameters. Following in this tradition, the diffusion becomes

$$
\begin{aligned}
Edx_i &= \alpha Bx_i(\mathcal{F}_k - x_i)dt \\
Edx_i dx_j &= [\alpha x_i x_j(\delta_{ij} + \mathcal{F}_k - x_i - x_j) + x_i(\delta_{ij} - x_j)]dt,
\end{aligned}
$$

where $\alpha = 2N\sigma^2$.

The most important consequence of adding drift is that the process no longer has a stationary distribution. The boundaries at zero have become accessible; they will be hit in a finite period of time. Once an allele is lost, it is gone forever. Thus, the eventual state of the population is to be made up entirely of a single allele. It is this process of losing alleles that we would like to describe.

The first problem that we encounter when applying the Matkowsky-Schuss technique is with the solution to the equation $L^*[v] = 0$. Recall that in obtaining the mean time for an allele to hit a barrier at ϵ in the infinite population case we required the integral of v over the domain of the process. As v is proportional to the stationary distribution, it is integrable over the entire domain of the process. However, when drift is added, v is no longer a distribution and will not be integrable over the domain of the process effectively aborting any effort to use the Matkowsky-Schuss approach in the obvious way. To add insult to injury, when drift is present the solution to $L^*[v] = 0$ is not known.

The reason for the breakdown of the technique is tied up with the behavior of the diffusion at the boundaries. In our previous application, the boundary at ϵ was imposed by us. When genetic drift is present, the boundary corresponds to edges where the diffusion coefficient is identically zero. Such things are not meant to happen in the usual application of the

Matkowsky-Schuss technique. Still, there must be some connection between the mean time for an allele to become rare when drift is absent and the mean time to be lost when drift is present, at least asymptotically.

The connection emerges when we consider the asymptotic form of the mean times in very large populations. In such populations, selection will dominate drift for common alleles, while rare alleles will be subject to the combined action of drift and selection. The time required for an allele that is initially common to become rare should be determined by selection alone. Once it becomes rare, its subsequent fate will be dictated by the combined action of drift and selection. This suggests that we should be able to use our previous results to obtain the mean time to become rare, and a new boundary layer analysis to describe what happens once an allele becomes rare. Clearly, a major hurdle in such an approach is deciding what we mean by rare.

The boundary between common and rare could be defined to lie at the point where the contributions of selection and drift are roughly equal in the diffusion coefficient. By this criterion, the ith out of k alleles will be rare when

$$\sigma^2 x_i^2(1 + \mathcal{F}_k - 2x_i) \approx x_i(1 - x_i)/2N.$$

When x_i is small, we can ignore higher powers to get

$$x_i \approx \frac{1}{2N\sigma^2(1 + E\mathcal{F}_{k-1})} = \frac{1}{\alpha(1 + E\mathcal{F}_{k-1})}$$

as a criterion for rareness. This only makes sense when selection is relatively strong, that is, when α is large.

When an allele is rare, its frequency changes more slowly than those of common alleles. Moreover, the homozygosity will be determined mostly by the $k - 1$ common alleles. This is why $E\mathcal{F}_{k-1}$ was used in place of $\mathcal{F}_k$ in the criterion. We could imagine that the mean time to lose an allele from a finite population is roughly equal to the mean time for an allele to become rare in an infinite population. Were this so, then we could take our results on the mean time to hit ϵ for an infinite population (equation 4.45) and substitute

$$\epsilon = \frac{1}{\alpha(1 + E\mathcal{F}_{k-1})} \tag{4.56}$$

to get the mean time to lose the first of k alleles from the interior. An obvious shortcoming of this argument is that it fails to recognize the role of the mean change of rare alleles. Nonetheless, the answer appears to be correct. We will be able to demonstrate this for two alleles, and provide some support for the k-allele case.

The role of α in this discussion should be emphasized. For the asymptotic expansion to apply, ϵ must approach zero. Equivalently, α must approach infinity. As α grows, selection dominates drift over an increasing fraction of the state space. We will say that a population is experiencing *strong selection* if α is much larger than one. This contrasts to the cases of *moderate* or *weak* selection where α is near one or much less than one, respectively. Notice that strong selection does not imply that selection is strong in some absolute sense, but only that it dominates drift. Thus, in large populations alphas that range from 10 to 100 will be compatible with very small values of σ^2.

Our derivation of the asymptotic expression for the mean time to lose an allele will rest heavily on intuition gained from the two-allele case. The two-allele version of the symmetrical SAS-CFF diffusion that includes genetic drift has drift and diffusion coefficients

$$
\begin{aligned}
b(x) &= \alpha Bx(1-x)(1-2x) \\
a(x) &= x(1-x)(2\alpha x(1-x)+1).
\end{aligned}
$$

The problem before us is to find an asymptotic expression for the mean time for one or the other of the alleles to be lost from the population when both alleles are common at the outset. That is, we want to find an asymptotic expression for the solution to the equation

$$
\frac{a(x)}{2}\bar{t}''(x) + b(x)\bar{t}'(x) = -1,
$$

with boundary conditions $\bar{t}(0) = \bar{t}(1) = 0$ as $\alpha \to \infty$.

The asymptotics will be performed on the general solution of the backward equation. Toward this end, let

$$
\psi(x) = e^{-2\int^x \frac{b(y)}{a(y)}dy} = [x(1-x)+1/2\alpha]^{-B}
$$

and let $u(x)$ be the probability that $x(t)$ hits zero before one. With these definitions, the general solution of the backward equation may be written*

$$
\bar{t}(x) = 2u(x)\int_0^x \frac{dy}{a(y)\psi(y)} \int_0^y \psi(z)dz + 2(1-u(x))\int_x^1 \frac{dy}{a(y)\psi(y)} \int_y^1 \psi(z)dz.
$$

As $\alpha \to \infty$, $u(x) \to 1/2$. Thus, we need only attack the two double integrals. They turn out to be asymptotically the same, so only the left one will be considered and it may be written in the suggestive form

$$
\frac{1}{2\alpha}\int_0^x [y(1-y)]^{B-2}\left[1+\frac{1}{2\alpha y(1-y)}\right]^{B-1}\int_0^y [z(1-z)+1/2\alpha]^{-B}dzdy.
$$

A quick and dirty analysis of this integral goes as follows. The inner integral, viewed as a function of y, increases rapidly from zero to a value that may be found by approximating the integral with

$$
\int_0^y [z+1/2\alpha]^{-B}dz = \frac{(2\alpha)^{B-1}}{B-1}[1-(1+2\alpha y)^{-(B-1)}] \sim \frac{(2\alpha)^{B-1}}{B-1}.
$$

---

*The solution to this equation may be found in any treatment of exit times for diffusions, including the books by Gardiner [79, p. 139] and Ewens [68, p. 120].

Since the increase to this value is rapid, the integral could be viewed as simply being equal to the constant $(2\alpha)^{B-1}/(B-1)$. This suggests writing the double integral as

$$\frac{(2\alpha)^{B-2}}{B-1} \int_0^x [y(1-y)]^{B-2} \left[1 + \frac{1}{2\alpha y(1-y)}\right]^{B-1} dy.$$

Turning a blind eye to the divergence of this integral, we could let α approach infinity, causing the bracketed expression to approach one, and the entire expression to approach

$$\frac{(2\alpha)^{B-2}}{B-1} \int_0^x [y(1-y)]^{B-2} dy.$$

To recover the mean time, incorporate the second double integral by continuing the upper limit of integration to one, giving

$$\bar{t}(x) \sim \frac{(2\alpha)^{B-2}}{B-1} \int_0^1 [y(1-y)]^{B-2} dy = \frac{\Gamma(B-1)^2}{(B-1)\Gamma(2B-2)} (2\alpha)^{B-2}.$$

To express the mean time in terms of generations gather than units of $2N$ generations, multiply the mean time by $2N$, giving

$$\bar{t}(x) \sim \frac{\Gamma(B-1)^2}{2\sigma^2(B-1)\Gamma(2B-2)} (2\alpha)^{B-1}.$$

Comparing this with the mean time to hit ϵ for the model without drift from equation 4.43, we see that the two are the same if

$$\epsilon = 1/2\alpha.$$

Since $E\mathcal{F}_1 = 1$, this corresponds exactly to the conjecture given in equation 4.56. For two alleles, the mean time to lose an allele from a finite population is asymptotically the same as the mean time for an allele to become rare in an infinite population, providing that rare is defined according to equation 4.56.

The problem lies with the asymptotic analysis of the integral. The approach that we used, while instructive, produced a divergent integral at an intermediate step. To do it correctly, one must use the fact that the inner integral approaches zero at zero to make the full integral converge. One method is to break the outer integral into two pieces: an integral from zero to δ, where δ is a small number, and a second integral from δ to x. It is easy to establish that the second integral approaches an expression that is in the same form as we claimed above. It is also easy to show that the first integral converges. By letting δ approach zero, the desired limit is obtained.

Unfortunately, this line of argument cannot be extended to multiple alleles because we do not have the general solution for the mean time to lose an allele. However, if we assume that the solution is asymptotically of the same form as the mean time for an allele to become rare in an infinite population, then all we need to do is find the appropriate value for ϵ. The most likely place to look is the boundary layer solution. Since the Matkowsky-Schuss technique only requires the derivative of the boundary layer solution at the boundary, a comparison of the derivatives at the boundary for the finite and infinite population models should suggest the correct value for ϵ.

Consider again the two-allele case. The boundary layer equation for the finite population model uses the stretched variable $y = \alpha x$. The equation for the mean time to lose allele one in the boundary layer is

$$(\alpha y/2)(2y + 1)T_1''(y) + \alpha By T_1'(y) = 0,$$

with boundary conditions

$$T_1(0) = 0, \ T_1(\infty) = C_0$$

and solution

$$T_1(y) = C_0[1 - (1 + 2y)^{-(B-1)}].$$

We need the derivative of T_1 with respect to x. Substituting αx for y, differentiating with respect to x, and evaluating the derivative at zero gives

$$\frac{dT_1(0)}{dx} = C_0(B - 1)2\alpha.$$

The derivative for the infinite population size case, evaluated at ϵ, was shown to be

$$\frac{dT_1(\epsilon)}{dx} = C_0(B - 1)/\epsilon$$

in equation 4.42. The two are equal if $\epsilon = 1/(2\alpha)$.

This result suggests an approach to the multiple-allele case: find a value for ϵ such that the derivative of the mean time to hit ϵ—evaluated at ϵ—in the infinite population size case equals the derivative of the mean time to lose an allele—evaluated at zero—in the finite case, all using boundary layer expansions.

For the k-allele case, the boundary layer equation for the ith allele is

$$(\alpha y/2)[(1 + E\mathcal{F}_{k-1})y + 1]T_i''(y) + \alpha B \, E\mathcal{F}_{k-1}y T_i'(y) = 0$$

with boundary conditions

$$T_i(0) = 0, \ T_i(\infty) = C_0$$

and solution

$$T_i(y) = C_0\{1 - [1 + (1 + E\mathcal{F}_{k-1})^{-(2BE\mathcal{F}_{k-1}/(1+E\mathcal{F}_{k-1})-1)}]\}.$$

The derivative of the solution with respect to x, evaluated at zero, is

$$\frac{\partial T_i(0)}{\partial x} = C_0\left(\frac{2BE\mathcal{F}_{k-1}}{1 + E\mathcal{F}_{k-1}} - 1\right)(1 + E\mathcal{F}_{k-1})\alpha.$$

Using equation 4.28 to evaluate $E\mathcal{F}_{k-1}$ yields

$$\frac{\partial T_i(0)}{\partial x} = \frac{C_0(B-1)(2B-1)}{kB-1}(1 + E\mathcal{F}_{k-1})\alpha.$$

From equation 4.44 we see that the derivative of the mean time to hit ϵ, evaluated at ϵ, for the infinite population size case will equal this finite population result if

$$\epsilon = \frac{1}{\alpha(1 + E\mathcal{F}_{k-1})}.$$

Using equation 4.45, we conclude that the mean time to lose the first of k alleles from the interior is

$$\bar{t}_{out}(k) \sim C_0 = \frac{A_k}{2N}[\alpha(1 + E\mathcal{F}_{k-1})]^{2(B-1)/k}, \qquad (4.57)$$

where

$$A_k = \frac{(kB-1)[2(B-1)(k-1)+k]\Gamma(2(B-1)/k)\Gamma(2(B-1)(k-1)/k)}{\sigma^2 k^2 B(B-1)(2B-1)\Gamma(2B-2)},$$

and

$$1 + E\mathcal{F}_{k-1} = \frac{2[B + (B-1)/(k-1)]}{2B-1}.$$

Time continues to be measured in units of $2N$ generations. This agrees with our conjecture based on the definition of rareness from equation 4.56.

It would be desirable to have a benchmark to decide how fast alleles are lost from the population. Neutral alleles provide a time-honored basis for comparison. Littler [199] showed that the mean time to lose the first of k interior alleles under the neutral model without mutation is proportional to N when time is measured in units of generations. From equation 4.57 we see that the mean time to lose the first of k interior SAS-CFF alleles is proportional to $N^{2(B-1)/k}$, which grows faster than the neutral time whenever $2(B-1)/k > 1$. This is also the condition that the stationary distribution has an interior mode with tails that approach zero. Clearly, if the stationary distribution is such that alleles seldom approach zero, then the mean time to lose an allele will be (asymptotically) much longer than the time to lose a neutral allele. If $2(B-1)/k = 1$, the stationary distribution is uniform and the mean time to lose an allele grows with N at exactly the neutral rate. Otherwise, the first SAS-CFF allele will be lost sooner than the first neutral allele.

Why should an allele be lost sooner at a locus experiencing balancing selection than at one with no selection whatsoever? When $2(B-1)/k < 1$, the stationary distribution is unbounded at zero. Selection will cause allele frequencies to move relatively rapidly toward zero where they become trapped by genetic drift before they can move to the interior again. This is very similar to Robertson's [247] observation that overdominance can speed up the loss of alleles if the deterministic equilibrium is close to zero.

However, we should not jump to the conclusion that there will be less variation when balancing selection is present, since in both SAS-CFF and overdominance the time for alleles to enter the interior when mutation is present is much less than for the neutral model.

From a mathematical point of view, our results could use some additional work to prove that we have identified the correct leading term in an asymptotic expansion. Our derivation depends very much on comparisons with the two-allele case rather than a direct attack on the k-allele diffusion. It might seem that genetic drift in large populations would make this problem formally like small noise problems that are so popular in the world of stochastic differential equations. However, there are two aspects to this problem that make it fundamentally different from those that are usually analyzed. The first is that the limiting process obtained by allowing α to approach infinity is not an ordinary differential equation, as is usual, but rather is a diffusion process. The second is that the mean time that we are most interested in is the time for the process to hit a boundary where the drift and diffusion coefficients vanish. Again, this is not the situation that is usually addressed. These models would appear to hold great promise for some interesting mathematical work that departs quite a bit from the standard fare.

Gaining alleles

Having allowed genetic drift to remove all of the variation from our populations, it is time to add mutation to bring it back. There are many ways to model mutation depending on the assumptions that are entertained about the mutational distances between alleles. The simplest scheme, and the one most often employed, assumes that the k alleles are separated from each other by one mutational step. While this may strain our topological understanding of the structure of DNA, it is convenient from a mathematical point of view. Fortunately, when mutation rates are small, the results for this scheme are readily modified to cover all others.

Let the nucleotide mutation rate be u_n. If there are k alleles, then each allele can mutate to $k - 1$ other alleles making the total mutation rate $(k - 1)u_n$. If the frequency of the ith allele is x_i, then the rate of mutation to this allele is $(1 - x_i)u_n$, whereas the rate away from the allele is $x_i(k - 1)u_n$. These rates produce an additional term in the drift coefficient of the diffusion equation

$$
\begin{aligned}
E dx_i &= [\alpha B x_i(\mathcal{F}_k - x_i) + \frac{k\theta_n}{2}(\frac{1}{k} - x_i)]dt & (4.58) \\
E dx_i dx_j &= [\alpha x_i x_j(\delta_{ij} + \mathcal{F}_k - x_i - x_j) + x_i(\delta_{ij} - x_j)]dt,
\end{aligned}
$$

where $\theta_n = 4Nu_n$. (We follow the conventional definition of θ_n, even though defining it as $2Nu_n$ would eliminate the factor of one half in the drift coefficient.)

Mutation prevents alleles from being permanently lost from the population. Thus, the new diffusion will have a stationary distribution. Unfortunately, we have no idea what it is. The usual approach to finding a stationary distribution through the zero probability flux condition fails. It should come as no surprise that the only known results are from asymptotics. The basic idea is the same as for the case of drift alone: try to keep the effects of mutation and drift small except near the boundary. One way to accomplish this is by allowing α to approach infinity just as was done in the previous case. A second way is to allow α to approach infinity while θ_n approaches zero.

Biological considerations make the latter route preferable. The nucleotide mutation rate is known to be very small, of the order of 10^{-9} to 10^{-8}. We do not know the effective population sizes of species, but for many it is probably smaller than 10^8. Thus, θ_n should be quite a bit smaller than one for many, if not most, species. This suggests the form of the asymptotics that will be developed. By allowing α to approach infinity and θ_n to approach zero, we are, in effect, assuming that

$$u_n << \frac{1}{2N} << \sigma^2.$$

In words, we are assuming that genetic drift dominates mutation and is, in turn, dominated by selection. The limiting results under this assumption have been termed the strong-selection, weak-mutation or SSWM limit.

The mean time until an allele leaves the interior for this new diffusion must be asymptotically the same as for the case with drift and selection alone. It is clear that mutation will have little effect in the interior, given that α is growing and θ_n is shrinking. Once an allele becomes rare, drift should continue to dominate mutation since θ_n is approaching zero. When the allele becomes so rare that mutation does affect its dynamics, a crash into the barrier at zero is almost a certainty. Thus, the mean time to lose an allele with drift alone should equal the mean time for the first crash into the boundary at zero when mutation as well as drift is present.

Mutation will provide a very weak push away from zero. Although it is unlikely that an allele that is pushed away will reenter the interior during any single trip off of the boundary, eventually mutation, drift, and selection will work their magic and the allele will reenter the interior. An allele that is trying to enter the interior will spend a very long time at a low frequency. In fact, it will be lost from the population many times before it finally enters the interior. During this period the time scale of its movement will be slow relative to that of interior alleles. It seems reasonable, therefore, to view the dynamics of a rare allele as a one-dimensional process that depends only on the average properties of interior alleles.

The appropriate one-dimensional process for a rare allele when there are i interior alleles is a linearization of equation 4.58 near zero. The drift and diffusion coefficients for the linearized process are

$$b(x) \quad = \quad \alpha BE\mathcal{F}_i x + \theta_n/2$$

$$a(x) = \alpha x^2 (1 + E\mathcal{F}_i) + x.$$

In deriving this diffusion, higher powers of x were ignored except when x^2 is multiplied by α. Similarly, $\theta_n x$ was ignored since θ_n is approaching zero.

As very rare alleles will hit the barrier at zero many times before entering the interior, we will restrict our attention to alleles whose initial frequencies are zero. Mutation's constant push makes zero a reflecting barrier. Thus, we are interested in the mean time for the process, beginning with $x(0) = 0$, to hit a small value, δ. The mean time is[*]

$$\bar{t}(0) = 2 \int_0^\delta \psi(x) \int_0^x [a(y)\psi(y)]^{-1} dy dx, \tag{4.59}$$

where

$$\psi(x) = e^{-2 \int^x \frac{b(y)}{a(y)} dy} = (1 + \alpha\eta x)^{-\gamma} x^{-\theta_n}$$

and

$$\gamma = 2BE\mathcal{F}_i/(1 + E\mathcal{F}_i), \quad \eta = 1 + E\mathcal{F}_i. \tag{4.60}$$

The latter two quantities are temporary constants that will streamline the notation during our analysis of the mean time. The task before us is to find an asymptotic form for the mean time as $\alpha \to \infty$ and $\theta_n \to 0$.

The first step is to change variables in equation 4.59 with $u = \alpha\eta x$ and $v = \alpha\eta y$:

$$\bar{t}(0) = \frac{2}{\alpha\eta} \int_0^{\alpha\eta\delta} (1 + u)^{-\gamma} u^{-\theta_b} \int_0^u (1 + v)^{\gamma-1} v^{\theta_n-1} dv du.$$

Write the integrand of the inner integral as

$$v^{\theta_n-1} + [(1 + v)^{\gamma-1} - 1]v^{\theta_n-1}$$

and then integrate to get

$$\bar{t}(0) = \frac{2}{\alpha\eta\theta_n(\gamma-1)}[1 - (1 + \alpha\eta\delta)^{-(\gamma-1)}] + \tag{4.61}$$

$$\frac{2}{\alpha\eta} \int_0^{\alpha\eta\delta} (1 + u)^{-\gamma} u^{-\theta_b} \int_0^u [(1 + v)^{\gamma-1} - 1]v^{\theta_n-1} dv du.$$

The first term on the right side of equation 4.61 approaches

$$\frac{2}{\alpha\eta\theta_n(\gamma-1)} \tag{4.62}$$

as $\alpha \to \infty$ because $\gamma - 1$ is always positive. The integral that makes up the second term is asymptotically insignificant to the first term and can be ignored. The reasons are as follows.

---

[*]The mean time for a diffusion with one reflecting barrier to hit an absorbing barrier may be found in Gardiner [79, p. 139] or Ewens [68, p. 123].

The integrand is bounded, suggesting that the asymptotic behavior of the integral will be determined by events when u and v are large. When this is so, the inner integrand will grow as $v^{\gamma+\theta_n-2}$, and its integral as $v^{\gamma+\theta_n-1}$. Similarly, the outer integrand should grow as $u^{-\gamma-\theta_n}$, suggesting that the double integral will grow as $\log(\alpha\eta\delta)$ and the entire term as

$$\log(\alpha\eta\delta)/\alpha.$$

This approaches zero as $\alpha \to \infty$. Thus, the integral term in the expansion will be insignificant providing

$$\frac{1}{\alpha\theta_n} >> \frac{\log(\alpha)}{\alpha}$$

or, more simply, if $\theta_n \log(\alpha) \to 0$. This condition is our first stab at trying to understand the relationship that must hold between α and θ_n for our asymptotics to be correct.

Using equation 4.28 for the mean homozygosity, equation 4.60 for the definitions of γ and η, and equation 4.62, we have

$$\bar{t}(0) \sim \frac{i}{\alpha\theta_n(B-1)} \tag{4.63}$$

for the mean time for an allele that is initially absent from the population to enter the interior.

The problem began with an effort to find the mean time to hit a barrier at δ, yet δ does not appear in the final answer. The reason is that an allele spends most of its time very close to zero, actually disappearing and reappearing many times before it gets close to δ. Once it breaks away from the influence of the boundary at zero, it rapidly moves into the interior where it moves on a much faster time scale. Thus, the mean time to hit any of the interior points will be asymptotically the same.

It appears that the time to enter the interior is exponentially distributed. The intuition comes from a remarkable theorem due to Gnedenko [101]. The theorem states that the distribution of a geometric number of positive random variables will approach an exponential distribution if the mean of the geometric approaches infinity and the positive random variables are suitably scaled.

To use Gnedenko's theorem for rare alleles, pick a very small allele frequency, say x^*, as the initial frequency of the process. An allele with frequency x^* will either hit zero before entering the interior or will enter the interior without hitting zero. Let $u(x^*)$ be the probability that it hits zero before entering the interior. Should it hit zero, then it will eventually return to x^*. Given that the process hits zero before entering the interior, let T_1 be a random variable representing the time from the beginning of the process until the process hits x^* again, *but only after having first hit zero*. Given that it is at x^* the second time, then the conditional time for it to hit zero and return to x^* the third time will be called T_2, and so forth.

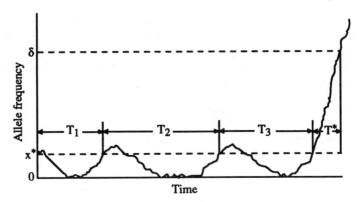

Figure 4.9. The sample path of a rare allele.

Eventually, the process will enter the interior from x^* without hitting zero. Let the conditional time for this to happen be T^*. These definitions are illustrated in Figure 4.9.

From this description it should be clear that the number of times that the process hits zero and returns to x^* will be geometrically distributed with mean $[1 - u(x^*)]^{-1}$. Call the number of these events M. The time to enter the interior may now be written

$$T_1 + T_2 + \ldots + T_M + T^*.$$

This representation is essentially the same as that required of Gnedenko's theorem. What needs to be done to complete the proof of the exponentiality is to let x^* approach zero, causing $u(x^*)$ to approach one and the mean number of regenerations before entering the interior to approach infinity. At the same time, the mean of the T_i will approach zero, allowing the convergence to occur. The contribution of T^* will become insignificant as x^* approaches zero.

Turning this intuition into a rigorous demonstration of the exponentiality of the waiting time entails a fair amount of work. In fact, this has yet to be done. Here we will make some observations to bolster confidence in the approach. What we will do is derive the mean of the geometric distribution and of the T_i, and show that the product of the two gives the same mean time to enter the interior that we obtained above.

The probability of hitting zero before entering the interior is given by

$$u(x^*) = 1 - \frac{\int_0^{x^*} \psi(x)dx}{\int_0^{\delta} \psi(x)dx}.$$

If we let $\alpha x^* \to 0$, then it is not difficult to show that

$$u(x^*) \sim 1 - \alpha\eta(\gamma - 1)x^*.$$

Thus, the mean number of times that the zero is hit before the allele enters the interior is $1/\alpha\eta(\gamma-1)x^*$, which increases without bound because of our assumption that $\alpha x^* \to 0$.

The other quantity that we need is the mean of the T_i. This is a difficult calculation since the mean is for a conditional process. However, we can assume that the conditional time to hit zero is small relative to the (unconditional) time to go from zero back to x^*. From equation 4.61 the latter mean is, asymptotically, $2x^*/\theta_n$. Multiplying this by the mean number of times that the process hits zero recovers the mean time to hit δ:

$$\frac{2x^*}{\theta_n} \times \frac{1}{\alpha\eta(\gamma-1)x^*} = \frac{2}{\theta_n\alpha\eta(\gamma-1)}.$$

In Gnedenko's proof, the means of the positive random variables are fixed, suggesting that we must set x^* equal to some constant times θ_n. This would presumably make the random variables T_i approach some limiting form. It also implies that $\alpha\theta_n$ must approach zero for the exponentiality to hold. However, this condition may well prove too restrictive. This whole issue is in desperate need for some more work to clear up each of these points.

Consider, now, the consequences of all of this on the composition of the population. Imagine that there are a k alleles at the locus, but that only K of them are currently in the interior and $k - K$ are waiting to enter the interior. The mean time for any one of them to enter is given by equation 4.63 with $i = K$. By our conjecture that the time for any one allele to enter is exponentially distributed, the time for the first of the $k-K$ alleles to enter should also be exponentially distributed with a mean that is $1/(k - K)$ times the mean time for any one of them to enter:

$$t_{in}(K) = \frac{K}{(k - K)\alpha\theta_n(B - 1)}. \tag{4.64}$$

The time to leave the interior is also exponentially distributed and independent of the initial conditions. In both cases the only dependence on the state of the population is through K, the number of interior alleles. This suggests that the number of interior alleles may be viewed as a continuous time Markov chain. Such chains will be called *SSWM Markov chains*.

The Markovian behavior of K is best summarized by the probability of increase of K at the next event

$$q(K) = \begin{cases} 1 & \text{if } K = 1 \\ \frac{t_{out}(K)}{t_{in}(K)+t_{out}(K)} & \text{if } K = 2,\ldots,k-1 \\ 0 & \text{if } K = k \end{cases}$$

and the mean time until the next event

$$t_e(K) = \begin{cases} t_{in}(1) & \text{if } K = 1 \\ \frac{t_{in}(K)t_{out}(K)}{t_{in}(K)+t_{out}(K)} & \text{if } K = 2,\ldots,k-1 \\ t_{out}(k) & \text{if } K = k \end{cases}. \tag{4.65}$$

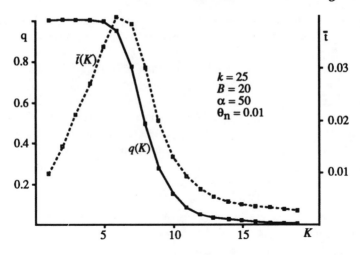

Figure 4.10. Two functions characterizing the SAS-CFF SSWM Markov chain.

The mean time may be derived by noting that the total rate of change of K is the sum of the rate of entry and the rate of exit:

$$1/t_{in}(K) + 1/t_{out}(K).$$

The mean time until a change occurs is the reciprocal of the rate of change, which gives the expression for $t_e(K)$.

Figure 4.10 illustrates the dependence of $q(K)$ and $t_e(K)$ on K for a particular set of values of B, α, k, and θ_n. A striking aspect of this figure is the strong S-shaped form for $q(K)$. For small values of K, the probability that the number of interior alleles increases is very nearly one. At a critical value of K this probability suddenly drops to nearly zero and remains low for higher values of K. The mean time between events changes in a coordinated way, with the fastest times being associated with values of K that are far away from the critical value. This behavior suggests that the number of interior alleles will generally be very close to a value of K, call it $\hat{K}$, for which $q(\hat{K}) \approx 0.5$.

The reason for this behavior lies mainly with the function $t_{out}(K)$. Referring to Figure 4.10, we see that the waiting time to lose an allele from the interior rises sharply once K falls below a value that is determined mainly by B. The radical change in the value of $t_{out}(K)$ is far greater than that of $t_{in}(K)$, suggesting that the value for $\hat{K}$ will be fairly insensitive to the values of the parameters θ_n and α. For example, the value for $\hat{K}$ that corresponds to the parameters in Figure 4.10 is 6.9. If θ_n is reduced by 2 orders of magnitude to 10^{-4}, $\hat{K}$ only changes to 4.4. These values for $\hat{K}$ were obtained numerically. It appears to be very difficult to find an approximation for $\hat{K}$ that is of value over a suitable wide ranges of parameter values.

With the SSWM assumptions, that is, with $\alpha \to \infty$ and $\theta_n \to 0$, the state space of the k-dimensional SAS-CFF diffusion (equation 4.58) collapses into a one-dimensional process. The time scale of change of this process is based on the mean times for alleles to enter or leave the interior. The alleles in the interior are undergoing changes on a much faster time scale. When an allele enters or exits, the interior process achieves stationarity in a time period that is instantaneous when compared with the time scale of entry or exit. The distribution of the interior alleles is given by the K-dimensional Dirichlet distribution (equation 4.27). The original diffusion may be said to converge to a one-dimensional, distribution-valued stochastic process. The identities of the alleles are not followed in this process suggesting that the process be called *unlabeled* to match the term applied to a similar situation that arises in the neutral allele theory [69]. We are not restricted to such esoterica as distribution-valued processes. It is usually easier to focus on just the number of interior alleles, K, which is a one-dimensional birth and death process whose state space is the set of integers $1, \ldots, k$.

There is a mathematical question lurking around concerning whether there is a proper limiting process as $\alpha \to \infty$ and $\theta_n \to 0$. We cannot hope to find this process unless an explicit assumption is made concerning the relationship between α and θ_n. Earlier we argued that the product $\alpha\theta_n$ must approach zero for the time to enter the interior to be exponentially distributed. Were this to hold, then the mean time for an allele to enter the interior will grow as $1/(\alpha\theta_n)$. At the same time, the mean time for the first of K interior alleles to exit will grow as

$$\alpha^{2(B-1)/K-1}.$$

For there to be a nontrivial limiting process, there must exist a value for K such that these two means grow at the same rate. An obvious candidate is

$$\tilde{K} = -\frac{2(B-1)\log(\alpha)}{\log(\theta_n)}. \tag{4.66}$$

Ignoring for the moment the fact that this is not an integer, note that a limiting value for K will only occur if

$$\lim_{\substack{\alpha \to \infty \\ \theta_n \to 0}} \log(\alpha)/\log(\theta_n) = \zeta,$$

where ζ is between zero and infinity. One way to guarantee this limit is to set $\alpha = \theta_n^{-\zeta}$, which is compatible with the requirement that $1/\alpha\theta_n \to 0$ providing that $\zeta < 1$. This suggests that a proper limiting Markov chain will exist if these two conditions are met. However, the limiting chain will be trivial in the sense that the limiting value of $q(K)$ will equal one for value of K less than $\tilde{K}$ and zero for values greater than $\tilde{K}$. The convergence to the limit will be very slow, probably logarithmic in θ_n and α. It is unlikely that in nature θ_n will be small enough and α large enough for the dynamics to match the extreme form of $q(K)$ in the limiting process.

4.6 Sticky boundaries

It is an extraordinary stroke of bad luck that such a fundamental model as captured in the diffusion process in equation 4.58 should be so difficult to analyze. Population genetics tends to be treated better by its models. We are usually able to derive most of our important results by relatively elementary techniques. Why should this model be so different?

Looking back over this chapter, it is clear that things turned sour when drift and mutation were added to the SAS-CFF diffusion, equation 4.53. Without drift and mutation, we were able to derive the stationary distribution exactly and could use an established asymptotic technique to solve hitting probability and waiting time problems. When drift and mutation were added, we could do neither. By contrast, for constant fitness models the stationary distribution for multiple alleles is known exactly [313] and the waiting times in large populations may be found by standard small noise approximations [200].

Mathematically, the difference may lie with the fact that the constant fitness model is reversible while the SAS-CFF model with drift and mutation is not. I can offer no evidence in support of this view; it is presented as a conjecture that may entertain someone skilled in these matters. Should our asymptotics ultimately prove to be correct, we will have in hand the most important properties of the model, though not a simple way to derive them. We will not have, on the other hand, a model with a very pleasing mathematical structure.

It is tempting to seek a model that gives up a little biology to simplify the mathematics much as we did in using the c-haploid model to approximate the dynamics of the SAS-CFF model. In doing this, we would like to use the pristine SAS-CFF diffusion (i. e., without drift or mutation) in the interior and to compress the complex behavior of rare alleles into the boundary. One approach is to impose a sticky boundary on the diffusion equation 4.53 at ϵ and $1 - \epsilon$.

Sticky boundaries represent a little known option for the behavior of sample paths that crash into regular barriers. They cause sample paths to behave in a manner that is remarkably like that of rare alleles that hit zero in the SAS-CFF diffusion with drift and mutation. In particular, whenever a process hits a sticky barrier, it will return to the barrier infinitely often before escaping from its influence. Although the process does not stay on the barrier for a finite length of time on any one hit, the time spent on the barrier after the infinite number of hits will be nonzero. Moreover, the distribution of the time to hit a point that is close to the sticky barrier is exponentially distributed.

It is difficult to find any discussion of stick barriers in the secondary literature on diffusion processes. Most of what I know comes from working out problem 11 in Chapter 16 of Breiman's book [23] and from a correspondence with M. Iizuka and Y. Ogura. Perhaps this situation will change as the relevance of sticky barriers to population genetics becomes more generally appreciated. Here we will only describe a two-allele process with sticky barriers to illustrate the idea.

Consider a two-allele symmetrical SAS-CFF diffusion without drift or mutation,

$$
\begin{aligned}
b(x) &= \sigma^2 Bx(1-x)(1-2x) \\
a(x) &= 2\sigma^2 x^2(1-x)^2,
\end{aligned}
$$

on the closed interval $[\epsilon, 1-\epsilon]$. The two points ϵ and $1-\epsilon$ will be the sticky barriers. When a sticky barrier is present, the mean time for a process that begins in the interval (ϵ, δ) to hit δ satisfies the equation

$$
\frac{a(x)}{2}\bar{t}''(x) + b(x)\bar{t}'(x) = -1
$$

with boundary conditions

$$
\bar{t}'(\epsilon) = -s_\epsilon, \quad \bar{t}(\delta) = 0.
$$

The parameter s_ϵ is a measure of the stickiness of the barrier. As s_ϵ increases, the barrier becomes stickier. If $s_\epsilon = 0$, the barrier behaves just like a reflecting barrier.

The solution to the differential equation is

$$
\bar{t}(x) = \frac{s_\epsilon}{\psi(\epsilon)} \int_x^\delta \psi(y)dy + 2\int_x^\delta \psi(y)dy \int_\epsilon^y \frac{dz}{a(z)\psi(z)},
$$

where

$$
\psi(x) = \exp^{-2\int^x \frac{b(y)}{a(y)}dy} = [x(1-x)]^{-B}.
$$

As ϵ approaches zero, the influence of the sticky barrier is lessened because of the longer intervals of time between visits. To counter this, the stickiness should be increased as ϵ decreases. This leads to an asymptotic expansion for the mean time to hit δ,

$$
\bar{t} \sim \frac{s_\epsilon \epsilon}{B-1},
$$

which is valid as long as s_ϵ grows faster than $\log(\epsilon)/\epsilon$.

The sticky boundary process will be asymptotically equivalent to the genetic process if the values for ϵ and s_ϵ are chosen appropriately. For the former, we have already seen that we should use $\epsilon = 1/(2\alpha)$. For the latter, we need only set the mean time to hit δ given above to the mean time for an allele to enter the interior (from equation 4.63) to get

$$
s_\epsilon = \frac{1}{\epsilon\sigma^2\theta_n} = \frac{1}{u}.
$$

In making this comparison, we have measured time in units of generations rather than units of $2N$ generations.

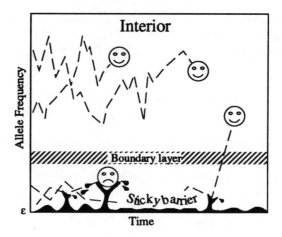

Figure 4.11. The fates of alleles in the sticky barrier process.

Of the two processes, the sticky barrier process is by far the simpler. The state space is broken into a sticky barrier and the interior. The dynamics of interior alleles are completely unpolluted by drift and mutation, not just asymptotically so. This means that the stationary distribution, conditioned on residencey in the interior, is a truncated Dirichlet distribution. The probability that the process is found in the interior is given by

$$\frac{\bar{t}_{out}(2)}{\bar{t}_{out}(2) + \bar{t}_{in}(1)},$$

just as it is for the genetic process.

The real advantage of the sticky barrier approach is for processes with more than two alleles. In this case the stationary distribution of interior alleles will also be a truncated Dirichlet. Recall that for the genetic case we were not able to write down the stationary distribution exactly. The stickiness of the barriers is specified by the mean times given by equation 4.64. This model is presented here as a carrot to lure workers to examine its fascinating structure. Figure 4.11 gives a cartoonist's view of the dynamics of SAS-CFF models with sticky barriers.

4.7 An historical note

In 1948, Sewall Wright initiated his mathematical work on selection in a temporally fluctuating environment with the following diffusion model for selection on additive alleles in a diploid population [312, p. 292]:

$$Edx = x(1-x)(s-\bar{s})dt \tag{4.67}$$

$$Edx_2 = \sigma_s^2 x^2 (1-x)^2 dt. \tag{4.68}$$

Wright apparently obtained his diffusion by first approximating the change in the allele frequency by

$$\Delta x \approx x(1 - x)(s_1 - s_2)$$

and then using the mean and variance of Δx for the drift and diffusion coefficients. In so doing, he set $E(s_1 - s_2) = s - \bar{s}$ and $\sigma^2 = \text{Var}(s_1 - s_2)$. The essential difference between his model and ours is the absence of the variance term in his drift coefficient. Significantly, when this term is present a polymorphism results if the appropriate conditions on the parameters are met; when it is absent, genetic variation is driven from the population. Wright viewed the effects of random fluctuations as being analagous to genetic drift. That temporal fluctuations in fitness could lead to a stable polymorphism appears to have escaped him.

In 1954, Kimura [152] obtained the complete transient solution to equation 4.67 using a transformation that converted the diffusion into Brownian motion. He noted that, although variation was driven from the population, alleles could not actually become fixed due to the assumption that the population size is infinite. To emphasize this point he called the loss of variation *quasi-fixation*. He, like Wright, appeared to be unaware of the error in the drift coefficient.

In 1955, Dempster [53] examined a haploid model and, as we saw earlier, was able to show by an exact anlaysis that the allele with the largest geometric mean fitness ultimately prevailed in the population. Kimura's solution gave a contradictory result: the allele with the largest arithmetic mean prevailed. Neither Dempster nor Kimura appears to have noticed the contradiction, perhaps because the more important result, that temporal fluctuations remove variation, was shared by both models.

In 1963, Haldane and Jayakar [113] analyzed a two-allele diploid model with deterministic fluctuations and showed that a polymorphism would occur if the geometric mean fitness of the heterozygote exceeded that of both homozygostes. Like Dempter's, theirs was an exact analysis, one based on the behavior of rare alleles. Unfortunately, Haldane and Jayakar considered neither the diffusion approximation of their model nor the additive case corresponding to equation 4.67. Thus, while their results were very important, they had little impact on the prevailing view that temporal fluctuations are a dispersive force.

The tide began to turn in the early 1970s when at least four population geneticists—independently and at about the same time—realized that Wright's diffusion was in error. Out of this came two papers on the diffusion analysis of haploid models by Jensen [141] and myself [81], one manuscript by Joe Felsenstein which he withdrew because Jensen and I were further along in getting ours published, and one blackboard derivation by Warren Ewens that was obliterated by an eraser. The correct calculation is sufficiently elementary that others undoubtedly repeated it at about the same time.

The new diffusion allows the genotype with the largest geometric mean to win, thus resolving the conflict between Kimura and Dempster in Dempster's favor. It is a simple step from the correct haploid diffusion to the additive diploid diffusion, a step that appears to have been taken first in 1974 [82]. With this paper it became known that temporal fluctuations in diploids should not be viewed as a wholly dispersive force, even for the additive model. A large number of papers on selection in a fluctuating environment were written during the 1970s. Felsenstein's review [71] should be consulted for a complete review.

Surprisingly, the interpretation that temporal fluctuations are a dispersive force like genetic drift lives on. In 1976, Nei and Yokoyama [219] devised a frequency-dependent model in a fluctuating environment whose (correct) diffusion approximation is the same as Wright's diffusion. Other than the fact that the model reproduces Wright's diffusion, it has little to recommend it. Nonetheless, as recently as 1987, Nei supported this model writing

> In Nei and Yokoyama's formulation, alleles are expected to behave just like neutral alleles when the mean of s is equal to zero, and the rate of gene substitution is not affected by population size. The only effect of this type of fluctuating selection is to increase the amount of genetic drift per generation and thus to reduce genetic variability. [216, p. 201]

I mention this bit of history as I find it interesting that a simple mathematical error could have had such a profound impact on a subject as important as the effects of temporal fluctuations of the environment on genetic variation.

5

SSWM approximations

In the previous chapter we made progress on a formidable diffusion model by using strong-selection weak-mutation (SSWM) limits to study the entry and egress of alleles from the population. Bolstered by this success, it is natural to seek other arenas to apply the SSWM methodology. Before setting off on the quest, however, we should step back for a moment and reflect on its purpose.

The SSWM analysis of the SAS-CFF model allowed us to collapse a complex high-dimensional process into a simple one-dimensional Markov process. As the simple process is fully specified by the mean times for alleles to enter or leave the interior, we can hope that other models for which the equivalent mean times are available will collapse similarly. Should this be the case, then the simple processes become objects of general interest in population genetics theory.

In this chapter we will show how directional selection and overdominance models may be collapsed via SSWM limits to simple processes as well. The limiting processes will henceforth be called SSWM Markov chains. In some of these cases the SSWM Markov chains may be solved completely to provide insights into molecular evolution and polymorphism. In others, they may be studied by computer simulations or numerical approximations.

5.1 Substitution processes

In this section we will use a few elementary ideas to make some interesting observations about the substitution of advantageous alleles in the strong-selection weak-mutation domain. Our goal is to see if there are situations that might lead to the episodic evolution that we inferred in Chapter 3: bursts of amino acid substitutions followed by latent periods.

As our aim is to provide an intuitively appealing route to the final results, we will use, whenever possible, the simplest model that captures the essential ideas. The time-honored simplest model for rare advantageous alleles is the Galton-Watson branching process.* Our use of this theory will

---

*My favorite introduction to branching processes is in Feller's book [70, Sections XII.3–5].

be confined to the approximation for the probability of ultimate survival of a new mutation. Let the fitness of the heterozygote for a new mutation be $1 + s$ and that of the common allele be one. Branching process theory tells us that the probability of ultimate survival of the mutation is approximately $2s$ if s is small.

In the SSWM world, mutations to the same allele recur. Thus, the probability of ultimate fixation of an advantageous allele is one. It may take a long time for the particular mutation that ultimately sweeps through the population to appear, but eventually it will show up. How long will it take? On average, $2Nu_n$ new mutations to a particular allele appear each generation. (Recall that N is the population size and u_n the nucleotide mutation rate.) If exactly $2Nu_n$ were to appear each generation, then the probability that at least one of these ultimately survives is

$$p_s = 1 - (1 - 2s)^{2Nu_n},$$

that is, one minus the probability that they all go extinct. If s and $4Nu_n s$ are both small, p_s may be approximated by

$$p_s = 1 - e^{2Nu_n \ln(1-2s)} \approx 1 - e^{-4Nu_n s} \approx 4Nu_n s.$$

Thus, the mean time until a mutation appears that ultimately survives is

$$ET_g = \frac{1}{4Nu_n s}, \tag{5.1}$$

a result that has appeared numerous times in the literature as befitting its importance. Here I will call attention only to an article by Maynard Smith who uses the same derivation as ours [206].

Each generation, either a mutation appears that will ultimately survive or it does not. If the ultimate survival of a mutation is independent of the survival of all other mutations, then the number of generations until the first surviving mutation appears, T_g, will be geometrically distributed:

$$\Pr\{T_g = k\} = p_s(1 - p_s)^{k-1}, \ k = 1, 2, \ldots .$$

The independence assumption seems reasonable in large populations because the relative frequencies of the new mutations are vanishingly small.

In the SSWM domain, N is very large (say greater than 10^6), $\theta_n = 4Nu_n$ is small (less than 0.1), and $\alpha = 2Ns$ is large (greater than 10). Together, these imply that the waiting time until a surviving allele appears will be large. A geometric distribution with a large mean may be approximated by an exponential distribution. To keep the mean of the exponential under control, time should be scaled in units of $2N$ generations. The exponential distribution of the time until the first surviving mutation appears, T, is

$$\Pr\{T < t\} = \frac{1}{\theta_n \alpha} e^{-t/(\theta_n \alpha)},$$

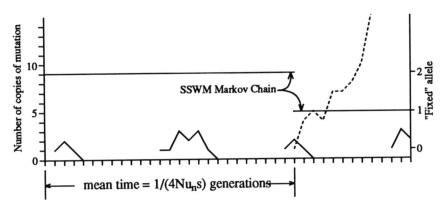

Figure 5.1. The substitution process described in the text. The dotted line is the trajectory of the first allele to sweep through the population.

where time is now measured continuously with a particular realization $T = t$ corresponding to $2Nt$ generations. The mean time is $(\theta_n \alpha)^{-1}$.

To define a SSWM Markov chain for a substitution process, we need to assign each allele a number. Let the allele that is initially fixed in the population be allele two and the advantageous allele be allele one. The state space for the SSWM Markov chain is the identity of the allele that is currently fixed—or nearly fixed—in the population. Thus, the chain for our first substitution process begins in state two where it remains for an exponentially distributed length of time before jumping to state one where it remains in perpetuity. The rate of change from state two to state one is the reciprocal of the mean time in state two, $\lambda_{2,1} = \theta_n \alpha$. These ideas are illustrated in Figure 5.1. It is hard to imagine a simpler process!

For a more traditional description of the SSWM Markov chain, we need to study the probability of being in state i at time t, $p_i(t)$, for a specified initial condition. The rate of change of $p_i(t)$ for an arbitrary continuous-time Markov chain is

$$\frac{dp_i(t)}{dt} = -p_i(t)\lambda_{ii} + \sum_{n \neq i} p_n(t)\lambda_{ni},$$

where λ_{ni} is the rate of transition rate from state n to state i and

$$\lambda_{ii} = \sum_{n \neq i} \lambda_{in}.$$

In all of our applications, the process will start in a particular state with probability one. If the process starts in state k, the initial conditions are

$$p_i(0) = \begin{cases} 1 & \text{if } i = k \\ 0 & \text{otherwise} \end{cases}.$$

The time spent in state i, given that the process is sitting there, is exponentially distributed with mean $1/\lambda_{ii}$.

It is often convenient to write Markov chains using matrix notation. Let $\mathbf{p}(t)$ be the column vector of the $p_i(t)$ and Λ the matrix with the λ_{ij} as off-diagonal elements and $-\lambda_{ii}$ as diagonal elements. The differential equation for the probabilities may be written concisely as

$$\frac{d\mathbf{p}(t)}{dt} = \Lambda'\mathbf{p}(t),$$

where the prime indicates the transpose of the matrix. For our simple two-allele genetic case,

$$\Lambda = \begin{pmatrix} 0 & 0 \\ \theta_n\alpha & -\theta_n\alpha \end{pmatrix}.$$

There is an ambiguity in the definition of the SSWM Markov chain stemming from the identity of the allele that is currently fixed in the population. What should we do while one allele is in the process of replacing another? In the SSWM domain the time spent in such nebulous states is small relative to the time spent waiting for an allele to begin its ascent. There are, in fact, two different time scales. The longer time scale applies to rare advantageous alleles waiting to enter the interior. The shorter time scale is the transient time required for an ascending allele to move through the interior. The former time scale is governed by three forces: drift, mutation, and selection. The latter is set by selection alone. Thus, we can adopt any convention we choose for identifying the allele that is currently "fixed." Figure 5.1 was drawn such that an allele that is destined to be fixed is called fixed at the moment it arises. We could have claimed an allele is fixed when its frequency exceeds one half. The difference between these definitions is unimportant when the process is observed on the time scale of rare alleles.

The power of the SSWM approach becomes apparent as we move to more complicated situations. Consider first the case where there are k different alleles, each with a different scaled fitness, α_i. What is the mean time until the first allele sweeps through the population? This is the same as asking for the minimum of k exponentially distributed random variables, each representing the time spent by one of the alleles in the boundary layer before entering the interior. The minimum of a collection of exponential random variables is also an exponential random variable but with mean

$$\frac{1}{\theta_n\alpha_1 + \theta_n\alpha_2 + \cdots + \theta_n\alpha_k} \tag{5.2}$$

when the mean of the ith exponential random variable is $1/\theta_n\alpha_i$. For example, if the fitnesses of all of the alleles were the same, the mean time until the first of them sweeps through the population is just $1/k$ times the mean time until a particular allele enters.

The fact that the minimum of a collection of exponential random variables is also exponential plays such an important role in what follows that a short proof of this and some other useful properties of collections of exponentials seems warranted. Consider first the case of two exponential random variables, X and Y, with means μ_x and μ_y. The probability that the minimum $Z = \min(X, Y)$ is less than z is equal to one minus the probability that X and Y are greater than z:

$$
\begin{aligned}
\Pr\{Z < z\} &= 1 - \Pr\{X > z\}\Pr\{Y > z\} \\
&= 1 - \frac{1}{\mu_x} \int_z^\infty e^{-x/\mu_x} dx \frac{1}{\mu_y} \int_z^\infty e^{-y/\mu_y} dy \\
&= 1 - e^{-z(1/\mu_x + 1/\mu_y)}.
\end{aligned}
$$

The final result will be recognized as the distribution function for an exponential random variable with mean

$$
\left(\frac{1}{\mu_x} + \frac{1}{\mu_y} \right)^{-1}.
$$

If we set $\mu_x = 1/(\theta_n \alpha_1)$ and $\mu_y = 1/(\theta_n \alpha_2)$, we get equation 5.2 for the special case of two alleles. The extension to an arbitrary number of alleles is obvious.

Next, we might ask: What is the probability that the ith allele is the first to sweep through the population? This is the same as asking for the probability that the ith exponential waiting time, T_i, is less than the others. For the genetic case the answer is

$$
\frac{\alpha_i}{\alpha_1 + \alpha_2 + \cdots + \alpha_k}. \tag{5.3}
$$

The most fit out of the k advantageous alleles is the most likely to sweep through the population. However, if there are a large number of alleles with similar fitnesses, the probability that the most fit allele is the first one through may be quite small. As a consequence, there are likely to be several substitutions; call it a burst of substitutions.

The proof of equation 5.3 may also be sketched with our two exponential random variables, X and Y. The probability that X is less than Y is

$$
\begin{aligned}
\Pr\{X < Y\} &= \int_0^\infty \Pr\{X = x\}\Pr\{Y > x\} dx \\
&= \frac{1}{\mu_x} \int_0^\infty e^{-x/\mu_x} e^{-x/\mu_y} dx \\
&= \frac{1/\mu_x}{1/\mu_x + 1/\mu_y}.
\end{aligned}
$$

Setting $\mu_x = 1/\theta_n \alpha_1$ and $\mu_y = 1/\theta_n \alpha_2$, we get equation 5.3 for the special case of two alleles.

The final question yields a surprising result: What is the mean time until the first allele sweeps through the population, given that it is a particular allele? We might expect, for example, that if the first allele to swept through were the most fit, the waiting time might be shorter than the time for an allele of lesser fitness. Of course this isn't true; the mean time is the same no matter which allele we condition upon.

The appropriate calculation in this case is

$$\Pr\{X < x \mid X < Y\} = \frac{\Pr\{X < x \text{ and } X < Y\}}{\Pr\{X < Y\}}$$

$$= 1 - e^{-x(1/\mu_x + 1/\mu_y)},$$

which is the same exponential distribution as for $Z = \min(X, Y)$.

With these simple observations under our belts, it is possible to attack a more substantial problem. Imagine a diploid population with k alleles with additive effects on fitness at a particular locus. Let the fitness of the homozygote for ith allele be $1 + s_i$ and that of the i/j heterozygote be $1 + (s_i + s_j)/2$. Label the alleles such that

$$s_1 > s_2 > \cdots > s_k.$$

Thus, the homozygote for allele one is the most fit and that for allele k is the least fit. Suppose the population is initiated with allele i fixed. Since there are $(i - 1)$ alleles that are more fit than the ith allele, we would expect a succession of substitutions ending up with allele one. On average, how many substitutions should occur? To find the answer we need only derive the SSWM Markov chain and use standard results from Markov chain theory to obtain the mean number of steps before absorption at state one.

The fitness of the i/j heterozygote $(j < i)$ relative to the common homozygote is

$$\frac{1 + (s_j + s_i)/2}{1 + s_i} \approx 1 + (s_j - s_i)/2.$$

Thus, the exponential waiting time associated with the jth allele, given that allele i is fixed in the population, has mean

$$\frac{1}{4Nu_n N(s_j - s_i)} = \frac{1}{\theta_n(\alpha_j - \alpha_i)}$$

when time is measured in units of $2N$ generations. The reciprocal of the mean time is the rate of change from state i to state j:

$$\lambda_{ij} = \theta_n(\alpha_j - \alpha_i).$$

For reasons that will become apparent shortly, it is helpful to write this rate as

$$\lambda_{ij} = \theta_n(v_j + v_{j+1} + \cdots + v_{i-1}), \tag{5.4}$$

where $v_n = \alpha_n - \alpha_{n+1}$ is the incremental fitness increase of the nth allele over the $(n+1)$st allele.

There is nothing special about the ith allele other than it is the one that is initially fixed in the population. If the jth allele should be the next one fixed, then the rate of flow to subsequent alleles will be in the same form as given in equation 5.4 with the obvious argument changes. Using equation 5.4, the SSWM Markov chain for this model is defined by

$$
\Lambda = \theta_n
\begin{pmatrix}
-\lambda_1 & v_1 & v_1 + v_2 & \cdots & v_1 + v_2 + \cdots + v_{i-1} \\
0 & -\lambda_2 & v_2 & \cdots & v_2 + v_3 + \cdots + v_{i-1} \\
0 & 0 & -\lambda_3 & \cdots & v_3 + v_4 + \cdots + v_{i-1} \\
. & . & . & \cdots & . \\
0 & 0 & 0 & \cdots & -\lambda_i
\end{pmatrix},
$$

where

$$
\lambda_j = \begin{cases} 0 & \text{if } j = 1 \\ (v_1 + 2v_2 + \cdots + (i-1)v_{i-1})/\theta_n & \text{if } j = 2, \ldots, k \end{cases} \tag{5.5}
$$

and the initial condition is

$$
p_n(0) = \begin{cases} 1 & \text{if } n = i \\ 0 & \text{otherwise} \end{cases}.
$$

The complete transient solution of this process is known [86]. Rather than present the details here—they are an entirely routine application of Markov process theory—we will only display the mean number of substitutions before allele one becomes fixed:

$$
\sum_{j=1}^{i-1} \left\{ \frac{1}{j} - \frac{\lambda_j}{\lambda_i} \frac{1}{i-1} - \sum_{n=j+1}^{i-1} \frac{\lambda_j}{\lambda_n} \frac{1}{n(n-1)} \right\}. \tag{5.6}
$$

The derivation is in [86, p. 208–209].

In one sense, the promise of the SSWM approach has been fulfilled in this example. We have derived a Markov chain for the substitution process with minimum effort. In another sense, it has not because the solution that we are most interested in (equation 5.6) is still rather messy. It depends, for example, on i parameters. To display the mean time we would first need to assign values to the s_j. There is little in the experimental literature that provides any guidance. One way around this dilemma is to assign the selection coefficients at random, perhaps chosen independently from a common probability distribution. But which distribution? The experimental literature will not help here either; extreme value theory will. If the number of alleles, k, is very large, then the distribution of the fitnesses of the top few alleles should converge to the extreme value distribution *no matter what distribution is used to assign the fitnesses.*

The use of extreme value theory is new to population genetics so a few words on its behalf are in order.* Consider a sample of n independent, identically distributed random variables that have been ordered and labeled such that

$$X_1 > X_2 > \cdots > X_n.$$

Assuming that certain conditions on the random variables are met, it is possible to find a sequence of numbers a_n and b_n such that the distribution of

$$Z_n = \frac{X_1 - a_n}{b_n}$$

converges to the extreme value distribution

$$\lim_{n \to \infty} \Pr\{Z_n < z\} = \exp(-e^{-z}). \tag{5.7}$$

The fact that the limiting distribution does not depend on the distribution of the X_i is reminiscent of the Central Limit Theorem. The theory turns out to be remarkably useful. An obvious application is the prediction of the size of the 100-year flood, this being the maximum of 100 random variables representing river heights.

A technical inelegance of extreme value theory is the derivations of the constants a_n and b_n. The best approach is to look them up in a book. Here I will give a couple of examples. If the X_i are standardized normal random variables, then

$$a_n = (2 \ln n)^{1/2} - \frac{\frac{1}{2}(\ln \ln n + \ln 4\pi)}{(2 \ln n)^{1/2}} \tag{5.8}$$

and

$$b_n = (2 \ln n)^{-1/2}. \tag{5.9}$$

If the X_i are exponentially distributed, $a_n = \ln n$ and $b_n = 1$. Both of these examples are taken from Galambos' book [78].

A technical detail involves the conditions placed on the distribution of the X_i to assure convergence of the maximum to the extreme value distribution. In fact, there are not one but three extreme value distributions. Bounded random variables converge to one, strange creatures like Cauchy random variables go to a second, and unbounded, well-behaved random variables like those with normal, exponential, gamma, or log normal distributions go to a third. The latter distribution is called the Type III extreme value distribution and is the one given in equation 5.7. In all that follows, we will assume that the random variables representing fitness belong to the latter class.

An obscure corner of extreme value theory involves the distribution of the spacings $X_i - X_{i-1}$ between the largest random variables. For a fixed

---

*A concise introduction to the theory may be found in David's book on order statistics [51, Section 9.3]. Galambos' book [78] should be consulted for a more complete account.

m, the asymptotic scaled spacings

$$V_i = \lim_{n \to \infty} \frac{i(X_i - X_{i-1})}{b_n}, \quad i = 1, 2, \ldots, m$$

are independent, exponentially distributed random variables [85,305]. The factor i multiplying the ith spacing corrects for the fact that the random variables become closer together as they move toward the median.

The definition of the V_i should look familiar. Recall that the eigenvalues given in equation 5.5 depend on the spacings between fitnesses multiplied by the same integers as used in the definition of the V_i. For a fixed n and as $k \to \infty$, the distribution of λ_n/b_n should approach that of a sum of $(n-1)$ independent exponential random variables. To obtain the average number of fixations we need only take the expectation of equation 5.6 with respect to the joint distribution of the scaled spacings.

The calculation is even easier than it might seem at first glance. We really need only the expectation of the ratios of eigenvalues:

$$\begin{aligned}
E\left\{\frac{\lambda_j}{\lambda_n}\right\} &= E\left\{\frac{v_1 + 2v_2 + \cdots + (j-1)v_{j-1}}{v_1 + 2v_2 + \cdots + (n-1)v_{n-1}}\right\} \\
&= (j-1)E\left\{\frac{v_1}{v_1 + 2v_2 + \cdots + (n-1)v_{n-1}}\right\} \\
&= \frac{j-1}{n-1}.
\end{aligned}$$

The final step follows from the symmetry of the jv_j. Using this result, the mean value of equation 5.6 is seen to be

$$\frac{1}{2} + \frac{1}{i} + \frac{1}{2}\sum_{n=2}^{i-1} \frac{n+3}{n(n+1)}.$$

The dependency of the mean number of substitutions on the allele that is initially fixed is illustrated in Figure 5.2.

The most remarkable aspect of this result is the slow growth of the mean number of substitutions with the number of the initial allele. Obviously, the first fixation usually involves an allele whose fitness is relatively high, moving the process rapidly toward allele one.

A lot more could be learned about this substitution process. However, there are aspects of its biological underpinnings that make it unrealistic as a model of molecular evolution and thus less worthy of further study. The process was introduced mainly to illustrate the power of an approach based on SSWM Markov chains and extreme value theory. We have taken a formidable problem—the waiting time properties of a k-dimensional stochastic process—and reduced it to a simple one-dimensional Markov chain. The reduction occurred because of the emergence of two time scales as the SSWM limit is approached: the time scale of rare alleles subject to the joint effects of drift, selection, and mutation and the much faster time

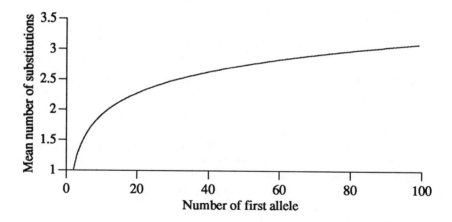

Figure 5.2. The mean number of substitutions for the simple substitution process.

scale of common alleles subject only to the action of natural selection. The time scale of the SSWM Markov chain is that of rare alleles. The jumps from one state to another occur on the common allele time scale, which is instantaneous on the rare allele time scale.

The SSWM approach is nestled comfortably between the deterministic and diffusion models commonly used in population genetics. The diffusion models usually assume that the parameters s, u, and $1/N$ are all of similar orders of magnitude. Thus, drift, mutation, and selection all contribute equally to the dynamics. The deterministic theory, on the other hand, assumes that $N = \infty$ and (frequently) that $u = 0$, making selection the only relevant force. In the SSWM approach, drift and mutation are entertained, but only for rare alleles whose dynamics may be studied by diffusion methods as we saw in the previous chapter. Common alleles, on the other hand, follow deterministic dynamics. Moreover, since our interest is usually in the time scale of rare alleles, the only aspect of the deterministic theory that we need is the equilibrium behavior. The time required to move from one equilibrium to another is negligible on the rare allele time scale. From this perspective SSWM Markov chains emerge as a bridge between the diffusion and deterministic approaches. They appear to be perfectly suited to study the role of natural selection in molecular evolution.

After that bit of proselytizing, we must make some effort to modify our first substitution process into one with more biological currency. The problem lies with the mutation structure. We assumed that each allele can mutate to every other allele in a single mutational step. The linear structure of DNA, on the other hand, mandates that if one allele mutates to a second by a base change, and the second changes to a third by a mutation at a different site, then the first and third cannot be reached from each other in a single mutational event.

A model that mimics the full mutational structure of DNA is an awesome thing to behold. Fortunately, under SSWM dynamics, back substitutions never occur allowing us to assume with impunity that back mutations do not occur either. The absence of back mutations makes some aspects of the model similar to those of the infinite-sites models that play such an important role in neutral allele theories. The similarity of the two will be more fully described at the end of this chapter.

The modification of our previous substitution model to one without back mutations is relatively easy. The best approach is to describe the new model verbally and to add some mathematics later. Imagine that we begin as before with one allele fixed in the population. This allele will be generating mutations that are one mutational step away. Mutations that are two mutational steps away will appear so infrequently that they may be ignored. (If the nucleotide mutation rate is 10^{-8}, a particular double mutation will occur at the rate 10^{-16}.) Let there be $k - 1$ alleles one step away that are engaged in SSWM dynamics. We must now assign fitnesses to these k alleles as we did before and label them such that allele one is the most fit, followed by allele two, and so forth. Let the currently fixed allele be allele i. This defines the starting condition of the model.

From equation 5.3 we see that the probability that the first allele to sweep through the population is allele j is

$$\frac{\alpha_j}{\alpha_1 + \alpha_2 + \cdots + \alpha_i}. \tag{5.10}$$

Once fixed, all subsequent mutations will be one mutational step away from the new allele, but two mutational steps away from the original allele. Consider the set of alleles containing the newly fixed allele plus the $k - 1$ that are one mutational step away. The newly fixed allele retains its fitness but we need to assign fitnesses to the others at random as was done for the first set of alleles. Once assigned, the alleles need to be labeled such that the most fit allele is allele one, etc. In general, the fixed allele must take on a new number reflecting its ranking among the new mutations. If it happens to be the most fit allele, then it will be allele one and the process will come to a grinding halt. Otherwise, one of the alleles that is more fit will become the newly fixed allele as determined by the probabilities in equation 5.3. At this point, we need to generate a new set of alleles, assign fitnesses, relabel and decide if the process will go for one more iteration or terminate. Figure 5.3 illustrates the process.

I have called this process the mutational landscape* [89]. The name was coined to emphasize its analogy with Sewall Wright's adaptive landscape. For the adaptive landscape, evolution stagnates when it reaches a peak on the adaptive surface. For the mutational landscape, evolution stagnates when it reaches a point where all alleles that are one mutational step away are less fit then the fixed allele. There may be an allele two mutational steps away that is more fit, but the mutation rate to that allele is so low that

---

*In fact, I have also called it the molecular landscape [93] process for reasons that even I don't understand.

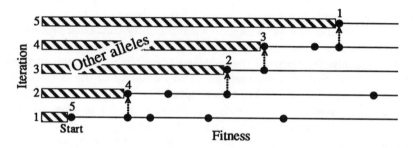

Figure 5.3. One realization of the mutational landscape process. The black dots represent the fitnesses of alleles. The numbers are the indices of the fixed alleles in the current iteration. Only the fixed alleles and those of higher fitnesses are represented. The dotted lines illustrate the inheritance of fitness through successive iterations.

the population is stuck at the current peak for a period of time that is long relative to the time scale of molecular evolution. The two landscapes are very similar, perhaps the main difference being one of emphasis. Factors other than mutation may hold the population on a peak under Wright's model, whereas mutation, or the lack thereof, is always the factor holding the population at a peak under the mutational landscape process.

The two aspects of the process that are most relevant to studies of molecular evolution are the mean number of substitutions before the process terminates, μ_x, and the *clumpedness*,

$$\mu_x + \frac{\sigma_x^2}{\mu_x},$$

where σ_x^2 is the variance in the number of substitutions before termination. Recall that if the occurrence of bursts follows a Poisson process, the clumpedness is the index of dispersion for the process (equation 3.7). There are no analytic results available for either of these moments. However, the model is easy to simulate. The results of one such simulation are illustrated in Figure 5.4. As with the simpler model, the striking aspect of the dynamics is the small mean number of steps that are taken before the process terminates. The clumpedness also grows slowly. In this regard the landscape process is compatible with the statistical description of molecular evolution that we outlined in Chapter 3.

5.2   Overdominance

Overdominance is a form of balancing selection. Consequently, our interest gravitates from substitutions to the maintenance of alleles in the population. Under SSWM assumptions, the dynamics of overdominant alleles are rather uninteresting in comparison with those of SAS-CFF alleles. The reason is simple: With overdominance, selection dominates drift, holding

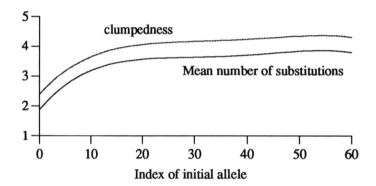

Figure 5.4. A simulation of the mutational landscape process. The curves are fourth-order polynomials that were fitted to the 50 initial conditions simulated. For this simulation there are a total of 500 alleles with exponentially distributed fitnesses. Each case was replicated 2000 times.

alleles in the interior essentially forever. With SAS-CFF, alleles meander around due to the vagaries of the environment, occasionally becoming rare enough to be captured by the sticky dynamics at the boundaries.

Our study of the SSWM dynamics of overdominant alleles could proceed in several different directions. In analogy with the development of the SAS-CFF model, we could derive the mean times for alleles to enter and leave the interior and use them to infer the number of segregating alleles. However, a more direct approach applies SSWM limits to the stationary distribution of the overdominance model as obtained from a standard diffusion equation. This approach has the advantage of being both easier and falling more in the tradition of theoretical population genetics. We will begin by displaying the k-allele diffusion with its stationary distribution. Next, the asymptotic analysis will be directed at the two-allele case as a way of introducing the approach. Finally, we will attack the k-allele model.

Consider a locus with k segregating alleles with frequencies

$$\mathbf{x} = (x_1, x_2, \ldots, x_k).$$

Let the fitness of the i/j genotype be

$$1 + \frac{\alpha s_{ij}}{2N},$$

a notation chosen to allow us to take SSWM limits without having to go through an extra round of symbols. The $(k-1)$-dimensional diffusion describing the dynamics of this population has mean incrementals

$$
\begin{aligned}
E dx_i &= [x_i \alpha (\bar{s}_i - \bar{s}) + \frac{k \theta_n}{2}(\frac{1}{k} - x_i)]dt \\
E dx_i dx_j &= x_i (\delta_{ij} - x_j)dt,
\end{aligned}
$$

where time has been scaled in units of $2N$ generations and

$$\bar{s}_i = \sum_{i=1}^{k} x_j s_{ij}$$

$$\bar{s} = \sum_{i=1}^{k} x_j \bar{s}_j = \sum_{i=1}^{k} \sum_{j=1}^{k} x_i x_j s_{ij}.$$

The stationary density of this diffusion, first derived by Sewall Wright [313] in 1949, is

$$\phi_k(\mathbf{x}) = C \prod_{i=1}^{k} x_i^{\theta_n-1} e^{\alpha \bar{s}}, \tag{5.11}$$

where C is the normalizing constant. Our task is to examine this distribution as $\theta_n \to 0$ and $\alpha \to \infty$ to discover where the probability mass accumulates. This will give us the number of alleles that are segregating in the population.

For two alleles, the density may be written

$$\phi_2(x) = C[x(1-x)]^{\theta_n-1} e^{\alpha \bar{s}},$$

where x is the frequency of allele one. An example of ϕ_2 for a symmetric model, $s_{ii} = -1$ and $s_{12} = 0$, with $\alpha = 20$ and $\theta_n = 0.01$ is illustrated in Figure 5.5. Note that the probability mass is concentrated in three regions. The central region is centered on the deterministic equilibrium (i.e. the equilibrium for an infinite population with no mutation). The two boundary regions correspond to the fixation of the one or the other of the two alleles. The height of the mode for the central equilibrium is determined entirely by the value of α. As $\alpha \to \infty$, the peak at $1/2$ narrows considerably.

The behavior at the end points is determined by the value of θ_n. As is apparent, the rise toward infinity as x approaches 0 or 1 occurs very close to the end points. This creates a valley with very little probability mass separating the central and the boundary regions. Alleles will stay in a region for a very long time before jumping to a neighboring region. The amount of time spent in a region is proportional to the probability mass associated with it. As the SSWM limits are approached, the distinction between the regions is magnified. In addition, unless some very delicate conditions are met, the mass in one of the regions will become infinity greater than that in the others as the SSWM limits are approached.

To obtain the probability mass near zero we need to examine the integral of ϕ_2 in a small region,

$$\delta\text{-mass}(0) \sim \int_0^{\delta} \phi_2(x) dx,$$

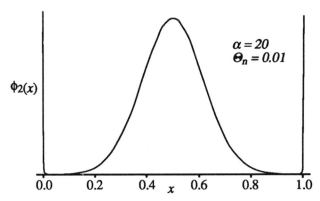

$\phi_2(x)$

$\alpha = 20$
$\Theta_n = 0.01$

0.0   0.2   0.4 x 0.6   0.8   1.0

Figure 5.5. The stationary distribution for two symmetric overdominant alleles. The near-vertical lines at the boundaries are not axes as they might appear, but rather are part of the distribution.

where δ is a small fixed constant. If δ is small enough, $\bar{s} \approx s_{22} = \bar{s}(0)$, allowing us to write

$$\delta\text{-mass}(0) \sim Ce^{\alpha\bar{s}(0)} \int_0^\delta x^{\theta_n-1}dx$$
$$= Ce^{\alpha\bar{s}(0)}\delta^{\theta_n}/\theta_n$$
$$\sim Ce^{\alpha\bar{s}(0)}/\theta_n,$$

where the asymptotics are meant to apply as $\theta_n \to 0$.

The mass around zero will be compared to the mass that accumulates around the stable deterministic equilibrium at

$$\hat{x} = \frac{s_{12} - s_{22}}{2s_{12} - s_{11} - s_{22}}.$$

The simple expedient of expanding $\bar{s}(x)$ around the equilibrium will make the analysis particularly easy. Use the Taylor series expansion

$$\bar{s}(x) = \bar{s}(\hat{x}) + \frac{1}{2}\bar{s}''(\hat{x})(x - \hat{x})^2$$

to obtain

$$\bar{s}(x) = \bar{s}(\hat{x}) - 2(2s_{12} - s_{11} - s_{22})(x - \hat{x})^2.$$

In the region around the deterministic equilibrium, we can approximate the mass of ϕ_2 by

$$\delta\text{-mass}(\hat{x}) \sim C[\hat{x}(1 - \hat{x})]^{-1}e^{\alpha\bar{s}(\hat{x})} \int_{\hat{x}-\delta}^{\hat{x}+\delta} e^{\alpha\bar{s}''(\hat{x})(x-\hat{x})^2} dx.$$

The asymptotic form of the integral (as $\alpha \to \infty$) follows immediately from the recognition that it is the integral of a normal function with "variance"

$[-2\alpha\bar{s}''(\hat{x})]^{-1}$. This yields

$$\delta\text{-mass}(\hat{x}) \sim C[\hat{x}(1-\hat{x})]^{-1}e^{\alpha\bar{s}(\hat{x})}\left(\frac{\pi}{-\alpha\bar{s}''(\hat{x})}\right)^{1/2}.$$

(Recall that $\bar{s}''(\hat{x})$ is negative by our assumption that $\hat{x}$ is a stable equilibrium.)

The ratio of the mass at $\hat{x}$ to that at zero will indicate the relative accumulation of probability mass at the internal fixed point:

$$\frac{\delta\text{-mass}(\hat{x})}{\delta\text{-mass}(0)} \sim C^*\theta_n e^{\alpha[\bar{s}(\hat{x})-\bar{s}(0)]}\alpha^{-1/2}.$$

The constant C^* contains all of the factors that are independent of α and θ_n.

As the SSWM limit proceeds, the ratio will approach infinity or zero unless a delicate relationship exists between θ_n and α. The mass will accumulate near zero if

$$\theta_n = o(e^{-\alpha[\bar{s}(\hat{x})-\bar{s}(0)]}\alpha^{1/2}).$$

For example, suppose that the model is symmetric with $s_{12} = 1$ and $s_{ii} = 0$. In this case the condition becomes

$$\theta_n = o(e^{-\alpha/2}\alpha^{1/2}).$$

If $\alpha = 100$, then θ_n would have to be smaller than about 10^{-21} for an appreciable fraction of the probability mass to accumulate at one of the end points! The message is obvious: overdominance is a potent force for maintaining variation in the population.

By contrast, we learned from equation 4.66 that the number of interior alleles under the SAS-CFF model is approximately

$$\tilde{K} = -\frac{2(B-1)\log(\alpha)}{\log(\theta_n)}.$$

For there to be only one,

$$\theta_n = o(\alpha^{-(B-1)}).$$

If $B = 2$, θ_n would have to be less than about 0.01 for the probability mass to pile up at one of the fixation points. Recall that when $B = 2$ the stationary distribution is uniform, implying that the allele frequency will wander freely through the unit interval including frequent skirmishes with the boundary dynamics. We conclude that, for values of B close to or less than two, balancing selection under the SAS-CFF model is not nearly as effective as overdominance at maintaining variation.

Once B exceeds two by a sizeable amount, SAS-CFF dynamics become just as effective as overdominance at maintaining variation. For example, if $B = 5$ and $\alpha = 100$, then θ_n would have to be much less than 10^{-8} for drift to be effective at reducing the number of segregating alleles. This is numerically much larger than 10^{-21}, but the biological implication is the same: alleles will remain in the interior for a very long time.

The extension of the overdominance analysis to multiple alleles uses the same approach as the two-allele case. It is easy to understand the gross behavior of ϕ_k by appealing to the deterministic dynamics of overdominant alleles. The deterministic system corresponding to the diffusion is described by the differential equations

$$\frac{dx_i}{dt} = x_i \alpha(\bar{s}_i - \bar{s}), \ i = 1, 2, \ldots, k.$$

This system may have a considerable number of fixed points. There may be an internal stable equilibrium with all k alleles in the population and a number of unstable marginal equilibria with a subset of segregating alleles. Alternatively, some of the marginal equilibria may be stable but not the internal equilibrium. Under the SSWM assumptions, selection dominates drift so we would expect the probability mass to accumulate around some or all of these equilibria.

Surprisingly, it is possible that the mass might accumulate around a fixed point that is unstable under the full deterministic dynamics. Consider that drift is always working to remove alleles from the population. If the mutation rate were zero, the probability mass would eventually accumulate at one or more of the k states with only a single allele in the population. With a very small amount of mutation, it may be possible for two or three alleles to be held in the population near their deterministic equilibrium, but perhaps no more than this. As θ_n grows, more alleles will be able to enter until finally the alleles accumulate around the fixed point with the highest mean fitness.

To locate all of these potential points of accumulation, we need to find all subsets of the k alleles that can coexist at an internal stable equilibrium. Next, we need to integrate ϕ_k (from equation 5.11) in the regions around these equilibria to see how much probability mass is nearby. By comparing the mass at each of the fixed points it will quickly become apparent where the mass is accumulating as $\theta_n \to 0$ and $\alpha \to \infty$.

Consider a fixed point of the form $\hat{\mathbf{x}} = (\hat{x}_1, \hat{x}_2, \ldots, \hat{x}_K, 0, \ldots, 0)$, where the $\hat{x}_i$ are the deterministic equilibrium allele frequencies for a population with K segregating and $k - K$ absent alleles. Assume that this equilibrium is stable in the subspace consisting of alleles one to K. (It may, however, be unstable when all k alleles are allowed to participate.) The probability mass around $\hat{\mathbf{x}}$ may be determined by integrating ϕ_k in a small region around $\hat{\mathbf{x}}$:

$$\int_{\Omega_{\hat{x}}} \phi(\mathbf{x}) d\mathbf{x}.$$

The asymptotic form of this integral will be examined in two steps.

Consider first the contribution to the integral of the absent alleles. They make essentially no contribution to $\bar{s}$ allowing the approximation

$$\bar{s}(\mathbf{x}) \approx \sum_{i=1}^{K} \sum_{j=1}^{K} x_i x_j s_{ij}.$$

The integral in the dimension of the kth allele may be approximated by

$$\int_0^\delta \phi \, dx_k \approx C \prod_{i=1}^{k-1} x_i^{\theta_n - 1} e^{\alpha \bar{s}} \int_0^\delta x_k^{\theta_n - 1} dx_k$$

$$= C \prod_{i=1}^{k-1} x_i^{\theta_n - 1} e^{\alpha \bar{s}} \frac{\delta^{\theta_n}}{\theta_n}$$

$$\sim C \prod_{i=1}^{k-1} x_i^{\theta_n - 1} e^{\alpha \bar{s}} \frac{1}{\theta_n}.$$

The same procedure should be carried out for the remaining absent alleles. In addition, it seems reasonable to approximate each of the x_i in the terms of the form $x_i^{\theta_n - 1}$ for the k interior alleles with their deterministic equilibrium. Then, as $\theta_n \to 0$, we have

$$C \theta_n^{-(k-K)} \prod_{i=1}^{K} \hat{x}_i^{-1} e^{\alpha \bar{s}} \tag{5.12}$$

as the asymptotic form of the integral of ϕ for the integration in the $(k - K)$ dimensions of the absent alleles.

Integration in the remaining dimensions is more orthodox as we require the integral of $\exp(\alpha \bar{s})$ as $\alpha \to \infty$. The usual approach to such integrals is via *Laplace's method*. It relies on the observation that the integral will be dominated by events near the maximum of $\bar{s}$. As $\bar{s}$ is proportional to the mean fitness of the population, the fixed point will sit at a maximum of $\bar{s}$ in the K-dimensional subspace. By expanding $\bar{s}$ around the fixed point, we will simultaneously focus our attention on the region of the integrand that determines the asymptotic value of the integral as well as putting the integral in the form of a normal distribution.

The obvious way to proceed is by expanding $\bar{s}$ as a Taylor series around the point $(\hat{x}_1, \ldots, \hat{x}_K)$. However, we must be careful since the allele frequencies add to one. The best approach is to begin by setting

$$x_K = 1 - \sum_{i=1}^{K-1} x_i$$

and breaking $\bar{s}$ into the components

$$\bar{s} = \sum_{i=1}^{K-1} \sum_{i=1}^{K-1} x_i x_j s_{ij} + 2 x_K \sum_{i=1}^{K-1} x_i s_{iK} + x_K^2 s_{KK}.$$

The expansion of $\bar{s}$ around the fixed point may be written

$$\bar{s}(\mathbf{x}) = \bar{s} + \sum_{i=1}^{K-1} \frac{\partial \bar{s}}{\partial x_i}(x_i - \hat{x}_i) + \frac{1}{2}\sum_{i=1}^{K-1}\sum_{j=1}^{K-1} \frac{\partial^2 \bar{s}}{\partial x_i \partial x_j}(x_i - \hat{x}_i)(x_j - \hat{x}_j).$$

All of the $\bar{s}$ functions and derivatives on the right side of the equation are evaluated at the fixed point. It is entirely routine to use the above to arrive at

$$\bar{s}(\mathbf{x}) = \bar{s}(\hat{\mathbf{x}}) + \bar{s}^*(\mathbf{x}),$$

where

$$\bar{s}^*(\mathbf{x}) = \sum_{i=1}^{K-1}\sum_{j=1}^{K-1} b_{ij}(x_i - \hat{x}_i)(x_j - \hat{x}_j)$$

and

$$b_{ij} = s_{ij} - s_{iK} - s_{Kj} + s_{KK}.$$

The integral of equation 5.12 over the remaining $(K-1)$ dimensions in the region around the fixed point may now be written

$$C\theta_n^{-(k-K)}\prod_{i=1}^{K}\hat{x}_i^{-1}e^{\alpha\bar{s}(\hat{\mathbf{x}})}\int e^{-\alpha\bar{s}^*(\mathbf{X})}d\mathbf{x}.$$

Although the integration is over a small region around the fixed point, the dominant contribution to the integral comes from an even smaller region very close to the fixed point. Thus, the limits of integration may be extended over the entire $(K-1)$-dimensional space without affecting the asymptotic value of the integral. The integral is now in the familar normal form

$$\int e^{-\frac{1}{2}[-2\alpha\bar{s}^*(\mathbf{X})]}d\mathbf{x} = \frac{(2\pi)^{\frac{K-1}{2}}}{(2\alpha)^{\frac{K-1}{2}}(-1)^{K-1}\mid\mathbf{b}\mid^{1/2}},$$

where $\mathbf{b}$ is the matrix with components b_{ij}. The quadratic form $\bar{s}^*(\mathbf{x})$ must be negative definite if the fixed point is a stable point in the $(K-1)$-dimensional space [153]. Thus, $-\bar{s}^*(\mathbf{x})$ is positive definite as required for the normal integral.

The final asymptotic form of the integral is

$$\delta\text{-mass}(\hat{\mathbf{x}}) \sim C^*\theta_n^{-(k-K)}e^{\alpha\bar{s}(\hat{\mathbf{x}})}\alpha^{-\frac{K-1}{2}},$$

where C^* absorbs all of the factors that are not functions of α or θ_n. Our only use of this result will be for the symmetric overdominance model. A discussion of asymmetric cases may be found in [88].

For the symmetric case, set $s_{ii} = 0$ and $s_{ij} = 1$, $i \neq j$. For the fixed point with K segregating alleles, $\hat{x}_i = 1/K$ and $\bar{s}(\hat{x}) = 1 - 1/K$. Plugging these into the asymptotic value of the integral gives

$$\delta\text{-mass}(\hat{\mathbf{x}}) \sim C^*\theta_n^{-(k-K)}e^{\alpha(1-\frac{1}{k})}\alpha^{-\frac{K-1}{2}}.$$

To compare the mass accumulating at two points, say ones with K_1 and K_2 segregating alleles, use the ratio of the masses at each of the points:

$$\frac{\delta\text{-mass}(K_1)}{\delta\text{-mass}(K_2)} \sim C^{**} \left[\theta_n e^{\alpha/(K_1 K_2)} \alpha^{-\frac{1}{2}} \right]^{K_1 - K_2},$$

where C^{**} is the ratio of the two constants.

As an example, we might ask under what conditions will fewer than k alleles be maintained in the population? The answer comes from setting $K_1 = k$ and $K_2 = k - 1$:

$$\frac{\delta\text{-mass}(k)}{\delta\text{-mass}(k - 1)} \sim C^{**} \theta_n e^{\frac{\alpha}{k(k-1)}} \alpha^{-\frac{1}{2}}.$$

If the mass were to accumulate at a fixed point with $k - 1$ alleles, this ratio would have to approach zero as $\theta_n \to 0$ and $\alpha \to \infty$. Note that α in argument of the exponential function is divided by $k(k - 1)$. For a large number of alleles, α would have to be very large indeed to maintain all alleles in the population. Since the average frequency of each allele is $1/k$, as k increases alleles find themselves closer and closer to the boundary where they can be snapped up by genetic drift.

The view that will be argued in the final chapter is that there are, at most, only a few alleles at a locus that will be under strong enough selection to be in the SSWM domain and, at the same time, be mutationally accessible. Other alleles that might participate in the push toward the interior are two or more mutational steps away from the K segregating alleles. If true, then we need only be concerned with the time scale of the build up to the k alleles that will ultimately segregate in the interior.

The mean time for an allele with selective advantage s to enter the population is, from equation 5.1, $1/(4Nu_n s)$. When there are K segregating alleles under the symmetric overdominance model, the average selective advantage of a rare allele is

$$\frac{\alpha}{2N}(\bar{s}_i - \bar{s}) \approx \frac{\alpha}{2N} \frac{1}{K}$$

as $\bar{s}_i \approx 1$ and $\bar{s} \approx 1 - 1/K$. Thus, the mean time for a particular allele to enter when time is measured in units of $2N$ generations is $K/(\theta_n \alpha)$. If there are $k - K$ alleles waiting to enter, the mean time for the first of these to arrive is

$$\frac{K}{k - K} \frac{1}{\theta_n \alpha}. \tag{5.13}$$

This is in the same form as the analogous result for the SAS-CFF model as given by equation 4.64. The two differ only in the factor of $(B - 1)$ that appears in the denominator of the SAS-CFF time. Thus, the dynamics of the buildup of alleles should be similar for the two models, at least when B is larger than two to prevent the loss of alleles before the buildup is completed. The mean time, in units of $2N/(\theta_n \alpha)$ generations, is illustrated

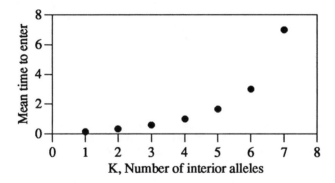

Figure 5.6. The mean time for an overdominant allele to enter the population as a function of the number of segregating alleles.

in Figure 5.6. As expected, the time decreases as the number of segregating alleles increases just as it does for the SAS-CFF model.

The most important point of this section is that the buildup of alleles for the overdominance model is, at the SSWM limit, very similar to that of the SAS-CFF model. If our only interest is in the entry of alleles into the interior, then we are moving toward a view that deemphasizes the detailed dynamics of a particular model and focuses only on the mean times for alleles to jump into and out of the interior. These times could be viewed as the parameters of models rather than derived quantities. Such a view would free us from the tyranny of population genetics algebra. This point will be taken up again in the final chapter.

5.3 Models of the gene

So far, we have dealt only with the dynamics of allele frequencies. Yet, the data we must eventually confront are DNA sequences of alleles that contain considerably more information than that found in an allele's frequency. The connection between neutral allele-frequency models and DNA sequences was made years ago by Kimura [157] and Watterson [297]. Kimura introduced a model of the gene that he called the *infinite sites model*. A locus is imagined to be composed of an infinite number of nucleotides with free recombination between them. While an infinite number of nucleotides may seem excessive, it is meant to be an approximation to a locus with a large, but finite, number of sites. The assumption was introduced to prevent more than one mutational event at a single site, thus allowing two-allele models to be used instead of the more difficult three- or four-allele models. More problematic is the assumption of free recombination, which is, in fact, an assumption that there is no linkage disequilibrium between sites. Watterson considered the other—perhaps more realistic—extreme: infinite sites but no recombination. Either extreme is much easier to deal with mathemati-

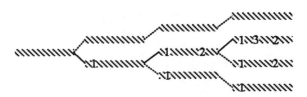

Figure 5.7. A realization of the buildup process ending with four alleles. The gray bars represent the sequences, the numbers designate the mutations in order of appearance, and the lines give the parentage of alleles. Solid lines connect alleles differing by a mutation, dotted lines connect alleles that are the same.

cally than are models with intermediate levels of recombination. A common practice is to analyze the two extremes and view them as bounds on the situation in nature. In this section we will concentrate on infinite-sites, no-recombination models in the context of our SSWM Markov chains.

No additional work needs to be done to graft the infinite sites structure onto the substitution models. Each substitution causes one nucleotide change, making the number of substitutions and the number of nucleotide differences separating a pair of sequences the same. Additional work is required to describe the numbers of mutations separating alleles held in the population by balancing selection.

The buildup process

Our results for the symmetric SAS-CFF and overdominance models at the SSWM limit suggest that both models will accumulate a moderate number of alleles fairly rapidly. We will refer to this as the *buildup process*. The models differ in what is likely to happen next. Overdominant alleles are likely to remain in the population for a very long time if the parameters remained unchanged. SAS-CFF alleles, on the other hand, begin an *allelic exchange process* that causes alleles to enter and leave the interior at a rate smaller than that of the buildup process.

Consider first the accumulation of mutations during the buildup process. Imagine that the population is initiated with an allele, the first allele, with a specified DNA or amino acid sequence. The sequence of the second allele to enter the interior will differ from the sequence of the first allele by a mutation at a single site as seen in the first bifurcation in Figure 5.7. For our symmetric models, the average frequency of each of two alleles is one half. The third allele to enter will be derived from one of the two existing alleles by a single mutational event. The parent allele is assumed to be chosen at random from the two segregating alleles. For example, in Figure 5.7, the allele with the first mutation happens to parent the third allele that contains both the first and second mutations. By symmetry, the frequencies each of the three alleles is one third.

The buildup process proceeds in this way until all of the alleles that can coexist and are mutationally accessible are in the interior at which point the process terminates. As is clear, the buildup process produces a genealogy for the segregating alleles. Each bifurcation of the tree yields two daughter alleles, one identical to the parental allele and one differing by a single mutational event. Whenever a new bifuration occurs, the parental allele is chosen at random from all of the contemporary alleles. These allelic genealogies are particularly easy to describe. In what follows we will give just two properties: the distribution of the number of mutations that are found on a randomly drawn allele and the mean and variance of the number of mutations that separate two randomly drawn alleles.

Consider first the number of mutations on a randomly drawn allele from a buildup that resulted in K segregating alleles. The probability that the chosen allele contains the first mutation to have entered the population is one-half, the second mutation, one-third, and so on up to the $(K-1)$st mutation. Let S_K be the number of mutations on the randomly drawn allele. S_K may be written as a sum of independent Bernoulli random variables:

$$S_K = \xi_1 + \xi_2 + \cdots + \xi_{K-1},$$

where

$$\xi_i = \begin{cases} 0 & \text{with probability } i/(i+1) \\ 1 & \text{with probability } 1/(i+1). \end{cases}$$

The mean number of mutations on the randomly drawn allele is thus

$$ES_K = \sum_{i=1}^{K-1} \frac{1}{i+1}. \tag{5.14}$$

Similarly, the variance of the number of mutations is just the sum of Bernoulli variances:

$$\text{Var} S_K = \sum_{i=1}^{K-1} \frac{i}{(i+1)^2}.$$

Note that both of these moments grow by approximately $1/i$ with successive alleles implying that their growth is logarithmic in K.

These results may be applied immediately to a simple model of molecular evolution to demonstrate that polymorphism can lead to bursts of substitutions just as did the mutational landscape. Imagine that the environment that led to the buildup of alleles occasionally changes in such a way that one of the segregating alleles becomes more fit than the others, resulting in its fixation. We will call the loss of alleles *allelic constrictions* to leave open the possiblity that they may be caused by mechanisms other than selection. In the new environment a set of alleles that are mutationally accessible from the fixed allele leads to another buildup process and so on as illustrated in Figure 5.8.

With each allelic constriction, a random number of mutations are fixed in the population. If we assume that the allele that is fixed is chosen at

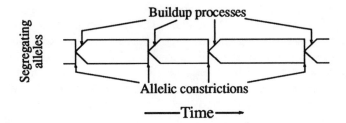

Figure 5.8. An illustration of the major features of molecular evolution involving an alternation of buildup processes and allelic constrictions.

random from the segregating alleles, the number of mutations that are fixed is given by the random variable S_K. From this and equation 3.7 we conclude that if the allelic constrictions follow a Poisson process, the index of dispersion for the process will be

$$I(t) = ES_K + \frac{\mathrm{Var}\,S_K}{ES_K}. \tag{5.15}$$

This result, which depends only on K, is illustrated in Figure 5.9.

A comparison of Figures 5.4 and 5.9 shows that both the mutational landscape and polymorphism can lead to bursts of evolution. They share the property that the clumpedness increases slowly, making large values unlikely.

The second property of our model concerns the number of mutations that separate a pair of distinct alleles drawn at random from the population. One approach to the problem is through allelic genealogies. When all K of the alleles in the population are considered, their ancestry may be represented by a binary tree, as illustrated in Figure 5.10. Each bifurcation of the tree produces one branch identical to the parental branch and one with a single new mutation. Thus, to find the number of mutations separating a randomly drawn pair of alleles we need to derive the distribution of the time back to the common ancestor of the two alleles and compound this with the probability of a mutation on the branch leading to the sampled allele.

The probability that the common ancestor of two randomly chosen alleles occurred at the most recent bifurcation is

$$p_1 = \frac{2}{K(K-1)}.$$

The probability that the first allele that was drawn participated in the most recent bifurcation is $2/K$; the probability that the second allele drawn also participated is $1/(K-1)$. As these events are independent, the probabilities may be multiplied to give p_1. Similarly, the probability that the two alleles

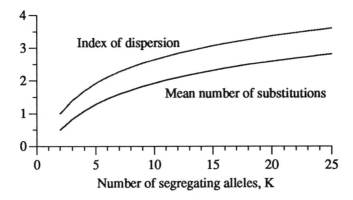

Figure 5.9. The mean number of substitutions and the index of dispersion for a process with Poisson allelic constrictions followed by buildups to K alleles.

came from the second most recent bifurcation is

$$p_2 = (1 - p_1) \frac{2}{(K-1)(K-2)}.$$

Proceeding in this fashion, we see that the probability that the common ancestor of the two chosen alleles occurred i bifurcations in the past is

$$p_i = \frac{(K+1)(K-i)}{(K-1)(K+2-i)} \times \frac{2}{(K+1-i)(K-i)}. \tag{5.16}$$

The probability is written as the product of the probability that the bifurcation did not occur up to the $(i-1)$st bifurcation times the probability that it did occur at the ith bifurcation.

The mean number of mutations that separate a randomly drawn pair of alleles whose common ancestor allele is known to have occurred j bifurcations in the past may be obtained by an argument that is summarized in Figure 5.11.

If the two alleles came from the most recent bifurcation, they are always separated by exactly one mutation. If the ancestor allele occurred two bifurcations in the past, the mean number of mutations separating the two alleles is

$$\mu_2 = 1 + \frac{2}{K+1}. \tag{5.17}$$

Referring to Figure 5.11 for the case $j = 2$, we see that the one in μ_2 comes from the step just before the bifurcation and $2/(K+1)$ comes from the initial step. The argument for the second term is as follows.

There are three events that our two alleles could experience during the first iteration. The two alleles could have emerged from the most recent bifurcation. This occurs with probability p_1. However, as we have conditioned on $j = 2$, this event is of no interest.

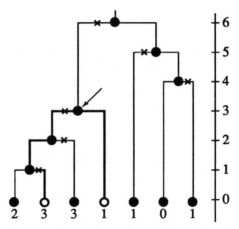

Figure 5.10. A typical realization of an allelic genealogy. Alleles are represented by circles, mutations are marked by an "x"; the number below each allele is the total number of mutations that have accumulated on the allele. The two open circles represent two randomly chosen alleles, and the arrow points to the common ancestor of these two alleles. Time, as measured backward in units of bifurcations, is given on the right-hand side. The figure is from [96].

Alternatively, the two alleles may not have participated in any bifurcations. This occurs with probability

$$\frac{(K-2)(K-3)}{K(K-1)}.$$

In this case neither of our alleles will receive a mutation so this event contributes nothing to μ_2.

Finally, one or the other of the two alleles could have participated in a bifurcation, but not both. This occurs with probability

$$\frac{4(K-2)}{K(K-1)}. \qquad (5.18)$$

In this case, the probability that the allele that participated in the bifurcation received the mutation that always accompanies a bifurcation is one half. The mean number of new mutations contributed by this event is given by the probability that one of the two chosen alleles participates in a bifurcation, given that both do not participate (equation 5.18) divided by p_1, multiplied by $1/2$, as in the second term in equation 5.17.

Carrying on this argument, using Figure 5.11 as a guide, we find that the mean number of mutations that differentiate a randomly drawn pair of alleles with a common ancestor allele known to have occurred j generations in the past is

$$\mu_j = 1 + \sum_{i=1}^{j-1} \frac{2}{K+2-i}, \quad j = 1, \ldots, K-1. \qquad (5.19)$$

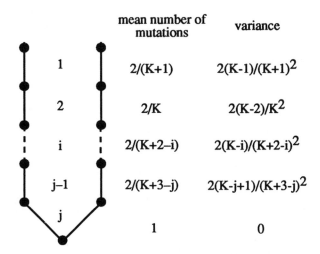

Figure 5.11. The history of a pair of randomly drawn alleles with a common ancestor j bifurcations in the past.

By convention, the sum will equal zero when $j = 1$. The mean number of mutations that separate a randomly drawn pair of alleles is given by

$$\sum_{j=1}^{K-1} p_j \mu_j, \tag{5.20}$$

which depends only on the number of segregating alleles, K. It is illustrated in Figure 5.12.

The variance in the number of mutations separating a randomly drawn pair of alleles may be obtained by a similar argument. Consider first the variance conditioned on the common ancestor allele having occurred j bifurcations in the past. The variance in the number of mutations contributed by the ith step is just the Bernoulli variance obtained by multiplying the probability of a mutation by one minus that probability:

$$\frac{2(K-i)}{(K+2-i)^2}, \quad i = 1, \ldots, j-1.$$

The total variance, given that the common ancestor allele occurred j bifurcations in the past, is

$$V_j = \sum_{i=1}^{j-1} \frac{2(K-i)}{(K+2-i)^2}, \quad j = 1, \ldots, K-1.$$

Let the random variable Z_i represent the number of mutations contributed by the ith step. The total variance may now be written as

$$E_j[Var(Z_1 + \ldots + Z_j \mid j)] + Var_j[E(Z_1 + \ldots + Z_j \mid j)].$$

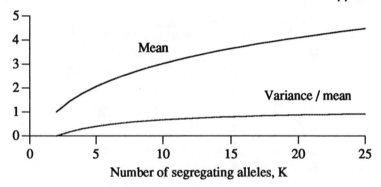

Figure 5.12. The mean and the variance-to-mean ratio of the number of mutations separating a randomly drawn pair of alleles at the end of the buildup process.

In terms of our previous results, this becomes

$$\sum_{j=1}^{K-1} p_j V_j + \sum_{j=1}^{K-1} p_j \mu_j^2 - \left(\sum_{j=1}^{K-1} p_j \mu_j\right)^2.$$

The ratio of this variance to the mean is illustrated in Figure 5.12.

These results may be obtained by an entirely different approach based on the probability distribution of the number of alleles that a particular mutation occupies. We refer to the number of distinct alleles occupied by a particular mutation as its *multiplicity*. The probability that the nth mutation to enter the population has multiplicity j at the end of the buildup process is

$$p_{n,j} = \frac{n(K-n-1)!(K-j-1)!}{(K-n-j)!(K-1)!}, \; j = 1, 2, \dots, K-n.$$

The derivation of this result may be found in [95]. It is a straightforward route from $p_{n,j}$ to equation 5.20.

The allelic exchange process

SAS-CFF models differ from overdominance models in that allele frequencies go on long excursions. Sometimes they get close enough to the boundary to become mired in the sticky dynamics that are the scourge of rare alleles. Should an allele be lost, a new mini-buildup process begins that increases the number of interior alleles from $K-1$ back to K. Alternatively, an allele sometimes enters the population bringing the number of interior alleles to $K+1$. This results in a relatively rapid loss of an allele to once again bring the number of interior alleles back to the most probable number, K.

The steady and gain and loss of alleles is called the *allelic exchange process*. With each allelic exchange there will be a change in the identity and perhaps number of segregating sites. The distibution of the number of segregating sites given the number of alleles, K, is of particular interest in the study of molecular variation. At the end of the buildup process to K alleles there are $K - 1$ segregating sites. When the allelic exchange process kicks in, the number of segregating sites becomes a random quantity.

A mathematic description of the allelic exchange process for the SAS-CFF model has yet to be achieved. In this subsection we will explore a crude approximation that exposes some of the major features of the process. The approximation is based on the assumption that the number of interior alleles, K, is constant. We saw in the provious chapter that K is, in fact, a Markov chain with transition probabilities $q(K)$ as illustrated in Figure 4.10. As the SSWM limit is approached, the transition probabilities tend to hold K tightly to its most probable state, but not sufficiently to allow us to claim that K is constant. A correct analysis is an open and interesting problem.

Assume from now on that the number of interior alleles is fixed at the most probable value of K. For this value, $q(K) \approx 1/2$, which implies that

$$t_{in}(K) \approx t_{out}(K).$$

Recall that $t_e(K)$ is the mean time between gains or losses of alleles as defined in equation 4.65. When $q(K) \approx 1/2$, $t_e(K) \approx t_{in}(K)/2$, where $t_{in}(K)$ is given by equation 4.64. Thus,

$$t_e(K) \approx \frac{K}{2(k - K)\alpha\theta_n(B - 1)}$$

is the mean time between allelic exchanges in units of $2N$ generations. If the number of available alleles, k, is less than or equal to the number that can be maintained in the population, then $t_e(K) = \infty$ and the allelic exchange process does not function. Otherwise, the rate of the process is

$$\rho_x = \frac{1}{4Nt_e(K)} = \frac{2u_n\alpha(B - 1)(k - K)}{K} \tag{5.21}$$

when time is measured in generations.

At this point we can exploit a remarkable analogy between the dynamics of mutations in the allelic exchange process and those of a haploid neutral model. Every time an allelic exchange occurs an allele is chosen at random to receive a new mutation and replace one of the existing alleles (possibly including itself). The dynamics of mutations on the K alleles is exactly like those of mutations on chromosomes in a haploid population of size $N = K$. The only difference between the allelic exchange process and the haploid neutral model is in the mutation process. In the neutral model a Poisson number of mutations accompanies each event; in the allelic exchange process each event includes a single mutation with probability one.

Watterson [297] gave a mathematical description of the haploid neutral model that is ideal for our purposes. His equation 4.2 is the generating function for the number of segregating sites in a sample of size i from an equilibrium population. The only change that we need to make to use his generating function for the allelic exchange process is in the mutation process. Rather than using a Poisson number of mutations for each event, we must assume that a single mutation occurs with each exchange with probability one. Thus, where Watterson used the Poisson probability generating function $g(s) = \exp[y(s-1)]$ for the number of mutations, we will use $g(s) = s$, allowing us to modify his equation 4.2 for the probability function of the number of segregating sites in a sample of size i to

$$P_i(s) = \prod_{j=1}^{i-1} \frac{s}{K/j - s(K/j - 1)}.$$

The mean number of segregating sites in the population may be obtained from $P_i(s)$ or, more easily, from Watterson's equation 1.4a:

$$K\left(1 + \frac{1}{2} + \frac{1}{3} + \cdots + \frac{1}{K-1}\right). \tag{5.22}$$

We see from this result that, at equilibrium, the number of segregating sites will exceed the number of alleles.

The connection between the allelic exchange process and the neutral model also allows us to write down the rate of substitution. The probability that a new mutation that enters the interior is ultimately fixed is equal to its mean initial frequency, $1/K$, in analogy to the probability of $1/N$ that a new mutation is ultimately fixed under the neutral model. The mean number of allelic exchanges to occur in a short period of time, δ, is $\rho_x \delta$. A fraction, $1/K$, of these are ultimately fixed. Thus, the rate of substitution of sites is

$$\rho_x/K. \tag{5.23}$$

Interestingly, the rate of substitution appears to be inversely proportional to the number of segregating alleles. The true dependency is much more complex. If we rely on our rough estimate of the number of segregating alleles (equation 4.66) combined with equation 5.21 and $k \gg K$, then

$$\rho_x/K \approx \left(\frac{\ln \theta_n}{\ln \alpha}\right)^2 \frac{k\theta_n \alpha}{2(B-1)}. \tag{5.24}$$

If B is increased, K is increased and the rate of substitution is decreased. If α is increased, then K is increased and the rate of substitution is increased as well. Obviously the dynamics of the allelic exchange process are complex and at this point not well understood.

The evolution of DNA as formulated in this section is the foundation of a theory of molecular evolution by natural selection that will be developed in Chapter 7.

6

Neutral allele theories

In this and Chapter 7 we will address the scientific issues raised by the observations on molecular variation and the mathematics of selection in a fluctuating environment. This chapter is about the neutralist side of the much-publicized "neutralist–selectionist" debate. The next chapter is about the selectionist side.

Our initial problem is to define exactly what we mean by "the neutral allele theory." Many neutral theories are not neutral at all, but assume that the mutations that contribute to molecular variation are slightly deleterious. In his lament of this situation, Kimura wrote

> One possibility would be to rename the theory the 'mutation-random drift theory', but the term 'neutral theory' is already widely used and I think it better not to change horses in midstream. I want the reader to realize that 'neutral theory' is shorthand for 'the theory that at the molecular level evolutionary changes and polymorphisms are mainly due to mutations that are nearly enough neutral with respect to natural selection that their behavior and fate are mainly determined by mutation and genetic drift.' [159, p. xii]

Although the range of neutral theories is large, there is a common thread tying them together: they all rely on mutation to introduce new variants and genetic drift to fix them in the population. For genetic drift to play its part, the selective differences between alleles must be small. But how small? The original neutral theories included the assumption that the selective differences between alleles are much less than the reciprocal of the population size. If we represent the selective difference between alleles by σ_s, we can write this initial assumption as $\sigma_s \ll 1/N$, where N is the effective size of the population. We will call selection of this magnitude *weak selection*.

As data on molecular evolution and polymorphism accumulated, the neutral theory based only on weak selection appeared unable to account for all of the observations. As a consequence, the theory was expanded to include alleles whose fitness differences were close to the reciprocal of the population size, $\sigma_s \approx 1/N$. Selection of this magnitude will be called *moderate selection*. However, not all moderately selected alleles are part of the

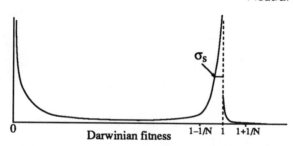

Figure 6.1. A selection coefficient distribution for the neutral allele theory.

theory. Only those that are deleterious with respect to a common allele are included. Moderately selected advantageous or overdominant alleles enter the population through the action of selection, not drift, so are excluded from the theory.

The neutral theory based on weakly and moderately selected deleterious alleles has been widely accepted by the scientific community. One can safely state that no other mechanistic theory of molecular evolution has received even a small fraction of the support that the neutral theory has received. The aim of this chapter is to judge whether this support is warranted.

Our investigation begins with a precise description of the theory; it is difficult to judge its success if some of its assumptions are left under the rug. From here we will move to an examination of the traditional arguments that support the theory. Finally, we will summarize the success of the theory.

6.1 Fitness distributions

Neutral theories are concerned with the evolutionary dynamics of mutations of very small effect. The key player in these theories is the fitness distribution of new mutations. Our initial goal is to describe the two fitness distributions that appear in the literature and to offer a combined distribution that appears to combine the best features of each.

The gross context of neutral fitness distributions is illustrated in Figure 6.1 in which it is assumed that natural selection has already moved the locus to such an exalted state that further improvements through selection on new mutations is extraordinarily unlikely. Rather, almost all new mutations are either strongly deleterious ($\sigma_s \gg 1/N$) or are weakly ($\sigma_s \ll 1/N$) to moderately ($\sigma_s \approx 1/N$) deleterious. In drawing Figure 6.1, I have assumed that the strongly selected mode is at lethality. For loci that are not lethal-mutable, the strong selection mode could be at some other value as long as it is much smaller than one. Our concern is not with this mode, but with the mode near one, which will be called the *neutral mode*. Mutations in the neutral mode are the raw material of neutral evolution.

As our interest is only with neutral mutations, assume that the area under the neutral mode is one, making it a proper probability distribution.

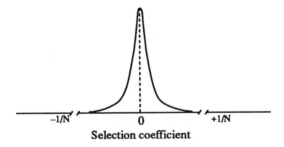

Figure 6.2. A selection coefficient distribution for the weak-selection neutral model.

The mode of the distribution will be placed at zero rather than one and the random fitnesses, now deviations from one, will be called *selection co-efficients* (except for occasional lapses when they will be called fitnesses because it sounds better). We must assume that the fitness distribution applies to all of the species in a particular study. For example, the same fitness distribution is used for all species of mammals.

The dispersion will be characterized by its standard deviation, σ_s. The fraction of the neutral mode occupied by weakly selected mutations will be called f_w; that by moderately selected mutations, f_m. If the total mutation rate to alleles in the neutral mode is u, then the mutation rate to weakly selected alleles is $f_w u$ and to moderately selected alleles is $f_m u$.

Under the weak-selection neutral model, $\sigma_s \ll 1/N$, as illustrated in Figure 6.2. There are two key points to make about the weak-selection model. The first is that σ_s is assumed to be so small that $N\sigma_s \ll 1$ holds for species with population sizes ranging over several orders of magnitude. Otherwise, the neutral mutation rate, $f_w u$, would vary as a function of population size and moderately selected alleles could make up a significant fraction of the mutations in the larger populations.

The second point is that the fraction of mutations that fall within the neutral mode, f_w, is locus specific. Loci that evolve more slowly are said to be more constrained and thus have a smaller f_w. In our terminology, we say that slowly evolving loci have greater site effects and are not environmentally challenged.

The fact that f_w varies from locus to locus, or from site to site within a locus, in the weak-selection model has some interesting implications about the nature of fitness effects of mutations. It is as if mutations sit near cusps: they can be either weakly selected or strongly selected, but not moderately selected. From a modeling point of view, this is perfectly reasonable as suggested by the distributions illustrated in Figures 6.1 and 6.2. Even as a biological statement about the nature of macromolecules this does not appear to be unreasonable a priori.

We do not have to specify any other properties of fitness distributions for weak-selection models. The dynamics should behave essentially the same no matter what the form of the fitness distribution. Even balancing selection will have only a small effect as long as $N\sigma_s \ll 1$. Not so for moderately selected mutations: almost all aspects of their dynamics depend critically on the form of the fitness distribution. For this reason we will spend somewhat more time on the actual form of the distribution than we did for weakly selected alleles.

The first detail in a discussion of moderate selection concerns the dominance relationships between alleles. It is generally assumed that heterozygotes are exactly intermediate between their two associated homozygotes. This assumption is motivated by experiments on both spontaneous mutations and naturally occurring variants that generally exhibit an inverse heterozygous–homozygous effect [260]. Mutations of large effect tend to be nearly recessive ($s \approx -1, h \approx 0.05$), those of small effect tend to be nearly additive ($|s| \approx 0, h \approx 0.5$).* Mukai et al. [215], for example, estimated that spontaneous mutations in *Drosophila* with an average homozygous effect of $s \approx -0.075$ have a heterozygous effect of $h \approx 0.4$. Presumably, mutations of smaller effect are even closer to exact additivity.

In most of the work on moderate-selection neutral models, the fitness distribution is assumed to represent the fitnesses of heterozygotes, each with one allele being a new mutation and the other contributing a selective coefficient of zero. The globally most-fit allele is assumed to be nearly fixed in the population and all others are derived from it.

Two fitness distributions have been commonly used in the literature. The first, due to Ohta [228], is the exponential distribution

$$f_e(s) = \sigma_{ms}^{-1} e^{s/\sigma_{ms}}, \; s < 0. \tag{6.1}$$

We use σ_{ms} instead of σ_s to emphasize that we are discussing moderately selected alleles. The second, due to Kimura [158], is the gamma distribution

$$f_g(s) = \frac{\alpha^\beta}{\Gamma(\beta)}(-s)^{\beta-1}e^{\alpha s}, \; s < 0, \tag{6.2}$$

where $\alpha = \beta/\sigma_{ms}$.

The two fitness distributions are illustrated in Figure 6.3 for the special case $\sigma_{ms} = 0.001, \beta = 0.5$ favored by Kimura [159]. They have the same means but differ greatly in their behaviors near zero. The gamma distribution has considerably more probability mass near zero, suggesting that f_w will be much larger than for the exponential distribution. Kimura was led to the gamma distribution precisely for this property:

> Ohta's model has a drawback in that it cannot accommodate enough mutations that behave effectively as neutral when the population size gets large. [158, p. 3440]

---

*The notation for heterozygous effects comes from the two-allele model using relative fitnesses with the most-fit homozygote having a fitness of one, the least fit homozygote $1 - s$, and the heterozygote $1 - hs$.

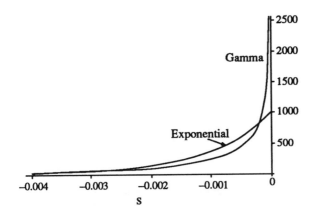

Figure 6.3. The exponential and gamma densities for selection coefficients of moderate-selection neutral models.

For large $N\sigma_{ms}$, the probability mass in the interval $(-0.1/N, 0)$ for the exponential distribution in equation 6.1 is

$$f_w^{(e)} \approx \int_{-0.1/N}^{0} f_e(s)ds = 1 - e^{-0.1/(N\sigma_{ms})} \sim \frac{0.1}{N\sigma_{ms}}. \qquad (6.3)$$

For the gamma (equation 6.2) it is

$$f_w^{(g)} \approx \frac{\sqrt{1/(2\sigma_{ms})}}{\Gamma(1/2)} \int_{-0.1/N}^{0} (-s)^{-1/2}ds = \sqrt{\frac{0.2}{\pi\sigma_{ms}N}}$$

for the special case $\beta = 0.5$. Thus, the ratio $f_w^{(g)}/f_m^{(e)}$ grows as $\sqrt{N}$ showing why Kimura's choice of the gamma distribution allows many more neutral mutations in large populations.

But why the gamma? Why did Kimura base his 1983 book on this particular distribution? He seems to have chosen the distribution solely for its ability to save the moderate selection neutral theory from evolutionary stagnation, not for any a priori biological reason. By one criterion, it appears not to have been the best choice.

The distribution of s is meant to reflect the selection coefficient relative to the most fit allele. By implication, there is an underlying distribution of absolute fitnesses from which the relative fitnesses are derived. Suppose, at a particular locus, the absolute fitnesses of m alleles are given by the random variables

$$X_1 > X_2 > \cdots > X_m,$$

which are ordered from m random variables drawn independently from some probability distribution. The selection coefficient of the second best allele, relative to the top allele, is given by

$$s = \frac{X_2}{X_1} - 1.$$

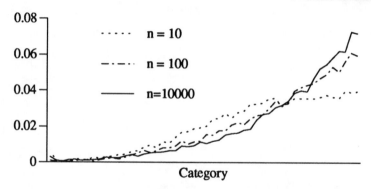

Figure 6.4. Simulation results illustrating the convergence of the selection coefficient of the second most fit allele to an exponential distribution. The lines are through points of three histograms obtained from 10,000 replicates of 10, 100, or 10,000 normal deviates.

As $m \to \infty$, extreme value theory tells us that the distribution of s approaches an exponential distribution rather than a gamma, no matter what the distribution of the X_i.

The proof is a straightforward extension of our previous observation that the spacings between the top order statistics are exponential. Recall from Chapter 5 that there are sequences a_m and b_m such that the distribution of

$$Z_i = (X_i - a_m)/b_m$$

approaches one of the three limiting extreme value distributions. This suggests rewriting s as

$$s = \frac{1 + \frac{b_m}{a_m} Z_2}{1 + \frac{b_m}{a_m} Z_1} - 1.$$

The ratio b_m/a_m approaches zero as $m \to \infty$, giving

$$s \sim -\frac{b_m}{a_m}(Z_1 - Z_2) + o(b_m/a_m).$$

We have already seen that the spacing $(Z_1 - Z_2)$ is exponentially distributed, so we conclude that s must be exponential as well.

Rates of convergence to extreme value limits are often quite slow, particularly for the normal distribution. To help assess the rate of convergence, Figure 6.4 presents the distribution of Z_1 for normally distributed X_i. The curve for $n = 10,000$ is convex, being similar to Ohta's exponential distribution illustrated in Figure 6.3. Note, however, that for smaller $n = 10$ the curve is concave. That is, the approach to the exponential is from the "opposite side" from Kimura's gamma distribution. From this we conclude that Ohta's exponential distribution is the preferred distribution for selection coefficients.

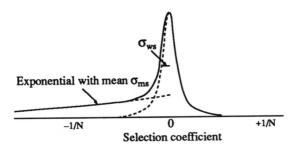

Figure 6.5. The distribution of selection coefficients for the combined model.

Kimura introduced the gamma as a means of assuring that there will be enough neutral mutations in large populations to prevent the stagnation of molecular evolution. The same end could be attained by assuming that the distribution of selection coefficients is a mixture of two components, one for alleles that are weakly selected and the other for alleles that are moderately selected. The mean of the weakly selected mode must be so small that σ_{ws}, the standard deviation of this component, is much less than the reciprocal of the largest population size of the taxa under discussion. The standard deviation of the moderately selected component, on the other hand, must be such that $\sigma_{ms} \approx 1/N$ for the population sizes that typify the taxa.

The two-component neutral model seems both reasonable and yet, at the same time, completely at variance with the extreme value argument used to defrock the gamma distribution. The difference lies with implicit assumptions about which alleles are parenting the mutations. In our extreme value argument, we assumed that the allele producing the mutations was the most fit allele. If we were to make the same assumption for the two-component model, we would necessarily end up with an exponential distribution for the relative fitnesses.

But the assumption that the most-fit weakly selected allele is fixed is absurd. The alleles within the weakly selected group are not influenced by natural selection. There is no reason to assume that the most fit among them is the one that is most frequent in the population. In fact, the most natural assumption is that the alleles that are frequent in the population are chosen at random from all of the weakly selected mutations with the same largest moderately selected component. In our two-component model we must assume that the alleles producing the mutations are chosen at random from among the weakly selected alternatives of the allele with the largest moderately selected component of fitness. When we do, we are led to a distribution as illustrated in Figure 6.5.

Putting these ideas together we arrive at what I feel is the most satisfactory version of the neutral fitness distribution. Let p_w be the fraction of mutations from the weak-selection component of the neutral mode. A fraction $1 - p_w$ comes from the moderate-selection component that is exponentially distributed with mean $-\sigma_{ms}$. The total fraction of mutations that are weakly selected is

$$f_w \approx p_w + (1 - p_w) \int_{-.1/N}^{0} \sigma_{ms}^{-1} e^{s/\sigma_{ms}} ds = 1 - (1 - p_w) e^{-0.1/(N\sigma_{ms})}$$

while the fraction that is moderately selected is

$$f_m \approx (1 - p_w) \int_{-10/N}^{-.1/N} \sigma_{ms}^{-1} e^{s/\sigma_{ms}} ds = (1 - p_w)[e^{-0.1/(N\sigma_{ms})} - e^{-10/(N\sigma_{ms})}].$$

In these approximations, I have somewhat arbitrarily assumed that moderately selected alleles are those with selection coefficients spanning two orders of magnitude from $-10/N$ to $-0.1/N$.

Our new fitness distribution appears to fit very well what Kimura intended for his gamma distribution. There is a real advantage in the explicit use of the parameter p_w in that it allows us to slide freely between the weak-selection neutral model ($p_w = 1$) and Ohta's moderately deleterious model ($p_w = 0$). Having arrived at the distribution, I now want to point out two fundamental problems with its use as a model for molecular evolution.

The first problem concerns the assumption that once a fitness is assigned to an allele, it is fixed *in perpetuity*. Consider that the fitness of an allele is a measure of its success in a particular environment relative to that of other alleles. Given that environments are in a constant state of flux, it is hard to imagine a situation that would lead to a very small—of the order $1/N$—selective advantage of one allele over another that would not flip-flop frequently as the environment changes from one generation to the next.

But even if such rapid fluctuations are rejected, it is even harder to imagine that fitnesses are constant on the time scale of molecular evolution. As the theory is usually developed, relative fitnesses are assumed to remain fixed for several substitutions, a time span of at least several million years. Given that such major climatic events as ice ages occur on time scales of tens of thousands of years, it seems unlikely that fitnesses would remain constant for periods of time that are larger by two or more orders of magnitude.

The constancy of fitnesses might not be viewed as a serious problem were it not that the dynamics of moderate selection neutral models are structurally unstable to the assumption. If the fitnesses fluctuate, the dynamics change substantially. We will return to this point in the next chapter.

The second problem is related to the first: is it not peculiar that we would assume that essentially all moderately selected mutations are deleterious? Not if we feel that selection has proceeded for a very long time—at least tens of millions of years—in a constant environment so that the most-fit allele has had an opportunity to displace the others. But if the fitnesses were fluctuating, even on a very slow time scale, then given that the fitness differences are very small (of order $1/N$), we might expect the population to be sufficiently far away from the most-fit allele that it is about equally likely that a moderately selected mutation is advantageous or deleterious.

To appreciate this argument, it must be borne in mind that the fitness differences are very small, perhaps as small as 10^{-10} to 10^{-5}, depending on the species. We have no experimental results to help decide whether mutations of such small effect are mostly deleterious or split evenly between positive and negative selection coefficients. One thing is clear: we cannot use the fact that strongly selected alleles are almost always deleterious to argue that moderately selected alleles should be deleterious as well.

Mutations of large effect usually involve loss of function through major disruptions of the integrity of the protein. Alleles of moderate effect, by contrast, alter the protein by a miniscule amount. I can see no reason to assume that this miniscule change is generally deleterious, particularly in the context of a changing environment. That the assumption that moderately selected mutations are almost always deleterious has never, to my knowledge, received much discussion, is unfortunate.

6.2 Genetic loads

Lewontin and Hubby [190] appear to be the first to use genetic load theory to argue against natural selection as a mechanism for maintaining molecular variation within populations. After some calculations, which will be reproduced below, they concluded that

> While we cannot assign an exact maximum reproductive value to the most fit multiple heterozygous genotype, it seems quite impossible that only one billionth of the reproductive capacity of a *Drosophila* population is being realized. No *Drosophila* female could conceivably lay two billion eggs. [190, p. 606]

Although load theory led them to this point, it did not compel Lewontin and Hubby to accept the neutral alternative, even though they clearly stated it as one of the possible explanations for molecular variation.

Two years later Kimura [155] also applied load theory to molecular variation. He was concerned with substitution load—Haldane's Cost of Selection—as it applied to mammals. He concluded that

> ... the calculation of the cost based on Haldane's formula shows that if new alleles produced by nucleotide replacements are substituted in a population at the rate of one substitution every 2 yr, then the substitutional load becomes so large that no mammalian species could tolerate it [155, p. 625].

Unlike Lewontin and Hubby, Kimura felt that the only escape from intolerable loads was to assume that molecular variation is neutral.

The invocation of genetic loads is a natural reaction to the suggestion that selection plays a major role in molecular evolution. It seems unlikely that selection could act simultaneously on tens of thousands of segregating nucleotides without resulting in extraordinary fitness differences between genotypes. Experience has shown that large fitness differences between outbred individuals do not occur: We have yet to see a female *Drosophila* lay a billion eggs! Thus, we are led to reject selection as a likely cause of molecular variation.

Load theory is one of those areas where intuition can be misleading. In this section we will develop the theory in an orthodox fashion, yet reach a conclusion that is entirely different from that of Lewontin, Hubby, and Kimura. In accord with history, we will consider segregation load first, followed by substitutional load. Segregation load is much easier to describe yet includes all of the concepts of substitutional load.

Consider a diploid species experiencing overdominant selection at n diallelic loci. Let the fitness contribution of each of the two homozygotes at a locus be $1 - s$ and that of the heterozygote, $1 + s$. (The restriction to two alleles and symmetry has no impact on the points to be made.) Assume that the loci interact multiplicatively; that is, that the fitness of a genotype that is homozygous at i loci is

$$w(i) = (1 - s)^i (1 + s)^{n-i}. \tag{6.4}$$

Because the marginal mean fitness at each locus is one, the mean fitness of the entire population, $\bar{w}$, is one as well.

The genetic load is, by definition, the difference in fitness between the most-fit genotype and the average fitness of the population:

$$L = w_{max} - \bar{w} = (1 + s)^n - 1.$$

If, as Lewontin and Hubby argue, $s = .01$ and $n = 2000$, then $L \approx 10^9$, suggesting that somewhere out there is a female with a billion eggs. The calculation becomes even more compelling if larger values of n are used, as seems appropriate for mammals or if silent as well as amino acid variation is included.

In response to Lewontin and Hubby's fecund female, a number of papers were written that pointed out that a true understanding of the significance of genetic loads can only come from a description of the distribution of fitness in the population [163,210,276]. The analysis of load theory that follows is taken from these papers and from one by Ewens [66].

For our case, we can obtain the distribution of fitness by randomizing $w(i)$ from equation 6.4 with respect to the distribution of the number of homozygous loci per individual. For weak linkage, the latter is a binomial distribution with mean $n/2$ and variance $n/4$.

The calculations will be somewhat easier if we use some approximations. For the fitness $w(i)$ use the Taylor series expansion

$$\log(1 + x) \approx x - x^2/2$$

to obtain

$$w(i) = e^{i \log(1-s) + (n-i) \log(1+s)} \approx e^Y, \tag{6.5}$$

where

$$Y = ns - 2si - \frac{1}{2} ns^2.$$

The moments of Y are

$$\mu = EY = -\frac{1}{2}ns^2, \ \sigma^2 = \mathrm{Var}Y = ns^2.$$

If n is large, the binomially distributed i may be approximated with a normal distribution. In so doing, e^Y becomes log normal with moments

$$
\begin{aligned}
Ee^Y &= e^{\mu + \frac{1}{2}\sigma^2} = 1 \\
\mathrm{Var}\, e^Y &= e^{2\mu}e^{\sigma^2}(e^{\sigma^2} - 1) = e^{ns^2} - 1.
\end{aligned}
$$

The significance of these calculations becomes apparent when we return to Lewontin and Hubby's original example, $s = 0.01$ and $n = 2000$. The coefficient of variation of fitness in this instance is

$$\frac{\sqrt{\mathrm{Var}\, e^Y}}{Ee^Y} = \sqrt{e^{ns^2} - 1} \approx \sqrt{ns} = 0.4472, \tag{6.6}$$

not nearly as large a number as we may have expected given what the celebrated fecund female contributes to the variance in fitness. The reason that the coefficient of variance is not astronomical is that most individuals are heterozygous for a number of loci that does not differ tremendously from the mean number, $n/2$.

We can use extreme value theory to discover the number of heterozygous loci that are likely to be found in the most heterozygous individual in a population of size N and to compare this to the fecund female. If Z_N is the maximum of N standardized normal random variables, then $(Z_N - a_N)/b_N$ converges to the extreme value distribution given in equation 5.7, where a_N and b_N are given in equations 5.8 and 5.9. "Un-standardizing" the normal and rearranging the extreme value scaling shows that the distribution of the maximum number of heterozygous loci in an individual approaches that of

$$n/2 + \sqrt{n/4}(b_N U + a_N),$$

where U is an extreme value random variable with extreme value distribution given in equation 5.7. As N grows, the mean number of heterozygous loci in the most heterozygous individual approaches

$$\sqrt{n/4}(2\ln N)^{1/2} + n/2.$$

Using equation 6.5, we see that the fitness of this genotype is

$$e^{2s\sqrt{(n\ln N)/2}}.$$

For example, in a population of 10^6 individuals with 2000 loci, the mean number of heterozygous loci in the most heterozygous individual is only 117 more than the mean (1000). The fitness of this individual is 3.23, 9 orders of magnitude less than that of the fecund female! Thus, when load is based on the most-fit individual that is likely to occur, rather than on a mythical individual that will never occur, the entire load argument for molecular variation evaporates. This conclusion could be strengthened by using values of s that are smaller, say 10^{-3} or 10^{-4}, as may be more appropriate for molecular variation.

Ewens [66] used substitution rather than segregation load to make the same argument. For substitution load caused by the fixation of additive alleles experiencing directional selection, he showed that the variance in fitness is s/ρ, where ρ is the rate of substitution of alleles for the entire genome in units of nucleotides fixed per generation. Using $s = 0.01$ and Kimura's estimate that $\rho = 1/6$, Ewens argued that the standard deviation of fitness is only 0.245, about half that obtained using Lewontin and Hubby's figures for segregation load. Thus, we are again led to the view that a great deal of selection could be operating without an unreasonable effect on the distribution of fitness.

We have seen in equation 6.6 that the coefficient of variation of fitness is about $\sqrt{n}s$. Dobzhansky and Spassky [57], showed that the variance in viability in outbred individuals for one of the four *Drosophila* chromosomes is around 0.05. We could use this to argue that $\sqrt{n}s < \sqrt{.05} = 0.22$. If $s = 10^{-4}$, then about 5 million loci could be experiencing balancing selection without fitness differentials that are out of line with experiments. If $s = 10^{-5}$, the number of loci jumps to 500 million. Clearly a large number of loci may be weakly selected without incurring a burdensome genetic load.

What about the fecund female? Her existence as part of our model, if not of the natural world, must be explained. One avenue is to claim that our multiplicative model is only viewed as an approximation to fitness interactions for genotypes that are close to the population mean. It simply does not apply to genotypes that are many standard deviations away. By adopting this view, we are throwing up our hands and saying that $L = w_{max} - \bar{w}$ cannot be discussed in the context of our model. Were we to be interested in L, we should produce a new model that places an upper bound on $w(i)$. Such a bound both appeals to our intuition and brings the genetic load under control.

I do not want to leave the impression that load theory has no place in population genetics. It is clearly the most expedient means of examining the consequences of mutation–selection balance, particularly for mutations with relatively large effects. This aspect of the theory, however, has little relevance to our discussion of molecular variation.

6.3 Substitutions

Under the weak-selection neutral model, the rate of substitution is equal to the neutral mutation rate per generation:

$$k_g = u_g. \tag{6.7}$$

If mutation rates and generation times are "reasonably constant" across a group of organisms, then the rate of evolution should be "reasonably constant" as well. By contrast, certain models of directional selection predict that the rate of molecular evolution is

$$k_g = 4Nu_g s.$$

For the same degree of constancy, some assumptions are required to keep Ns under control. The general feeling has been that there are no such assumptions that appeal to our biological intuition. For these reasons, Kimura and Ohta concluded (in 1971) that

> Probably the strongest evidence for the theory is the remarkable uniformity for each protein molecule in the rate of mutant substitutions in the course of evolution. This is particularly evident in the evolutionary changes of haemoglobins, where, for example, the number of amino-acid substitutions is about the same in the line leading to man as in that leading to the carp from their common ancestor. [161, p. 467]

Today, it is still true that the rough constancy of rates of molecular evolution is the strongest and most appealing argument in favor of the neutral allele theory.

Yet, in Chapter 3 we saw that rates of molecular evolution are not constant. How does this impact the neutral allele theory? There are two distinct aspects of rate constancy that must be addressed. In our statistical study we called them lineage effects and residual effects.

Lineage effects

Our observations on lineage effects in Chapter 3 could be summarized as follows. Within mammals, the magnitude of lineage effects differs for silent and replacement substitutions, being more pronounced in the former. Moreover, lineage effects for silent substitutions appear to be due to a generation-time effect: species with shorter generation times evolve more rapidly. By contrast, the generation-time effect for replacement substitutions is very weak.

The weak-selection neutral theory appears ill-equipped to handle this dichotomy. Assuming that the mutation rate, u_g, is relatively constant per generation across mammals, equation 6.7 clearly predicts that the rate of substitution should vary with generation time, just as seen for silent substitutions. The dependency of the mutation rate on generation time must be a genome-wide property. In particular, if we assume that u_g is independent of the generation time for silent substitutions, we must assume that it is independent for replacement substitutions as well. If so, then how are we to account for the absence of a generation-time effect for replacement substitutions? The answer is clear: we can't under the weak-selection neutral model.

Historically, this argument was turned on its head. Even though a generation-time effect had been noted in the late 1960s in DNA hybridization studies, what impressed population geneticists at the time was the rough clock-time dependence of amino acid substitutions inferred from protein sequence data. This led to the assumption that the rate of mutation was clock-time dependent as well, $u_g = g u_y$, where the mutation rate per year, u_y, was viewed as constant across species for each protein.

For example Kimura wrote in 1969,

> The remarkable constancy per year is most easily understood by assuming that in diverse vertebrate lines the rate of production of neutral mutations per individual per year is constant. [156, p. 347]

It should be noted that the constancy of mutation rates per year was not a well-established biological phenomenon then, nor is it today. Thus, the neutral theory in no sense *predicted* the clock-time dependency of amino acid substitutions. Rather, the theory was modified in such a way as to make it compatible with the observations.

Kimura himself quickly retreated from the constancy of u_y when he adopted Ohta's mildly deleterious theory. For example, in his 1983 book he wrote

> Unless the mechanism of mutation differs fundamentally for neutral alleles from other type of mutations, we should expect that the frequency of neutral mutations is roughly constant per generation, contrary to observations.
>
> I must admit that this is a difficult problem for the neutral theory to cope with (and even more so for the 'selectionist' theory). [159, p. 246]

Others have retained the assumption that u_y rather than u_g should be held constant. The justification is that the rate of mutation may, in fact, be constant per cell generation rather than per creature generation. If the number of cell generations in spermatogenesis per unit time is roughly the same in all mammals, then the clock-time dependence of the overall mutation rate is a simple consequence [308].

We thus have two models of mutation and two dynamics of substitutions. The choices seem obvious:

- u_g *constant*: Under this assumption we must conclude that silent substitutions, because they exhibit a generation-time effect, are compatible with the weak-selection neutral model while replacement substitutions are not.

- u_y *constant*: Under this assumption we must conclude that replacement substitutions, because they are clock-time dependent, are compatible with the weak-selection neutrality while silent substitutions are not.

Most will find the first alternative more attractive. The choice that cannot be accepted is that *both* silent and replacement substitutions are weakly selected.

We can accommodate both phenomena under a neutral theory that includes moderate selection as was done originally by Ohta [226] in 1972. She assumed that mutation rates are constant per generation, that silent substitutions are purely neutral ($p_w = 1$) and that amino acid substitutions are moderately deleterious ($p_w = 0$). It is clear that this can account for the generation-time effect among silent substitutions, but it is not at all obvious how the absence of a generation-time effect among amino acid substitutions is accommodated. With good reason: it isn't unless we introduce the additional assumption that the generation time is inversely proportional to the population size. We will look first at the mathematical argument that leads to this conclusion and then at the assumption itself.

Mathematical results on the substitution process for the moderately selected deleterious alleles are surprisingly sparse. All that is known comes from an approximate analysis based on the assumption that the population is monomorphic. The probability of fixation of a mutation with selection coefficient $s < 0$ is approximately

$$\frac{-2s}{e^{-4Ns} - 1}$$

when only two alleles are in the population. If s is exponentially distributed, as in equation 6.1, the probability of fixation, randomized over all possible mutations, is

$$\sigma_{ms}^{-1} \int_{-\infty}^{0} \frac{-2se^{s/\sigma_{ms}}}{e^{-4Ns} - 1} ds.$$

The change of variable $y = -4Ns$ transforms this expression into

$$\frac{1}{2N} \frac{1}{4N\sigma_{ms}} \int_{0}^{\infty} \frac{ye^{-[1+1/(4N\sigma_{ms})]y}}{1 - e^{-y}} dy = \frac{1}{2N} \frac{1}{4N\sigma_{ms}} \zeta(2, 1 + \frac{1}{4N\sigma_{ms}}),$$
(6.8)

where ζ is Reiman's zeta function.

Traditionally (for want of a better explanation), equation 6.8 is approximated by

$$\frac{1}{2N} \frac{1}{4N\sigma_{ms}}.$$

The approximation can be justified only for large $4N\sigma_{ms}$. Note that if $4N\sigma_{ms} < 1$, the rate of substitution of deleterious alleles exceeds that of neutral alleles, an obvious absurdity.

The rate of substitution per generation, k_g, is approximately the mean number of deleterious alleles introduced each generation times the fraction that are ultimately fixed, or

$$k_g \approx \frac{u_g}{4N\sigma_{ms}} \zeta[2, 1 + 1/(4N\sigma_{ms})].$$

For large $4N\sigma_{ms}$, we have

$$k_g \approx \frac{u_g}{4N\sigma_{ms}}. \tag{6.9}$$

Thus, substitutions occur more rapidly in smaller populations, as would be expected given that they are deleterious.

If the generation time is inversely proportional to the population size, $g = C_g/N$, the rate of substitution per year,

$$k_y \approx \frac{k_g}{g} = \frac{u_g}{4C_g\sigma_{ms}}$$

is independent of the generation time, as we wanted to show.

Ohta's model provides a natural explanation for the contrast in the strength of the generation-time effect for silent and replacement substitutions. Although there are some mathematical details that need to be cleaned up, the foundation for a neutral theory that encompasses both sorts of substitutions is firmly in place. Our judgment of the scientific validity of the theory must begin with an examination of the assumption that the generation time is inversely proportional to the population size.

Ohta herself provides no direct evidence, merely noting that

> We know as an empirical fact that there is a negative correlation between population size and generation time. [228, p. 149]

Although the assumption might seem reasonable—there are a lot of *Drosophila* and not many elephants—the only direct test that I am aware of is that by Nei and Graur [218] who failed to find a significant correlation between N and g among 77 species. This is a serious blow to the theory and could quite reasonably be used to reject it altogether. My own view, however, is that this remains an open question until a more thorough examination of the correlation of N and g within mammals is attempted.

Beyond this, we need more results on the rate of substitution as a function of the population size. It is clear from equation 6.8 that the rate of substitution is not (exactly) inversely proportional to population size. Whatever the relationship is, we require that the generation time be proportional to it.

Residual effects

Once lineage effects are removed, there is still some residual variation in numbers of substitutions beyond that expected were the substitution process a Poisson process. In Chapter 3 we quantified residual effects with the index of dispersion,

$$I(t) = \frac{\operatorname{Var}\mathcal{N}(t)}{E\mathcal{N}(t)},$$

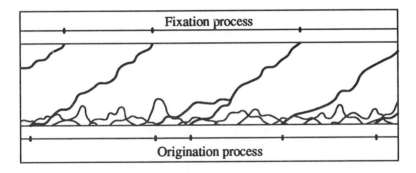

Figure 6.6. An illustration of the connection between the trajectories of nucleotides, the origination process, and the fixation process.

where $\mathcal{N}(t)$ is a random variable representing the number of substitution on a lineage of length t.* From Figure 3.7, we see that, for mammals, $R(t) \approx 7.8$ for replacement substitutions and approximately 3.3 for silent substitutions, although we expressed little confidence in the latter figure. Are these results compatible with the constancy of rates predicted by the neutral theory?

A short digression is in order to explain the connection between the way data are gathered and the predicted index of dispersion of the neutral theory. There are actually two point processes that could be used to describe fixations under the neutral model as illustrated in Figure 6.6. One represents the instants in time when nucleotides become fixed; call this the *fixation process.* The other represents the instants in time when mutations that ultimately become fixed first appear in the population; call this the *origination process.* The two processes are intimately connected since each origination is attached to one fixation, although each fixation may correspond to more than one origination.

The two processes differ dramatically in complexity. The origination process is, to very good approximation, a Poisson process with constant rate u_g when time is measured in units of generations.

The fixation process is much more complex. Because of hitchhiking, the fixation of one site increases the probability of the fixation of another site within a small interval of time. The resulting clustering of substitutions is moderated somewhat by a refractory period between successive substitutions due to a reduction in the genetic variation that accompanies fixations. A mathematical description of the fixation process may be found in two papers by Watterson [301,302]. Fortunately, our sampling procedure, which looks at the cumulative number of substitutions, applies to the origination rather than the fixation process.

To see this, suppose we have sequences from two species whose common

---

*Recall that the statistic $R(t)$ is often used to estimate the index of dispersion, $I(t)$.

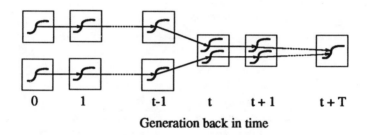

Figure 6.7. The history back in time of two sequences sampled in generation 0.

ancestor lived t generations ago. Each of these sequences is replicated from a sequence in the previous generation. Each of these is a copy of a sequence from two generations before present, and so forth back to the population that existed t generations ago, the common ancestor population, as illustrated in Figure 6.7. The two ancestor sequences in the common ancestor population will have a common ancestor sequence at some random time, T generations further back. For weakly selected alleles, T is geometrically distributed with mean $2N$. Thus, the time back to the common ancestor sequence of our two sampled sequences is the random time $t + T$.

Any nucleotide site that differs between our two sampled sequences must have appeared for the first time in one of the ancestral sequences. Thus, the times of origination of fixed mutations, rather than the times of their fixation, are what determine the distribution of the number of nucleotide differences between sequences chosen from a pair of species.

The mutations appear at random along the lines of descent. Were the time back to the common ancestor a fixed number t, then the number of mutations would be Poisson distributed with mean $2u_g t$. However, the time is a random quantity so the distribution is the sum of two random variables. The first, X_t, is the number of mutations that occurred during the fixed time interval t. X_t is a Poisson random variable with mean $2u_g t$.

The second, Y, is the number that occurred during the random period of time T. The distribution of Y is obtained by randomizing a Poisson with an exponential (an approximation of a geometric) random variable with mean $4Nu_g$. A Poisson distribution randomized by an exponential is a geometric distribution. Thus, Y is geometrically distributed with mean $\theta = 4Nu_g$ and variance $\theta(1 + \theta)$. Adding these two independent random variables we conclude that the mean number of mutations separating the two species has mean

$$\mu(t) = EX_t + EY = 2u_g t + \theta$$

and variance

$$\sigma^2(t) = \text{Var} X_t + \text{Var} Y = 2u_g t + \theta(1 + \theta).$$

Thus,

$$R(t) = \frac{\sigma^2(t)}{\mu(t)} = 1 + \frac{\theta^2}{2u_g t + \theta}, \tag{6.10}$$

as was originally shown by Gillespie and Langley [99]. From this we conclude that the apparent index of dispersion for the neutral model is greater than one.

There is a problem: on the one hand, the origination process is claimed to be a Poisson process (with $I(t) = 1$); on the other hand, the estimated index of dispersion is greater than one. The resolution comes with the realization that we are, in effect, following a Poisson process for a random length of time when we examine two sequences. That extra bit of randomness introduced by the time back to the common ancestor sequence, T, inflates the variance in the number of substitutions beyond the mean. The estimator, $R(t)$, is thus not an unbiased estimator of $I(t)$ for the neutral model.

The error is small, however, for the sequences typically used to estimate the index of dispersion. For example, the average number of substitutions in β hemoglobin between representatives of different orders of mammals is 30 [159, Table 4.4], which we can use as an estimate of $2u_g t + \theta$. We do not know θ for replacement sites in β-globin, but $\theta = 0.1$ is representative of proteins. Putting these into equation 6.10 gives $R(t) \approx 1.003$.

In general, we would expect the apparent index of dispersion for neutral substitutions to be very close to one unless θ is unreasonably large. Rearranging equation 6.10 gives

$$\theta = \sqrt{(R(t) - 1)E\mathcal{N}(t)},$$

where $E\mathcal{N}(t)$ is the mean number of substitutions separating a pair of species. For $R_n = 7.8$ and $E\mathcal{N}(t) = 30$, $\theta = 14.28$. Were all of the alleles weakly selected, then $\theta = 14.28$ implies that the expected homozygosity is $1/(1 + \theta) = 0.065$, far lower than seen in protein polymorphism studies.

Our conclusion must be that the index of dispersion of replacement substitutions is too high to be accounted for by the weak-selection neutral allele theory. The same conclusion was reached by Hudson [134] in a more complete analysis using all of the data in the Langley and Fitch studies [182]. Given our reservations about the estimate of $R(t)$ for silent substitutions, there remains the possibility that they are weakly selected.

Certain modifications of the neutral model might allow it to exhibit a higher index of dispersion. One possibility is that linked loci undergoing directional or balancing selection might raise $R(t)$. However, it is easy to see that this is not the case. The sampling process illustrated in Figure 6.7 applies no matter what dynamics may be changing the frequency of linked sites. The only place where linked loci can have an effect is in the distribution of T. Even if T has a distribution that is wildly different from an exponential, the effects on $R(t)$ would be minor as long as t is much larger than the mean of T, as is the case for comparisons involving orders of mammals. A direct demonstration that the fixation probability of a neutral mutation is independent of selection at linked sites, recently published by Birky and Walsh [18], also argues for the lack of sensitivity of $R(t)$ to events at linked loci.

An obvious way to increase the variability of rate of substitution is by allowing the mutation rate to vary. For this to work, the time scale of change of the mutation rate must be delicately balanced. If it were much faster than the rate of molecular evolution, the variation would be averaged out and the process would be identical to a constant mutation-rate process. If it were much slower, the mutation rate would be inherited down the separate lineages and the process would, once again, exhibit little variability.

This time-scale argument should sound familiar: it is the same one that led us to an episodic model for molecular evolution in Chapter 3. There we had the luxury of allowing the rate of molecular evolution to vary without bound; here we must constrain the mutation rate within reasonable levels, mitigating against an episodic model of mutation. The restrictions on time scales and the bounds on the variation in mutation rates do not rule out fluctuations of mutation rates as an explanation for the high $R(t)$, but they do argue that such an explanation would depend in a very delicate way on the parameters.

Takahata's *fluctuating neutral space* model [277] is a way of circumventing these problems. It provides a connection between the rate of change of the mutation rate and the rate of molecular evolution by assuming that the mutation rate changes with each substitution. Our sampling model, shown in Figure 6.7, may be easily modified to include the fluctuating neutral space.

As it currently stands, we represent the number of substitutions separating the two species as a Poisson process with rate u_g that has been running for the random time, $2(t+T)$. The fluctuating neutral space model simply replaces the Poisson process with a more complicated point process. Takahata [277] chose a renewal process for mathematical convenience, but any stationary point process will do. In fact, the renewal process is not the most biologically compelling choice since it does not exhibit any autocorrelation of mutation rates. Each substitution changes the rate to a value that is independent of the current rate.

A complete mathematical description of the neutral space model is complicated as it involves the moments of the numbers of events for a stationary point process over finite intervals. There are no general expressions for these moments. They are complicated even for the relatively simple renewal process. However, if we choose species for which $t \gg ET$, then the measured index of dispersion will equal the asymptotic $(t \to \infty)$ index of dispersion of the mutation process. In this way, we can easily account for the high index of dispersion for replacement sites within the context of a purely neutral model by using our estimates of $R(t)$ as estimates of the index of dispersion of the mutation process.

But is a mutational process with a high index of dispersion biologically reasonable? Recent work on contextual effects in mutagenesis [175,245] shows that one mutation can dramatically alter the frequency of subsequent mutations. Thus, we have little difficulty in identifying a biological mechanism for elevating the index of dispersion of mutation. However, if contextual effects account for the index of dispersion for replacement substitutions, why don't silent substitutions, which one might feel are less affected by selection, show a high index of dispersion as well? I can see no answer to this other than to assume that silent mutations are subject to forces other than drift and mutation, a choice I feel is much less attractive than rejecting contextual effects as the cause of variable rates.

Alternatively, we could attribute the high index of dispersion for replacement substitutions to properties of the proteins themselves. Takahata argues that

> The [fluctuating neutral space] model assumes that the substitution rate fluctuates through changes of selective constraints as new substitutions occur. [277, p.174]

Picture a protein with a certain fraction of amino acid sites undergoing neutral evolution and the remainder being held invariant by natural selection. A change in one of the neutral sites is assumed to cause a previously selected site to suddenly become a neutral site. In the neutralist jargon, this is a "relaxation of constraints," in ours it is a lowering of site effects. The lowering of site effects is believable; that this could be accomplished by purely neutral substitutions is less so. That such a mechanism could cause a many-fold change in rates, as seen in the data, seems extraordinary. Yet, this is the model that is currently used to account for the high index of dispersion for replacement substitutions in the context of the weak-selection neutral theory.

Could a moderate-selection netural model account for high values of $R(t)$? Just as Ohta's theory of mildly deleterious mutations salvaged the neutral theory from the generation-time effect, we might hope that it can provide salvation from residual effects as well. An obvious start is to exploit the fact that the rate of substitution depends on the population size. Since population sizes fluctuate in nature, we might expect that the fluctuations will elevate $R(t)$. In fact, they do [93,277], although the effect does not appear to be strong enough to elevate $R(t)$ to the level seen in replacement substitutions. The basic problem can be understood without resorting to mathematics.

Imagine a species whose population size continually oscillates between large and small values. While small, substitutions occur at a rapid rate; while large, they occur very slowly. This is exactly what we need to elevate $R(t)$. For such a scenario to succeed, several substitutions must occur while the population is in each of its sizes. Since, on average, substitutions occur on a time scale of millions to tens of millions of years, we require that the population size oscillate on a somewhat longer time scale. Our demographic intuition says that fluctuations occur much more rapidly than this. If they do, the substitution process proceeds as if the population size were constant at its average value.

An approximate mathematical demonstration of this point is possible using our results from Chapter 3 on the doubly stochastic Poisson process. Assume that the population size shifts to new sizes at the end of time intervals that are exponentially distributed with mean μ_t and that each size is chosen independently from some probability distribution. The rate of substitution corresponding to each population size will be a random quantity as well. Its mean may be written Ek_g and its autocovariance

$$r(x) = \text{Var}(k_g)e^{-x/\mu_t}.$$

Using equation 3.9, we see that the asymptotic (large t) value of the index of dispersion is

$$I(\infty) = 1 + \frac{2\mu_t \text{Var}\, k_g}{Ek_g}.$$

As an example, consider a species whose population size is chosen at random from two values leading to two rates of substitution, k_0 and k_1, that occur with equal probability. The mean rate is $(k_0 + k_1)/2$ and the variance is $(k_0 - k_1)^2/4$. The index of dispersion is

$$I(\infty) = 1 + \frac{\mu_t(k_1 - k_0)^2}{k_0 + k_1}.$$

The situations most likely to yield large indices of dispersion will have very different rates corresponding to the two population sizes. Let $k_0 \gg k_1$, giving

$$I(\infty) \approx 1 + k_0\mu_t.$$

If the fast rate of substitution is, say, $k_0 = 10^{-5}$, we see immediately that the population size must remain constant for hundreds of thousands of years ($\mu_t = O(10^5)$) to elevate the index of dispersion beyond one. However, the more likely situation is for $\mu_t \ll 1/k_0$. From this we are forced to conclude that fluctuating population sizes and moderate selection of deleterious alleles is not a likely model to account for high values of $R(t)$.

There is another mechanism that could elevate $R(t)$: multiple mutational events such as caused by gene conversion or replication slippage. However, such events should elevate the index of dispersion for both silent and replacement substitutions, which isn't observed in the sequence data. Perhaps when we finally have a solid estimate of $R(t)$ for some region of the genome that we are confident is undergoing neutral evolution we can use that estimate to indicates the fraction of the replacement $R(t)$ that is attributable to complex mutational events.

Patterns of substitutions are our best available evidence that speaks to the scientific validity of the neutral allele theory. In this section we have seen that the evidence is compatible with a weak-selection neutral theory for silent substitutions, but strains the theory for amino acid substitutions.

If a weak-selection neutral theory is to be invoked for all substitutions, then it must be one that includes a fluctuating neutral space for replacement substitutions and an orthodox mutational pattern for silent substitutions. The moderate-selection neutral theory does not, in its current incarnation, offer any explanation for the high values of $R(t)$ for replacement substitutions.

6.4 Constraints

Two conspicuous properties of molecular evolution that have been commonly used to argue for the neutral theory, as stated by Kimura [159, p. 103], are

- "Functionally less important molecules or parts of molecules evolve (in terms of mutant substitutions) faster than more important ones."

- "Those mutant substitutions that are less disruptive to the existing structure and function of a molecule (conservative substitutions) occur more frequently in evolution than more disruptive ones."

Basically, substitutions with only a small functional consequence occur more frequently than those with a large effect.

King and Jukes [164] were among the first to use the inverse relationship between the effect of a substitution and its rate of occurrence as evidence for the neutral allele theory. They argued that certain amino acid replacements, such as leucine for isoleucine, are chemically so similar as to be purely neutral. They also argued that the sensitivity of a protein to a particular amino acid substitution depends on where the substitution occurred. There may be regions of some proteins where amino acid substitutions of even moderate chemical effects could be purely neutral. In Figure 1.12 we saw that the rates of amino acid substitution may not exhibit the pattern predicted by the neutral theory. The chemically most conservative changes appear not to occur as rapidly as some less conservative changes.

Kimura [159, p. 155] contrasted the predictions of the neutral theory to those of a Fisherian model of evolution, deciding that the graphs supported the former. The Fisherian model is a geometric representation of the notion that mutations with large effect are less likely to be favorable than those of small effect. The probability depends on the magnitude of effect, r; the number of pleiotropic effects that mutations are thought to have, n; and the distance of the mean phenotype from the optimal phenotype, d. The probability of a favorable mutation is, under Fisher's model,

$$p(x) = \frac{1}{\sqrt{2\pi}} \int_x^\infty e^{-y^2/2} dy,$$

where $x = r\sqrt{n/d}$ [75, p. 43]. Kimura argued that the probability of fixation of an advantageous mutation is proportional to its effect, suggesting that rate of fixation of advantageous mutations should be proportional to

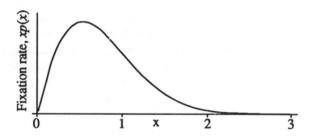

Figure 6.8. The rate of fixation as predicted by Kimura's adaptation of Fisher's geometric model of adaptive evolution.

$xp(x)$. This function is graphed in Figure 6.8. The similarity of the curve to the sixth-order polynomials fitted to the data in Figure 1.12 is striking.

Taken at face value, the amino acid substitutions appear to be due to the fixation of advantageous rather neutral mutations. However, such a conclusion must be viewed with extreme caution. Our data represent average properties taken from a large number of proteins and species. As such, there are many opportunities for biases that could obscure the true relationship. For example, the more rapidly evolving pairs may reflect a tendency for such pairs to be located in regions of proteins far away from ligand binding sites rather than reflecting their chemical differences. Such biases make me uncomfortable using Figure 1.12 to argue for directional selection; they make me even more uncomfortable using it to argue for neutrality.

There is a simple argument for the neutrality of conservative amino acid substitutions that illustrates the pitfalls of using averages across proteins. We could declare that substitutions between pairs of amino acids with the highest rate of substitution are purely neutral. If so, then the rate between these pairs should be similar to that of a region of the genome, say silent sites or processed pseudogenes, where we believe that neutral evolution is occurring. Kimura [159, p. 154] did exactly this and concluded that the highest rate of substitution between amino acids was about one half that of silent substitutions, concluding that

> considering the large statistical error of this estimation procedure, we may conclude that the data on synonymous substitution are consistent with the protein data...

Consider, however, that we know at the outset that certain proteins (e. g., histones) evolve very slowly while others (e. g., fibrinopeptide) evolve very rapidly. The absolute rates that appear in Figure 1.12 reflect, in the main, the particular mix of proteins in *The Atlas* used to calculate the rates. Had only histones been used, for example, then the comparison of the absolute rates to silent rates would have been very different. From this we can only conclude we cannot use the absolute rates from this data set to decide whether or not the fastest substitution rates reflect neutral events.

A better approach to finding some amino acid sites that are evolving at the "neutral rate" is to examine the most rapidly evolving sites within a set of proteins and check whether these rates are similar across the proteins as they should be if all of the fast evolving sites are neutral. To my knowledge, this has not been attempted.

The evolution of codon usage and GC% may be one of the best examples of evolution under constraints. As we saw in Chapter 2, the rate of silent substitution is negatively correlated with the degree of codon bias in unicellular organisms and *Drosophila*. The usual explanation for this is based on the existence of an optimal codon that allows for the fastest rate of translation. Efficiency of translation is more important in highly expressed proteins, hence the stronger selection for codon bias with the consequent lowering in the rate of substitution of moderately selected deleterious mutations to the suboptimal codon.

6.5   Polymorphisms

Although polymorphism studies fueled much of the original debate over the neutral theory, they have done little to help settle the issue. The reasons will emerge as we discuss their use in arguments for and against the theory.

When faced with both polymorphism and molecular evolution data, the obvious first question is whether the two are mutually compatible under the weak-selection neutral allele theory. In 1971, Kimura and Ohta [161] concluded that for proteins they are compatible, using the following argument.

The neutral mutation rate, u_y, is equal to the rate of amino acid substitution, which is "typically" 10^{-7} amino acid substitutions per locus per year in mammals. The expected homozygosity at equilibrium,

$$EF = \frac{1}{1 + 4Nu_yg}, \tag{6.11}$$

is "typically" 0.9 in mouse and *Drosophila* populations. If mice and *Drosophila* reproduce twice annually ($g = 0.5$) and if their effective population sizes are approximately $N = 5 \times 10^5$, then the substitution rate and homozygosity are mutually compatible with the weak-selection equilibrium neutral allele theory.*

The compatibility is very sensitive to the effective population size. Were the true size an order of magnitude smaller or larger, the compatibility dissolves. In fact, it has been argued that the effective size of *Drosophila* populations could be as large as 10^{10} [9], in which case the predicted homozygosity is 0.0005, far below the observed values. *Drosophila* is not unique. In a study of 77 species for which protein heterozygosities and

---

*Their argument is slightly more detailed than this in an effort to accommodate the lack of resolution of gel electrophoresis. The frills do not significantly affect the conclusion.

(crude) population size estimates were available, Nei and Graur [218] concluded that the homozygosities of most species are well above that expected under the weak-selection neutral allele theory.

High homozygosities are readily accommodated under the weak-selection neutral theory by assuming that most populations are not at equilibrium due to historic effects such as bottlenecks or hitchhiking. The time for a population that is initially homozygous to achieve one half of its equilibrium homozygosity is approximately

$$\frac{\ln(2)}{1 + 4Nu)}2N$$

generations, a very long time for a species to evolve in the relative homogeneity required of the neutral theory. It is likely that some event will interfere with the attainment of equilibrium and raise the homozygosity. As we shall see, hitchhiking is a better candidate than bottlenecks.

We can imagine two sorts of models of population size fluctuations that fall under the rubric of bottlenecks. The first assumes that the population size fluctuates at random on a time scale that is faster than that of genetic drift. Such a model will behave essentially like a constant population size model, but one with the effective size of the population, N_e, satisfying

$$E\ln[1 - 1/N(t)] = \ln(1 - 1/N_e).$$

Were this the correct model, some species should be found with larger heterozygosities than expected given the current population size and others with smaller heterozygosities. Nei and Graur's finding that almost all species exhibit greater than the expected homozygosities effectively argues against short time scale population size fluctuation as the reason for the excess.

Alternatively, imagine that all species experienced a severe bottleneck in the relatively recent past and that their heterozygosities are still climbing toward their equilibrium values. Nei and Graur argue that most species experienced such a bottleneck during the most recent ice age. Unfortunately, we have no way to test this hypothesis. It is clear that the bottleneck would have to be severe and would have to last a very long time. Beyond this, there is little to add. We did see in Chapter 1 that the average heterozygosity of temperate species is about 15% below that of tropical species, but this is not particularly informative since tropical species may have had their population sizes reduced during the last glaciation as did their temperate counterparts.

Hitchhiking appears to be a much stronger candidate to account for low heterozygosities in the context of the weak-selection neutral model. Maynard Smith and Haigh [207] presented an approximate analysis suggesting that hitchhiking of neutral alleles on chromosomes bearing favorable mutations could be a more potent force than genetic drift for removing variation.

Recently, Kaplan et al. [149] showed that if one substitution out of every 400 is selected, the heterozygosity at linked neutral sites will be reduced to 20% of the expected value under the equilibrium neutral model. This is an important calculation. Supporters of the neutral theory frequently claim that 1 out of 10 substitutions are selected. Were this the case, observed heterozygosities should be severely limited by hitchhiking. Moreover, hitchhiking provides a natural explanation for our failure to find a strong correlation between population size and heterozygosity.

We cannot accept this role for hitchhiking without some qualifications. In our discussion of the polymorphism data in Chapter 1, we noted the presence of locus effects. Some loci tend to be more monomorphic than others among species. The reduced variation at these loci cannot be attributed to hitchhiking without postulating that transient selection at closely linked loci is similar across species, an interesting idea but one that has no empirical support. If we are to use hitchhiking, we should use it only to explain the fact that the heterozygosities at the most polymorphic loci are much lower than would be expected under the neutral theory. In so doing, we also avoid discussions of average heterozygosities as we advised earlier.

Our development of the neutral theory has reached a critical point. If, as our argument appears to have taken us, populations are not at equilibrium, then much of what we have held to be relevant to the neutral theories as it applies to natural populations is not relevant at all. For example, the formula for the mean homozygosity, equation 6.11, does not apply. Nor does the Ewens sampling distribution, nor many of the results from coalescent theory, nor stepping-stone models, and on and on. The specter of nonequilibrium dynamics is so daunting that we must have embraced the equilibrium theory despite many observations and theoretical results that should have warned us away. The neutral theory may not be the correct theory, but I feel strongly that if it is to be invoked, it should not be used as an equilibrium theory.

The alternative explanation for low heterozygosities is Ohta's hypothesis that most alleles are moderately deleterious [227]. While the extra parameter reflecting the average strength of selection in her model should make the fit to the data better than for the weak-selection model, the mathematical properties of the model are not known in sufficient detail to allow us to check the fit. What follows are some crude approximations that will illustrate some of the important qualitative features of Ohta's model.

If all mutations come from the moderate-selection component of the fitness distribution ($p_w = 0$), we would expect only those with deleterious effects very close to zero to attain high enough frequencies to appear in a sample. The dynamics of these mutations may be close enough to weak-selection neutral dynamics to use equation 6.11 with a doctored mutation rate as an approximation to the mean homozygosity for the moderate-selection model. Mutations with selection coefficients in the interval $(-0.1/N, 0)$ will behave very much like neutral alleles suggesting that we use the approximation in equation 6.3 to replace the mutation rate, u_y, in equation 6.11 with

$$u_y[1 - e^{-0.1/(N\sigma_{ms})}].$$

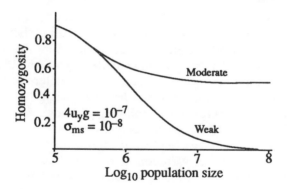

Figure 6.9. The homozygosity under weak and moderate selection as a function of population size.

The resulting approximation of the mean homozygosity compared with that for the weak-selection neutral model is illustrated in Figure 6.9.

Figure 6.9 clearly illustrates one of the most important properties of Ohta's model, the restriction of the range of mean homozygosities imposed by the upper limit:

$$\lim_{N \to \infty} E\mathcal{F} = \frac{1}{1 + 0.4 u_{y}g/\sigma_{ms}}.$$

The largest protein heterozygosities for individual loci are around 0.4. If the weakest mean selection coefficient were around $\sigma_{ms} \approx 0.6u_y$ and if N were large enough, we could nicely account for the upper limit on heterozygosities and the weak correlation between heterozygosity and population size illustrated in Figure 1.17. Examination of equation 6.9 shows that we cannot be too cavalier about the magnitude of N. If it is too large $(N\sigma_{ms} \gg 1)$ molecular evolution will grind to a halt. If it is too small, we loose the insensitivity of $E\mathcal{F}$ to N. To make Ohta's theory work it appears that a delicate balance between N, σ_{ms} and u_y must be assumed.

We can examine silent variation in much the same way as we did replacement variation, except that we will concentrate on properties of sites rather than of the entire locus. The only data that we have confidence in is for the *Adh* locus in *Drosophila melanogaster* for which, as we saw in Table 2.8, one site in 166 is polymorphic in a pair of randomly drawn chromosomes. Were this variation weakly selected and were the population in equilibrium (which it cannot be if we acknowledge the role of hitchhiking), then the estimate for $\theta_n = 4Nu_n$ is (from equation 6.11), 0.006. If the nucleotide mutation rate is somewhere in the range 10^{-9} to 10^{-8}, the effective population size of *D. melanogaster* must be around 10^5 to 10^6, ominously close to the figure from protein data, but too low for the reasons discussed previously.

This glimpse into silent variation suggests that it is depauperate as well. If it were weakly selected, then hitchhiking could be responsible. Support for this view comes from Table 2.8 where we saw that regions of the *Drosophila* chromosome with reduced recombination also appears to have reduced heterozygosity. As with amino acid variation, should silent variation be out of equilibrium, we are severely restricted in the statistical procedures available to test hypotheses.

Ohta's moderate-selection deleterious allele model may provide a viable alternative explanation for the reduced heterozygosity in the exons of the *Adh* locus. Recall that codon bias is pronounced at this locus suggesting that silent variation may be deleterious. If so, this may account for the reduced levels of variation. We clearly need a study that examines silent variation in exons from loci with low and high codon biases. Ohta's hypothesis cannot explain the lowered variation in regions of low recombination suggesting that deleterious alleles can account for only a portion of the reduction in heterozygosity.

In Chapter 2 we noted Aquadro's observation that *D. melanogaster* has higher protein variation but lower silent variation than its sibling species *D. simulans*. Aquadro accounted for this disparity by invoking weak selection for silent variation and moderate selection for protein variation and assuming that the effective population size of *D. simulans* is greater than that of *D. melanogaster*. Figure 6.9 suggests that this explanation needs some additional assumptions as the curves for silent and replacement substitutions do not cross. They can be made to cross by assuming that the silent mutation rate is less than that of replacement mutations, an assumption which appears to be compatible with the genetic code. With this additional assumption Aquadro's explanation becomes viable.

This brief discussion of the polymorphism data shows that the level of replacement and silent variation is too low to be accounted for by a weak-selection equilibrium neutral model. The low levels of variation are compatible with nonequilibrium and moderate-selection neutral theories, although in both cases the parameters must be chosen carefully.

6.6 The status of neutral theories

The most important conclusion from our examination of molecular evolution and polymorphism data is that silent and replacement mutations are experiencing different dynamics. As a consequence, we cannot conclude that both are undergoing the same brand of neutral evolution. There cannot be one neutral theory to accept or reject.

The case for the neutrality of replacement substitutions seems particularly weak. Not only does the theory have difficulty accounting for the high value of $R(t)$ and the weaker generation-time effect, but the theory cannot even speak to the examples of microadaptations that we documented in Chapter 1. In my view, the neutral theory must be abandoned for replacement substitutions.

Silent substitutions, on the other hand, may well be neutral, although the evidence at the time of this writing is incomplete. Should silent variation be neutral, then there are two important observations that must be made. The first is that silent variation is probably not in dynamic equilibrium because of historic events such as hitchhiking or recent bottlenecks. The second is that the patterns of codon usage and GC% evolution imply that at least some of the silent variation is moderately selected. Together, these two observations suggest that the genetic structure of populations is far more complex than we have hitherto assumed. An unfortunate consequence of this view is that we cannot rely on statistical procedures that assume that silent variation is weakly selected and at equilibrium.

7

Selection theories

In this, the final chapter, I will present a theory of molecular evolution and polymorphism based on the combined forces of natural selection, genetic drift, and mutation. The theory is intended to apply to amino acid variation, although it may eventually be extended to include silent variation as well. Before jumping in, I will summarize some of the evidence that created the need for such a theory.

7.1 Selection on proteins

In Chapters 1 and 3 we described studies that point to natural selection as a major force contributing to the evolution of proteins. Here I will review the major features of these studies and argue that, collectively, they imply that most amino acid substitutions are adaptive.

The case for selection begins with stories: anecdotes about amino acid substitutions that can reasonably be called adaptive. Such stories bolster our intuition about what is possible. We saw, for example, that the broad patterns of LDH adaptations to temperature are mirrored in the few amino acid substitutions that separate closely related species of fish living in waters that differ by only a few degrees centigrade. We saw amino acid substitutions in hemoglobins that increase oxygen affinities in species living at high altitudes. We saw examples of species or populations living in warmer environments having more thermostable proteins then their colder relatives. In each case, an adaptive story unfolded because of the original experimenter's ability to recognize an environmental factor that is likely to elicit an evolutionary response in a protein. The pairing of a functional aspect of a protein with a relevant environmental factor is key to a successful investigation. The pairing also forces us to recognize that, since environments are in a constant state of flux, so must be the evolutionary forces acting on proteins.

Our most convincing anecdotes used comparisons of different species, but we also described a number of studies of allelic variation within species which also suggested—albeit less convincingly—a role for natural selection. The fitnesses of PGI alleles in *Colias* butterflies, for example, appear to be affected by temperature as do the fitnesses of LDH alleles in *Fundulus*. The dynamics of alleles affecting osmoregulation in *Tigriopus* and *Mytilus* are also likely to be influenced by natural selection. Even though direct estimates of fitness differences are usually lacking, in each of these cases there are measureable physiological differences between genotypes that can reasonably be attributed to the variation in the enzymes.

While anecdotes expand our horizons about what is biologically plausible, there remains the lingering uneasiness that we are being misled by a small fraction of observations from a large scientific enterprise that has, in the main, failed to uncoverer direct evidence for selection. In our assessment of the role of examples, we must pay careful attention to the studies of null alleles in *Drosophila* populations that tell us, as we saw in Chapter 1, that selection coefficients for enzymes are likely to be bounded above by 10^{-3}. If all naturally occurring amino acid variants were subject to selection intensities on the order of 10^{-4} to 10^{-3}, we would be unable to measure any fitness differences; yet, such intensities represent very strong selection in species, such as *Drosophila*, with effective population sizes greatly in excess of 10^4. In this context, our examples should be viewed as extremes, instances where experimentalists were clever enough to choose systems with very large effects. They should be cherished as windows into a world of selection that will forever remain beyond the resolution of our techniques.

We should not give up our quest for generality: there is evidence in support of the thesis that *most* amino acid substitutions are adaptive. The first of this evidence is summarized in Table 1.3, which argues that most allelic variation in enzymes in *Drosophila* has both kinetic and physiological effects. Had we been unable to measure such effects, the case for selection would be weakened considerably. While Table 1.3 certainly makes a strong case that most allelic variation is functionally significant, it is unfortunate that more isn't known about the kinetic and physiological effects of naturally occuring amino acid variation in *Drosophila* and other species. It is surprising that no one has chosen a pair of sibling species and carefully compared the kinetic properties of, say, 20 enzymes between the two species. At the present time we can conclude that the best evidence supports the hypothesis that most allelic variation has measureable physiological consequences, and plead for more such experiments in the future.

Indirect studies into the effects of selection holds more promise for establishing generalities. In moving from Chapter 1 to Chapter 3, we saw a series of examples designed to connect the action of selection with accelerations in the rates of amino acid substitutions. We saw, for example, that the rate of substitution in insulin in the hystricomorph rodents accelerated by an order of magnitude as these rodents evolved a modified gastroenteropancreatic hormonal system. Similarly, we documented accelerated evolution of lysozymes in two independent groups of mammals, langurs and ruminants, that evolved rumins.

Most changes in rates of substitution should be more subtle. Yet, in Table 3.5 we saw that significant rate variation could be detected in 12 out of 20 proteins using only three species in the analysis. Rates of silent substitution are much less variable, suggesting that the rate variation in proteins is functionally significant. Given the crudeness of our measures, the fact that we can measure significant variation in as many as one half of the proteins compels us to conclude that variable rates are the norm for protein evolution. In the previous chapter, we argued that neutral models have difficulty accounting for rate variation, leading us to the general conclusion that most amino acid substitutions result from the action of natural selection.

Yet, one could argue that the high values of $R(t)$ are due to a few selected substitutions in a sea of neutral substitutions. We need some quantitative argument to rule out this possibility if we are to claim the most amino acid substitutions are selected. One approach is as follows.

Suppose the substitution process is the sum of a Poisson process, $X(t)$, representing neutral substitutions and a compound Poisson process, $Y(t)$, representing episodically selected substitutions:

$$N(t) = X(t) + Y(t).$$

Let p be the fraction of substitutions contributed by the Poisson process $X(t)$. The index of dispersion for $N(t)$ is

$$I(t) = p + (1 - p)I_Y(t),$$

the average of the indices of dispersion of the two component processes.

As the fraction of Poisson (neutral) substitutions increases, so must the index of dispersion of the selected alleles:

$$I_Y(t) = \frac{I(t) - p}{1 - p}.$$

If, for example, 90% of the substitutions were neutral and $I(t) = 7.75$, then the index of dispersion for the selected substitutions would be $I_Y(t) = 67.5$. Such a high value should alert us to the possibility of strange dynamic. Just how strange is illustrated in Figure 7.1, which provides a histogram of the estimated indices of dispersion from Table 3.5 compared with the expected histograms (using the same simulation of the estimation procedure as in Figure 3.7) for a case with 90% and 10% Poisson substitutions. When $p = 0.9$, the expected histogram has a mode near one and a rapid fall off for higher values of the index of dispersion. The reason for this behavior is that the high value of $I_Y(t)$ forces the episodic process into a bimodal pattern: in a fixed period of time it is likely to have either no substitutions or a large number of substitutions. As the mean contribution of $Y(t)$ is only 10% that of $X(t)$, most of the time no episodic burst occurs. Thus, most of the time the process looks very Poisson-like, with only occasional lineages with large numbers of substitutions. The data do not exhibit this behavior, being much closer to the histogram with only 10% neutral substitutions.

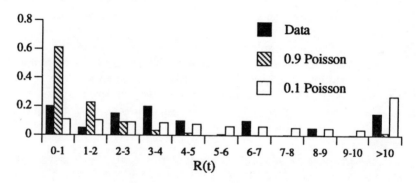

Figure 7.1. Histograms of the indices of dispersion for the data in Table 3.5 and from simulations with 10% and 90% neutral (Poisson) substitutions.

From this we must conclude that the available evidence supports the view that the fraction of selected substitutions is closer to 90% than 10%.

Other indirect studies are also suggestive. For example, we saw parallel clines in allele frequencies in *Menidia* and *Drosophila* that strongly suggest some role for natural selection. The studies of ADH in *Drosophila* show that the amino acid difference at that locus is following a dynamic that differs from the dynamics of silent mutations.

I am persuaded by this evidence that most amino acids substitutions and polymorphisms are selected. I will go further and claim that most are under strong selection in our sense that $N\sigma_s \gg 1$. Otherwise, it is difficult to account for the high values of $R(t)$. (This particular point will be taken up again in the next section.)

If we accept that strong selection is at work, we are faced with the difficult question: What kind of selection is operating? All of our examples point to selection in response to environmental factors, either external or internal, that are changing through time and/or space. Those cases implicating temperature are the most obvious examples. If they serve as guides, then we must be concerned with models of selection in a variable environment. How could it be otherwise? Natural selection is the force adapting species to their environments. Environments are in a constant state of flux; selection coefficients must be in a constant state of flux as well. Models of selection should reflect this; that in the bulk of population genetics theory they do not may have contributed to our failure to make significant progress in our understanding of the forces shaping protein evolution.

7.2 Strong selection

The aim of this section is to develop a model of molecular evolution under strong selection that is compatible with the major features of protein evolution. There are two observations that are crucial in determining the nature of the model.

- The average value of the index of dispersion of replacement substitutions, once lineage effects are removed, is about 7.8 (see Fig. 3.7). In our discussion of this value we concluded (see equation 3.12) that an episodic model of amino acid substitutions is appropriate,

$$\mathcal{N}(t) = X_1 + X_2 + \cdots + X_{M(t)}, \qquad (7.1)$$

  where $\mathcal{N}(t)$ is the total number of substitutions, X_i is a positive random variable representing the number of substitutions in the ith episode, and $M(t)$ is a Poisson process representing the number of episodes.

- The rate of replacement substitution is more clock-time than generation-time dependent. There appears to be a weak generation-time effect, but not nearly as strong as that for silent substitutions (see Fig. 3.6).

When completed, our model must exhibit these two features and be compatible with the rates of substitution and heterozygosities documented in Chapter 1.

The clock-time dependency of rates of amino acid substitutions suggests that the process is being driven by external factors, presumably a restless environment. Imagine that the times at which environmental changes occur may be represented by a point process, $M_e(t)$, and let the number of selected amino acid substitutions that occur in response to the ith environmental change be Y_i. We can immediately write down the total number of substitutions in a form,

$$\mathcal{N}(t) = Y_1 + Y_2 + \cdots + Y_{M_e(t)}, \qquad (7.2)$$

that is formally identical to equation 7.1. In doing so, we have made the most important conceptual leap in our model.

While equation 7.2 is formally the same as equation 7.1, there is nothing in our description of equation 7.2 to assure that the number of substitutions accompanying each episode, Y_i, are distributed like the empirically determined X_i nor that $M_e(t)$ is similar to a Poisson process. Establishing these similarities using the theory of gene frequency dynamics is our main challenge.

Consider first the number of substitutions accompanying each environmental change as captured in Y_i. From Table 3.6 we see that the estimated mean values of X_i, $\hat{\mu}_b$, are between one and five with most values between two and three. Is there anything to suggest that most of the adaptive substitutions accompanying each burst should be similarly restricted? In Chapters 4 and 5 we saw that there are two distinct mechanisms that could lead to bursts of substitutions during an episode and that both typically involve small numbers of substitutions.

One process leading to bursts of substitutions is excursions through the mutational landscape for loci that are generally monomorphic. For these loci, the fixed allele will not be the globally most fit, but will be the one that is most fit in the current environment among all those that are one mutational step away from it. This allele will remain fixed until the environment changes in such a way that one or more of the alleles that are one mutational step away become more fit than the fixed allele. (Mutations two or more mutational steps away occur too infrequently to enter the population.)

After the environmental change, one of the more fit mutations will sweep through the population to produce mutations one step away from itself and two steps away from the original allele. One or more of these mutations may be more fit and may displace the current allele. This process will continue until an allele is fixed that is more fit than any others one mutational step away, at which point the process stagnates. If the fitnesses of the alleles are assigned at random, then the mean number of substitutions per episode is small, as illustrated in Figure 5.4. Recall that we used extreme value theory to argue that the distribution of the excursions through the mutational landscape is insensitive to the distribution of fitness effects.

In Chapter 1 we reviewed the evidence that our initial estimates of protein heterozygosities may have been inflated and that most loci may be monomorphic. If future evidence supports this view, then the mutational landscape model may be appropriate for a majority of loci and provides a ready explanation for the small mean value of Y_i.

The second process leading to small bursts of substitutions is a combination of the fixation of polymorphic sites and the mutational landscape. Our process is illustrated in Figure 5.8. We imagine an alternation of buildup processes and allelic constrictions. The buildup process is the relatively rapid accumulation of alleles in the population due to strong balancing selection. Allelic constrictions are events, such as extreme environmental changes or hitchhiking, that render the population homozygous.

We saw in Chapters 4 and 5 that the buildup process is the same for the SAS-CFF and overdominance models and argued that it should be essentially the same for other models of balancing selection as well. The accumulation of mutations on chromosomes during the buildup process is illustrated in Figure 5.7. The limitation on the total number of segregating alleles is imposed either by the mutational landscape—no more alleles satisfying the polymorphism conditions are one mutational step away from the segregating alleles—or, in the case of the SAS-CFF model, the values of parameters (see equation 4.66). When an allelic constriction occurs, one allele is fixed in the population. At that time, all of the mutations that accumulated on the allele are fixed. The mean number of fixed mutations, as a function of the number of segregating alleles, is illustrated in Figure 5.9. As with the mutational landscape alone, the mean number of mutations fixed in each episode is small.

From the above we see that the small number of substitutions associated with each episode is a natural property of our SSWM models. The independence of the number of substitutions at different episodes follows from the fact that each episode unfolds in a different region of the mutational landscape. Thus, we have succeeded in our attempt to equate Y_i in equation 7.2 with X_i in equation 7.1.

The next problem concerns the point process $M_e(t)$ that represents the times of environmental change or allelic constrictions. If $M_e(t)$ is to correspond to the empirical $M(t)$ in equation 7.1, we need some reason to think that $M_e(t)$ will be close to a Poisson process. There is a simple argument that appears to do just that.

The times at which episodes of substitutions occur are widely separated; a typical locus experiences one amino acid substitution every 10 million years. Yet, the environment is changing on a considerably faster time scale. Obviously, not every environmental change results in an amino acid substitution. For a change to result in a substitution, it must alter the relative fitnesses of the alleles that are accessible on the mutational landscape and the new ordering must be maintained long enough for the burst of substitutions to run its course or for polymorphic alleles to accumulate. From the point of view of a particular locus, such changes must be very rare.

For many changes, there may be a large number of loci that have alleles available on the mutational landscape that can mollify whatever challenge the environment may have offered. Should the alleles at a particular locus be more strongly selected than those at other loci, then this locus is more likely to experience a burst of substitutions or an accumulation of polymorphic alleles. Under the epistatic scheme that I envision, the changes at this locus will restore the rank ordering of alleles at the other loci and, in so doing, prevent substitutions at these loci.

We can capture these ideas in a model by supposing that the times of environmental change are represented by a point process $\mathcal{M}(t)$, that the probability that a change in the environment leads to a burst of substitutions or the accumulation of a new set of alleles at a particular locus is p, and that the probabilities that successive environmental changes lead to bursts of substitutions or polymorphisms are independent. Set $M_e(t)$ equal to the point process obtained by including a point from $\mathcal{M}(t)$ in $M_e(t)$ with probability p.

The act of choosing points at random from a point process to create a new point process is called *thinning*. A thinned point process will approach a Poisson process if the rate of the process increases while the probability of choosing a particular point for the thinned process decreases in such a way that the rate of the thinned process remains fixed [46, p. 98]. In our

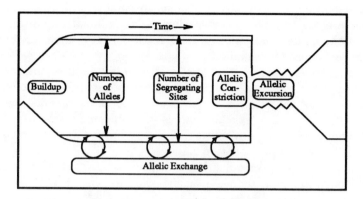

Figure 7.2. A summary of the elements of the SSWM model of molecular evolution.

case, we imagine that the rate of the environmental process $\mathcal{M}(t)$ is very high and that p is very small. As a consequence, $M_e(t)$ should be close to a Poisson process and our demonstration that equations 7.1 and 7.2 are similar is complete.

The two essential ingredients in the model are the limitations placed on the number of substitutions by the mutational landscape and the Poisson character of the environmental changes that lead to substitutions. What differentiates the model from others is that substitutions are "waiting" for environmental changes rather than mutations. The model is environmentally limited rather than mutationally limited, even though the population spends most of its time sitting on a peak in the mutational landscape.

The SAS-CFF model differs from the overdominance model in that it has an allelic exchange process in addition to buildup processes and allelic constrictions. Recall that the fluctuations in the frequencies of SAS-CFF alleles due to the vagaries of the environment mean that alleles may occasionally become rare enough to be sucked into the boundary layer and replaced in the interior by a new allele. This leads to a steady exchange of alleles in a process that is remarkably like the origination process of the weak-selection neutral model. In particular, the allelic exchange process is a Poisson process and is mutation limited (see equation 5.24).

Both substitution processes may be included in a single model as illustrated in Figure 7.2. The rate of substitution per year for the combined model is, from equations 5.23 and 3.13,

$$k_y = \rho_e \mu_b + \frac{\rho_x}{gK}, \tag{7.3}$$

where ρ_e is the episodic rate, μ_b is the mean burst size, ρ_x is the rate of allelic exchange, and K is the number of segregating alleles. In this expression, ρ_x is expressed in units of generations so it must be divided by the generation time, g, to yield a clock-time rate.

The weak generation-time effect suggests that the contribution of the allelic exchange process, which will only operate at polymorphic loci experiencing SAS-CFF style dynamics, will be less important than the episodic process. Moreover, the observation that the level of polymorphism and the rate of substitution are correlated (see Fig. 1.18) also suggests that the episodic component dominates. (Recall that μ_b is an increasing function of K as given by equation 5.14.)

It is tempting to extend the analysis of the SSWM model to test for agreement with polymorphism data. For example, the SAS-CFF model has the same sampling distribution as the weak-selection neutral model and necessarily fits the allele frequency data as well as does the neutral model. However, it does not seem profitable to head down this path. The distribution of the frequency of alleles in the population depends critically on the details of the model. One thing we can be certain of is that whatever model we choose it will not be a faithful mimic of nature. Should we reject, say, the symmetric overdominance model we need only move to an asymmetric overdominance model to achieve agreement. We could accept the asymmetric overdominance model, but at the risk of committing a blatant Type II error. The problem is compounded by the distinct possibility that the population is out of equilibrium.

These complications do not arise when discussing substitutions under the SSWM assumptions because all models converge to the fixation process in equation 7.1; the differences between models are only reflected in the moments of X_i and $M(t)$. Just as with the neutral model, substitutions separating species are much more instructive than are polymorphisms within species.

At this early stage in the development, the SSWM model of molecular evolution and polymorphism appears to fit the protein sequence data better than do weak-selection models. Moreover, the model can directly address the numerous examples of amino acid variations that appear to be related to aspects of a changing environment, a connection that is not embraced by weak-selection models. The model, as presented here, is in its most specialized form. Generalities may be found in [95,96].

There is, at present, no compelling evidence concerning the strength of selection acting on silent mutations. Our current estimate of the index of dispersion for silent substitutions is so confounded by corrections for multiple substitutions that it is premature to use the index in any scientific judgments about forces acting on silent mutations. The fact that silent substitutions exhibit an apparent generation-time effect in mammals means that, were they strongly selected, they would be mutation limited.

7.3 Moderate selection

Moderate-selection models have dominated the literature on stochastic theories of selection. In classical population genetics the standard assumption in models that mix constant selection and finite population effects is

$s = O(1/N)$. More recently, a common alternative model to the neutral model in discussions of molecular polymorphism is overdominance with moderate selection (e. g., [298]). While constant-fitness models spanning the time scale of molecular evolution are biologically unrealistic, moderate-selection models with varying fitness are of interest.

The most thoroughly studied random environment moderate-selection model is the TIM model, named for the three authors of its original incarnation: Takahata, Iishi, and Matsuda [278]. The model, which is concerned with selection on additive alleles in a moderately autocorrelated environment, is approximated by the diffusion process

$$Edx_i = [\alpha x_i(\mathcal{F}_k - x_i) - \theta x_i/2]dt$$
$$Edx_idx_j = [\alpha x_i x_j(\delta_{ij} + \mathcal{F}_k - x_i - x_j) + x_i(\delta_{ij} - x_j)]dt.$$

To place this diffusion in the context of our previous models, it should be compared with equation 4.58, which is the symmetric SAS-CFF diffusion.

The first, and most important, observation is that the TIM model corresponds to a SAS-CFF diffusion with $B = 1$. This is the value of B that is appropriate for a moderately autocorrelated environment as was recorded in Table 4.1. The second observation is that $k = \infty$ and θ corresponds to the locus rather than a site within the locus. In this regard, the TIM model is similar to neutral models, which also assume an infinite number of alleles and a locus θ.

Recall that SAS-CFF models with $B = 1$ are equivalent to haploid models. In haploid models with only temporal fluctuations, selection is a dispersive rather than a balancing force. Consequently, variation must be held in the population by the balance between mutation and the combined effects of drift and fluctuating selection. For mutation to be a powerful enough force either we need to increase the mutation rate or the number of alleles over what was assumed for SSWM SAS-CFF models. As the nucleotide mutation rate is fixed, our only choice is to assume that the number of moderately selected alleles is very large, hence the assumption that $k = \infty$. Despite the apparent simplicity of the TIM diffusion, very few analytic results are available. The most complete description, based of computer simulations, is by Takahata and Kimura [279]. From their paper we can describe some of the qualitative features of the model.

As the strength of selection increases, it begins to dominate both drift and mutation and variation is driven from the population. In addition, the time scale of selection is shortened, so alleles move through the population faster, leading to an accelerated rate of substitution. Takahata and Kimura showed that the rate of substitution approaches

$$k_g \sim \frac{u\alpha}{\ln(2\alpha)}$$

as selection begins to dominate drift. From this we see that the rate of substitution is mutation limited, hence we should expect to see a generation-time effect under the TIM model.

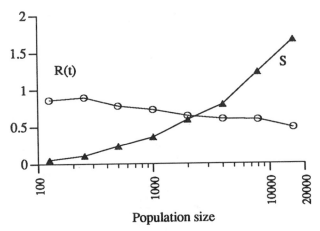

Figure 7.3. A simulation of the TIM model. R(t) is the index of dispersion of the origination process and S is the average number of segregating sites.

For the TIM model to be a candidate to explain protein evolution, it must be able to account for the high index of dispersion. Since no analytic results are available on this point, I simulated the infinite-sites, no recombination TIM model and recorded both the index of dispersion for the origination process and the average number of segregating sites. The results for one case are illustrated in Figure 7.3.

Surprisingly, the index of dispersion is less than one. If the mutation rate and strength of selection are held fixed as the population size increases, the index of dispersion decreases. The only explanation I can offer is that fixations occur fairly rapidly, thereby wiping out the standing variation and introducing a refractory period during which variation builds to spawn another substitution. If such a process occurs, then the substitutions will be more regular than for a Poisson process, thus accounting for the low index of dispersion for the TIM model.

The TIM model does not appear to be a viable candidate for protein evolution but its two major features, low index of dispersion and pronounced generation-time effect, make it a viable model for silent substitutions as will be discussed more fully in the next section.

It should be noted that the TIM model is very similar to Ohta's model of moderately selected deleterious alleles. If we were to examine the fitnesses of genotypes under the TIM model at one instant in time, they would be distributed in exactly the same way as assumed under Ohta's model. The essential difference, of course, is that under the TIM model the fitnesses change slowly through time, whereas under Ohta's model they remain fixed *in perpetuity*. Depending on one's views on the time scale of change of fitnesses, the TIM model might well be viewed as an improvement, or at least an extension, of Ohta's model. However, the two are dynamically very different. Under Ohta's model, genetic drift is the only force causing

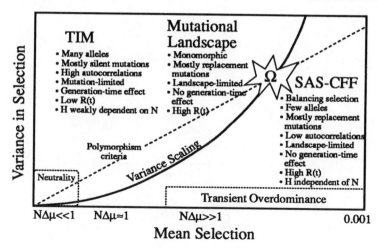

Figure 7.4. A unified model of selection in a fluctuating environment.

the fixation of mutations whereas under the TIM model, selection always plays a role and when α is large, plays the dominant role. This difference shows that a lot rides on Ohta's assumption that fitnesses are constant. If her model is to be used as an explanation for certain phenomena, then the explanation must carry with it a clear justification for maintaining constant fitnesses.

7.4 Whither?

I have argued the case for strong selection acting on amino acid variation but have said little about silent variation. I feel that at the time of this writing the data on silent variation are too sparse to form a clear picture of the phenomenology, much less of the responsible forces. It does seem to be true that silent substitutions are mutation limited and that their rates of substitution are less variable than are those of replacement substitutions. It also seems true, based on the evolution of codon usage, that natural selection plays some role in the dynamics of silent mutations.

It is of some interest to try to fit silent and replacement dynamics into a single unified model. The approach that I will take makes the fundamental assumption that selection on silent mutations is weaker than that on replacement mutations. Few will find this assumption unpalatable, although it must be stressed that there is no direct evidence to support it. If our model is to be unified, it must contain some elements that slide smoothly from the stronger selected amino acid mutations to the more weakly selected silent mutations. Figure 7.4 is a rendition of the slide.

In our discussion of the conditions for polymorphism under the SAS-CFF model, we observed that variation will be maintained if the variance in the effects of alleles is greater than the difference in their mean effects. Typically—for example, equation 4.31—the conditions for polymorphism are of the form

$$\sum_{j=1}^{k}(\mu_j - \mu_i) < c\sigma^2, \ i = 1, 2, \ldots, k, \tag{7.4}$$

where the constant c reflects the particular details of the model. If the variance is large enough, all k alleles will be held polymorphic.

In our derivation of the SAS-CFF diffusion we assumed that the mean and variance of allelic effects on the additive scale were very small and of the same order of magnitude. One way to express this assumption is through a parameter, ϵ, and the order of magnitude relationships:

$$(\mu_j - \mu_i) = O(\epsilon), \ \sigma^2 = O(\epsilon). \tag{7.5}$$

As $\epsilon \to 0$, the order of magnitude of the moments on both sides of equation 7.4 remain the same relative to each other. Consequently, polymorphism is possible no matter how small ϵ may be.

Is this scaling appropriate? In biological systems one often constrains the coefficient of variation when scaling. In equation 7.5, the coefficient of variation is of magnitude $1/\sqrt{\epsilon}$. As $\epsilon \to 0$, the coefficient of variation blows off to infinity. While we have no a priori reason to be distressed by this revelation, it does suggest that we entertain another scaling. If our criterion is that the coefficient of variation remains fixed, then we must have

$$(\mu_j - \mu_i) = O(\epsilon), \ \sigma^2 = O(\epsilon^2).$$

With this scaling, the mean effects on the left side of equation 7.4 grow in proportion to ϵ, while the variance effects on the right side grow in proportion to ϵ^2. These two cases are illustrated in Figure 7.4 by the lines marked "Polymorphism criteria" and "Variance scaling," respectively. The slope of the former line is chosen such that when the lines cross, at Ω, we move from a domain where balancing selection is not operative to a region where it is.

In the region of strong selection, marked $N\Delta\mu \gg 1$ in Figure 7.4, balancing selection is seen to incur the largest fitness differences. Perhaps this is related to the ease of finding kinetic and physiological differences between polymorphic alleles as documented in Table 1.3 and the correlations of developmental and fitness components with the number of heterozygous loci that we documented in the subsection *On Being Heterozygous.*

As we slide from strong to moderate selection, the variance in fitness goes to zero more rapidly than the mean. It appears that the effects of environmental stochasticity become insignificant in comparison with mean effects. To correct this we need to introduce another element to the model: autocorrelations in the temporal fluctuations. Accordingly, assume that as $\epsilon \to 0$, the autocorrelation increases as required for the continued presence of stochastic selection (see equation 4.52).

The delicate balance between the variance and autocorrelation required by equation 4.52 may seem overly restrictive. However, rather than viewing equation 4.52 as a restriction on the model, it is preferable to view it as a filter on the full power spectrum of environmental fluctuations. Only those fluctuations with autocorrelations given by equation 4.52 will contribute to the dynamics of moderately selected mutations. Those components fluctuating on a faster time scale will average out and contribute nothing to the dynamics. Those on a longer time scale will give long-term mean advantages to certain sets of alleles from which the moderately selected alleles will be chosen.

The final assumption of the model concerns the numbers of alleles participating in the dynamics. If we accept the Fisherian view that mutations of small effects are more likely to be advantageous in the current environment than alleles of large effect, then the number of mutations participating in the dynamics of our model should increase as selection gets weaker. Once we enter the moderate-selection domain, variation is maintained by the balance between mutation and the combined effects of drift and fluctuating selection, so the number of alleles must be very large.

At the present time the theory of selection in a fluctuating environment is not developed sufficiently to assess fully the merit of the model summarized in Figure 7.4. In each domain we have a model that has been investigated in some detail:

- *Neutral model:* In the lower left hand corner we have the weak-selection neutral model. As the figure is drawn, the neutral domain appears to occupy a small fraction of the space of mutations. However, as the effective population size gets smaller, the relative region occupied by the shaded neutral region will grow. If population sizes were small enough relative to the strength of selection, most mutations could be weakly selected. In the neutral domain populations are not likely to be in equilibrium due to the effects of hitchhiking.

- *TIM model:* In the moderate selection domain alleles are continually being brought into and driven out of the population by a moderately autocorrelated fluctuating environment. C. H. Langley once suggested to me that these dynamics be referred to as "churning haplotypes." The time scale of the TIM model is faster than that of the weak-selection neutral model so it is possible that moderately selected alleles are in equilibrium. Silent mutations are good candidates for this domain.

- *Mutational landscape model:* This strong-selection substitution model produces the bursts of substitutions required to elevate the index of dispersion. Polymorphism is ruled out if the mean effects, which change on a time scale of millions of years, are larger than the variance effects.

- *SAS-CFF model*: In the right domain variance effects are large enough to allow balancing selection under the SAS-CFF model. Superimposed on these dynamics are occasional allelic constrictions operating on a time scale of millions of years that result in bursts of substitutions. Overdominance may occur for short periods of time relative to the time scale of molecular evolution. This is indicated by "Transient overdominance" in the lower right hand corner.

I will leave the description of the unified model at this incomplete stage.

A critical aspect of the unified model, one that has not been explored mathematically, concerns the role of the autocorrelation of the environment. Environmental fluctuations may be decomposed into components operating on time scales of different lengths. The greatest power is presumably concentrated at shorter time scales, hours to years. These are the components that lead to polymorphism under the SAS-CFF model. The components with time scales similar to the time scale of moderate selection will allow the TIM dynamics to proceed. Very long time scale changes will be responsible for substitutions in the mutational landscape and allelic constrictions. These long time-scale fluctuations may be due, in part, to an evolving biological environment as well as an epistatic internal environment. At the present time, we do not have a theory that begins with a spectrum of environmental noise and demonstrates how each component leads to evolution on the corresponding time scale.

The theories outlined in this chapter do not mesh well with some of the standard paradigms of population genetics, the most cherished of which is Sewall Wright's adaptive landscape. Under this model, populations are imagined to spend most of their time on selective peaks, genetic drift providing the push when a population jumps from one peak to another. In our random environment models, there are no analogs to adaptive peaks. The essential reason is that the adaptive landscape is changing faster than the genetic system. The population is always running uphill, but the peak is always two steps ahead. All the population ever sees, in effect, is the side of the mountain. Should it stop evolving, it will face extinction. This view is essentially Fisher's description of the deterioration of the environment [75, p. 45]. It is also closely related to his model on the nature of adaptation [75, p. 41] that assumes that a population is never exactly at its optimal phenotype.

If selection is responsible for much of the protein polymorphism and some of the silent polymorphism, then some of this variation must contribute to the variation observed in quantitative characters through its pleiotropic manifestations. The standard paradigm claiming that most quantitative variation is due to the balance between mutation and selection must be reexamined in light of our model. Perhaps the reader will be stimulated to work in this challenging area of evolutionary theory.

References

[1] Abramowitz, M. and I. A. Stegun 1965. *Handbook of Mathematical Functions*. Dover Publ. Inc., New York.

[2] Alahiotis, S. 1979. Biochemical studies of supernatant malate dehydrogenase allozymes in *Drosophila melanogaster*. *Comp. Biochem. Physiol.* **62B**:375–380.

[3] Anderson, P. R. and J. G. Oakeshott 1984. Parallel geographic patterns of allozyme variation in two sibling *Drosophila* species. *Nature* **308**:729–731.

[4] Aota, S.-I. and T. Ikemura 1986. Diversity in G+C content at the third position of codons in vertebrate genes and its cause. *Nucl. Acids. Res.* **14**:6345–6355.

[5] Aquadro, C. F. 1991. Molecular population genetics of *Drosophila*. In *Molecular Approaches to Pure and Applied Entomology*. ed. Oakeshott, J. G. and M. Whitten, (in press). Springer-Verlag, New York.

[6] Aquadro, C. F., S. F. Desse, M. M. Bland, C. H. Langley, and C. C. Laurie-Ahlberg 1986. Molecular population genetics of the alcohol dehydrogenase gene region of *Drosophila melanogaster*. *Genetics* **114**:1165–1190.

[7] Atkinson, D. E. 1969. Limitations of metabolic concentrations and the conservation of solvent capacity in the living cell. In *Current Topics in Cellular Regulation*. ed. Horecker, B. L. and E. B. Stadtman, pp. 29–43. Academic Press, New York.

[8] Avise, J. C. and R. K. Selander 1972. Evolutionary genetics of cave-dwelling fishes of the genus *Astyanax*. *Evolution* **26**:1–19.

[9] Ayala, F. J., J. R. Powell, and M. L. Tracey 1972. Enzyme variability in the *Drosophila willistoni* group. V. Genic variability in natural populations of *Drosophila equinoxialis*. *Genet. Res. Camb.* **20**:19–42.

[10] Ayala, F. J., J. W. Valentine, D. Hedgecock, and L. Barr 1975. Deep-sea asteroids: High genetic variability in a stable environment. *Evolution* **29**:203–212.

[11] Azlarov, T. A. and N. A. Volodin 1986. *Characterization Problems Associated with the Exponential Distribution.* Springer-Verlag, New York.

[12] Beintema, J. J. and R. N. Campagne 1987. Molecular evolution of rodent insulins. *Mol. Biol. Evol.* 4:10–18.

[13] Bernardi, G. 1989. The isochore organization of the human genome. *Annu. Rev. Genet.* 23:637–661.

[14] Bernardi, G. and G. Bernardi 1985. Codon usage and genome composition. *J. Mol. Evol.* 22:363–365.

[15] Bernardi, G., D. Mouchiroud, C. Gautier, and G. Bernardi 1988. Composition patterns in vertebrate genomes: Conservation and change in evolution. *J. Mol. Evol.* 28:7–18.

[16] Bijlsma, R. 1978. Polymorphism at the G6PD and 6GPD loci in *Drosophila melanogaster.* II. Evidence for interaction in fitness. *Genet. Res., Camb.* 31:227–237.

[17] Bird, A. P. 1980. DNA methylation and the frequency of CpG in animal DNA. *Nucl. Acids Res.* 8:1499–1504.

[18] Birky, C. W. and J. B. Walsh 1988. Effects of linkage on rates of molecular evolution. *Proc. Natl. Acad. Sci. USA* 85:6414–6418.

[19] Blundell, T. L. and S. P. Wood 1975. Is the evolution of insulin Darwinian or due to selectively neutral mutations. *Nature* 257:197–203.

[20] Bonner, T. I., R. Heinemann, and G. J. Todara 1980. Evolution of DNA sequences has been retarded in Malagasy primates. *Nature* 286:420–423.

[21] Borgmann, U. and T. W. Moon 1975. A comparison of LDHs from an ectothermic and endothermic animal. *Can. J. Biochem.* 53:998–1004.

[22] Borowsky, R. 1977. Detection of the effects of selection on protein polymorphisms in natural populations by means of a distance analysis. *Evolution* 31:341–346.

[23] Breiman, L. 1968. *Probability.* Addison-Wesley, Reading.

[24] Britten, R. J. 1986. Rates of DNA sequence evolution differ between taxonomic groups. *Science* 231:1393–1398.

[25] Brown, A. J. L. and C. H. Langley 1979. Reevaluation of level of genic heterozygosity in natural populations of *Drosophila melanogaster* by two-dimensional electrophoresis. *Proc. Natl. Acad. Sci. USA* 76:2381–2384.

[26] Brown, A. J. L. and C. H. Langley 1979. Correlation between heterozygosity and subunit molecular weight. *Nature* **277**:649–651.

[27] Bulmer, M. 1986. Neighboring base effects on substitution rates in pseudogenes. *Mol. Biol. Evol.* **3**:322–329.

[28] Bulmer, M. 1987. Coevolution of codon usage and transfer RNA abundance. *Nature* **325**:728–730.

[29] Bulmer, M. 1987. A statistical analysis of nucleotide sequences of introns and exons in human genes. *Mol. Biol. Evol.* **4**:395–405.

[30] Bulmer, M. 1988. Are codon usage and patterns in unicellular organisms determined by selection-mutation balance? *J. Evol. Biol.* **1**:15–26.

[31] Bulmer, M. 1989. Estimating the variability of substitution rates. *Genetics* **123**:615–619.

[32] Burton, R. S. and M. W. Feldman 1982. Changes in free amino acid concentrations during osmotic response in the intertidal copepod *Tigriopus californicus*. *Comp. Biochem. Physiol.* **73A**:441–445.

[33] Burton, R. S. and M. W. Feldman 1983. Physiological effects of an allozyme polymorphism: Glutamate-pyruvate transaminase and response to hyperosmotic stress in the copepod *Tigriopus californicus*. *Biochem. Genet.* **21**:239–251.

[34] Cann, R. L., W. M. Brown, and A. C. Wilson 1984. Polymorphic sites and the mechanism of evolution in human mitochondrial DNA. *Genetics* **106**:479–499.

[35] Catzeflis, F. M., F. H. Sheldon, J. E. Ahlquist, and C. G. Sibley 1987. DNA-DNA hybridization evidence fo the rapid rate of Muroid rodent DNA evolution. *Mol. Biol. Evol.* **4**:242–253.

[36] Cavener, D. R. and M. T. Clegg 1981. Evidence for biochemical and physiological differences between enzyme genotypes in *Drosophila melanogaster*. *Proc. Natl. Acad. Sci. USA* **78**:4444–4447.

[37] Chakraborty, R. 1981. The distribution of the number of heterozygous loci in an individual in natural populations. *Genetics* **98**:461–466.

[38] Chakraborty, R., P. A. Fuerst, and M. Nei 1980. Statistical studies on protein polymorphism in natural populations. III. Distribution of allele frequencies and the number of alleles per locus. *Genetics* **94**:1039–1063.

[39] Chappell, M. A. and L. R. G. Snyder 1984. Biochemical and physiological correlates of deer mouse α-chain hemoglobin polymorphisms. *Proc. Natl. Acad. Sci. USA* **81**:5484–5488.

[40] Charlesworth, B. and C. H. Langley 1989. The population genetics of transposable elements. *Annu. Rev. Genet.* **23**:251–287.

[41] Christiansen, F. B. 1975. Hard and soft selection in a subdivided population. *Amer. Natur.* **109**:157–166.

[42] Cockburn, A., I. M. Mansergh, L. S. Broome, and S. Ward 1990. Molecular clocks and generation time in burramyid marsupials. *Mol. Biol. Evol.* **7**:283–285.

[43] Coulthart, M. B. and R. S. Singh 1988. Low genic variation in male reproductive-tract proteins of *Drosophila melanogater* and *D. simulans*. *Mol. Biol. Evol.* **5**:167–181.

[44] Coulthart, M. B. and R. S. Singh 1988. Differing amounts of genetic polymorphism in testes and male accessory glands of *Drosophila melanogaster* and *Drosophila simulans*. *Biochem. Genet.* **26**:153–164.

[45] Courant, R. and F. John 1974. *Introduction to Calculus and Analysis, Volume Two*. John Wiley & Sons, New York.

[46] Cox, D. R. and V. Isham 1980. *Point Processes*. Chapman and Hall, London.

[47] Coyne, J. A. 1976. Lack of genetic similarity between two sibling species of *Drosophila* as revealed by varied techniques. *Genetics* **84**:593–607.

[48] Coyne, J. A. 1984. Correlation between hererozygosity and rate of chromosome evolution in animals. *Amer. Natur.* **123**:725–729.

[49] Crawford, D. A. and D. A. Powers 1989. Molecular basis of evolutionary adaptation at the lactate dehydrogenase-B locus in the fish *Fundulus heteroclitus*. *Proc. Natl. Acad. Sci. USA* **86**:9365–9369.

[50] Daley, D. J. and D. Vere-Jones 1988. *An Introduction to the Theory of Point Processes*. Springer-Verlag, New York.

[51] David, H. A. 1970. *Order Statistics*. John Wiley & Sons, Inc., New York.

[52] Dayhoff, M. O. 1978. Survey of new data and computer methods of analysis. In *Atlas of Protein Sequence and Structure. Vol. 5, Suppl. 3*. ed. Dayhoff, M. O., pp. 1–8. National Biomedical Res. Found., Washington.

[53] Dempster, E. R. 1955. Maintenance of genetic heterozygosity. *Cold Spring Harbor Symp. Quant. Biol.* **20**:25–32.

[54] Dickerson, R. E. and I. Geis 1983. *Hemoglobin: Structure, Function, Evolution, and Pathology* . Benjamin/Cummings, Menlo Park.

[55] DiMichele, L. and D. A. Powers 1982. LDH-B genotype-specific hatching times of *Fundulus heteroclitus* embryos. *Nature* **296**:563–564.

[56] DiMichele, L. and D. A. Powers 1982. Physiological basis for swimming endurance differences between LDH-B genotypes of *Fundulus heteroclitus*. *Science* **216**:1014–1016.

[57] Dobzhansky, Th. and B. Spassky 1954. XXII. A comparison of the concealed variability in *Drosophila prosaltans* with that in other species. *Genetics* **39**:472–487.

[58] Dykhuizen, D. E., J. de Framond, and D. L. Hartl 1984. Selective neutrality of glucose-6-phosphate allozymes in *Escherichia coli*. *Mol. Biol. Evol.* **1**:162–170.

[59] Dykhuizen, D. E., J. de Framond, and D. L. Hartl 1984. Potential for hitchhiking in the *eda-edd-zwf* gene cluster of *Escherichia coli*. *Genet. Res., Camb.* **43**:229–239.

[60] Dykhuizen, D. E. and D. L. Hartl 1983. Functional effects of PGI allozymes in *Escherichia coli*. *Genetics* **105**:1–18.

[61] Dykhuizen, D. and D. L. Hartl 1980. Selective neutrality of 6PGD allozymes in *E. coli* and the effects of genetic background. *Genetics* **96**:801–817.

[62] Easteal, S. 1988. Rate constancy of globin gene evolution in placental mammals. *Proc. Natl. Acad. Sci. USA* **85**:7622–7626.

[63] Easterby, J. 1973. Coupled enzyme assays: a general expression for the transient. *Biochim. Biophys. Acta* **293**:552–558.

[64] Ethier, S. N. and T. G. Kurtz 1986. *Markov Processes: Characterization and Convergence*. John Wiley & Sons, New York.

[65] Evans, M. J. and R. C. Scarpulla 1988. The human somatic cytochrome gene: Two classes of processed pseudogenes demarcate a period of rapid molecular evolution. *Proc. Natl. Acad. Sci. USA* **85**:9625–9629.

[66] Ewens, W. J. 1970. Remarks on the substitution load. *Theor. Popul. Biol.* **1**:129–139.

[67] Ewens, W. J. 1972. The sampling theory for selectively neutral alleles. *Theor. Popul. Biol.* **3**:87–112.

[68] Ewens, W. J. 1979. *Mathematical Population Genetics*. Springer-Verlag, Berlin.

[69] Ewens, W. J. and K. Kirby 1975. The eigenvalues of the neutral alleles processes. *Theor. Popul. Biol.* **7**:212–220.

[70] Feller, W. 1968. *An Introduction to Probability Theory and Its Applications*. John Wiley & Sons, Inc., New York.

[71] Felsenstein, J. 1976. The theoretical population genetics of variable selection and migration. *Ann. Rev. Genet.* **10**:253–280.

[72] Fersht, A. 1985. *Enzyme Structure and Mechanism*. W. H. Freeman and Co., New York.

[73] Filipski, J. 1987. Correlation between molecular clock ticking, codon usage, fidelity of DNA repair, chromosome banding and chromatin compactness in germline cells. *FEBS Lett.* **217**:184–186.

[74] Filipski, J., J. Salinas, and F. Rodier 1987. Two distinct compositional classes of vertebrate gene-bearing DNA stretches, their structures and possible evolutionary origin. *DNA* **6**:109–118.

[75] Fisher, R. A. 1958. *The Genetical Theory of Natural Selection*. Dover, New York.

[76] Fitch, W. M. 1971. Toward defining the course of evolution: Minimum change for a specific tree phylogeny. *Syst. Zool.* **20**:406–416.

[77] Fitch, W. M. 1971. Rate of change of concomitantly variable codons. *J. Mol. Evol.* **1**:84–96.

[78] Galambos, J. 1978. *The Asymptotic Theory of Extreme Order Statistics*. John Wiley & Sons, Inc., New York.

[79] Gardiner, C. W. 1985. *Handbook of Stochastic Methods*. Springer-Verlag, Berlin.

[80] Gillespie, J. H. 1972. The effects of stochastic environments on allele frequencies in natural populations. *Theor. Popul. Biol.* **3**:241–248.

[81] Gillespie, J. H. 1973. Natural selection with varying selection coefficients—a haploid model. *Genet. Res. Camb.* **21**:115–120.

[82] Gillespie, J. H. 1974. Polymorphism in patchy environments. *Amer. Natur.* **108**:145–151.

[83] Gillespie, J. H. 1977. Sampling theory for alleles in a random environment. *Nature* **266**:443–445.

[84] Gillespie, J. H. 1978. A general model to account for enzyme variation in natural populations. V. The SAS-CFF model. *Theor. Popul. Biol.* **14**:1–45.

[85] Gillespie, J. H. 1982. A randomized SAS-CFF model of selection in a random environment. *Theor. Pop. Biol.* **21**:219–237.

[86] Gillespie, J. H. 1983. A simple stochastic gene substitution process. *Theor. Popul. Biol.* **23**:202–215.

[87] Gillespie, J. H. 1984. The molecular clock may be an episodic clock. *Proc. Natl. Acad. Sci. USA* **81**:8009–8013.

[88] Gillespie, J. H. 1984. Some properties of finite populations experiencing strong selection and weak mutation. *Amer. Natur.* **121**:691–708.

[89] Gillespie, J. H. 1984. Molecular evolution over the mutational landscape. *Evolution* **38**:1116–1129.

[90] Gillespie, J. H. 1985. The interaction of genetic drift and mutation with selection in a fluctuating environment. *Theor. Popul. Biol.* **27**:222–237.

[91] Gillespie, J. H. 1986. Variability of evolutionary rates of DNA. *Genetics* **113**:1077–1091.

[92] Gillespie, J. H. 1986. Rates of molecular evolution. *Annu. Rev. Ecol. Syst.* **17**:637–665.

[93] Gillespie, J. H. 1987. Molecular evolution and the neutral allele theory. *Oxford Surveys Evol. Biol.* **4**:10–37.

[94] Gillespie, J. H. 1989. Lineage effects and the index of dispersion of molecular evolution. *Mol. Biol. Evol.* **6**:636–647.

[95] Gillespie, J. H. 1989. Molecular evolution and polymorphism: SAS-CFF meets the mutational landscape. *Amer. Natur.* **134**:638–658.

[96] Gillespie, J. H. 1990. The molecular nature of allelic diversity for two models of balancing selection. *Theor. Popul. Biol.* **37**:91–109.

[97] Gillespie, J. H. and H. A. Guess 1978. The effects of environmental autocorrelations on the progress of selection in a random environment. *Amer. Natur.* **112**:897–909.

[98] Gillespie, J. H. and K. Kojima 1968. The degree of polymorphism in enzymes involved in energy production compared to that in nonspecific enzymes in two *Drosophila ananassae* populations. *Proc. Natl. Acad. Sci. USA* **61**:582–585.

[99] Gillespie, J. H. and C. H. Langley 1979. Are evolutionary rates really variable? *J. Mol. Evol.* **13**:27–34.

[100] Gillespie, J. H. and C. Langley 1975. Multilocus behavior in a random environment. I. Random Levene models. *Genetics* **82**:123–137.

[101] Gnedenko, B. V. 1970. Limit theorems for sums of a random number of positive independent random variables. *Proc. 6th Berkeley Symp. Math. Stats. Prob.* **2**:537–549.

[102] Gojobori, T. 1982. Means and variances of heterozygosity and protein function. In *Molecular Evolution, Protein Polymorphism and the Neutral Theory.* ed. Kimura, M., pp. 137–148. Springer-Verlag, Berlin.

[103] Gojobori, T., W.-H. Li, and D. Graur 1982. Patterns of nucleotide substitution in pseudogenes and functional genes. *J. Mol. Evol.* **18**:360–369.

[104] Goldberg, A. L. and J. F. Dice 1974. Intracellular protein degradation in mammalian and bacterial cells. *Annu. Rev. Biochem.* **43**:835–869.

[105] Goodman, M., J. Barnabas, G. Matsuda, and G. W. Moore 1971. Molecular evolution and the descent of man. *Nature* **233**:604–613.

[106] Grantham, R., C. Gautier, M. Gouy, M. Jacobzone, and R. Mercier 1981. Codon catalog usage is a genome strategy modulated for gene expressivity. *Nucleic Acids Res.* **9**:r43–r74.

[107] Grantham, R., C. Gautier, M. Gouy, R. Mercier, and A. Pave 1980. Codon catalog usage and the genome hypothesis. *Nucleic Acids Res.* **8**:r49–r62.

[108] Graur, D. 1985. Amino acid composition and the evolutionary rates of protein-coding genes. *J. Mol. Evol.* **22**:53–62.

[109] Graur, D., Y. Shuali, and W.-H. Li 1989. Deletions in processed pseudogenes accumulate faster in rodents than in humans. *J. Mol. Evol.* **28**:279–285.

[110] Graves, J. E., R. H. Rosenblatt, and G. Somero 1983. Kinetic and electrophoretic differentiation of lactate dehydrogenases of teleost species from the Atlantic and Pacific coasts of Panama. *Evolution* **37**:30–37.

[111] Graves, J. E. and G. N. Somero 1982. Electrophoretic and functional enzymic evolution in four species of eastern Pacific barracudas from different thermal environments. *Evolution* **36**:97–106.

[112] Guess, H. A. and J. H. Gillespie 1977. Diffusion approximations to linear stochastic difference equations with stationary coefficients. *J. Appl. Prob.* **14**:58–74.

[113] Haldane, J. B. S. and S. D. Jayakar 1963. Polymorphism due to selection in varying directions. *J. Genet.* **58**:237–247.

[114] Hall, F. G., D. B. Dill, and E. S. Gutzman Barron 1936. Comparative physiology in high altitudes. *J. Cellular Comp. Physiol.* **8**:301–313.

[115] Hall, J. G. 1987. The adaptation of enzymes to temperature: Catalytic characterization of glucosephosphate isomerase homologues isolated from *Mytilus edulis* and *Isognomon alatus*, bivalve mulluscs inhabiting different thermal environments. *Mol. Biol. Evol.* **2**:251–269.

[116] Harris, H. 1966. Enzyme polymorphisms in man. *Proc. Roy. Soc. Ser. B* **164**:298–310.

[117] Harris, H., D. A. Hopkinson, and Y. H. Edwards 1977. Polymorphism and subunit structure of enzymes: Contribution to the neutralist-selectionist controversy. *Proc. Natl. Acad. Sci. USA* **74**:698–701.

[118] Harris, S., J. R. Thackeray, A. J. Jeffreys, and M. L. Weiss 1986. Nucleotide sequence analysis of the lemur β-globin family: Evidence for major rate fluctuations in globin polypeptide evolution. *Mol. Biol. Evol.* **3**:465–484.

[119] Hartl, D. L. and D. E. Dykhuizen 1985. The neutral theory and the molecular basis of preadaptation. In *Population Genetics and Molecular Evolution*. ed. Ohta, T. and K Aoki, pp. 107–124. Springer-Verlag, Berlin.

[120] Hayashida, H., H. Toh, R. Kikuno, and T. Miyata 1985. Evolution of influenza virus genes. *Mol. Biol. Evol.* **2**:289–303.

[121] Heinstra, P. W. H., W. Sharloo, and G. E. W. Thorig 1988. Alcohol dehydrogenase polymorphism in *Drosophila*: Enzyme kinetics of product inhibition. *J. Mol. Evol.* **28**:145–150.

[122] Hiebl, I., G. Braunitzer, and D. Schneeganss 1987. The primary sequence of the major and minor hemoglobin-components of adult Andean goose (*Chloephaga melanoptera*, Anatidae): The mutation Leu→Ser in position 55 of the β chains. *Biol. Chem. Hoppe-Seyler* **368**:1385–1390.

[123] Hiebl, I., D. Schneeganss, and G. Braunitzer 1986. The primary structure of the α^D-chains of the bar-headed goose (*Anser indicus*), the greylag goose (*Anser anser*) and the Canada goose (*Branta canadensis*). *Biol. Chem. Hoppe-Seyler* **367**:591–599.

[124] Hiebl, I., D. Schneeganss, F. Grimm, J. Kösters, and G. Braunitzer 1987. High altitude respiration of birds. The primary structures of the major and minor hemoglobin component of adult European black vulture (*Aegypius monachus, Aegypiinae*). *Biol. Chem. Hoppe-Seyler* **368**:11–18.

[125] Hiebl, I., R. Weber, D. Schneeganss, and G. Braunitzer 1989. The primary structure and functional properties of the major and minor hemoglobin components of the adult white-headed vulture (*Trigonoceps occipitalis*, Aegypiinae). *Biol. Chem. Hoppe-Seyler* **370**:699–706.

[126] Hiebl, I., R. Weber, D. Schneeganss, J. Kösters, and G. Braunitzer 1988. Structural adaptations in the major and minor hemoglobin components of adult Rüppell's Griffon (*Gyps rueppelli*, Aegypiinae):

a new molecular pattern for hypoxic tolerance. *Biol. Chem. Hoppe-Seyler* **369**:217–232.

[127] Hilbish, T. J. and R. K. Koehn 1985. The physiological basis of natural selection at the *LAP* locus. *Evolution* **39**:1302–1317.

[128] Hill, R. E. and N. D. Hastie 1987. Accelerated evolution in the reactive centre regions of serine protease inhibitors. *Nature* **326**:96–99.

[129] Ho, C. and I. M. Russu 1987. How much do we know about the Bohr effect of hemoglobin? *Biochemistry* **26**:6299–6305.

[130] Hochachka, P. W. and G. N. Somero 1984. *Biochemical Adaptation.* Princeton University Press, Princeton.

[131] Hoffman, R. J. 1983. Temperature modulation of the kinetics of phosphoglucose isomerase genetic variants from the sea anemone *Metridium senile*. *J. Exp. Zool.* **227**:361–370.

[132] Holmquist, G. P. 1989. Evolution of chromosome bands: Molecular ecology of noncoding DNA. *J. Mol. Evol.* **28**:469–486.

[133] Holmquist, R., M. Goodman, T. Conroy, and J. Czelusniak 1983. The spatial distribution of fixed mutations within genes coding for proteins. *J. Mol. Evol.* **19**:437–448.

[134] Hudson, R. R. 1983. Testing the constant rate neutral model with protein sequence data. *Evolution* **37**:711–719.

[135] Hudson, R. R., M. Kreitman, and M. Aguadé 1987. A test for neutral molecular evolution based on nucleotide data. *Genetics* **116**:153–159.

[136] Iizuka, M. 1987. Weak convergence of a sequence of stochastic difference equations to a stochastic ordinary differential equation. *J. Math. Biol.* **25**:643–652.

[137] Iizuka, M. and H. Matsuda 1982. Weak convergence of discrete time non-Markovian processes related to selection models in population genetics. *J. Math. Biol.* **15**:107–127.

[138] Ikemura, T. 1981. Correlation between the abundance of *Escherichia coli* transfer RNAs and the occurrence of the respective codons in its protein genes. *J. Mol. Biol.* **146**:1–21.

[139] Ikemura, T. 1985. Codon usage and tRNA content in unicellular and multicellular organisms. *Mol. Biol. Evol.* **2**:13–34.

[140] Ikemura, T. and S.-I. Aota 1988. Global variation in G+C content along vertebrate genome DNA. *J. Mol. Biol.* **203**:1–13.

[141] Jensen, L. 1973. Random selective advantages of genes and their probabilities of fixation. *Genet. Res. Camb.* **21**:215–219.

[142] Johnson, F. M., C. G. Kanapi, R. H. Richardson, M. R. Wheeler, and W. S. Stone 1966. An analysis of polymorphisms among isozyme loci in dark and light *Drosophila ananassae* strains from American and Western Samoa. *Proc. Natl. Acad. Sci. USA* **56**:119–125.

[143] Johnson, M. S. 1974. Comparative geographic variation in *Menidia*. *Evolution* **28**:607–618.

[144] Johnson, N. L. 1949. Systems of frequency curves generated by methods of translation. *Biometrika* **36**:149–176.

[145] Johnson, N. L. and S. Kotz 1969. *Distributions in Statistics: Discrete Distributions*. Houghton Mifflin Co., Boston.

[146] Jollès, J., P. Jollès, B. H. Bowman, E. M. Prager, C.-B. Stewart, and A. C. Wilson 1989. Episodic evolution in the stomach lysozymes of ruminants. *J. Mol. Evol.* **28**:528–535.

[147] Kacser, H. and J. A. Burns 1981. The molecular basis of dominance. *Genetics* **97**:639–666.

[148] Kamin, S. 1978. On elliptic perturbation of a first order operator with a singular point of attracting type. *Indiana Univ. Math. J.* **27**:935–951.

[149] Kaplan, N. L., R. R. Hudson, and C. H. Langley 1989. The hitchhiking effect revisited. *Genetics* **123**:887–899.

[150] Keith, T. P. 1983. Frequency distribution of esterase-5 alleles in populations of *Drosophila pseudoobscura*. *Genetics* **105**:135–155.

[151] Kimura, M. 1990. The present state of the neutral theory. In *Population Biology of Genes and Molecules*. ed. Takahata, N. and J. F. Crow, pp. 1–16. Baifukan, Mishima.

[152] Kimura, M. 1954. Process leading to quasi-fixation of genes in natural populations due to random fluctuations of selection intensities. *Genetics* **39**:280–295.

[153] Kimura, M. 1956. Rules for testing stability of selective polymorphism. *Proc. Natl. Acad. Sci. USA* **42**:336–372.

[154] Kimura, M. 1964. Diffusion processes in population genetics. *J. Appl. Prob.* **1**:177–232.

[155] Kimura, M. 1968. Evolutionary rate at the molecular level. *Nature* **217**:624–626.

[156] Kimura, M. 1969. The rate of molecular evolution considered from the standpoint of population genetics. *Proc. Natl. Acad. Sci. USA* **63**:1181–1188.

[157] Kimura, M. 1971. Theoretical foundations of population genetics at the molecular level. *Theor. Popul. Biol.* **2**:174–208.

[158] Kimura, M. 1979. Model of effectively neutral mutations in which selective constraint is incorporated. *Proc. Natl. Acad. Sci. USA* **76**:3440–3444.

[159] Kimura, M. 1983. *The Neutral Allele Theory of Molecular Evolution.* Cambridge University Press, Cambridge.

[160] Kimura, M. 1987. Molecular evolutionary clock and the neutral theory. *J. Mol. Evol.* **26**:24–33.

[161] Kimura, M. and T. Ohta 1971. Protein polymorphism as a phase of molecular evolution. *Nature* **229**:467–469.

[162] Kimura, M. and T. Ohta 1974. On some principles governing molecular evolution. *Proc. Natl. Acad. Sci. USA* **71**:2848–2852.

[163] King, J. L. 1967. Continuously distributed factors affecting fitness. *Genetics* **55**:483–492.

[164] King, J. L. and T. H. Jukes 1969. Non-Darwinian evolution. *Science* **164**:788–798.

[165] Kingman, J. F. C. 1975. Random discrete distributions. *J. Roy. Stat. Soc. B* **37**:1–22.

[166] Kingman, J. F. C. 1977. The population structure associated with the Ewens sampling formula. *Theor. Popul. Biol.* **11**:274–283.

[167] Kingsolver, J. G. 1983. Ecological significance of flight activity in *Colias* butterflies: Implications for reproductive strategy and population structure. *Ecology* **64**:546–551.

[168] Kingsolver, J. G. and W. B. Watt 1983. Thermoregulatory strategies in *Colias* butterflies: Thermal stress and the limits to adaptation in temporally varying environments. *Amer. Natur.* **121**:32–55.

[169] Koehn, R. K., W. J. Diehl, and T. M. Scott 1988. The differential contribution of individual enzymes of glycolysis and protein catabolism to the relationship between heterozygosity and growth rate in the coot clam, *Mulinia lateralis. Genetics* **118**:121–130.

[170] Koehn, R. K. and W. F. Eanes 1978. Molecular structure and protein variation within and among populations. *Evolutionary Biology* **11**:39–100.

[171] Koehn, R. K. and J. F. Siebenaller 1981. Biochemical studies of aminopeptidase polymorphism in *Mytilus edulis*. II. Dependence of reaction rate on physical factors and enzyme concentration. *Biochem. Genet.* **19**:1143–1162.

[172] Kohne, D. E., J. A. Chiscon, and B. H. Hoyer 1972. Evolution of primate DNA sequences. *J. Hum. Evol.* **1**:627–644.

[173] Kojima, K., J. H. Gillespie, and Y. Tobari 1970. A profile of *Drosophila* species' enzymes assayed by electrophoresis. I. Number of alleles, heterozygosities, and linkage disequilibrium in glucose-metabolizing systems and some other enzymes. *Biochem. Genet.* **4**:627–637.

[174] Kreitman, M. 1983. Nucleotide polymorphism at the alcohol dehydrogenase locus of *Drosophila melanogaster*. *Nature* **304**:412–417.

[175] Kunkel, T. A. and K. Bebenek 1988. Recent studies of the fidelity of DNA synthesis. *Biochim. BioPhys. Acta* **951**:1–15.

[176] Kunkel, T. A. and A. Soni 1988. Mutagenesis by transient misalignment. *J. Biol. Chem.* **263**:14784–14789.

[177] Kushner, H. J. and H. Huang 1981. On the weak convergence of a sequence of general stochastic difference equations to a diffusion. *SIAM J. Appl. Math.* **40**:528–541.

[178] Laird, C. D., B. L. McConaughy, and B. H. Hoyer 1969. Rate of fixation of nucleotide substitutions in evolution. *Nature* **224**:149–154.

[179] Lanave, C., G. Preparata, C. Saccone, and G. Serio 1984. A new method for calculating evolutionary substitution rates. *J. Mol. Evol.* **20**:86–93.

[180] Langley, C. H. 1990. The molecular population genetics of *Drosophila*. In *Population Biology of Genes and Molecules*. ed. Takahata, N. and J. F. Crow, pp. 75–91. Baifukan, Tokyo.

[181] Langley, C. H. and W. M. Fitch 1973. The constancy of evolution: a statistical analysis of the α and β haemoglobins, cytochrome c, and fibrinopeptide A. In *Genetic Structure of Populations*. ed. Morton, N. E., pp. 246–262. Univ. of Hawaii Press, Honolulu.

[182] Langley, C. H. and W. M. Fitch 1974. An estimation of the constancy of the rate of molecular evolution. *J. Mol. Evol.* **3**:161–177.

[183] Langley, C. H., E. A. Montgomery, and W. F. Quattlebaum 1982. Restriction map variation in the *Adh* region of *Drosophila*. *Proc. Natl. Acad. Sci. USA* **79**:5631–5635.

[184] Langley, C. H., R. A. Voelker, A. J. Leigh Brown, S. Ohnishi, B. Dickson, and E. Montgomery 1981. Null allele frequencies at allozyme loci in natural populations of *Drosophila melanogaster*. *Genetics* **99**:151–156.

[185] Leary, R. F., F. W. Allendorf, and K. L. Knudsen 1984. Superior developmental stability of heterozygotes at enzyme loci in salmonid fish. *Amer. Natur.* **124**:540–551.

[186] Levene, H. 1953. Genetic equilibrium when more than one ecological niche is available. *Amer. Natur.* **87**:311–313.

[187] Levins, R. 1968. *Evolution in a Changing Environment.* Princeton Univ. Press, Princeton.

[188] Lewontin, R. C. 1974. *The Genetic Basis of Evolutionary Change.* Columbia Univ. Press, New York.

[189] Lewontin, R. C. 1985. Population genetics. *Annu. Rev. Genetics* **19**:81–102.

[190] Lewontin, R. C. and J. L. Hubby 1966. A molecular approach to the study of genic heterozygosity in natural populations of *Drosophila pseudoobscura. Genetics* **54**:595–609.

[191] Li, W.-H. and D. Graur 1991. *Fundamentals of Molecular Evolution.* Sinauer Assoc., Inc., Sunderland.

[192] Li, W.-H., C.-C. Luo, and C.-I. Wu 1985. Evolution of DNA sequences. In *Molecular Evolutionary Genetics.* ed. MacIntyre, R. J., pp. 1–94. Plenum Press, New York.

[193] Li, W.-H. and L. A. Sadler 1991. Low nucleotide diversity in man. *Genetics* (in press).

[194] Li, W.-H., M. Tanimura, and P. M. Sharp 1987. An evaluation of the molecular clock hypothesis using mammalian DNA sequences. *J. Mol. Evol.* **25**:330–342.

[195] Li, W.-H., M. Tanimura, and P. M. Sharp 1988. Rates and dates of divergence between AIDS virus nucleotide sequences. *Mol. Biol. Evol.* **5**:313–330.

[196] Li, W.-H., C.-I. Wu, and C.-C. Luo 1985. A new method for estimating synonymous and nonsynonymous rates in nucleotide substitution considering the relative likelihood of nucleotide and codon changes. *Mol. Biol. Evol.* **2**:150–174.

[197] Li, W.-H. and C.-I. Wu 1987. Rates of nucleotide substitution are evidently higher in rodents than in man. *Mol. Biol. Evol.* **4**:74–77.

[198] Li, W.-H., C.-I. Wu, and C.-C. Luo 1984. Nonrandomness of point mutation as reflected in nucleotide substitutions in pseudogenes and its evolutionary implications. *J. Mol. Evol.* **21**:58–71.

[199] Littler, R. A. 1975. Loss of variability at one locus in a finite population. *Math. Biol.* **25**:151–163.

[200] Ludwig, D. 1975. Persistence of dynamical systems under random perturbations. *SIAM Rev.* **17**:605–640.

[201] Mandel, S. P. H. 1959. Genetic equilibrium under selection. *Heredity* **13**:289–302.

[202] Mandl, P. 1968. *Analytic Treatment of One-Dimensional Markov Processes*. Springer-Verlag, New York.

[203] Manly, B. F. J. 1985. *The Statistics of Natural Selection on Animal Populations*. Chapman and Hall, London.

[204] Matkowsky, B. J. and Z. Schuss 1977. The exit problem for randomly perturbed dynamical systems. *SIAM J. Appl. Math.* **33**:365–382.

[205] Matthew, J. B., F. R. N. Gurd, E. B. Garcia-Moreno, M. A. Flanagan, K. L. March, and S. J. Shire 1985. pH-dependent processes in proteins. *CRC Crit. Rev. Biochem.* **18**:91–197.

[206] Maynard Smith, J. 1976. What determines the rate of evolution? *Amer. Natur.* **110**:331–338.

[207] Maynard Smith, J. and J. Haigh 1974. The hitch-hiking effect of a favorable gene. *Genet. Res. Camb.* **23**:23–35.

[208] McKechnie, S. W. and B. W. Geer 1988. The epistasis of *Adh* and *Gpdh* allozymes and variation in the ethanol tolerance of *Drosophila melanogaster* larvae. *Genet. Res., Camb.* **52**:179–184.

[209] McLachlan, A. D. 1972. Repeating sequences and gene duplication in proteins. *J. Mol. Evol.* **64**:417–437.

[210] Milkman, R. D. 1967. Heterosis as a major cause of heterozygosity in nature. *Genetics* **55**:493–495.

[211] Miller, S., R. W. Pearcy, and E. Berger 1975. Polymorphism at the *alpha*-glycerophosphate dehydrogenase locus in *Drosophila melanogaster*. I. Properties of adult allozymes. *Biochem. Genet.* **13**:175–188.

[212] Miyata, T., H. Hayashida, K. Kuma, K. Mitsuyasu, and T. Yasunaga 1987. Male-driven molecular evolution: A model and nucleotide sequence analysis. *Cold Spring Harbor Symp. Quant. Biol.* **70**:863–867.

[213] Miyata, T., K. Kuma, N. Iwabe, H. Hayashida, and T. Yasunaga 1990. Different rates of autosome-, X chromosome-, and Y chromosome-linked genes: Hypothesis of male-driven molecular evolution. In *Population Biology of Genes and Molecules*. ed. Takahata, N. and J. F. Crow, pp. 341–357. Baifukan, Mishima.

[214] Miyata, T., S. Miyazawa, and T. Yasunaga 1979. Two types of amino acid substitution in protein evolution. *J. Mol. Evol.* **12**:219–236.

[215] Mukai, T., S. I. Chigusa, L. E. Mettler, and J. F. Crow 1972. Mutation rate and dominance of genes affecting viability in *Drosophila melanogaster*. *Genetics* **72**:335–355.

[216] Nei, M. 1987. *Molecular Evolutionary Genetics.* Columbia University Press, New York.

[217] Nei, M., P. A. Fuerst, and R. Chakraborty 1978. Subunit molecular weight and genetic variability of proteins in natural populations. *Proc. Natl. Acad. Sci. USA* **75**:3359–3362.

[218] Nei, M. and D. Graur 1984. Extent of protein polymorphism and the neutral mutation theory. *Evol. Biol.* **17**:73–118.

[219] Nei, M. and S. Yokoyama 1976. Effects of random fluctuations of selection intensity on genetic variability in a finite population. *Japan. J. Genet.* **51**:355–369.

[220] Nevo, E., A. Beiles, and R. Ben-Shlomo 1984. The evolutionary significance of genetic diversity: Ecological, demographic and life history correlates. In *Evolutionary Dynamics of Genetic Diversity*. ed. Mani, G. S., pp. 13–213. Springer-Verlag, Berlin.

[221] Notohara, M., K. Ishii, and H. Matsuda 1978. Use of orthogonal transformations in populations genetics theory. *J. Math. Biol.* **6**:249–263.

[222] O'Brien, S. J. and R. J. MacIntyre 1969. An analysis of gene-enzyme variability in natural populations of *Drosophila melanogaster* and *D. simulans*. *Amer. Natur.* **103**:97–113.

[223] Oakeshott, J. G., S. W. McKechnie, and G. K. Chambers 1984. Population genetics of the metabolically related *Adh*, *Gpdh*, and *Tpi* polymorphisms in *Drosophila melanogaster*. I. Geographic variation in *Gpdh* and *Tpi* allele frequencies in different continents. *Genetica* **63**:21–29.

[224] Oberthür, W., G. Braunitzer, and I. Würdinger 1982. Das Hämoglobin der Streifngans (*Anser indicus*) Primärstruktur und Physiologie der Atmung, Systematik und Evolution. *Hoppe-Seyler's Z. Physiol. Chem.* **363**:581–590.

[225] Ogasawara, N. 1985. Markedly unbiased codon usage in *Bacillus subtilis*. *Gene* **40**:145–150.

[226] Ohta, T. 1972. Evolutionary rate of cistrons and DNA divergence. *J. Mol. Evol.* **1**:150–157.

[227] Ohta, T. 1976. Role of very slightly deleterious mutations in molecular evolution and polymorphism. *Theor. Pop. Biol.* **10**:254–275.

[228] Ohta, T. 1977. Extension of the neutral mutation drift hypothesis. In *Molecular Evolution and Polymorphism.* ed. Kimura, M., pp. 148–167. National Institute of Genetics, Mishima.

[229] Ohta, T. and M. Kimura 1971. On the constancy of the evolutionary rate of cistrons. *J. Molec. Evol.* **1**:18–25.

[230] Osawa, S., T. H. Jukes, A. Muto, F. Yamao, T. Ohama, and Y. Andachi 1987. Role of directional mutation pressure in the evolution of the Eubacterial genetic code. *Cold Spring Harbor Symp. Quant. Biol.* **70**:777–789.

[231] Osheroff, N., S. H. Speck, E. Margoliash, E. C. I. Veerman, J. Wilms, B. W. König, and A. O. Muijsers 1983. The reaction of primate cytochromes c with cytochrome c oxidase. *J. Biol. Chem.* **258**:5731–5738.

[232] Pakula, A. A. and R. T. Sauer 1989. Genetic analysis of protein stability and function. *Annu. Rev. Genet.* **23**:289–310.

[233] Palese, P. 1986. Rapid evolution of human influenza viruses. In *Evolutionary Processes and Theory.* ed. Karlin, S. and E. Nevo, pp. 53–68. Academic Press, Inc., New York.

[234] Palese, P. and J. F. Young 1982. Variation of influenza A, B, and C viruses. *Science* **215**:1468–1474.

[235] Parvin, J. D., A. Moscona, W. T. Pan, J. M. Leider, and P. Palese 1986. Measurement of the mutation rates of animal viruses: Influenza A virus and poliovirus type 1. *J. Virol.* **59**:377–383.

[236] Perutz, M. F. 1983. Species adaptation in a protein molecule. *Mol. Biol. Evol.* **1**:1–28.

[237] Perutz, M. F., J. V. Kilmartin, K. Nishikura, J. H. Fogg, P. J. G. Butler, and H. S. Rollema 1980. Identification of residues contributing to the Bohr effect of human haemoglobin . *J. Mol. Biol.* **138**:649–670.

[238] Petschow, D., I. Würdinger, J. Baumann, G. Braunitzer, and C. Bauer 1977. Causes of high blood O_2 affinity of animals living at high altitude. *J. Appl. Physiol.* **42**:139–143.

[239] Place, A. R. and D. A. Powers 1984. Kinetic characterization of the lactate dehydrogenase (LDH-B_4) allozymes of *Fundulus heteroclitus.* *J. Biol. Chem.* **259**:1309–1315.

[240] Powers, D. A. 1980. Molecular ecology of teleost fish hemoglobins: Strategies for adapting to changing environments. *Amer. Zool.* **20**:139–162.

[241] Powers, D. A. and A. R. Place 1978. Biochemical genetics of *Fundulus heteroclitus* (L.). I. Temporal and spatial variation in gene frequencies of *Ldh-B, Mdh-A, Gpi-B,* and *Pgm-A. Biochem. Genet.* **16**:593–607.

[242] Riggs, A. 1960. The nature and the significance of the Bohr effect in mammalian hemoglobins. *J. Gen. Physiol.* **43**:737–752.

[243] Riggs, A. F. 1988. The Bohr effect. *Annu. Rev. Physiol.* **50**:181–204.

[244] Riley, M. A. 1989. Nucleotide sequence of the *Xdh* region in *Drosophila pseudoobscura* and an analysis of the evolution of synonymous codons. *Mol. Biol. Evol.* **6**:33–52.

[245] Roberts, J. D. and T. A. Kunkel 1988. Fidelity of a human cell DNA replication complex. *Proc. Natl. Acad. Sci. USA* **85**:7064–7068.

[246] Roberts, J. D., B. D. Preston, L. A. Johnston, A. Soni, L. A. Loeb, and T. A. Kunkel 1989. Fidelity of two retroviral transcriptases during DNA-dependent DNA synthesis in vitro. *Mol. Cell. Biol.* **9**:469–476.

[247] Robertson, A. 1962. Selection for heterozygotes in small populations. *Genetics* **47**:1291–1300.

[248] Russu, I. M., N. T. Ho, and C. Ho 1982. A proton nuclear magnetic resonance investigation of histidyl residues in human normal adult hemoglobin. *Biochemistry* **21**:5031–5043.

[249] Saitou, N. and M. Nei 1986. Polymorphism and evolution of influenza A virus genes. *Mol. Biol. Evol.* **3**:57–74.

[250] Sarich, V. M. and J. E. Cronin 1977. Generation time and rates of hominoid molecular evolution. *Nature* **269**:354–355.

[251] Scott, A. F., H. F. Bunn, and A. H. Brush 1977. The phylogenetic distribution of red cell 2,3 diphosphoglycerate and its interaction with mammalian hemoglobin. *J. Exp. Zool.* **201**:269–288.

[252] Seino, S., S. J. Blackstone, S. J. Chan, J. Whittaker, G. I. Bell, and D. F. Steiner 1988. Appalachian Spring: Variations on ancient gastro-entero-pancreatic themes in New World mammals. *Horm. Metabol. Res.* **20**:430–435.

[253] Selander, R. K. 1976. Genetic variation in natural populations. In *Molecular Evolution.* ed. Ayala, F. J., pp. 21–45. Sinauer Associates, Inc., Sunderland.

[254] Seno, S. and T. Shiga 1984. Diffusion models of temporally varying selection in population genetics. *Adv. Appl. Prob.* **16**:260–280.

[255] Sharp, P. M. and W.-H. Li 1987. The rate of synonymous substitution in Enterobacterial genes is inversely related to codon usage bias. *Mol. Biol. Evol.* **4**:222–230.

[256] Sharp, P. M. and W.-H. Li 1989. On the rate of DNA sequence evolution in *Drosophila*. *J. Mol. Evol.* **28**:398–402.

[257] Shaw, J.-P., J. Marks, C. C. Shen, and C.-K. J. Shen 1989. Anomalous and selective DNA mutations of the Old World monkey α-globin genes. *Proc. Natl. Acad. Sci. USA* **86**:1312–1316.

[258] Shields, D. C. and P. M. Sharp 1987. Synonymous codon usage in *Bacillus subtilis* reflects both translational selection and mutational balance. *Nucleic Acids Res.* **15**:8023–8040.

[259] Shields, D. C., P. M. Sharp, D. G. Higgens, and F. Wright 1988. "Silent" sites in *Drosophila* genes are not neutral: Evidence of selection among synonymous codons. *J. Mol. Biol. Evol.* **5**:704–716.

[260] Simmons, M. J. and J. F. Crow 1977. Mutations affecting fitness in *Drosophila* populations. *Annu. Rev. Genet.* **11**:49–78.

[261] Singh, R. S., D. A. Hickey, and J. David 1982. Genetic differentiation between geographically distant populations of *Drosophila melanogaster*. *Genetics* **101**:235–256.

[262] Singh, R. S., R. C. Lewontin, and A. A. Felton 1976. Genetic heterozygosity within electrophoretic alleles of xanthine dehydrogenase. *Genetics* **84**:609–629.

[263] Singh, R. S. and L. R. Rhomberg 1987. A comprehensive study of genic variation in natural populations of *Drosophila melanogaster*. II. Estimates of heterozygosity and patterns of geographic differentiation. *Genetics* **117**:255–271.

[264] Skibinski, D. O. F. and R. D. Ward 1982. Correlations between heterozygosity and evolutionary rate of proteins. *Nature* **298**:490–492.

[265] Smith, S. C., R. R. Racine, and C. H. Langley 1980. Lack of variation in the abundant proteins of the human kidney. *Genetics* **96**:967–974.

[266] Smouse, P. E. 1986. The fitness consequences of multiple-locus heterozygosity under the multiplicative overdominance and inbreeding depression models. *Evolution.* **40**:946–957.

[267] Snyder, L. R. G. 1981. Deer mouse hemoglobins: Is there genetic adaptation to high altitude? *BioScience* **31**:299–304.

[268] Somero, G. N. 1978. Temperature adaptation of enzymes: Biological optimization through structure-function compromises. *Annu. Rev. Ecol. Syst.* **9**:1–29.

[269] Somero, G. N. 1983. Environmental adaptation of proteins: Strategies for the conservation of critical functional and structural traits. *Comp. Bioch. Physiol.* **76A**:621–633.

[270] Springer, M. S. and J. A. W. Kirsch 1989. Rates of single-copy DNA evolution in Phalangerform marsupials. *Mol. Biol. Evol.* **6**:331–341.

[271] Starmer, W. T. and D. T. Sullivan 1989. A shift in the third-codon-position nucleotide frequency in alcohol dehydrogenase in the genus *Drosophila*. *Mol. Biol. Evol.* **6**:546–552.

[272] Steiner, D. F., S. J. Chan, J. M. Welsh, and S. C. M. Kwok 1985. Structure and evolution of the insulin gene. *Annu. Rev. Genet.* **19**:463–484.

[273] Stewart, C.-B. and A. C. Wilson 1987. Sequence convergence and functional adaptation of stomach lysozymes from foregut fermenters. *Cold String Harbor Symp. Quant. Biol.* **52**:891–899.

[274] Sueoka, N. 1962. On the genetic basis of variation and heterogeneity of DNA base composition. *Proc. Natl. Acad. Sci. USA* **48**:582–592.

[275] Sueoka, N. 1988. Directional mutation pressure and neutral molecular evolution. *Proc. Natl. Acad. Sci. USA* **85**:2653–2657.

[276] Sved, J. A., T. E. Reed, and W. F. Bodmer 1967. The number of balanced polymorphisms that can be maintained in a natural population. *Genetics* **55**:469–481.

[277] Takahata, N. 1987. On the overdispersed molecular clock. *Genetics* **116**:169–179.

[278] Takahata, N., K. Iishi, and H. Matsuda 1975. Effect of temporal fluctuation of selection coefficient on gene frequency in a population. *Proc. Natl. Acad. Sci. USA* **72**:4541–4545.

[279] Takahata, N. and M. Kimura 1979. Genetic variability maintained in a finite population under mutation and autocorrelated random fluctuation of selection intensity. *Proc. Natl. Acad. Sci. USA* **76**:5813–5817.

[280] Tavaré, S. 1986. Some probabilistic and statistical problems in the analysis of DNA sequences. In *Lectures on Mathematics in the Life Sciences.* ed. Miur, R. M., pp. 57–86. American Mathematical Society, Providence.

[281] Tindall, K. R. and L. F. Stankowski Jr. 1989. Molecular analysis of spontaneous mutations at the *gpt* locus in Chinese hamster ovary (AS52) cells. *Mutation Res.* **220**:241–253.

[282] Turelli, M. 1981. Temporally varying selection on multiple alleles: A diffusion analysis. *J. Math. Biol.* **13**:115–129.

[283] Turelli, M. and J. H. Gillespie 1980. Conditions for the existence of stationary densities for some two-dimensional diffusion processes with applications in population biology. *Theor. Popul. Biol.* **17**:167–189.

[284] Uzzell, T. and K. W. Corbin 1971. Fitting discrete probability distributions to evolutionary events. *Science* **172**:1089–1096.

[285] Van Beneden, R. J. and D. A. Powers 1989. Structural and functional differentiation of two clinally distributed glucosephosphate isomerase allelic isozymes from the teleost *Fundulus heteroclitus*. *Mol. Biol. Evol.* **6**:155–170.

[286] van Delden, W. 1984. The alcohol dehydrogenase polymorphism in *Drosophila melanogaster*, facts and problems. In *Population Biology and Evolution*. ed. Wohrmann, K. and V. Loeschcke, pp. 127–142. Springer-Verlag, Berlin.

[287] Varenne, S., J. Buc, R. Lloubes, and C. Lazdunski 1984. Translation is a non-uniform process: Effect of tRNA availability on the rate of elongation of nascent polypeptide chains. *J. Mol. Biol.* **180**:549–576.

[288] Voelker, R. A., C. H. Langley, A. J. Leigh Brown, S. Ohnishi, B. Dickson, E. Montgomery, and S. C. Smith 1980. Enzyme null alleles in natural populations of *Drosophila melanogaster*: Frequencies in a North Carolina population. *Proc. Natl. Acad. Sci. USA* **77**:1091–1095.

[289] Wabl, M., P. D. Burrows, A. von Gabain, and C. Steinberg 1985. Hypermutation at the immunoglobulin heavy chain locus in a pre-B-cell line. *Proc. Natl. Acad. Sci. USA* **82**:479–482.

[290] Wallace, B. 1968. *Topics in Population Genetics*. W. W. Norton & Co., Inc., New York.

[291] Walsh, J. B. 1984. Hard lessons for soft selection. *Amer. Natur.* **124**:518–526.

[292] Ward, R. D. and D. O. F. Skibinski 1985. Observed relationships between protein heterozygosity and protein genetic distance and comparisons with neutral expectations. *Genet. Res. Camb.* **45**:315–340.

[293] Watt, W. B. 1977. Adaptation at specific loci. I. Natural selection on phosphoglucose isomerase of *Colias* butterflies: Biochemical and population aspects. *Genetics* **87**:177–194.

[294] Watt, W. B. 1983. Adaptation at specific loci. II. Demographic and biochemical elements in the maintenance of the *Colias* PGI polymorphism. *Genetics* **103**:691–724.

[295] Watt, W. B. and C. L. Boggs 1987. Allelic isozymes as probes of the evolution of metabolic organization. In *Isozymes: Current Topics in Biological and Mendical Research. Vol. 15.* ed. Rattazzi, M. C., J. G. Scandalios, and G. S. Whitt, pp. 27–47. Alan R. Liss, Inc., New York.

[296] Watt, W. B., R. C. Cassin, and M. S. Swam 1983. Adaptation at specific loci. III. Field behavior and survivorship differences among *Colias* PGI genotypes are predictable form in vitro biochemistry. *Genetics* **103**:725–739.

[297] Watterson, G. A. 1975. On the number of segregating sites in genetic models without recombination. *Theor. Popul. Biol.* **7**:256–276.

[298] Watterson, G. A. 1977. Heterosis or neutrality? *Genetics* **85**:789–814.

[299] Watterson, G. A. 1978. The homozygosity test of neutrality. *Genetics* **88**:405–417.

[300] Watterson, G. A. 1978. An analysis of multi-allelic data. *Genetics* **88**:171–179.

[301] Watterson, G. A. 1982. Mutant substitutions at linked nucleotide sites. *Adv. Appl. Prob.* **14**:206–224.

[302] Watterson, G. A. 1984. Substitution times for mutant nucleotides. *J. Appl. Prob.* **19A**:59–70.

[303] Weber, R. E. and F. B. Jensen 1988. Functional adaptations in hemoglobins from ectothermic vertebrates. *Annu. Rev. Physiol.* **50**:161–179.

[304] Weber, R. E., R. Lalthantluanga, and G. Braunitzer 1988. Functional characterization of fetal and adult yak hemoglobins: An oxygen binding cascade and its molecular basis. *Arch. Biochem. BioPhys.* **262**:199–203.

[305] Weisman, I. 1978. Estimation of parameters and large quantities based on the k largest observations. *J. Amer. Stat. Assoc.* **73**:812–815.

[306] White, M. M., S. D. Mane, and R. C. Richmond 1988. Studies of esterase-6 in *Drosophila melanogaster*. XVII. Biochemical differences between the slow and fast allozymes. *Mol. Biol. Evol.* **5**:41–62.

[307] Wilbur, W. J. 1985. On the PAM matrix model of protein evolution. *Mol. Biol. Evol.* **2**:434–447.

[308] Wilson, A. C., S. S. Carlson, and T. J. White 1977. Biochemical evolution. *Annu. Rev. Biochem.* **46**:573–639.

[309] Wilson, A. C., H. Ochman, and E. M. Prager 1987. Molecular time scale for evolution. *Trends in Genet.* **3** 3:241–247.

[310] Winkler, H. H. and D. O. Wood 1988. Codon usage in selected AT-rich bacteria. *Biochemie* **70**:977–986.

[311] Wolfe, K. H., P. M. Sharp, and W.-H. Li 1989. Mutation rates differ among regions of the mammalian genome. *Nature* **337**:283–285.

[312] Wright, S. 1948. On the roles of directed and random changes in gene frequency in the genetics of populations. *Evolution* **2**:279–294.

[313] Wright, S. 1949. Adaptation and selection. In *Genetics, Paleontology, and Evolution.* ed. Jepson, G. L., G. G. Simpson, and E. Mayr, pp. 365–389. Princeton Univ. Press, Princeton.

[314] Yokoyama, S. and R. Yokoyama 1990. Molecular evolution of visual pigment genes and other G-protein-coupled receptor genes. In *Population Biology of Genes and Molecules.* ed. Takahata, N. and J. F. Crow, pp. 307–322. Baifukan, Tokyo.

[315] Zera, A. J. 1987. Temperature-dependent kinetic variation among phosphoglucose isomerase allozymes from the wing-polymorphic water strider, *Limnoporus canaliculatus. Mol. Biol. Evol.* **4**:266–285.

[316] Zouros, E. and D. W. Foltz 1987. The use of allelic isozyme variation for the study of heterosis. *Curr. Top. Biol. Med. Res.* **13**:1–59.

[317] Zuckerkandl, E. and L. Pauling 1962. Molecular disease, evolution, and genetic heterogeneity. In *Horizons in Biochemistry.* ed. Kasha, M. and B. Pullman, pp. 189–225. Academic Press, New York.

Index